I0809850

Two Armies
ON THE
RIO GRANDE

NUMBER 148

Williams-Ford Texas A&M University Military History Series

Two Armies on the Rio Grande

The First Campaign of the US-Mexican War

DOUGLAS A. MURPHY

Texas A&M University Press
College Station, Texas

Copyright © 2015 by Douglas A. Murphy
Manufactured in the United States of America
All rights reserved
First edition
This paper meets the requirements of ANSI/NISO Z39.48-1992
(Permanence of Paper).
Binding materials have been chosen for durability.
♾ ♻

Library of Congress Cataloging-in-Publication Data

Murphy, Douglas A., author
Two armies on the Rio Grande: the first campaign of the US-Mexican War /
Douglas A. Murphy. — First edition.
pages cm — (Williams-Ford Texas A&M University military history series; number 148)
Includes bibliographical references and index.
ISBN 978-1-62349-189-5 (cloth: alk. paper) — ISBN 978-1-62349-225-0 (ebook)
1. Palo Alto, Battle of, Tex., 1846. 2. Resaca de la Palma, Battle of, Tex., 1846. 3. Mexican War, 1846–1848—Texas—Lower Rio Grande Valley. I. Title. II. Series: Williams-Ford Texas A&M University military history series; no. 148.
E406.P3M87 2014
973.6'2—dc23
2014013154

For Karen

CONTENTS

ACKNOWLEDGMENTS

IN MY PERSONAL campaign to write this book, I have had the support of valuable allies. Some were with me from the very beginning. Bob Spude set me on my original course and offered valuable advice in the early stages of planning and information gathering. Dale Steinhauer shared his encyclopedic knowledge of US Army history and archives and had the uncanny ability to produce the exact reference I needed at the exact moment I needed it. Kevin Young similarly directed me to many sources on the Mexican military of the 1840s and enthusiastically encouraged me to finish the project. I am only sorry that he did not live to see it.

I also encountered new allies along the way. Two anonymous readers for the Texas A&M University Press provided thoughtful comments about the manuscript and suggested changes that vastly improved the final product. Mary Lenn Dixon and Katie Duelm patiently guided me through the publication process. Margret Kerbaugh did not just improve this manuscript with her editing, she made the process surprisingly painless, even pleasant.

Others provided me with ammunition for my mission. Ted Lusher welcomed me into his home and allowed me to explore the treasure trove of documents in his personal collection. Bill Hudson was equally generous in providing access to his image collection. And dozens of dedicated archivists—too many to possibly name—provided me access to documents and paper collections located around the United States and Mexico.

Success in battle often comes down to proper training and drilling, and I am fortunate to have been schooled by some of the finest instructors. My parents Michael and Barbara Murphy have influenced me in all facets of my life, and I follow their guidance more than they will ever know. Bob Fulks spurred my interest in history during my high school years and inspired me to continue studying it. Judith Ewell introduced me to Mexican history and first led me to consider history as a career. Gil Joseph helped me continue down that road. Although many years have passed since he formally advised me, his counsel on research and writing was well remembered as I worked on this project.

Tim Henderson, Don MacDonell, and Michael Van Wagenen offered support and friendship that extended far beyond the call of duty. Each member of this trio assisted with research and source materials, read various drafts, and offered constructive criticism. More importantly, they listened when I needed to talk, provided motivation when my energy flagged, offered counsel when I veered off course, and never hesitated to hit me with an insult when the situation called for one. I salute each of them.

I am most thankful, however, for support on the home front. My son Harrison helped me pore over historic newspapers for elusive articles, fed parking meters so that my research could continue uninterrupted, and hand-delivered manuscript drafts to the Texas A&M University Press. My daughter Katherine helped locate obscure reels of microfilm, retrieved books from far corners of libraries, and came to the rescue many times when I had questions about how to format computer documents. Both endured the stacks of papers and books that littered the house, the many nights and weekends when I monopolized the computer, and the family vacations that repeatedly gravitated toward a nearby archive or library. I thank them for their patience and assistance—usually cheerfully given.

Most of all I express my gratitude to my wife, Karen. She has stood shoulder to shoulder with me for the duration of this campaign and provided cover in every battle. Rather than try to list the ways in which she has contributed to this project, I will simply acknowledge that without her help and encouragement, I could not have completed it. I dedicate this book to her.

Two Armies
ON THE
RIO GRANDE

INTRODUCTION

ON MAY 18, 1846, two very different scenes unfolded near the Mexican city of Matamoros. To the southwest of town, Mexican troops were on the road after abandoning their barracks in the dark of night. Leaving behind hundreds of wounded compatriots who could not make the march, weary and demoralized men trudged toward the Sierra Madre and the distant city of Monterrey. Meanwhile, to the north, on the banks of the Rio Grande, a small, spontaneous ceremony unfolded. Thousands of American soldiers stood at water's edge on the north shore, watching a small group of their countrymen slowly hoist the Stars and Stripes over an abandoned Mexican fort. As the banner reached the top of its staff and unfurled in the breeze, the troops erupted in cheers, and military bands began to play, shattering the morning silence. With forlorn resignation on one side of town and joyous celebration on the other, Matamoros had fallen, and the first campaign of the war between the United States and Mexico came to a close.

Perspectives on the events that led up to this moment also diverged widely, with attitudes largely dependent upon whether the observer identified with the troops on the north side of the city or those to the south. Soldiers of the US Army focused on their successes in the recent battles of Palo Alto (May 8) and Resaca de la Palma (May 9) and the utter decimation of the Mexican forces arrayed against them. "They are really glorious victories," Lt. Nathaniel Wyche Hunter wrote of the two encounters, "and I have no doubt that they will be appreciated as such by the Country at large." The American press agreed. "The battles of Palo Alto and Resaca de la Palma," proclaimed the Charleston, South Carolina *Mercury*, for example, "are destined to occupy a page in history never to be effaced." Mexicans focused instead on the disastrous effects of these clashes, most notably the raising of the enemy flag over the frontier city of Matamoros. The *Gaceta de Tamaulipas* presented that act as the crowning shame of "ten days of sorrowful memory" and called failure on the Rio Grande "a transcendent event that threatens the most important interests of the nation, its respect, and its dignity." The Mexico City newspaper *El Monitor Republicano* offered more measured but equally earnest wording, referring to lost battles and the surrender of a city as "a terrible shift of capricious fortune."[1]

These conflicting sentiments quickly found their way into the first chronicles of the military campaign. In the United States, authors rushed to celebrate victory in books that extolled the campaign as one of the grand events of military history, and the American participants as epic heroes worthy of great acclaim. Just weeks after the occupation of Matamoros, the popular Louisiana-based writer and humorist Thomas Bangs Thorpe traveled to that city as part of a delegation from New Orleans charged with bestowing several ceremonial awards upon Gen. Zachary Taylor. Thorpe seized the opportunity to collect reports of the battles, interview American participants, and tour the area before returning home in mid-June. By October he had written and published a book titled *Our Army on the Rio Grande.* Though hastily assembled and focused on praising the US troops, who "exhibited a most perfect concentration of courage, tempered by constant acts of generosity," the volume nonetheless provided a detailed portrayal of the first military campaign against Mexico.[2]

More works soon followed. William Seaton Henry, an officer of the US 3rd Infantry, documented his military adventures, beginning with the Rio Grande campaign and continuing through the battles of Monterrey and Buena Vista. What started as a series of articles for the *Spirit of the Times* newspaper became a travelogue of the conflict, published in 1847 under the title *Campaign Sketches of the War with Mexico.* The popularity of this book on the heels of Thorpe's hot-selling account encouraged other, more distant observers to tackle the subject, too.

John Frost never travelled to the war zone, but relied on previous histories, official documents, and accounts of participants to develop his own narratives of events. In 1848, just months after the fighting had come to a conclusion with the US occupation of Mexico City, the historian published two lavishly illustrated volumes about the war. By the close of 1849 several other authors had placed their own contributions before a receptive American public as well. These weighty volumes still detailed the early maneuvers and engagements of the war, but the first campaign was now relegated to a few chapters preceding lengthy accounts of gallant deeds and military heroes.[3]

Mexican writers, meanwhile, were forced to address the sad reality of defeat. Like their American counterparts, several Mexican officers printed their own brief accounts of events of the spring of 1846. Unlike their foes, however, they spurned travelogues and lighthearted descriptions of military life for treatises—often formal testimonies—that defended their conduct in battle and attempted to apportion blame for defeat. Pedro de Ampudia, second in command during battles on the Rio Grande, fired an initial volley with the publication of *El ciudadano general Pedro de Ampudia ante el tribunal respetable de la opinión pública,* which heaped blame on the Mexican general-in-chief, Mariano Arista. A second account, *Campaña contra los Americanos del norte,* offered a more positive portrayal of Arista—and indeed has sometimes been attributed to him—while casting Ampudia in a less favorable light. Other narratives and testimonies by lesser officers soon followed, filling the bookstalls of Mexico with battle accounts that combined equal measures of fact, defensiveness, and wild accusation.[4]

As the first campaign gave way to more devastating losses that culminated in the occupation of their capital city, other Mexican authors documented failures and assigned culpability for a conflict that started badly and grew increasingly worse. In his work *El Nuevo Bernal Díaz,* statesman and historian Carlos María Bustamante assumed the role of Bernal Díaz del Castillo, a chronicler of Spain's subjugation of the Aztec Empire, and recounted the shortcomings and miscues that made his country vulnerable to another foreign conquest. Similarly, a group of young army officers, in a book titled *Apuntes para la historia de la guerra entre México y los Estados Unidos*, provided an extensive account of the military errors and breakdowns that resulted first in the fall of Matamoros, and finally in the surrender of the national capital and the loss of territory. They, like Bustamente, confessed that it was painful to look back upon the causes of defeat, but stressed that Mexicans should thoroughly examine the events in order to "reform [their] conduct and take the necessary precautions to avoid repetition of these disgraceful occurrences."[5]

The desired assessment took place—later, and to an extent. Decades after the conflict with the United States drew to a close, raw feelings had subsided and Mexicans were finally willing to turn their attention to documenting the tragic events of 1846 and 1847. In the intervening years their country had endured a civil war, confronted and expelled another foreign force, and emerged as a more stable nation, and a new generation of authors was eager to reevaluate the war in the light of lessons learned. An overriding theme of their studies was lack of national unity. The historians carefully detailed how, from the first campaign to the final cession of territory, Mexico had let political divisions supersede efforts to resist a common foe. Although soldiers often fought valiantly to defend their homeland, discord among politicians and military leaders made the task impossible, often deadly. Equally important to these new narratives, however, was the emphasis on the culpability of the United States. The authors admitted Mexico's vulnerability but bitterly criticized the United States for exploiting it in a bid to gain territory. They wanted to leave no doubt that their northern neighbor was ultimately the aggressor—a view that is often evident even in judging their books by the covers. Titles like *La invasión norte americana en 1846* and *Recuerdos de la invasión norte-americana* make clear that this was not merely a war, but an invasion forced upon an innocent nation.[6]

What these studies did not provide was a meaningful reappraisal of the first—or any—campaign of the war. All the authors devoted the majority of their writing to the political context of the war, providing details of the disputes and divisions that brought the nations to blows and determined the results. Against this expansive backdrop, the discussion of actual battles was usually perfunctory, consisting of little more than excerpts of previous testimonies and histories. And authors who did offer more detail rarely took pains to break new ground. In *Recuerdos de la invasión*, for example, José María Roa Bárcena drew heavily upon the work of American authors for clarification of certain points in the Mexican accounts. Similarly, in *Invasión de los norte-americanos en México*, Emilio del Castillo Negrete relied almost entirely on verbatim copies of previously published military dispatches and letters. In his introduction to the book, F. Javier Gaxiola justified including these sections as a way to expose the failures and carelessness of the military and thereby demonstrate "the government's commitment to emerge victorious from a war in which reason, justice and right were on its side even if force and power assisted the bold invader." Such reasoning provided little motivation for authors to investigate new sources and develop full and clear summaries of the specifically military aspects of the war.[7]

This disinclination of Mexican historians to delve into the actual clash of battle has continued into the present. Since the start of the twentieth century, and with interest rising near the centennial and sesquicentennial of the event, Mexican authors have produced a wealth of scholarship on the history of the war between the United States and Mexico. The majority of their works continue to focus on the diplomatic struggles that produced conflict and the internal dissentions on the national stage. Other more recent studies examine similar issues at the regional level or delve into the theme of popular resistance to occupation.[8] But in a country without a significant tradition of writing military history, only a few isolated researchers have attempted to produce detailed studies of individual battles. None have revisited the initial campaign. In his study of the US-Mexican War and its legacy, Michael Van Wagenen described the manner in which the Mexican government has carefully cultivated public awareness of the conflict and kept themes of unity and of resistance to intervention in the public consciousness. Ironically, but perhaps not surprisingly, information about the actual fighting has been repeatedly overlooked and, in the case of the first campaign, all but forgotten.

The military aspects of the US-Mexican War have been more thoroughly documented by authors from the United States. The initial enthusiasm for narratives about the Mexican campaigns faded in the 1850s and was swept away entirely when the United States plunged into the much bloodier Civil War. Nevertheless, the latter conflict eventually helped introduce a new generation to the events in Mexico. Many of the generals who became household names in the War between the States traced their military careers back to the Mexican War. By the end of the nineteenth century, when these aging veterans were attempting to profit from their service by writing about their experiences, their chronicles included not only accounts of the confrontations between the Union and the Confederacy, but also recollections of their campaigns to the "Halls of the Montezumas." Ulysses S. Grant's *Memoirs,* one of the best-known examples of these works, contained extensive recollections of his actions in and impressions of the Mexican campaigns, from the initial engagements to the fall of Mexico City. Works by Grant's peers offered similar fare, some summing up the war in a few pages, while others devoted multiple chapters to the exploits in Mexico.[9]

Many of these recountals became research material for scholars compiling the next round of US historical studies on the war. The new works, which started appearing early in the twentieth century, followed a formula established by the accounts of a half century before. They began with a general history of US-Mexican relations, continued with a more specific discussion of the causes of the war, and then proceeded to a campaign-by-campaign narrative.

These later books, however, were intended to provide a much more deliberative analysis of the conflict than had emerged during the excitement of the struggle. Toward that end, the new generation of authors drew not only from the work of its predecessors, but also from more recently available documents and accounts to provide a better-detailed picture of events. The pinnacle of these efforts was Justin Harvey Smith's thoroughly researched, carefully annotated two-volume opus *The War with Mexico.* Although Smith has since been challenged for his disparaging portrayal of Mexican character and his determination to depict Mexico as naked aggressor in the conflict, his attention to detail is indisputable and the study remains an authoritative source on the subject.[10]

Still, *The War with Mexico* is not the final word, especially with regard to initial maneuvers. Even though he churned out more than a thousand pages, Smith was forced to be selective in them because of his determination to review the entire course of the war. In the case of the first campaign, he emphasized the US advance to the Rio

Grande in March of 1846 and the major clashes that ensued in May. Unfortunately, this approach led him to gloss over the month of April 1846, during which events took place that lacked the drama of the clashes to follow, but that nevertheless played a significant role in shaping the campaign and its outcome.

More frustrating is Smith's apparent unwillingness to let Mexican perspectives help him construct a fuller, clearer picture of what transpired along the Rio Grande. There is no question that Smith stood out from his predecessors and, to a great degree, his successors, in his determination to locate and delve into Mexican sources. Even before publishing his epic work, he had written authoritatively on the subject of Mexican documents and archives, and the long list of sources cited in *The War with Mexico* demonstrates that he had consulted those materials.[11] But Smith often appeared intent on using the information he uncovered to depict Mexicans and their martial decisions and actions in the worst possible light. He dismissed one general's vow to halt the US advance to the Rio Grande at the start of the campaign as little more than an attempt "to win a sheaf of laurels," and he presented General Arista's difficult decision to abandon the city of Matamoros and end the campaign as an easy choice for a man who felt "no violent wish to sacrifice himself." In covering the intervening details, Smith did not hesitate to paint the Mexican leaders as variously foppish, self-aggrandizing, or savage men who sealed their fates in battle by consistently underestimating their US counterparts, whom they considered "more contemptible than the lowest of Mexican tailors," and failing to understand the bravery and quality of "our troops."[12] In an effort to support his contention that the United States was justified in waging the war, he exaggerated character flaws, ignored private views behind public bluster, and deliberately obscured important details that might have presented the Mexican foe in a more sympathetic light. The result is a well-documented but flawed interpretation of the events of the first campaign and the war that followed it.

Smith's perspectives eventually came under fire. In his 1942 book *Year of Decision, 1846,* Bernard DeVoto provided a broad overview of one year in the history of the United States. This work included both an examination of the conflict between the United States and Mexico and some direct words of criticism for Smith. DeVoto expressed admiration for Smith's investigative skills, but was contemptuous of his attempt to cast blame for the war solely upon Mexico. While he lauded Smith's research, which he called some of "the most exhaustive ever made by an American historian," he nevertheless observed that "it is frequently—very frequently—altogether impossible to understand how Smith's conclusions could exist in the presence of facts which he himself presents." Setting aside his own efforts at objectivity, he concluded, "If there is a more consistently wrongheaded book in our history . . . I have not encountered it." Some twenty years later, in *The Monroe Doctrine and American Expansionism*, Frederick Merk was somewhat more charitable in his challenge to *The War with Mexico*. He referred to Smith's argument merely as "unorthodox," dismissed it, and carefully laid out his own case implicating Pres. James Polk as a driving force behind the outbreak of hostilities.[13]

Since the mid-twentieth century, US authors of narratives about the war have tried to strike a balance in their assessment of causes, focusing on perspectives from both the United States and Mexico and analyzing motivation rather than assessing blame. In his 1961 offering, Otis Singletary firmly rejected Smith's views and called the war an offensive one on the part of the United States. But he was also quick to note that it was much more than a simple "land-grab" and that "there were causes other than greed and consequences other than gain." Robert Selph Henry was even less eager to find fault. He avoided any direct statement on responsibility and instead called the dispute "inescapable" and largely the result of "a fog of misunderstanding" between the United States and Mexico. A decade later, John Weems similarly stressed that the histories and actions of both nations contributed to the outbreak of fighting in a "needless but inevitable war." Meanwhile, K. Jack Bauer asserted that although James K. Polk's actions provoked the confrontation, Polk had nevertheless hoped to avoid armed conflict and resorted to war only when Mexico refused to yield to "graduated pressure."

More recent authors accept the premise that this was very much "Mr. Polk's War," but they also point to other influences at work. "The fact is that Mexico stood in the way of the American dream of Manifest Destiny," wrote John S. D. Eisenhower in *So Far from God.* He thought the outbreak of war resulted as much from social pressure as from any specific policy action. And, as Timothy Henderson observes in *A Glorious Defeat,* Mexico resisted not because any politician actually believed war was a good choice, but rather because "the desperate glory of death on the battlefield seemed preferable to the ignominy of compromise and surrender." In other words, researchers have come to agree that when the irresistible force of the United States met the immovable object that was Mexico, war became unavoidable.[14]

No such reappraisal has been applied to the campaigns of the war. From the 1960s to the present, editors have discovered, edited, and published dozens of diaries, letter collections, and manuscripts that reveal vital new details about battles, maneuvers, and military decision making. Narrative writers have incorporated these materials into their research and substantially broadened their interpretations of events. But for the most part, the supplemental materials are from the perspective of US soldiers and observers and do little to expand knowledge of what happened in the Mexican ranks. Modern chroniclers of the war have also felt little impulse to explore the Mexican perspective. Most seek to address issues in US history—the development of the military and its officers, perceptions of the war by the US population, or the effect of the war on the United States in general—and see little need to delve into Mexican archives to do so. When a Mexican perspective is required, these authors rely on published Mexican sources on the battles. Unfortunately, since few Mexican scholars have addressed the military aspects of the war, the American authors continue to draw from the shallow, often muddy, well of mid-nineteenth century publications. The result is that, aside from Smith's flawed *War with Mexico,* the history of the military campaigns has been largely a one-sided affair that tells the story almost exclusively from the point of view of the United States and its warriors. As noted, a number of Smith's views have been discredited, but in the arena of military operations they have never been revised.

This failure to examine the Mexican perspective necessarily distorts our understanding of the initial campaign of the war. The opening engagement of any military conflict is, as military historian John Shy asserts, particularly important. In advance of a first clash, military commanders often lack important information about the strengths, weaknesses, and weaponry of the foe they are about to face, and they are often uncertain about the skills of their own troops and the reliability of their own weaponry. Unpredictable political negotiations and decisions can add to the confusion as leaders prepare to fight. But combat answers many questions. It produces winners and losers; sometimes it transforms politics, and often it sets the course of the conflict to follow. It is, therefore, the events before and during the first battles of a war that provide real insight into the policies, perspectives, and preparations of the armies and nations involved.[15] In the case of the US-Mexican War, the first battles were the culmination of the first campaign. By neglecting to develop a full picture of these operations, informed by perspectives from both nations, researchers have overlooked an opportunity to better understand the causes of the war and the goals of its combatants on the eve of conflict.

They have also missed an opportunity to truly understand what occurred in the maneuvers and battles themselves. The narrow focus on US documents and accounts has created a standardized chronology of events that parallels the discussion of causes of the war. If Polk was the driving influence behind the outbreak of hostilities and his actions forced Mexican leaders to respond, it stands to reason that the US Army was the driving force in the initial campaign as well. The usual description of events has Mexico responding to General Taylor's advance to the Rio Grande, attempting to drive his troops from established positions, seeking to block American maneuvers, and ultimately retreating in the face of overwhelming pressure from the US Army. These modern accounts brush aside Justin Smith's portrayal of ambitious, egotistical, incompetent, and overconfident Mexican generals, but only to replace it with a picture of them as hapless and helpless pawns in a complex and masterful US plan.

In reality, the first campaign of the war between the United States and Mexico was very much a shared creation. Mexico was far more than just a reactionary foil for US policy. Officials of the Mexican government established the initial theater of war by deciding where to draw the line against an American advance. Mexican military officers took the lead in selecting the time and place of battles against US forces within that area of operations. Moreover, the dynamics of the Mexican Army, including its training, weaponry, personnel, organization, and the relationships among its officers, proved to be as significant as the corresponding dynamics of the US forces in determining the fortunes of war. This part of the story has escaped attention since the fall of Matamoros in 1846. Unfortunately, lack of perspective from south of the Rio Grande has insured that descriptions of this important military campaign have remained at best incomplete, and at worst, erroneous and misleading.

This book provides a narrative view of the campaign that draws on perspectives from both sides of the river. It builds on the foundation established by Thomas Bangs Thorpe's pioneering work, but it also adds new detail to a familiar story and uses Mexican sources to cast new light on decisions and actions in the opposing ranks. The book also revisits Justin Smith's impressive research, reviewing many of the same documents he used in 1916, but with the object of explaining rather than condemning Mexican motives and actions.

Like other accounts, this one follows the movements of the US Army from its occupation of the Rio Grande through to the triumphant capture of Matamoros. But it also traces the activities of the Mexican Army from its hopeful arrival at the river through its humiliating retreat from Matamoros. In the process, it focuses attention not only on the major clashes of the campaign, but also on the fighting itself—and on events before, between, and after the battles. One advantage of this approach is to show how profoundly periods of planning, construction, and maneuvering affected the course of the first campaign.

But generally this account follows a path beaten out by many pioneers and travelers who have gone before. Its purpose is principally to smooth out the occasional bump in the road, add signposts and directional markers, and open up some scenic vistas that make the journey to historical understanding clearer, easier and more worthwhile.

A Note on Place Names

Many of the places visited by the armies over the course of the first campaign of the conflict were known by one name to the Mexicans and another to the US troops. Most obvious was the river at the center of the dispute. In the United States of 1846, it was occasionally referred to as the Río del Norte or Río Grande del Norte, but it was known most commonly as the Rio Grande. In Mexico that same stream was called the Río Bravo del Norte, commonly shortened to Río Bravo. Rather than choose which of those names is the proper one, this study will rely on the name Rio Grande when describing events from the US perspective and Río Bravo when describing them from the Mexican.

That naming convention will be used for other sites as well. Any mention of the US coastal supply depot from an American point of view will use the name Point Isabel. In the context of Mexican planning and strategy, it will be referred to as the Frontón de Santa Isabel or simply as the Frontón. Likewise, the scene of the second major battle of the war will be called both Resaca de la Palma and Resaca de Guerrero, the former being the name regularly applied in the United States and the later more commonly used in Mexico.

A pair of US forts, one situated at Point Isabel/Frontón and the other on the bank of the Rio Grande/Río Bravo, presents a different nomenclature challenge—because for a long time, neither had any formal name at all. The US supply depository at the Point eventually became known as "Fort Polk," but only in the celebratory atmosphere at the close of the campaign. For most of the period covered in this narrative, troops referred to the site simply as "the depot" located at "the Point." Similarly, the primary US fort at the river was called "the camp opposite Matamoros," "the fort," and a variety of other informal names, but it was not officially dubbed "Fort Brown" until the close of fighting.

Historians deal with these places in several ways. Many only briefly touch upon the campaign and are able to gloss over the issue without really addressing it. Others have adopted the tactic of calling the forts by the names that were applied in the end. This simplifies talking about them, but it also creates an awkward situation in which the designation "Fort Brown" is applied to the fortification long before its namesake, Maj. Jacob Brown, died in its defense. Brown himself used another name for the fort. In a letter to Zachary Taylor, written during the siege of the post, Brown stated his location as "Fort Texas." Numerous authors have since then latched onto that name as a practical designation for the fort during the period of the campaign. But this approach is also problematic. Aside from Brown's single mention of "Fort Texas," there is little, if any, evidence that the soldiers referred to their post by that name. Six days after Major Brown used it, Capt. Edgar Hawkins, who took over for the mortally wound Brown, wrote a report in which he called the site "Fort Taylor."[16] But neither of these names—Fort Texas or Fort Taylor—gained widespread currency in 1846. Indeed, "Fort Texas" seems to have first found traction in history books of the mid-twentieth century as authors sought a practical, though not necessarily accurate, solution to the name problem.

This book will follow a different approach, leaving the forts unnamed, as did the soldiers who built them. Although not an ideal solution, it is the one that best captures the perspectives of the troops and the temporary nature of the sites. The sites will become Fort Polk and Fort Brown only at the proper point in the narrative. In the interval before those names are applied, the early Fort Polk will be called the depot or the Point and the unchristened Fort Brown will be known simply as the riverside fort or the fort across from Matamoros.

A final issue that invariably arises in any account involving US-Mexican relations is what to call the residents of the United States. Today many Latin Americans bristle at the use of "American" for US citizens, because all residents of the Western Hemisphere are, in fact, American. But in 1846, US citizens had already been calling themselves "American" for decades and had little doubt that the term applied only to their nation, the United States of America. Even in the heat of conflict, their foes did not appear to object. As they headed toward war, Mexicans referred to their northern neighbors by many names, including North Americans, Yankees, and Gringos, and often with adjectives like "perfidious," "haughty," and "ambitious" attached. With great frequency, however, they too relied on the simple word "American," without any in-depth analysis of the correctness or even justice of doing so. For the sake of simplicity, this study will also refer to US citizens as "Americans."

CHAPTER 1
The Road to War

★

IN HIS FIRST message to Congress, on December 2, 1845, Pres. James K. Polk spoke proudly of the incorporation of Texas into the American Union. "This accession to our territory has been a bloodless achievement," he announced. "No arm of force has been raised to produce the result. The sword has had no part in the victory." He also generously distributed credit for the accomplishment: Congress had developed a joint resolution for annexation, his predecessor had signed it into law, and the people of Texas had overwhelmingly voted in favor of the decision "to share the blessings of our Union." For his part, the freshman president accepted credit only for helping shepherd Texas through its transformation from republic to statehood. The steps in that transformation would be complete by the end of the year, and Congress could sign the legislation that officially joined the "'lone star' with our glorious constellation." It was a moment, Polk said, for which "the history of the world may be challenged to furnish a parallel," in that it added a huge expanse of territory to the United States and did so bloodlessly—the border had been "peacefully extended to the Del Norte."

Delving deeper into the topic, Polk conceded that relations with Mexico had deteriorated and had not been of the "amicable character which it is our desire to cultivate with all nations." He noted that the Foreign Minister of that republic considered the annexation "a violation of Mexican rights and demanded his passports." In the months that followed, Mexican officials had assumed an "attitude of hostility," claiming that Texas remained part of their territory and challenging the right of the United States to seize it. These protests, Polk insisted, were entirely baseless. He had, he assured his audience, informed the complainants "that the Republic of Texas was an independent power, owing no allegiance to Mexico and constituting no part of her territory or rightful sovereignty and jurisdiction." Indeed, the president suggested that the United States was the true victim in the relationship. The southern republic refused to pay its mounting debts to its American creditors, declined to address "injuries inflicted by the Mexican authorities and people on the persons and property of citizens of the United States," and generally failed to end the "insults repeatedly offered to American citizens and the American flag." Mexico now threatened to add to its outrages. It vowed to attack Texas, and the threat was credible enough that Polk had to order army and naval forces there.

Still, hope remained for a peaceful solution. Although the troops occupied a forward position, they had been instructed "to commit no act of hostility against Mexico unless she declared war or was herself the aggressor by striking the first blow." Mexico had also refrained from hostilities, and Polk was pleased to announce that "the peace of the two Republics has not been disturbed." That show of discretion by both nations had opened the door to another round of diplomacy. In November, the Mexican government had agreed to receive an envoy and discuss differences with the United States. This diplomat had already set out on his mission and would arrive in Mexico "with full powers to adjust and definitively settle all pending differences between the two countries, including those of boundary between Mexico and the State of Texas."[1]

Polk's speech concisely, though one-sidedly, described the major issues that would prevent Texas' annexation from being a "bloodless achievement," and it established the backdrop for the first campaign of a war with Mexico. Although the president declared that annexation was solely the business of the United States and Texas, Mexican officials certainly had concerns in the merger. After the Lone Star Republic had split away from Mexico in 1836, authorities in Mexico City stubbornly refused to recognize the independence of the region. Although internal turmoil and fiscal problems continually foiled Mexico's goal, many of its leaders retained hope of one day having the resources to retake the wayward province. With each passing year, more and more Mexicans recognized that Texas was unlikely to return to the fold, but this did not translate into willingness to see it appended to the United States. Most believed that the United States had actively supported the revolution in Texas, and they did not want to see that country rewarded with the bounty of land. They also were aware that their northern neighbor coveted the rich lands and ports of California and believed that an independent Republic of Texas would at least provide an obstacle between the ambitious Yankees and Mexico's distant northwestern territories. When President Polk added a demand for Mexico to sell these territories to help pay its debts, he erased any doubt of the ultimate US objective and made it even more imperative that annexation should not take place.[2]

Thus Polk played a far more important role in creating a dispute than his speech implied. His portrayal of himself as a sort of observer and custodian to an annexation that had started before he arrived on the scene was far from accurate. He had run for his high office with a vow to extend US boundaries westward, and his victory in the fall of 1844 was widely viewed as a mandate for action. Desire to annex Texas had persisted in some quarters of the United States for almost a decade but had never been able to overcome the resistance of abolitionists and anti-expansionists. In the wake of Polk's election, Congress quickly seized the opportunity to craft a resolution to make Texas the twenty-eighth state. John Tyler, a longtime advocate of annexation and Polk's predecessor in the Oval Office, eagerly signed the bill into law as one of his final duties. Nevertheless, there was little doubt that it was the incoming president who provided the driving force behind annexation.[3]

Polk immediately stamped his name on the dispute. No sooner had he taken the oath of office on March 4, 1845, than he made clear that he would tolerate no interference from Mexico or any other nation. "I regard the question of annexation as belonging exclusively to the United States and Texas," he stated in his inaugural address. "They are independent powers competent to contract, and foreign nations have no right to interfere with them or to take exceptions to their reunion." The Mexican minister to Washington, Juan Almonte, responded angrily several days later, declaring the annexation to be "an act of aggression, the most unjust which can be found recorded in the annals of modern history."[4]

Polk also escalated tensions when he proposed his boundary for the new state. Since Mexico had never officially recognized the independence of Texas, no official border had been established between the two republics. Nevertheless, for years Texans had claimed title to the vast expanse of territory bounded by the Rio Grande, from its origins high in the Rocky Mountains to its mouth on the Gulf of Mexico. They frequently traced this jurisdiction to the 1836 Treaties of Velasco. In those documents, signed after his defeat and capture in the battle of San Jacinto, Mexico's president, Gen. Antonio López de Santa Anna, had publicly promised to withdraw his forces south of the river and secretly vowed to seek congressional approval for the independence of Texas and the establishment of a boundary. To a great degree, however, Texan possession of this territory was evident only on maps. Communities along the great waterway from Santa Fe all the way to the lower river delta remained distinctly Mexican and beyond the control of Texan authorities. The joint resolution for annexing Texas had not addressed the thorny issue of a border with Mexico, but Polk did not hesitate. He quickly embraced the expansive boundary claimed by Texas, and, as evidenced in his first annual speech, almost casually asserted that the United States now extended to the "Del Norte" as well.[5]

Mexican leaders strongly contested this logic, insisting that the province of Texas retained the borders established by the Spanish long ago. They described a much smaller territory, bounded to the south by the course of the Nueces River and then taking a northerly course toward the Red River on a zigzag line drawn just west of

James K. Polk. *Courtesy of Library of Congress.*

San Antonio. The rebellion of 1836 had not changed their maps, and the extensive lands between Texas and the Rio Grande were assigned to the states of Tamaulipas, Nuevo Léon, and Coahuila as well as the territory of Nuevo México. The Treaty of Velasco they recognized as nothing more than a cease-fire agreement, signed under duress, and certainly not a document that transferred the territory of loyal states to the rebellious residents of Texas. The secret portion of that accord the Mexican Congress had repudiated entirely, going so far as to pass a law voiding any agreement made by a president while being held captive. The legislators could do little to erase the reality that Texans had exercised their autonomy after defeating Santa Anna by force of arms. They could and did remain defiant in their unwillingness to cede to Texas portions of multiple other states of the Mexican federation.[6]

The question of whether or not to fight for their position presented Mexicans with a difficult decision. Some called for an immediate declaration of war and a march to retake Texas. Others questioned their nation's will to fight, believing that lawmakers would bluster loudly, then "go mildly to work," seeing little benefit to adopting "high-handed measures against their powerful neighbors." The Mexican Congress adopted a middle course, refusing to declare war but proclaiming Mexico's duty "to take up arms in her defense, to oppose such usurpation and . . . to use all her resources and power to prevent the annexation." A month later, on June 4, 1845, Pres. José Joaquín Herrera pronounced US actions in Texas to be "an insult to [Mexico's] dignity as a sovereign nation, threatening her independence and political right to exist," and called upon citizens to defend their country. He also mobilized the country's military forces in preparation for a fight. No declaration of war followed, however, and it remained uncertain whether this was the aforementioned bluster or the precursor to conflict.[7]

Polk responded to these pronouncements with the military forces mentioned in his annual address. On May 28, 1845, he issued orders for Gen. Zachary Taylor to gather the troops under his command in readiness for a march into Texas. Since 1844, Taylor had commanded a "Corps of Observation" at Fort Jesup, Louisiana. It was primarily charged with monitoring the relations between Texas and Mexico as the United States prepared the groundwork for annexation. Now that the "Lone Star" had been invited to join the American constellation, Taylor was to have his troops prepared "to promptly and efficiently act in the defense of Texas in the event it shall become necessary or proper to employ them." A second command, issued in June, offered clarification. Texans had scheduled a vote for July 4 to decide whether to accept the offer of statehood, and all indicators—including the symbolic date of the polling—suggested that approval would be forthcoming. Taylor was expected to act quickly after this vote, marching his force into the new state and occupying a point in "western" Texas on or near the Rio Grande. As Polk would later remind the nation in his annual address, Taylor had strict orders to "limit [himself] to the defense of the territory of Texas, unless Mexico should declare war against the United States."[8]

Though Taylor's official mission was to repel any armed attack from Mexico, the president intended this "Army of Occupation" to achieve other goals as well. By ordering his general into a position on the Texas frontier, Polk effectively claimed the land in dispute and obliged the Mexican military to try to wrest it away. With his show of force in Texas, Polk also sent a message to Mexican politicians that he was willing to risk a war for the territory and thereby forced them to consider whether they had the same level of commitment to fight. In particular, Polk especially wished to exert influence on President Herrera. Herrera had already expressed doubts about the wisdom of plunging his bankrupt and fractious nation into a costly and potentially devastating war with the United States and appeared willing to reach a settlement over Texas. Polk hoped that the buildup of forces in the vicinity of the Rio Grande would push his Mexican counterpart to the bargaining table and lead him to make territorial concessions without resorting to warfare.[9]

This optimism faded quickly. The Texan vote to accept annexation on July 4 stirred politicians in Mexico City into a state of fury and ended the ambivalence that had prevailed just a month before. Although President Herrera remained unconvinced that a conflict would be in the best interests of Mexico, now he swam against a political current that promised to wash him away. In a bid to silence his opponents and retain his tenuous hold on power, he reluctantly took action. On July 21, he succumbed to the demands of an inflamed Mexican congress and announced a resolution promising to declare war the moment annexation was formally completed or when US troops "invaded" Texas. His only caveat, a significant one, was that the Congress also had to find money to pay for the military campaign.[10]

General Taylor arrived in the disputed territory as these events unfolded. In spite of his orders to march to Texas, the general found the long overland trek to be impractical and decided instead to advance with the majority of his troops by sea. He relocated his headquarters to New Orleans, summoned scattered US military units to join him there, and scoured the coast of the Gulf of Mexico for a suitable spot to land his growing force. He had plenty of time for the search. Troops trickled in from camps and barracks in all corners of the nation, and by mid-July his force remained inadequate for any real defense of Texas. Nevertheless, Taylor saw the need to press onward. Texas had approved annexation, Mexican politicians were venting their anger, and New Orleans newspapers were filling their columns with tales of huge Mexican armies marching northward, heavily armed and bent on vengeance. On July 22, as soldiers continued to congregate at the Crescent City and just hours after President Herrera had called for war if US troops entered Texas, Taylor set sail aboard the steamship *Alabama* with eight companies of the 3rd US Infantry.[11]

His destination was the tiny settlement of Corpus Christi, situated on a large bay at the mouth of the Nueces River. The location was by no means impressive. Lt. Arthur Tracy Lee recalled the spot as "a bleak sandy plain for two miles to the southeast (of the river), dotted here and there with scrub live-oaks and dwarf mesquite, terminating at a bare, forbidding bluff, or ridge, under which slept in those days the sweet-scented village, hamlet, town or ranch of Corpus Christi—the most murderous, thieving, gambling, cut-throat, God-forsaken hole in the 'Lone Star State.'"[12]

This assessment notwithstanding, Corpus Christi was a healthful place to set up camp, had relatively easy access to the Gulf of Mexico, and provided a secure spot for Taylor to build up his command and mold it into a fighting force. It also served as a suitable location from which troops could sally forth to counter any attacks on the population centers of Texas, whether by Mexico or the roving Indian bands of the region. More importantly, the distance from the Rio Grande made a surprise Mexican attack unlikely and afforded Taylor time to get his bearings and overcome a woeful lack of intelligence about the region. In the interim, Col. Henry Lawrence Kinney, a Texan who had established the trade outpost in 1838, offered valuable guidance and passed along information gleaned from the traders who journeyed through the area. At almost 170 miles' distance from the Rio Grande, the camp site was not really on the river as specified in Polk's orders, but Taylor did occupy the south bank of the Nueces, just within the disputed strip between the two rivers, demonstrating an effort to comply with the spirit of the command.[13]

Taylor was wise to be cautious in situating his base, as his arrival in Texas hardly made an awe-inspiring show of force. The first units appeared off Saint Joseph's Island—a barrier island on the Texas coast—on July 25, but heavy winds and high seas prevented a landing. The weather relented the next day, but the US troops had not been alerted to the presence of a sand bar that prevented them from landing by boat and forced them instead to splash their way seventy-five yards through the surf. With a depot finally established, the troops then had trouble reaching their destination on the mainland. Shoals across portions of Corpus Christi Bay blocked the movement of all but the smallest boats, and it was not until July 31 that the first parties reached their intended destination. As the latest arrivals began to explore the plains and bluffs of their new home, transports slowly shuttled additional forces, company by company. By the end of the first week of August, the Army of Occupation had grown significantly stronger but still had only around three hundred men in the lightly defended camp.[14]

A slow build-up of American strength ensued. During the early weeks of August, seven companies of the US 4th Infantry and several companies of the 3rd Artillery arrived and struck their tents beside the 3rd Infantry on the Corpus Christi beachfront. On August 6, Robert Jones, adjutant general of the army, informed Taylor that the US 7th Infantry, units of the engineers and topographic engineers, and ten thousand muskets would soon follow. To ease the process of ferrying men and supplies between the Saint Joseph depot and Corpus Christi, the War Department also contracted a small fleet of low-draught steamboats that could cross the treacherous shoals. General Taylor welcomed these reinforcements but noted that he still faced a daunting challenge if Mexico intended to attack. The delayed arrival of the dragoons meant that he had no mounted troops available to conduct vital reconnaissance missions into the surrounding countryside. A lack of artillery forces similarly limited his ability to defend the camp. Most notably, as of August 14, he still had only 699 troops present in his command.[15]

Reports from the south sounded alarm bells about the deficiencies of this force. As troops continued to trickle in, the New Orleans press reported that President Herrera had called for the governors of northern provinces to raise troops for an invasion of Texas. Gen. Mariano Arista, they said, had already marched from the northern city of Monterrey at the head of fifteen hundred troops, a mix of one thousand infantry and five hundred cavalry. The Crescent City tabloids were a major source for information from Mexico City, and their accounts created a stir in both Washington and Corpus Christi. Suddenly, Taylor's force appeared to be extremely vulnerable—likely to be overwhelmed before it had adequately established itself. True, Taylor had received word from one of Colonel Kinney's spies, a Mexican known as Chepito, that Arista's force lacked money and would not be a threat, but the danger could not be ignored.[16]

Taylor immediately called for more men and more artillery pieces, and the War Department, which had heard rumors that Mexico had already invaded, readily complied. The adjutant general's office rapidly dispatched two companies of Louisiana volunteer artillery, four additional companies of light artillery, the 5th Infantry, and the 8th Infantry. These allotments would increase Taylor's force to four thousand men, which the secretary of war considered sufficient for the circumstances as they stood. If war should to break out, however, the secretary authorized Taylor to request more volunteer forces from the states of Louisiana, Alabama, Mississippi, Tennessee, and Kentucky to meet the crisis.[17]

But the troop numbers were adequate to meet the crisis, because the threat had been greatly overstated. In the midst of the outrage created by the vote to annex Texas, many Mexicans had been caught up in a spirit of nationalism and called for an immediate assault on the United States. They believed that the American Army was unorganized and vulnerable and would give way to a determined onslaught. But in their confidence they did not take into account the tenuous condition of their own military, especially the 4th Military Division, which was responsible for the defense of the provinces of Nuevo León, Coahuila, and Tamaulipas. Mariano Arista, the general-in-chief of this Northern Army, headed a force that included the 7th Cavalry Regiment, the 1st Infantry, the 2nd Light Infantry, the 2nd Artillery, the presidial companies, the 7th and 11th Auxiliary Squadrons, and the Batallión de Auxiliares de Monterrey. This army had never been sufficient to serve the needs of the region, and the ranks of those units had grown thin over time.[18]

Shortly after taking command in January 1845, Arista had documented his need for more troops and reminded the secretary of war that he had been promised enough reinforcements to raise his troop total to four thousand. Instead, he complained, he had been left with the same small force as before and reduced to begging for more. The letter apparently had little effect, for in April he issued additional requests arguing the urgency of his situation. He predicted that hostilities were likely to erupt near the Rio Grande and advised that the government would be "well served to provide me with everything necessary." Given adequate troops, Arista vowed that he would have "the determination to repel any assault"; without them, he warned, he could not prevent further insult. This brought no better result. By July, reinforcements still had not arrived. Despite confident statements about the abilities of his men, Arista viewed the situation as a crisis.[19]

Arista also struggled to meet the needs of the troops he did have. In addition to his regular requests for more men, he issued repeated complaints that his current army lacked sufficient uniforms, weapons, horses, and ammunition. Even worse, many of his soldiers had a limited supply of poor food—it amounted to little more than small rations of corn and lard. He warned that an "absolute lack of resources" had put his army in a state of "immobility" and Mexico in danger of losing "a precious portion of its territory." Although money would solve many of these problems, he had little to spare. Those who had preceded him in the northern command had made liberal use of credit, guaranteeing that ranchers, traders, and other producers of the area would be paid at some later date. By the time Arista took over, the term had ended on many promissory notes and the general found his command deeply in debt. Patience had also run out, and few merchants were willing to heed calls to extend additional lines of credit to the military. As US troops headed toward Corpus Christi, Arista still saw no evidence of the long-awaited provisions, and he reminded the minister of war somewhat dryly that the lack of resources would make it difficult for his army to achieve glorious results. "The enemy may be despicable," he wrote, "but when he advances toward our line he will have abundant provisions for mouth and war."[20]

Lack of men and funding provided ample reason for Mexican troops to forego an attack on the US force at Corpus Christi, but the northern forces also faced an additional obstacle. Even as US-Mexican relations spiraled downward, 1845 was proving to be an especially trying year for Indian attacks along the northern frontier. Throughout the spring and summer, large bands of Apaches and Comanches were staging frequent raids along the Rio Grande. These attacks brought death and destruction to many of the scattered settlements of Northern Mexico and severely tested the ability of the 4th Division to repel them. By July the boldness of the assaults had grown, and Arista reported that six hundred Indian warriors had formed a war party and ridden from their settlement in the north to engage in full-scale combat against Mexico. For these attacks Texas bore a large share of the blame. Earlier in the year, Texas had signed peace treaties with a number of tribes, and Mexico believed that an alliance had been struck to create havoc and weaken Mexican resistance. Although Texas may have urged them on, the Indians hardly needed encouragement. The Comanches had been engaged in a war of attrition with Mexico for years, and these latest attacks came as they attempted to seize advantage from the distraction caused by the arrival of US troops. In any event, the far-flung strikes obliged Arista to spread his forces across a wide area of the frontier, so that he could not consolidate his power to face the larger threat.[21]

The Mexican government was sympathetic to Arista's plight but was unable to give him much help. Though the country claimed to have an army of more than thirty-three thousand men ready to rise to its defense, the turmoil and revolts of recent years had reduced that number by at least five thousand. Many of the remaining soldiers were enlisted in militias dedicated to state or local defense or were stationed in forts and presidios that could not be abandoned, and many were raw recruits. In total, there were fewer than nineteen thousand permanent troops available—and these were scattered around a big country, one whose transport problems made moving armies from one end of it to the other extremely difficult. Moreover, the troops of the other divisions of the Mexican Army were, for the most part, no better clothed, armed, or fed than those under Arista's command. They too were clamoring for assistance. In addition to all these problems, the federal government was mired in debt and credit problems of its own. It simply could not pay for the troops and equipment Arista needed.[22]

The Herrera administration responded to the threat as best it could. In July, Minister of War Pedro García Conde, who had been on the receiving end of dozens of Arista's calls for support, promised that supplies and troops were at last on their way. Two entire divisions of the Mexican Army had been ordered northward to provide help. The 1st Division, under the command of Gen. Vicente Filisola, was to march for the northern city of San Luis Potosí, then move on to the Río Bravo to garrison the city of Matamoros. The 3rd Division, commanded by Gen. Mariano Paredes y Arrillaga, was also directed toward San Luis Potosí, but would soon move on to Monterrey, where Arista currently had his headquarters. Paredes' troops were to serve as a rear guard, allowing Arista to move forward against Taylor. García Conde noted that this army represented a substantial commitment by the federal government and that the states and provinces of the north needed to show their commitment as well. For this reason, President Herrera had called for them to establish new volunteer militia units, the Defensores de la Independencia y de las Leyes, also known as the Defensores de las Villas del Norte, to assist in the northern defense.[23]

Arista, however, viewed García Conde's response as inadequate. In late July, he warned that reinforcements and supplies had not arrived and that he was in no way prepared to assume an offensive. He noted that he had 929 soldiers of the 2nd Brigade stationed at Matamoros, 755 men of the 3rd Brigade to guard the Port of Tampico, 1323 troops in Monterrey as a reserve corps able to respond to multiple locations, and a few scattered detachments around the state of Coahuila. With a total force of only 3455 men, he found it nearly impossible to guard a 450-mile-long segment of the river. The eventual arrival of additional troops would simplify the matter, but it did not erase the continuing problem of supplies. Whereas the US forces could be supplied easily via the coast, Mexico would have to ship its war matériel on an arduous journey overland that could take days or weeks. Even that appeared impossible. Though resolute in his desire to combat the occupation as far to the north as possible, Arista evidently saw establishing a limited line of defense along the Río Bravo as his only option. Reports of Mexican troop levies and movements continued to foment American speculation that Mexico intended a large-scale assault on Corpus Christi, but Arista had resigned himself to waiting for Taylor and his troops to approach the disputed river boundary.[24]

That advance would not come soon. Like Arista, officials of the Polk administration expected Zachary Taylor to summon his strength at Corpus Christi and then head southward toward the Rio Grande as quickly as possible. Even at the height of concern over a pending Mexican attack, Secretary of War William Marcy frequently reminded Taylor that his goal should be to extend his protection of Texas all the way to the Rio Grande, move as close to the river "as prudence dictates," and challenge any Mexican attempt to cross it. Taylor, however, took a different view. As additional regiments arrived to supplement his force, he grew convinced that a Mexican assault was not coming. Even if it did, he now felt comfortable in his ability to defend his position and the frontier villages of Texas, as his orders demanded. A move toward the Rio Grande, he surmised, would merely prod the Mexican army to respond with force, and he wanted to limit provocation until he had his entire army in place. Throughout the month of September he held his position, allowing his reinforcements to arrive and settle into camp. One month after the initial landing at Saint Joseph's Island, the secretary of war continued to warn of the need to adopt a forward position to meet a Mexican incursion. But as September gave way to October, Taylor held fast in Corpus Christi and gave no sign that he intended to move.[25]

The general had an additional motive for his deliberate approach to the campaign. Though he hailed from Louisiana, which was part of the block of southern states that supported national expansion and a possible territorial war with Mexico, Zachary Taylor had no great desire to initiate that conflict. As a stalwart member of the Whigs, who were currently in opposition to Polk's Democrats in Congress, Taylor had endorsed his party's stance against the annexation of Texas and questioned the president's claims of a boundary on the Rio Grande. He also understood that the president faced an uphill battle to win public approval for a war with Mexico and could hope to achieve support only if the Mexican army crossed the Rio Grande and attacked his forces. From the moment he arrived in Corpus Christi, Taylor expressed concern that his true mission was not to prevent the Mexicans from crossing the river, but to provoke them to do so, thereby providing Polk with justification for waging war if diplomacy failed. Junior officers noted that Taylor did not have his heart in his duties, and they resented having been selected to serve as high-stakes pawns in the political chess match.[26] They were not surprised that in the absence of a direct Mexican threat, their commander avoided actions that might inflame the enemy and remained as far from the Rio Grande as his orders permitted.

During this time, Taylor's camp at Corpus Christi began to evolve into a semi-permanent home for the US Army of Occupation. Throughout August and September of 1846, hundreds of Infantry troops poured into the area—first the 7th Infantry, then companies of the 4th, 5th, and 8th. Artillery units arrived as well, including heavy guns, the light horse artillery units of Maj. Samuel Ringgold and Capt. James Duncan, and two companies of the Louisiana Volunteer Artillery. Perhaps most importantly, the camp received the long-awaited companies of the 2nd Dragoons and several topographic engineers, allowing scouting and mapping of the region to begin. By October, Taylor placed his troop strength at just over four thousand officers and men. The four-hundred-yard strip of sand between the Corpus Christi Bay and a row of low, sandy bluffs, had previously harbored perhaps fourteen "shabby shanties," but now supported a "canvas town" consisting of hundreds of tents. Establishments to support this thriving community soon followed. "The arrival of Hart's theatrical company from Savannah was a prelude to the erection of quite a pretentious theatre," recalled Arthur Tracey Lee. "Restaurants, billiard-rooms, gambling hells, and all the usual adjuncts to such an establishment appeared like magic." Real estate brokers also appeared, surveyed the grounds of the camp, and divided it into lots, which they quickly sold to investment-minded men like Lt. Forbes Britton.[27]

During the months of September and October, as fears of a Mexican attack faded, the troops enjoyed the balmy climate and other offerings of this thriving community. With the gentle surf of Corpus Christi Bay directly to the east and an abundance of game just over the bluffs to the west, many soldiers filled their idle hours with fishing trips and hunting expeditions. Other leisurely pursuits like horse racing and sea bathing also thrived, as did the opportunities for socializing and gaming in the busy saloons. At times the soldiers described their situation in terms better fitting a resort than a military encampment. Capt. Ephraim Kirby-Smith called the climate "perfectly delicious and healthy; no possibility of sickness, and so cool from the trade winds, which blow steadily, that our cloth clothing is very comfortable."[28] Lt. Richard Cochrine agreed and appeared to forget the dangerous purpose of his mission for a moment when he said, "I think we are truly fortunate in coming South at the season we did and in getting such a delightful situation."[29]

Not all of camp life was pleasurable, however, and the army experienced its share of alarms and casualties. Newcomers to the area were often startled to find their peace ful night's sleep interrupted by rattlesnakes in the tents. Experienced troops learned to construct makeshift raised beds that permitted them to slumber in relative safety. And despite the much-touted healthfulness of Corpus Christi, the soaring population of the military encampment brought on a corresponding rise in disease. While cases of dreaded tropical fevers remained mercifully scarce, growing numbers of men suffered from bouts of dysentery and other digestive ailments. The presence of thousands of firearms in the hands of idle soldiers also took a toll in the form of accidents and injuries. In one incident a soldier fired his pistol at a tree and the bullet ricocheted off the trunk, striking Lt. Lafayette McLaws, who happened to be riding past. McLaws suffered a relatively minor injury, but a number of hunting accidents and some quarrels among troops resulted in additional shootings with more serious, occasionally fatal, results.[30]

By far the most notable incident, however, was the explosion of the steamship *Dayton* on September 12, 1845. One of the low-draft boats contracted to transport troops and supplies across the shallow Corpus Christi Bay, the aging *Dayton* had left the encampment and was headed for Saint Joseph Island with about twenty-seven men onboard when its straining boilers exploded, firing large pieces of iron in all directions across the deck. As the smoke cleared, the boat settled to the bottom of the bay, leaving the "sea covered with pieces of wreck and floating bodies."[31] Fortunately, the deck of the ship remained above the waterline, permitting many onboard to be rescued. But flying debris struck and killed seven soldiers immediately, and another died later of his wounds. All but two of the passengers suffered some degree of injury. For those who viewed the scalded, burned, and battered victims, the explosion served as a solemn reminder of the dangers that might lie ahead. The bodies of the fallen were laid to rest on a bluff overlooking the Nueces River.

But neither the pleasures of camp life nor the occasional disaster deterred the troops from readying themselves for the primary business at hand. Though he may have been opposed to starting a war, General Taylor was well aware that he might have to wage one, and he took measures to ensure that his army was properly prepared. Upon the arrival of the dragoons and engineers, he undertook tentative explorations of the countryside. Several parties made forays westward on the Nueces River and north and south along the coast, directed to map the army's current position and the initial stages of any march toward the Rio Grande. Taylor also tended to his transportation needs. Since the march to the Rio Grande would require a sizable supply train, he began looking for the horses, mules, and oxen necessary to make the overland trek. In this he had a clear advantage over his Mexican counterpart. With money in hand, he found many Mexican traders willing to do business with him, and he quickly acquired a substantial herd of draft animals.[32]

Taylor's highest priority was to ready his army for field combat. From the moment the first troops arrived at Corpus Christi, he focused on melding the incoming units into a single, cohesive force. "Discipline was not required by the 'Army of Occupation,'" recalled Lt. Alexander Hays, "but consolidation was essential and in this delightful locality, time and opportunity were afforded to perfect its organization by combining all its effective, but hitherto scattered elements." Although the US Army was composed of well-trained, veteran professionals, many of whom had combat experience in conflicts like the Florida Seminole Wars, it had not fought a full-scale European-style battle since the War of 1812. In many cases the American career soldiers had never gone to battle with a force larger than a few military companies. And because most of the troops were dispersed among far-flung frontier outposts, officers had never even had an opportunity to pull their units together for training exercises. Mexico, meanwhile, had fought many large clashes in its war of independence and in the more recent Texas Revolution. Whatever deficiencies its army faced in manpower and supplies, it had the upper hand in experience on a traditional battlefield. Taylor hoped to compensate for his disadvantage by devising an extensive regimen of drills that required cooperation among all branches of the service: infantry, cavalry, and artillery. He devoted hours each day to training the troops to work at a variety of organizational levels, including battalions, regiments, brigades, and divisions. He also began to enforce a strict dress code, designed to reinforce the notion that the army should look and act like a unified organization.[33]

By October this training began to show results, and Taylor finally had his full complement of troops at his disposal. In a letter to the adjutant general of the army, dated October 15, he reported that the final units had arrived at camp and that his force now stood at 3,860 men. Other sources placed the figure at 3922; this number included 251 officers and 150 dragoons nearby in the interior of Texas. Taylor had deployed these men into three brigades: the first consisted of the 8th Infantry and twelve companies of artillery and dragoons; the second, of the 5th and 7th Infantries along with four companies of horse artillery; and the last, of the 3rd and 4th Infantries, supported by two companies of Louisiana volunteer artillery. These latter companies Taylor deemed unnecessary because of the other, better-trained regular units, and he let them go home when their enlistment period ended in November. He restated his concerns about the need to continue drilling the troops in brigade maneuvers but otherwise appeared pleased, telling the adjutant, "I feel a satisfaction which I cannot doubt will be shared by the department, in being able thus to report the completion, without disaster or notable accident, of the transfer of so many bodies of troops from remote points to this coast at an unfavorable season of the year."[34]

This strength in numbers also permitted Taylor to give some thought to advancing toward the Rio Grande, and he broached the subject to his superiors in Washington. In a somewhat defensive tone he explained his reasons for remaining so long in Corpus Christi—he cited the absence of artillery, limited infantry, a lack of military engineers, and other points. He also expressed his belief that his presence in Corpus Christi was sufficient to deter any Mexican intrigue along the disputed frontier and recommended that he remain there. But he added that if the United States wanted to give a clear, unequivocal ultimatum about the Rio Grande as boundary, it should be accompanied by a bold show of force closer to the river. In that event, he recommended occupying the coastal port at Point Isabel and the inland city of Laredo, as these offered the best opportunities for defense and for monitoring Mexican movements. He declined to advance there, however, without a direct command from the War Department. Whether Taylor was trying to force the Polk administration to openly state its intentions or merely seeking to legitimize his actions is unclear, but whatever his purpose, he awaited orders.[35]

What Taylor did not know was that the Polk administration believed a diplomatic breakthrough to be near at hand. President Herrera had won reelection in August and had temporarily solidified his hold on power. His stipulation that Mexico not declare war without the funding to wage it had also tempered the drumbeats for war. By October, Herrera felt sufficiently secure to accept Polk's request for a new round of negotiations.[36] Seizing the opportunity, Polk dispatched Louisiana Congressman John Slidell, the envoy noted in his annual address, to sail for Mexico to begin discussions as soon as possible. With tensions dissipating, Secretary of War Marcy issued a note to Taylor advising him to turn his attention to locating winter quarters for his troops. This letter again encouraged Taylor to approach the Rio Grande as closely as possible, but it gave him considerable leeway in choosing his position and deploying his forces. The only proviso was that Taylor should continue to collect information to support any future campaign.[37]

Not surprisingly, Taylor responded to these directions with caution. He continued to believe that Corpus Christi offered the best haven for his troops, and with no

Camp of the Army of Occupation, Corpus Christi. *Courtesy of H. R. Hudson Collection.*

sign of hostilities along the Rio Grande, he saw no pressing reason to make an advance. News that the US negotiator John Slidell had left for Mexico City in early November strengthened his view. With a diplomatic resolution to the Texas crisis in the works, Taylor appeared unwilling to initiate an inflammatory march to the Rio Grande. Perhaps most notably, he had not received the direct order that he had requested. So he elected to remain in Corpus Christi—thus making a decision that would keep the US Army there until March of 1846.[38]

Life in the winter quarters at Corpus Christi continued much as before, with one significant difference—the weather. Taylor maintained the daily regimen of training and continued to hone the ability of troops to work in the newly established brigades. The town of Corpus Christi carried on as well, attracting thousands of traders, hangers-on, and "worthless characters" from both Texas and Mexico who hoped to make a living from the semipermanent base. Saloons and gaming places conducted a booming business and were soon joined by grocers, a newspaper, and additional theaters and churches. Mexican merchants found their wares in high demand as soldiers purchased textiles and other souvenirs to send home to family and friends.

But beginning in late October, the camp by the bay no longer seemed the exotic paradise of its early days. A bitter norther blasted through, ushering in an unusually cold and wet winter. With the frigid temperatures came sickness, and hundreds of soldiers suffered from a catalog of ailments that included fevers, diarrhea, dysentery, catarrh, rheumatism, abscesses and ulcers. Lack of suitable barracks added to the misery. One physician who tended to the ill described the quarters as being "of the worst quality."The rain, he said, "drizzled through the new tents, so as to wet everything, and many of the tents were worn out and useless. Officers could do something in the way of protection, by means of rubber coverings to their camp beds, etc.; but what could the poor soldier do?"

As temperatures dipped into the twenties, many men turned to a desperate search for wood that could be used to stoke camp fires, and brush that could be placed around tents to block the biting wind off the coast. Though remarkably few soldiers succumbed to their ailments, the wretchedness they endured created discord and dissatisfaction within the ranks. By December, words of praise for the glittering tent-city by the sea had been replaced by complaints and desertions.[39]

These dismal conditions also played havoc with Taylor's efforts to prepare his forces. Illness and poor weather kept troops away from the drilling fields and parade grounds, delaying efforts to develop the army's coordination. Reconnaissance missions suffered as well. Sent to scout a boat route along the Laguna Madre—the 150-mile-long waterway that stretches south from Corpus Christi between the mainland and the barrier island known as Padre Island—George Meade, a lieutenant of the Corps of Engineers, traveled only forty miles before shallow waters made further progress impossible. The "cold, miserable" weather encouraged him to make a speedy return to camp. On a similar journey, Capt. Charles May led a party of dragoons inland from Corpus Christi to determine the condition of the road south to the Mexican city of Matamoros. His party had traveled only twenty miles from camp when he discovered that heavy rains had turned the route into an impassable quagmire. Other surveys of the countryside did proceed, with scouts fanning out in all directions from the camp. Nevertheless, as 1845 came to a close, General Taylor did not have a clear picture of where he could place depots and establish camps along the main road to the Rio Grande, and he was not even certain that his force could advance along the route at all.[40]

This shortfall in intelligence took on greater importance with the arrival of the New Year. President Polk's annual address of December 1845 had held out promise that

Mexico would soon come to terms, but complications now chipped away at optimism. John Slidell arrived in Mexico City with a long list of discussion topics, including Texas, Mexican debts to American creditors, and the possible purchase of the New Mexico and California territories. President Herrera was willing to negotiate on Texas, possibly to tie an agreement about it to forgiveness of Mexican debts, but he was not willing to discuss surrendering additional territory. Concerned about the proposed range of talking points and about Slidell's title, "Envoy Extraordinary and Minister Plenipotentiary," which might imply a US attempt to restore full diplomatic relations, Herrera refused to meet, fearing that his enemies would brand him a traitor and cast him from office. As days of delay turned into weeks, Polk grew frustrated and decided to raise the pressure on Herrera. On January 13, 1846, he issued orders through the secretary of war for Taylor to proceed to the Rio Grande and take up a position there as soon as weather permitted.[41]

The orders reached Taylor at Corpus Christi in early February and caused an abrupt transformation in the US camp. The dull routine of the past several months gave way to a burst of activity as the army made last-minute efforts to acquire pack animals and supplies for the march. As sunny weather drove away the frigid rain of January, scouts ramped up efforts to locate the most suitable route from Corpus Christi to Matamoros, on the Rio Grande. Taylor had selected that city as his objective over locations near Mier and Laredo because its proximity to the Gulf Coast and the port of Frontón de Santa Isabel (or Point Isabel) would considerably shorten his supply lines. Unfortunately, since the army lacked the boats to transport all his troops and supplies, he still had to prepare for a laborious land march instead of a short sea voyage to his destination.[42]

The arid brushlands between Corpus Christi and the Rio Grande offered limited options for Taylor's advance. The most obvious choice was to head west from the camp on the Nueces until the path intersected the Matamoros-to-San Patricio road—about twenty-five miles away. From there the army could turn south and follow the 150-mile route until it ended on the Rio Grande. Frequently used by Mexican forces during their campaigns in Texas, this route ran past established water and pasturage areas and had proven that it could sustain troops and trains of pack and food animals. But it would require the army to ford several wide streams, and without pontoon bridges to help them make the crossings, Taylor feared the way might be impassable after the heavy winter rains. The alternative was to transport his troops to Padre Island and follow that narrow strip of land down to its terminus on the Brazos Santiago strait, near Point Isabel. This path was free of water crossings, but Taylor was not sure that the coastal dunes could provide enough fresh water and grass to support the advance. Confronted with two uncertain choices, he ordered investigations of both routes as soon as the weather broke in early February.[43]

By the middle of the month, the reports from both reconnaissances came in. The exploration of Padre Island, headed by the dragoon captain William Hardee, had traversed the length of the barrier island with little difficulty, finding a smooth, hard path and enough game to help feed the advancing troops. Upon reaching Brazos Santiago at the southern tip of the strand, the soldiers had encountered a Mexican revenue officer from Point Isabel who demanded their passports. The American soldiers, who carried no such documents, countered with assurances that the pending US occupation would bring improved trade and good treatment to the people of the region.[44]

The other expedition along the inland road had also proceeded without incident. Capt. Henry Hopkins Sibley, joined by Lt. Fowler Hamilton, had led a small detachment of the 2nd Dragoons on a hundred-mile journey along the Matamoros road. They had taken with them a small train of lightly loaded wagons to test whether a supply convoy could successfully make its way along this route, and their findings were highly encouraging. Although heavy rains had fallen in the days leading up to the journey and the road was muddy and occasionally flooded, the party had no difficulty following the route. Sibley concluded that the inland path was "perfectly practicable" for wagons and artillery, pointing out that the very worst conditions were along the first twenty-five miles of the march. He also noted that the route offered suitable stopping points for an extended march, often with plentiful firewood, pasturage, and water—resources that would make the advance considerably easier. Moreover, by the time of the return trip, road conditions had improved dramatically, indicating that a few sunny days might completely conquer the mud. In his report on the journey, which he concluded on February 21, the captain observed with some satisfaction that "a more favorable time for marching the army with its baggage and supply train from hence to the Rio Grande could not be selected than the present."[45] General Taylor apparently agreed and made immediate plans to advance along this corridor.

With the route selected, preparations moved forward rapidly. On February 24 Taylor gave notice that a march was imminent, possibly within the next forty-eight hours. The troops responded with a fevered effort to break down their camp, pack their gear, and write a few final letters home. Meanwhile, quartermasters gathered the last items on their supply lists. When these goods arrived, there were not enough mules to transport them, so Taylor hired a number of Mexican rancheros to round up some of the wild horses that roamed the area, break them, and train them to pull wagons. These activities pushed his original two-day timetable back, so that some of the soldiers were able to see a final play and attend a sermon in the camp theater before it was brought to the ground. But the delay was slight. On March 4, Maj. William Graham set out with a vanguard of about sixty men to establish a supply depot near Santa Gertrudis Creek, about fifty miles along the route. The rest of the army received word that, at long last, it would follow.[46]

During his final days in Corpus Christi, General Taylor also attended to some pre-march diplomacy. He wrote a proclamation to the people of Matamoros in which he alerted them to the march, promised that his intentions were peaceful, and vowed to respect the religious freedom and civil rights of the people he encountered. He also vowed to pay fair market value for any goods required. These words were in keeping with the administration's belief that the advance would pressure the Mexican government into complying with territorial demands, rather than provoke it to war. Although Gen. Mariano Paredes had recently seized power and vowed to fight for Texas, many Americans considered his words mere bluster and doubted that he would act on them. Even if Paredes did intend to pursue the dispute to a military conclusion, Polk and his administration held out hope that pressure might work on another audience. Politicians in the Northern states of Mexico had long exhibited an independent streak and resisted control from Mexico City. Some northern leaders had previously expressed interest in forming their own republic. If these leaders observed the US commitment to claiming the Rio Grande, coupled with assurances of religious and property rights for the Mexican people north of it, they might be induced to break away from Mexico, reach their own terms with the United States, and put a sizable amount of currency into their treasury. With this in mind, the secretary of war advised Taylor to tend to military affairs while also keeping a close eye on the sentiments of the people along the border.[47]

Some in Taylor's army suspected that war would be the inevitable consequence of an advance. In a letter to his fiancée, Julia Dent, Lt. Ulysses S. Grant wrote that the Mexicans "will make us fight for our ground before we will be allowed to occupy it." Col. Ethan Allen Hitchcock, in letters and diary notations, cited reports that sixty thousand to one hundred thousand Mexican troops had mobilized for war and were prepared to respond to the provocation of an American march. Residents of Corpus Christi agreed, offering dire warnings that a move toward Matamoros would lead to immediate conflict. Whether or not these merchants had any real knowledge is unclear.

They may, as many US soldiers believed, have been principally concerned with the income they would lose if the Americans left the Nueces River.[48]

Still uncertain how much threat lay ahead, the Army of Occupation began to file out of Corpus Christi on March 8, 1846. After four months of intensive drill, the soldiers who left the bayside camp had evolved from the loose collection of companies that had arrived in the fall into a true, structured army that advanced in three well-disciplined divisions. These divisions had changed slightly from the original organization established in October. On the morning of March 8, an advance unit consisting of the 2nd Dragoons and Samuel Ringgold's light artillery company set out to blaze a path. The next day, Gen. William Jenkins Worth moved out with the 1st Brigade, which now consisted of the 8th Infantry and ten artillery companies. The day after that, the 2nd Brigade—led by Col. James McIntosh and composed of the 5th and 7th Infantries along with James Duncan's light artillery battery—followed. At last, on March 11, the 3rd and 4th Infantries and Braxton Bragg's light artillery battery marched out as the 3rd Battalion, under the command of Col. William Whistler. The 3rd Battalion had in tow some three hundred wagons laden with supplies. Taylor and his staff also left on the eleventh and brought up the rear of this grand procession.[49]

Not everyone traveled overland. Maj. John Monroe and his company of infantrymen remained behind to supervise the loading of ships at Saint Joseph's Island. Although provisions needed to sustain the march had been sent with the army, Monroe had the responsibility of escorting most of the supplies and heavy artillery pieces via the Gulf to Point Isabel, where he was to rendezvous with the rest of the army. The ships also carried several of the topographic engineers and a number of the camp women who would be needed to cook and clean for the army upon its arrival, but who were not expected to brave the long, hazardous march.[50]

Also left behind were the shops, saloons, and merchants of the bustling town of Corpus Christi. Although the traders, hustlers, and layabouts who had congregated around the American camp had been ordered to remain behind, few of the soldiers expected them to do that. Many would dissolve back into the surrounding countryside, pursuing the livelihoods they had followed before the first troops arrived. But others would ignore Taylor's wishes and follow the troops at a safe distance. "Many of them," wrote Lt. Robert Hazlett, "will 'take up their beds and walk' to the Rio Grande to prey upon us." The town that these hangers-on had constructed along the bay was expected to wither and die. As Capt. Joseph King Fenno Mansfield of the engineer corps noted, the booming commerce of the port had been entirely the result of the army, without which the area offered "no inducements or advantages." Lieutenant Hazlitt made the same assessment, observing that "this move of the army is a sad blow to Corpus Christi. It rose with the army and it will fall without it." He went on to wax poetic about the wretched town and the unpleasant people who had populated it: "Oh! Corpus Christi, the child of the army, how thou hast fallen! Thy streets are deserted, thy public places no longer resound with mirth and revelry—thy theatres are closed and thy gamblers are gone. Thus lament the Corpus Christians, the worst set of Christians perhaps under the sun."

Many of Hazlitt's companions who had previously enjoyed the town now shared his disillusionment with it. Even with the threat of war hanging over their march, few expressed regret at leaving this home of the last seven months.[51]

The Mexican forces were aware of Taylor's move south. In addition to his own bold announcement of his intended march, military leaders in the north also had detailed spy reports submitted by Mexican traders and observers who had infiltrated the American camp.[52] They had little else. Although the Americans heard rumors of thousands of troops pouring into the region along the Rio Grande, in reality the Mexican military situation had not improved and in some ways had grown even worse.

As the direct result of plotting by Gen. Mariano Paredes y Arrillaga, troop levels in northern Mexico had failed to climb significantly during the period that US forces occupied Corpus Christi. After receiving assurances in July 1845 that Paredes had been ordered northward, Gen. Mariano Arista gratefully awaited his arrival. But as the month of August passed with no sign of the promised troops, Arista grew increasingly frustrated. In correspondence with Paredes, he learned that the 3rd Brigade was in a "disagreeable state" and could not march until it received funding for supplies. Troops of the 1st Brigade reportedly had been held up in San Luis Potosí for the same reason. This news spurred Arista to write another round of letters to the newly appointed Minister of War, Pedro de Anaya, in which he restated his plight and begged for assistance. At that point, Anaya revealed that Paredes had in fact been given more than seventy thousand pesos to fund his advance and that the troop movement should have been well underway. Pressed by Arista to explain his delay, Paredes offered vague excuses, but promised to send five hundred infantry troops and two hundred cavalry as an advance party.[53]

Paredes did not explain that he was preoccupied with a plan to overthrow the Herrera government. As tensions between Mexico and the United States simmered, longtime politician Lucas Aláman and Spanish foreign minister Salvador Bermúdez de

Castro plotted to replace Herrera's weak liberal government with a conservative regime that would rein in individual states, reestablish strong central authority, and produce the political stability required to defend the country. To this end, they actually hoped to see Herrera sell Texas to the United States. In the aftermath of such an act, they could denounce the president for disloyalty, expel him from office, and use the proceeds from the territorial sale to fund their efforts to rebuild Mexico. Ultimately, they hoped to place a Spanish prince at the head of government. To accomplish this rather cynical program, however, they required military support, and they selected Paredes as their co-conspirator. The experienced general, who supported the conservative cause, had

Mariano Paredes y Arrillaga. *Courtesy of Benson Latin American Collection, University of Texas at Austin.*

participated in an 1844 revolt against General Santa Anna and resented Herrera's having been selected in his stead for the presidency at that time. Most importantly, Paredes had command of a force of almost eight thousand men who could be directed to the capital when the opportune moment arose.[54]

A significant hitch to a harmonious partnership was Paredes' desire to take Texas back. The general strongly disapproved of American meddling in the region and wanted to reclaim it for Mexico. This ambition of course undermined the entire foundation of the plan devised by Aláman and Bermudez, who tried to persuade Paredes that the opportunity to save Texas had long since passed. But Paredes remained unconvinced and insisted upon his desire to restore Mexico's territorial integrity. He feared, moreover, that failure to defend the border would bring disgrace on the army and damage the organization at the center of his career.

This rift was resolved when the early arrival of the US envoy forced the conspirators to advance their timeline. John Slidell's appearance in Mexico City angered Mexico's liberal faction, and the conservative conspirators feared that group might oust Herrera before they themselves could act. It was also possible that Herrera might broker a quick resolution to the Texas dispute. In that event, the president could declare that peace reigned and disband the army before it could march against him. Sensing that their window of opportunity might snap shut, they modified their plan and decided to condemn the president simply for allowing an enemy envoy into the country. Herrera tried to stave off rebellion by delaying his meeting with Slidell, but to no avail. On December 15, 1845, Paredes and his garrison declared against the president and marched on the capital. On December 29—the same day that James Polk signed the legislation making Texas the twenty-eighth US state—troops in Mexico City joined the rebellion and forced Herrera to resign. Paredes himself entered the city on January 2, 1846, and installed himself as interim president of the republic.[55]

Arista sensed the political intrigue unfolding to his south long before Paredes proclaimed against Herrera, and he attempted to keep both factions focused on border defense. As early as the end of August, he realized that Paredes intended to use the garrison at San Luis Potosí for an assault on Mexico City. Nevertheless, he maintained an active correspondence with the rogue general in the forlorn hope that a common desire to protect Mexican territory might induce him to spare some troops for the frontier. Referring to Paredes as "my dear compatriot and fine friend," he pleaded that "the urgent moment has arrived for you to make whatever sacrifice is necessary and I beg you to order the immediate advance of the troops that I am supposed to receive and that are so necessary to defend Matamoros and repel the advance of the enemy."[56] At the same time, he continued to press Mexico City for troops so that he could seize the initiative and carry war to the US camp. "We have already passed the point at which we could have preserved a minimum of our national honor," he wrote to the minister of war. "We must initiate hostilities at any cost and in any event, whether our troops be many or few." His words failed to produce an effect on either front. With Herrera focused on self-preservation and Paredes bent on seizing control, neither was willing to spare troops for the common goal of combating the United States.[57]

Arista did what he could to prepare a defense. In August he sent Gen. Francisco Mejía and several hundred men of the 2nd Brigade to reinforce the vital frontier city of Matamoros and ordered the small garrison to shore up the town's crumbling defenses.[58] He also focused on activities north of the Río Bravo. He sent dozens of spies into the US camp in the guise of travelers and traders and used their reports to develop a remarkably accurate picture of enemy troop strength and activities. Unable to purchase horses for his troops, he encouraged some of the infiltrators to steal mounts from American soldiers and turn them over to needy Mexican forces.[59] In November, after Mexican scouts sighted US reconnaissance parties in the barren lands between Corpus Christi and Matamoros, Arista ordered Mejía to establish a small garrison on the Arroyo Colorado—a distributary channel of the Río Bravo some twenty-five miles north of Matamoros—as a first line of defense. That outpost became an important base of operations for the dozens of scouts and spies who roamed the rangeland to the north and monitored Taylor's every move.[60]

Concerns about troop and supply levels understandably dominated Arista's attention throughout the autumn of 1845, but he soon found himself plagued with other troubles as well. He continued to issue a steady stream of letters to the secretary of war in Mexico City and General Paredes in San Luis Potosí, filled with well-rehearsed lines about his need for help and the risks of ignoring his pleas. These appeals subsided only slightly when Arista realized that Taylor had decided to settle in at Corpus Christi for the winter. But the semi-permanent presence of the American camp also created a new challenge: smuggling and illicit trade between Mexican traders and US troops. The Mexican general, who had to struggle to feed and clothe the men under his command, watched with chagrin as residents of towns as far off as Reynosa and Matamoros rushed to the American camp to sell food, cloth, oxen, and horses. In an attempt to halt this assistance to the enemy, in November he issued a decree banning such trade. But a month later the movement of contraband continued. The same shortages that limited Arista's effectiveness against the Americans prevented his clamping down on the smugglers, whom he clearly viewed as betrayers of their homeland.[61]

Perhaps more damaging, Arista's own loyalties were called into question. As the general maintained his heated correspondence with Mariano Paredes, rumors suddenly began to circulate that Arista, a longtime resident of Mexico's north, supported the independence of that region and even maintained secret ties to Texas. In November, the newspaper *El Amigo del Pueblo* denounced Arista as a traitor, asserting that even as he was clamoring for more money and troops, he had been quietly using soldiers as laborers on his private estate, and that he benefited from food contracts and had even helped the US Army acquire mules that would be used to transport troops to the Rio Grande. Arista downplayed the report, noting that since the periodical "preoccupies itself with a dual policy of promoting indecent personalities and attacking public officials, I have made it a point not to read this incendiary paper." But he also vehemently denied the charges, which he suspected had been initiated by Paredes. In messages to his superiors he justified his efforts to gather supplies, explained that he relied on informants selling mules to gather information about the enemy, and reiterated his allegiance to the country. "I assure you that there is nothing capable of disturbing my loyalty and that of the troops," he wrote. "We remain firm in our will to defend the supreme government and to preserve the integrity of our territory, and we will stand as the strongest pillar of support of the current administration."[62]

Curiously enough, however, it was Arista's loyalty to the Herrera administration that caused him the greatest trouble. As it became increasingly evident that General Paredes intended to rise against Mexico City, Arista sent multiple messages southward, pledging his enduring fealty to Mexico and the existing government. When Paredes actually initiated his march in December, Arista refused to support the insurgency and instead issued a proclamation stating that it was vital to the "salvation of the Republic" that troops remain loyal to the existing government. He declared the entire 4th Division to be in opposition to the San Luis movement and vowed to resist this step toward anarchy. No other major military leader embraced his opinion, and as Paredes established his control over the capital and the government, Arista found himself isolated from the new regime. When Paredes accepted the mantle of interim president on January 6, it became clear that Arista's tenure as commander of the northern forces had reached its end. On January 14, 1846, Arista accepted the inevitable. Declaring that national defense and territorial preservation remained his overriding goals, he announced that he now felt those causes could best be served by his resignation from the army. After pledging that he would return to service if Mexico ever needed him, he turned his command over to Gen. Rómulo Díaz de la Vega and retired to his home near Monterrey.[63]

Arista's resignation added one more problem for an already troubled administration. Mariano Paredes had declared his rebellion against Herrera by promising a "necessary and glorious war" to defend Mexican territory. In one of his first speeches as interim president he renewed his denunciation of his predecessor for the indecision and weakness that had encouraged the United States to undertake a "scandalous usurpation" of Texas. Meanwhile, Paredes had significantly undermined Mexico's northern defenses by marching his troops to seize the capital. Uncertain of his own hold on power, he then hesitated to send his army on to reinforce the frontier. Instead, he ordered Gen. Pedro de Ampudia back to San Luis Potosí to assemble a new force for that purpose. The new troops were far from ready to advance, leaving only the Army of the North—which lacked manpower, supplies, and now its best leader—to hold the line against the Americans. Faced with these circumstances, Paredes hesitated to expel John Slidell from Mexico and push Mexico to the brink of war. Yet throughout January and February of 1846, he also remained adamant in his determination not to negotiate with the US envoy. In short, he found himself powerless to act and relying on the same feeble tactics used by President Herrera during his final days in office.[64]

Paredes' paralysis was noted both at home and in the United States. In Mexico City, friends and foes alike had been stirred by the interim president's fiery demands to fight for Texas, and newspapers did not conveniently forget his earlier rhetoric. "War, and only war, is the honorable path that Mexico must follow in order to preserve her rights," thundered the editors of the *Monitor Republicano*. "Triumph or failure: in the first case she would present herself to the world crowned in glory, freed from the stain that has engulfed her, and respected by her enemies. If the second case occurs, we would rather perish in a fight for the most just of causes than lose our name in humiliation and infamy."[65]

But the *Monitor* also had grown frustrated over the timid treatment of the US envoy, the woeful state of national defenses, and the endless stream of excuses for the government's lack of money and resources with which to make a strong stand. "Didn't they tell us," its editors wrote, "that the Herrera government had all the resources it needed at its disposal? . . . Why then does the current administration not put them to use? The nation is the same, the resources the same, the skills no better, only the men have changed. In what way have we improved?"[66]

Observing this discord from afar, James Polk grew convinced that Mexico would bow to necessity and ultimately seek to avoid a costly war. It seemed just a matter of time before the embattled Paredes regime would agree to meet with John Slidell and discuss a settlement of differences with the United States. But Polk also believed that he could speed the process up with the proper application of military pressure. He had already ordered Taylor to march to the Rio Grande as part of an effort to influence the Herrera administration. Now he allowed Taylor's preparations to go forward, continued to pledge that US troops would treat Mexico as a friendly nation and use military force only if fired upon, and waited to see if an advance would push Paredes to the negotiating table.[67]

News from the northern frontier indicated that it would be wise for Mexico to avoid a fight. In the aftermath of Arista's resignation, the officers of the 4th Division quickly realigned themselves with the new regime. Díaz de la Vega, who had previously commanded the 1st Brigade in Monterrey, Gen. Francisco Mejía of the 2nd Brigade in Matamoros, and Gen. Antonio Parrodi with the 3rd Brigade in Tampico each vowed loyalty to the Paredes government as soon as Herrera stepped down. But their oaths could not obscure divisions within the ranks. While Mejía and Díaz had remained loyal to Arista during his resistance to the San Luis uprising, Parrodi had been more willing to endorse Paredes. This stance earned him Arista's derision as a traitor and apparently created a rift that carried over after Arista's resignation as general-in-chief. Shortly after Díaz de la Vega assumed command of the Army of the North, he suggested that Parrodi's brigade be removed from his command and placed under the authority of the Army of the East, based in Veracruz. Juan Almonte, the former minister to Washington now serving as Paredes minister of war, refused this proposal and ordered the generals to continue to work together. Almonte recognized that, despite their rivalries, this core group of generals shared a familiarity with the northern frontier and a desire to preserve their country, and he expected them to set aside their differences for the common cause of protecting the border.[68]

That cause remained understaffed and under-funded. One of Arista's final acts as general-in-chief of the north was to remind Paredes that he still needed more troops—at least twelve hundred infantry and four hundred cavalry—as well as additional supplies. His successors immediately took up his familiar tune, this time in a chorus of three voices. Just days after Arista's resignation, Parrodi issued a plea to military commanders in Veracruz to shift three hundred troops to bolster his command. General Díaz de la Vega made more detailed appeals for assistance. Upon accepting his commission as general-in-chief, Díaz de la Vega touted the discipline, training, and readiness of his troops but reiterated that he needed more of them and lamented that his current force was short on uniforms, food, and weapons. A month later he wrote to the president through the minister of war, saying that spies embedded in the US camp at Corpus Christi had informed him of a pending advance. He despaired of being able to respond and pleaded for help: "Up to this point," he wrote, "I have tried to make clear to you that the moment of danger approaches, and I lack sufficient forces to successfully preserve national honor by repelling the advances of the enemy. It only remains for me to tell you that, since these critical circumstances continue and since I also lack any means to provide for the subsistence of my troops, duty makes me present this situation once again in the hope that you, as president, can use you superior position to devise a solution."

In detailing his difficulties, Díaz de la Vega reiterated many other points that Arista had made the previous summer. His troops were scattered sparsely along a vast frontier, and he lacked means to transport them easily. In any case, a move to meet the invading Americans at Matamoros or Frontón would expose Laredo and other communities to attacks from the roving bands of Comanches. In closing, he reasserted that the only way to resolve this situation was through a prompt and determined effort to reinforce and sustain the northern command.[69]

The most forceful declaration of need, however, came from General Mejía in Matamoros. Positioned on the front line of the looming conflict, Mejía was keenly aware of the deficiencies of his force and anxious for help. In a letter written in January and forwarded to the new minister of war through Parrodi, Mejía detailed his plan to move troops of the 10th Infantry Regiment and the Sapper Battalion forward to the Arroyo Colorado. Not only did the steep ravine offer natural advantages for men defending its banks, it also blocked the approach to Matamoros, the Frontón de Santa Isabel, and other Mexican settlements in the lower Rio Grande delta, making it an efficient place to garrison troops. In announcing his decision to deploy troops there, Mejía boldly promised that in any confrontation, the American enemy "will surely perish." Yet he quickly qualified the boast by admitting that his troops would be "in a difficult position at the moment fighting erupts." He went on to note that detachments along the Rio Grande had received very little in aid or rations for the last months, the troops lacked food for subsistence, and often the only supplies they had were those stolen from the enemy. Departing from his previous rosy assessment, Mejía warned that only poor weather was to thank for delaying the American advance, and he pleaded for assistance so that his troops would "not be forced to abandon their positions to the US troops out of sheer misery and thereby bring shame upon the army."[70]

Leaders in Mexico City responded to these anguished pleas with platitudes and delays. Although the dire warnings generated concern among the upper echelons of the military, few troops were available to help. Many reserve troops remained in the capital, but they were propping up the shaky Paredes regime. Around the country, other military divisions were busy rushing to fortify ports against threatened American occupations or to put down uprisings by opportunistic rebel groups, leaving few regiments available for the north. In San Luis Potosí, Gen. Pedro de Ampudia assembled a new force, but his soldiers lacked the training, weaponry, and supplies necessary to permit an advance. As a result, Minister of War Almonte had little to offer the northern command, other than to recommend that Díaz de la Vega move the 1st Brigade and his base of operations from Monterrey to Matamoros as quickly as possible to provide support for Mejía at the apparent target of the US advance. Díaz de la Vega could not comply. Without mules, wagons, and food, or the funds to get them, he had no way to make the march. He remained in Monterrey while Almonte offered him assurances that the government was aware of his situation, would give his concerns serious consideration, and would respond as quickly as possible.[71]

The muted response to these calls for help may also have been influenced by evidence that the American force was experiencing difficulties of its own. Beginning in November and December of 1845, a number of deserters from the American camp at Corpus Christi began appearing along the Rio Grande. In January and February of 1846, as preparations began for an immediate advance to the river, the trickle of fugitives developed into a minor flood that carried dozens of discontented US soldiers into Matamoros, Laredo, and communities in between. Interrogated by Mexican authorities, these defectors gave accounts of miserable cold and rain, brutal discipline, and widespread sickness. Some merely sought relief by wandering toward more southerly climes. Others said that they were immigrants to the United States and had little desire to risk their lives for their new country. A few specifically stated their opposition to war with Mexico, though it was not clear if they were sincere or just currying favor with their Mexican captors. In any case, the defections captured the attention of officials like Minister of War Almonte in Mexico City and General Ampudia at his headquarters in San Luis Potosí. At this distance, the deserters' tales of woe created a perception of widespread discontent and simmering insubordination within the American regiments. They also nurtured hope, which would endure up until the first battle of the war, that the US Army—loaded with immigrants and malcontents—might simply dissipate in the face of Mexican resistance.[72]

But the generals Díaz de la Vega and Mejía took a different message from the Corpus Christi fugitives. Spies within the American camp had provided enough descriptions of well-armed, well-fed, well-trained, and well-disciplined troops, that the leaders of the northern division gave little credence to tales of pervasive dissatisfaction. Instead they viewed the unhappy deserters as the exception to the general rule of order in Taylor's army. They did rely on the runaways to verify details about the American base and questioned them extensively about troop strength and military objectives. By means of these interviews they acquired significant forewarning of the US march, knew the proposed route, and verified that Taylor's goal was to take control of the Frontón de Santa Isabel and to occupy the Río Bravo near Matamoros. This afforded the Mexican generals a certain small level of comfort. They began to shift their troops away from Laredo and other frontier towns to concentrate them in the delta of the lower Río Bravo.[73]

But information from deserters did not compensate for lack of reinforcements. By February, no additional Mexican troops had arrived in the northern theater, and the generals of the brigade began to despair of their situation. Once again, it was Mejía in Matamoros who adopted the most pessimistic tone. In a letter to Minister of War Almonte, dated February 4, 1846, the general unleashed all of his pent-up fury. According to the latest intelligence, he wrote, General Taylor planned to march with four thousand infantry troops, one thousand cavalry, and twenty-six cannon. He also cited reports that the American general might be expecting an additional three thousand volunteer soldiers to arrive by boat at the Frontón de Santa Isabel. By contrast, Mejía pointed out, his own command had only eight hundred men, and they were charged with defending the five important but scattered towns of Laredo, Revilla, Reynosa, Matamoros, and Frontón. This placed the 2nd Brigade in an impossible situation. So uneven was the balance of manpower that, even if US forces divided to attack all five towns simultaneously and Mejía consolidated his troops, he would still find himself outnumbered at any point along the defense line. He chided the war minister, the president, and other officials in the capital for neglecting the frontier and leaving their army in such a plight. "To meet their responsibility to the nation," he wrote, "my superiors must sooner or later tend to the defense of the border." Until they did he was on his own and lacking answers as to how he could make a stand. "What do I do?" he asked in frustration. "Any choice is difficult."[74]

Mejía provided a catalog of other problems as well. He noted that the veteran US troops were especially proficient with artillery, while Mexican cannon were largely manned by new recruits, and they were obliged to use gunpowder that had never performed well in the humid climate of the region. Finally, the troops still lacked food, and the effects of the chronic shortage would only be more evident when combat erupted. Outmanned, outgunned, and outsupplied, Mejía could not even rely on Matamoros as a safe haven in an attack. The town's defenses and powder magazines had been destroyed in a recent hurricane. And Mejía believed that despite his efforts, Matamoros could not be defended. He was less than certain that its citizens even wanted to hold back an American invasion. Residents of the area had frequently been enticed by the lure of commerce with the United States, and many were pursuing a brisk, if illicit, trade with the US forces. Powerless to stop the contraband, Mejía felt equally helpless to prevent local merchants from welcoming foreign occupation.[75]

Despite his pessimism, Mejía believed that Mexico still had opportunities. He considered the Arroyo Colorado and the Frontón to be the keys to national defense. Eight hundred men entrenched at the Frontón could protect the important port indefinitely against an assault from land and sea, and he recommended fortifying it at once. He also continued to assert that the arroyo was the best location from which to challenge the advancing US Army. Here the Mexicans could make use of their superior cavalry and reduce the impact of American artillery, while at the same time protecting both Frontón and Matamoros. But success, Mejía insisted, would require many more troops and supplies—preferably delivered before the American advance began. If reinforcements, troops, weapons, and horses arrived in time, he promised to fight hard for the honor of Mexico. If they did not arrive, he would be forced to abandon his forward position and leave the nation to its fate.[76]

Letters like this one eventually struck a chord, though not with the intended audience. In addition to extensively critiquing the situation on the Río Bravo, Mejía referred to rumors that Almonte had resigned, and he blasted the minister of war for abandoning the republic in time of crisis. He soon discovered, however, that Almonte's replacement lent a more responsive ear. In February, Gen. José María de Tornel y Mendívil took over from Almonte and immediately forced a shift in operations. A hard-liner who strongly disliked the United States, Tornel began to push the interim president Paredes to bolster his northern defenses and prepare for hostilities against the United States. Within days of assuming his office, he had initiated a flow of funds and supplies to the hungry, cash-strapped soldiers. He also began to push in earnest to get more manpower up to the border. Orders went out for troops from the state of Veracruz to move forward to Tampico, for troops from Zacatecas to go to Tampico, and for Gen. Pedro de Ampudia to gather his reserve force in San Luis Potosí and advance quickly to Monterrey, where he would assume command as general-in-chief. These maneuvers would enable Díaz de la Vega to transfer his operations to Matamoros without endangering other frontier cities, while Parrodi could spare some of his limited force in Tampico, and Mejía could call his troops away from other outposts on the Río Bravo to join detachments at Frontón and the Arroyo Colorado. After months of watching and waiting, Mexican forces finally began to mobilize for action.[77]

Relieved to be free of a long-standing paralysis, the northern generals eagerly sprang into action. By the end of February, Díaz de la Vega had been furnished funds with which he began purchasing wagons, mules, and other necessities to reposition the four hundred men of the 1st Brigade and troops of the 7th Cavalry Regiment. Parrodi sent eighty dragoons of the Tampico Coast Guard Regiment and some presidial troops northward even before his promised reinforcements had arrived. Still monitoring the situation in the US camp, Mejía began gathering together presidial soldiers and the auxiliary regiments from the northern towns, the Defensores de las Villas del Norte, to support his vanguard troops, and he requested additional cavalry and artillery as well.[78]

Most importantly, Mariano Paredes abandoned his lethargy. Responding to both the criticisms of his regime and positive evidence that Mexico could mount a defense, the embattled interim president abandoned the cautious course he had followed since January. On March 12, foreign Minister Joaquín María del Castillo y Lanzas forwarded a message to John Slidell announcing that the interim president refused to accept him as envoy extraordinary and minister plenipotentiary. The strongly worded notice asserted Mexico's desire to avoid conflict and willingness to settle the Texas issue peacefully, but made clear that Paredes was not considering any surrender of territory. Paredes then clarified his position in a powerful proclamation issued March 21, in which he vowed that Mexico "does not recognize the American flag on the soil of Texas, will defend its invaded territory, and will never, ever permit new conquests and new advances by the government of the United States of America."[79] Belatedly but resolutely, the Mexican president had determined to go to war.

Hovering like a cloud over all these proceedings was the sense that it might be too little, too late. Despite the sudden flurry of movement, in the final weeks of February the first line Mexican defenses consisted only of three hundred infantry troops and a handful of cavalry positioned to defend the crossing of the arroyo and the Frontón de Santa Isabel. Behind this thin cordon, the city of Matamoros had two hundred volunteer troops, several companies of artillery, and a small detachment of cavalry to man the sagging defenses and the single small fort that protected the bank of the Rio Grande. Without immediate support, General Mejía had no illusions that he could halt a determined American attack. Assistance was on the way, but it came slowly. Díaz de la Vega was not able to send his first units out on the long march from Monterrey until February 24. Ampudia, at the head of the 4th Infantry and Anastasio Torrejón's cavalry, did not attempt his advance north until March 11. Additional delays occurred en route when he was forced to put down an insurrection by troops who hesitated to march to war armed with inferior weapons and equipped with inadequate supplies. Meanwhile, General Taylor's army had already started its movement southward, and whether enough Mexican defenders could reach the Arroyo Colorado and Frontón to halt the American advance was far from certain.[80]

CHAPTER 2
To the Rio Grande

★

AS MEXICAN FORCES rushed to the Rio Grande, uncertain about their preparedness for defense, the US Army left Corpus Christi for the river with their own doubts about what lay ahead. "From the accounts received here," wrote Lt. Ulysses S. Grant in early March, "I think the chances of a fight on our first arrival on the Rio Grande are about equal to the chances for peace." Reports from the south had done little to clarify the situation. Traders traveling northward reported that thousands of Mexican troops had assembled near the river and were ready to push onward to a fight, but conflicting accounts claimed that the route ahead was undefended. Some correspondents from Mexico reported that the republic was teetering on the verge of rebellion and that the American march would lead the northern states to break away from Mexico and form a separate nation. Others insisted that the population would rise up *en masse* against an occupying force. In the absence of reliable intelligence, Grant and his fellow travelers could only conclude that time would tell. "In sixteen days we shall have reached the Rio Grande or have been driven back by the Mexicans in disgrace," Lt. John Peck wrote in his diary on the eve of the march toward the unknown. His words captured the mood among the troops: "We are going there if we can force our way, if whipped it will be a sore battle."[1]

Resolved to fight if necessary, the soldiers nevertheless had mixed emotions about the advance. Some felt morally justified in the task ahead and eagerly awaited any confrontation that lay ahead. Others, however, questioned the boundary demands and the move to enforce them. The crusty old colonel Ethan Allen Hitchcock was among the latter. He strongly disapproved of US claims to the Rio Grande as the southwest border and dreaded any move to defend it. "I have said from the first that the United

States are the aggressors," he wrote. "We have outraged the Mexican government and people by an arrogance and presumption that deserve to be punished." For his part, Gen. Zachary Taylor, who according to Hitchcock had once denounced Texas annexation as "injudicious in policy and wicked in fact," approached the march as a necessary undertaking that need not have dire consequences. In the days before striking out, he again enjoined Mexican military leaders not to respond to the provocation and to allow diplomatic efforts to take their course. Most of the soldiers in the Army of Occupation probably shared the emotions of Lieutenants Grant and Peck, who were not necessarily seeking a fight but were eager to have the prolonged dispute resolved in one way or another.[2]

Indeed, at the outset of the journey to the Rio Grande, the only points of certainty involved the route the army would take and the formations it would employ. Last-minute reconnaissance efforts had successfully pinpointed an ideal location for an advance supply depot—at Santa Gertrudis Creek some fifty miles south of Corpus Christi—as well as a number of good campsites on the road before and after that point. This information enabled Taylor to prepare a detailed plan of march. The troops would set out with five days' supplies and replenish their stores at the depot before completing their ten-day trek to the Rio Grande delta. Split into the three brigades to ease movement along the narrow track, the groups would stop at common points along the way—each at a day's interval behind the preceding party. This division of units would make them somewhat vulnerable to attack if a Mexican force lay in wait, but Taylor doubted they would face any real danger before they reached the Arroyo Colorado, a deep river about 150 miles to the south. Therefore he ordered the brigades to congregate just north of that point to make the final push to the Rio Grande as a unified force.[3]

The first stages of the march passed without incident and even proved enjoyable. The brigades set out westward across the prairie, relieved to escape what had become the dreary routine of life in Corpus Christi. The sun shone pleasantly and springlike weather prevailed as the troops passed across fields blanketed in bright flowers. Stopping near the banks of the Nueces River after an easy march of about thirteen miles, the army camped on a beautiful, broad plain covered with native bluebonnets. "It was pleasant to look at," wrote Lt. Samuel French, "an enchanting scene that would have been drowsy and dreamlike from the fragrance of the flowers had we not discovered nearly every man grazing his horse carrying a small pole with which he was killing rattlesnakes."[4]

The rattlesnakes were everywhere and remained a hazard for the duration of the advance. Horsemen often rode ahead of the column to look out for them and shout the warning "Wake! Snake!"[5]

On the second day of travel the troops followed the banks of the Nueces River before striking out overland for an additional nine miles and camping at a spot used by Mexican soldiers in the 1835 Texas campaigns. But when their path turned southward, conditions deteriorated and made passage difficult. The muddy areas described in the reconnaissance reports of February had not dried, and men and wagons got mired down in what was soon dubbed "Hogwallow Prairie." At the front of the column, troops of the 1st Brigade slogged through the muck for an entire day but covered only four miles. The brigades trailing behind them benefited from the paths established and moved somewhat faster, but still took two days to escape their surroundings. Even after passing the worst of the bogs, the columns struggled through yet more mud, this created by driving rains that had drenched the prairies north of the Santa Gertrudis depot. The men also suffered through wild fluctuations in temperatures. They sweltered through intolerably hot conditions one day and woke the next morning to heavy frost.[6]

Once they were past the supply depot, conditions grew even worse. The land southward was increasingly dry, and pleasant prairies gave way to fields of stunted brown scrub. Temperatures climbed, and the sun flamed hot in the sky. The sandy ground absorbed the heat and burned through the soles of the troopers' shoes. Even worse, water grew scarce. In one desolate stretch of about forty miles, where no streams crossed the dusty ground, the men relied for water primarily on small puddles that dotted the route. At times they marched for miles in the blazing heat, making many fruitless forays off the trail before locating a pond. All too often, desperate men rushed toward inviting, shimmering pools, threw themselves to the ground, and drank deeply—only to taste a sharp brine that exacerbated their thirst. Whenever possible, soldiers in the lead brigades left behind guides to point the way to precious fresh water sources. At one point the brigades gratefully made use of the spot they called Filisola Wells, which had waterholes dug by that Mexican general's troops when they had faced similar adversity during their retreat from San Jacinto in 1836.[7]

All too often, however, parched soldiers were left with no alternative but to stumble along for miles with empty canteens through an overwhelming heat that left the road "strewed with men who had fallen in their tracks from utter exhaustion." Few perished in these conditions, but Lt. William Brooks later avowed, "In all the marching I ever made, I never experienced such a day as this was. I can't think any of the great deserts worse than this one in miniature." He also noted, however, that the harsh wasteland had a galvanizing influence on the troops. "It has produced one effect, I believe in all, that we shall suffer anything, even to death, rather than retreat to it."[8]

Such resolve was needed when Mexican soldiers began to make their appearance. On the first days of the march, the troops encountered nothing more than decades-old Mexican camps, and some traders with vague but menacing tales about war preparations ahead. Occasionally the sound of thundering hooves and the appearance of dust clouds on the horizon would provoke alarm before proving to be nothing more than herds of wild horses roaming the prairies. But, as the American forces pressed beyond the Santa Gertrudis depot, camping at places named San Fernando, Santa Clara, Cavancio, and Chiltipins, the enemy presence grew more pronounced. During their daily marches, soldiers of the various brigades noted that Mexican horseman regularly monitored their progress from a distance. On one occasion, officers pausing to water their horses at a small pond suddenly found themselves beside a group of Mexican lancers doing the same. After a tense moment, the two groups exchanged muted greetings and then parted without hostilities. But the animosity of the Mexican troops became clear when they set fire to the dry grasslands and scrub brush in advance of the American columns. The leading US brigade was obliged to drive its way through leaping flames and dense smoke. The soldiers in trailing units found themselves moving through great expanses of windblown ash that added to the misery of the parched desert environment and that blackened them from head to toe.[9]

This demonstration of Mexican displeasure with the American march was reinforced by verbal warnings as well. On March 14, Lt. Fowler Hamilton, one of the dragoons who set out in advance of the army, came across a group of Mexican scouts north of the Arroyo Colorado. When they accosted him and demanded to know his mission, Hamilton repeated General Taylor's already-published words about the army's intent to peacefully occupy the left bank of the Rio Grande. The Mexicans countered with grave warnings that their army would contest any attempt by the Americans to cross the arroyo. Hamilton suggested that the men should discuss the matter with someone of higher rank, and the Mexicans agreed to meet with Col. David Twiggs, commander of the 1st Brigade, later that afternoon. Twiggs arrived for the meeting, but no Mexican representative showed up. It was clear, however, that the Mexican troops intended a more confrontational encounter. Several days later, traders from Matamoros passed through the camps and notified the Americans that a large force had taken up

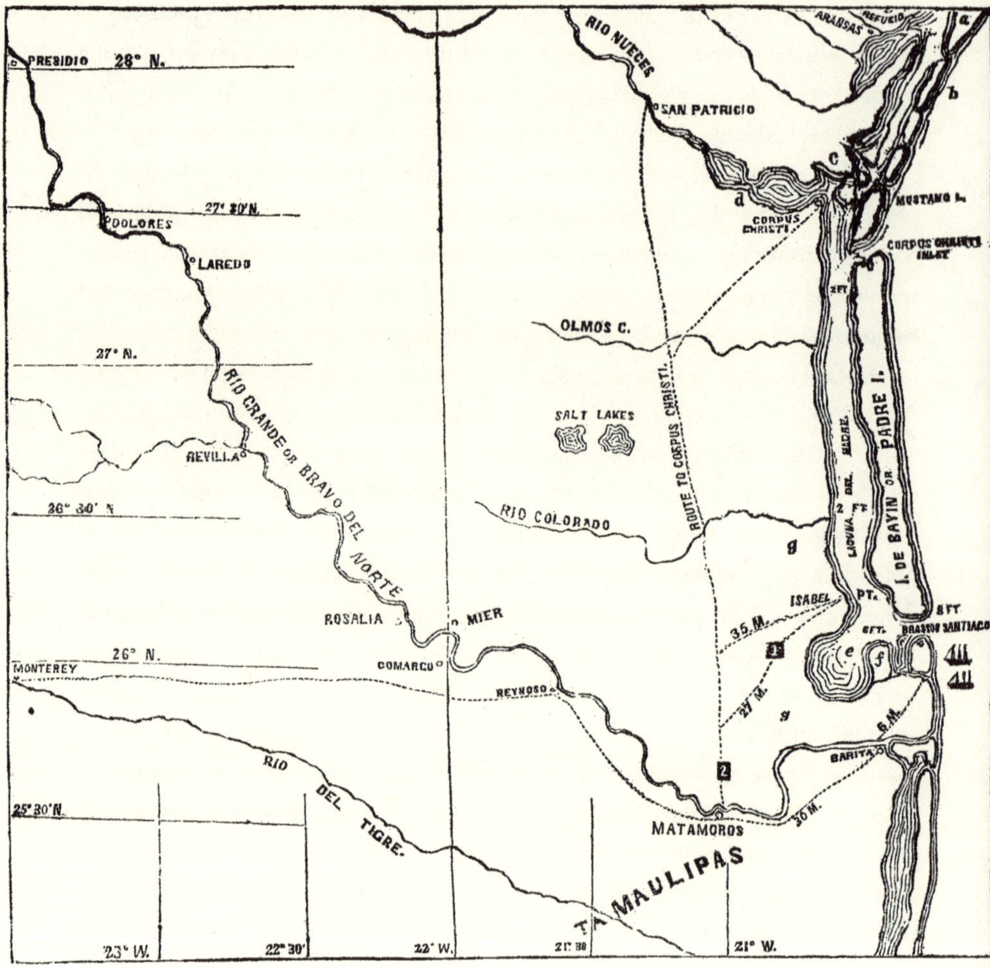

Theater of War and the US Advance to the Rio Grande. *Niles' National Register.*

position on the south bank of the arroyo and intended to contest their crossing. In response to both of these incidents, Taylor—who had worked his way up to the vanguard of the US force—ordered the 2nd and 3rd Brigades to quicken their steps and prepare to rendezvous with the advance units and the 1st Brigade at the ravine on March 21.[10]

Word of a possible fight traveled quickly through the scattered brigades and changed the atmosphere of the march. Men who had stumbled through the scorching, waterless plains obligingly picked up their pace now, suddenly alert to possible danger ahead. Both the 2nd and 3rd Brigades, which had averaged about twelve miles each day on the first stages of the march, covered fifteen to twenty miles daily in its later stages as they sought to close the distance with the lead units. In fact, so fast was their progress that the supply trains accompanying each brigade lagged far to the rear. Eventually the soldiers forged on ahead, issuing weapons to the teamsters who guided the ox-drawn wagons and leaving them to catch up when they could. This risky move did not imply a decline in vigilance. With each step toward the Arroyo Colorado, the troops grew increasingly cautious, marching with weapons primed and loaded and treading warily when the road narrowed to pass through areas of chaparral. At night, the camps posted double sentries to prevent unexpected attacks.[11]

Caution gave way to determination on March 19. On that evening General Taylor established his camp at a point about three miles north of the arroyo and sent a reconnaissance party to investigate ahead. His scouts advanced to the waterway and immediately encountered a group of thirty Mexican cavalrymen—a unit of the soldiers of the Defensores de las Villas del Norte, who had occupied the southern bank. The Mexican soldiers permitted the investigation to proceed without interference, but they informed the Americans that any attempt to ford the stream would be treated as an act of hostility and met with resistance. The reconnaissance party reported these findings but was not able to provide an accurate estimate of Mexican troop strength, and Taylor could not be certain whether the force he might confront numbered in the hundreds or the thousands. Moreover, he had only a fraction of his army on hand. Having united his small command party with the original advance units and the soldiers of the 1st Brigade, he traveled with just over a thousand men. The 2nd Brigade trailed by only four miles, but the 3rd Brigade remained a full day's march behind. Nevertheless, the threat of resistance drove Taylor to take immediate action. Shortly after the reconnaissance returned, he issued orders to the 1st Brigade that detailed a plan for crossing the arroyo under possible fire. He also sent a dispatch to the commanders of the 2nd Brigade advising them to press their troops onward early the following morning and to be prepared for a forced crossing of the arroyo immediately upon their arrival.[12]

The confrontation came early the next morning. Taylor and the 1st Brigade crossed a broad, grassy plain and arrived on the north bank of the arroyo shortly after seven. They took up position on the established crossing, a point where the road carved a gentle slope through the fourteen-foot-high banks of the arroyo and disappeared into the brackish water. On the far shore a group of horsemen—the same who had greeted the reconnaissance the evening before—occupied the road where it climbed the opposite bank, about seventy yards away. As the US artillery batteries rolled forward on either side of the road, Capt. Joseph King Fenno Mansfield spoke with the leader of the opposing party and once again was warned that an advance would be met by fire.[13]

Taylor ignored the warning, and, apparently wanting to demonstrate his resolve before the 2nd Brigade arrived, ordered a number of his troops to begin widening and smoothing the roadway for better passage of the wagon trains that would follow. This display prompted another response from the far bank as two more officers appeared and requested a parlay—Capts. José Barragán and Jean-Louis Berlandier, who splashed their horses through the four-foot-deep water and informed General Taylor in person that they had orders to fire on him if he moved to cross the river. They also presented him with a proclamation, issued by Gen. Francisco Mejía, denouncing the US advance as a "violation of every rule of morality and justice" and promising that the Mexican army would turn back the American invasion and launch a counterstrike for the reconquest of Texas.[14]

Taylor responded with equal force. He announced that he intended to cross the waterway in fifteen minutes' time and that any Mexican troops who appeared to challenge the crossing would come under fire from his guns. The brief meeting was conducted with polite formality, and the two groups "parted as friends," but battle lines apparently had been drawn. Beyond the brush on the south side of the arroyo, bugles sounded a call to arms, and men rushed about in preparation for the fight. On the north bank, cannon crews stood with their guns primed and loaded with grapeshot as Captain Mansfield rode down the bank, collected a long stalk of river cane, and used it to plumb the depth of the water. Upon learning that the fording site was indeed passable, Taylor ordered Major C. F. Smith and four companies of artillery to begin the crossing.[15]

The timely arrival of American reinforcements accompanied this decisive move. In response to Taylor's dispatch of the previous night, the 2nd Brigade had set out at daybreak intending to reach the arroyo at the same time as the 1st. Despite the best intentions, the march was delayed when the troops of the 2nd found themselves trapped behind the lagging wagon train of the lead brigade. Informed that General Taylor had already made contact with Mexican troops, the soldiers pushed their way past the obstacle and arrived at the riverbank around eight, just in time to witness the closing words of the parlay. The incoming companies immediately took up a support position to the right of the 1st Brigade, and no doubt emboldened Taylor in his determination to push forward. Still recovering from their seven-mile march, the troops of the 2nd Brigade joined their compatriots, anxiously watching as the two hundred advance troops waded into the water.

The crossing began as a tense drama. At the last moment, Gen. William J. Worth splashed forward to lead the advance. Behind him, moving through the chest-high water with guns and powder held high above their heads, the advance troops plodded forward—dangerously exposed to any fire from the opposite shore. Mexican troops continued to sound their horns and move about behind the brush. Apparently in preparation for an attack that might erupt at any moment, the American ranks grew solemnly quiet. "The utmost silence reigned everywhere," wrote Lt. John Henshaw, "every ear and every being on the 'qui vive' for the opening of the Mexican cannon." But the shooting did not come, and at the halfway point, the spirit of the proceedings changed significantly: "When they had reached the middle of the stream unmolested, one prolonged and deafening 'Huzza,' broke from every mouth as they continued to pour onward, and as the head of each regiment reached the opposite bank, the band struck up Yankee Doodle and Garry Owen while our troops moved up the steep sides in column, pushing through the chaparral or thicket."[16]

In a matter of minutes, a dangerous passage had become a celebratory march.

The successful crossing of the advance companies did not signal an end to danger. Although these troops had cleared a major hurdle in their path, the rest of the army still awaited passage. Taylor also remained concerned whether the Mexican troops had prepared an attack on the plain just beyond the arroyo with the intention of pinning his troops along the southern bank. Once again he sent out a reconnaissance party of dragoons to cross the stream and scope out the situation beyond the brushy banks. Picking their way through the chaparral, the cavalrymen found the clearing beyond free of Mexican troops. Indeed, the only sign of the enemy was the same group of horsemen that had earlier occupied the road. No longer challenging the advance, these soldiers remained visible only for a moment as they rode off into the distance.[17]

With the danger past, the remainder of the army began the process of fording the arroyo. Infantrymen had to follow the example of the advance companies and cross holding their weapons and haversacks high. Horsemen struggled to drive their mounts and many found themselves thrown into the salty water. Nevertheless, the regiments made the journey in about thirty minutes. The supplies took considerably longer. The ox-drawn wagons of the two brigades creaked slowly down the sides of the ravine, foundered in the muddy water, and struggled up the far bank, consuming the better part of the day in the crossings. As a result, the 1st and 2nd Brigades and their trains covered only four more miles before establishing camp for the night near a freshwater pond.[18]

Pausing to reflect on the day's events, the American soldiers congratulated themselves on having escaped what could have been a deadly confrontation. In a diary entry, Lt. John Peck noted that the broad stream, high banks, and brush cover would have made the Arroyo Colorado an ideal place for Mexican resistance. Taylor agreed, stating in his official report that the ravine "would have formed a serious obstruction to our march had the enemy chosen to occupy its right bank, even with a small force." Lt. Brooke pointed out that if Mexican forces had attacked the first American troops as they reached the south bank of the river, the American artillery would have been useless since it would have showered friend and foe alike. By withdrawing, he added, the Mexicans had abandoned "the only defensible spot between the Nueces and the Rio Grande" and "let their golden opportunity pass."[19]

The relieved American troops entertained a variety of explanations for the evaporation of Mexican force on the arroyo. Capt. Ephraim Kirby-Smith declared that the Mexicans had never intended to fight and that the display on the ravine had been "all gasconade intended to intimidate General Taylor and delay our advance." William S. Henry agreed, noting that "there were very few men at the river, and they thought to frighten us away with the sounds of bugles and big threats." Others, including Taylor, thought that the Mexicans had planned a fight, but, faced with such an overwhelming force, had decided that "discretion was the better part of valor" and withdrawn. Still others cited the retreat from the arroyo as evidence of a complete lack of Mexican will for this conflict. Among these was Lt. Ulysses S. Grant, who in a letter to his fiancée observed that the dissipation of resistance along the arroyo "shows anything but a decided disposition to drive us from the soil."[20]

To some degree, each of these assessments was correct, but the real motives behind the Mexican decision to cede the arroyo were far more complex. It was certainly true that Mexican troops lacked the numbers they would have preferred for a confrontation. Taylor's march had initiated a series of Mexican countermarches, but not many of these had yet reached their destination. General Ampudia, having quashed a rebellion over inadequate supplies in the barracks at San Luis Potosí, took to the march only to find his progress halted yet again by troops who complained that they lacked "indispensable resources" and who therefore refused to advance toward Texas. When word of this insubordination reached Mexico City, Mariano Paredes himself prepared to march to bring the troops back under control. Ampudia eventually restored order, making that drastic step unnecessary, but, as of March 20, he remained far from Monterrey and nowhere near the Arroyo Colorado. Though General Díaz de la Vega experienced less difficulty with his movement from Monterrey, he still needed a considerable amount of time to get the carts necessary for transporting not only supplies, but also the soldiers who were too weak from hunger and illness to undertake the march. As the confrontation unfolded on the arroyo, Ampudia had advanced only as far as Mier—more than a hundred miles away. To the south, in Victoria, General Parrodi had not sent any troops at all. Beset by a wave of Indian attacks and seeing no sign of the reinforcements that were supposed to arrive from Veracruz, Parrodi had announced, "I cannot send a single man more to Matamoros."[21]

This meant that the only reinforcements available were a few squadrons of mounted militia troops under the command of Gen. Antonio Canales. In a letter to Mejía announcing his approach, Canales described a difficult journey. "What a job I have had moving this squadron," he wrote. "The troops have been miserable and there is a complete lack of horses." Nevertheless, he cheerfully added that he had been seizing mounts wherever he could find them, promised that he would arrive soon, and assured Mejía of confidence in the latter's success: "I believe that you will have the privilege of striking the blow that will drive back the ambitious gringos."[22]

But the depth of Canales' commitment remained open to question. Several years previously, the general had been involved in a movement to separate the northern frontier from the rest of Mexico and establish an independent Republic of the Rio Grande. He and his allies had abandoned the effort only after their troops were crushed by Mexican forces. His separatist sentiments apparently had not entirely faded. Only weeks before, Canales had written to Zachary Taylor in Corpus Christi offering assistance in securing the boundaries of Texas if the Americans would provide him with the weapons and time necessary to establish his own breakaway republic. Taylor's rejection of the offer had, at least temporarily, forced the wily general back into the Mexican fold, and he presented the contact with Taylor as little more than an opportunity to spy on the American army. Mejía welcomed the assistance of this elusive ally for as long as he would remain loyal but had no illusions that Canales and his ragged militia would turn back an invasion. If he hoped to make a stand, he would have to do so with only three hundred infantry troops.[23]

Nevertheless, Mejía remained committed to taking action along the ravine, and he offered a range of arguments to support his case. He felt that it was important to establish a defensive position there as a political statement. Although Mexico lacked the resources to carry the fight as far as Corpus Christi, by positioning troops in this forward location Mejía could at least demonstrate that his country was prepared back up its claim to territory north of the Río Bravo. He also viewed the arroyo as a point of strategic importance. In keeping with the theme he had first asserted months before, his primary goal was to use his advance troops to protect the Frontón de Santa Isabel and preserve Mexican control of that port, which was a vital trade lifeline for Matamoros and the northern towns. Doing this would also place a line of troops between the US Army and the city of Matamoros, which Mejía feared would rise up in insurrection once Taylor's army reached the northern bank of the Bravo.[24]

Most importantly, Mejía firmly believed that the arroyo represented the best, perhaps the only, place for the Mexican military to counter the superior assets of the US force. Having already identified the American advantage in artillery, he felt certain that any clash on an open field would be disastrous to the Mexican cause. And any attempt to withdraw to Matamoros would prove futile, since the city remained unprotected and impossible to defend. But the arroyo, with its steep banks and deep water, would provide his forces with an ideal defensive position. As the American soldiers themselves noted, the ravine reduced the effectiveness of artillery, left the larger force extremely vulnerable at the time of crossing, and significantly leveled the playing field. With or without a large body of troops at his command, Mejía was determined to take advantage of the opportunity, and no matter the result, strike a blow for Mexico.[25]

For a time this sentiment prevailed throughout the military chain of command. As Mexican armies rushed to the war zone, they did so with the understanding that the arroyo would be their ultimate destination. As a case in point, when Minister of War Tornel directed Ampudia to begin his march, he specified that the general's mission was to lead the entire 4th Division northward to defend the Frontón. And the minister promised his waiting northern generals that the troops would arrive in time. "Rest assured," he wrote, "that the Supreme Government will provide the most efficacious means to preserve the national honor."[26]

This broad-based consensus to defend the arroyo soon broke down, as the result of a decision at the highest level of the Mexican government. The constant complaints from Mejía and other generals did spur President Paredes to respond with troops, supplies, and funding, but it also raised his awareness of the abject weakness of the country's northern defense. The insubordination within the ranks of Ampudia's army could only have magnified Paredes' concern. Despite the assurances of his minister of war that troops and other assistance would reach the Río Bravo in time to halt an

American advance, Paredes knew better. He realized that the promises were hollow and could not possibly be kept. He appreciated that the Mexican troops on the arroyo were prepared to make a heroic stand in defense of their motherland, but he suspected that the confrontation would end in a crushing Mexican defeat.

And such an outcome to the opening act of war would have dramatic effects. It would demoralize the nation and the army, possibly opening the way for Zachary Taylor's army to occupy Matamoros and other areas south of the Río Bravo. This in turn would jeopardize Paredes' efforts to elicit international support in his struggle against the United States. From the moment that American troops had begun to mobilize along the Corpus Christi bay, Mexican envoys had actively sought assistance from Great Britain and France to counter the Yankee threat. Although there was no clear sign that either nation had any interest in providing this aid, Paredes recognized that an early defeat would prove that Mexico could not sustain a viable defense and would eliminate any possibility of getting help from abroad.[27]

Most troubling for Paredes, however, was the danger that a loss would pose to his personal ambitions. By virtue of troops and weapons that should have been positioned on the Arroyo, he maintained a tenuous hold on the reins of power in Mexico City. A devastating loss in a region he had vowed to defend would almost certainly lead to a wave of accusations and recriminations that would topple him from his precarious perch. Instead of risking these dire consequences, Paredes called for Mejía to avoid "defeats of immense consequence" and concentrate on protecting Matamoros. From the security of that city, he insisted, the northern army could "focus on later glorious triumphs of national arms." Generals Díaz de la Vega and Ampudia subsequently received new orders directing them to march to Matamoros instead of the Frontón. Speaking with far more bravado than he must have felt, Paredes offered each of his generals assurances that US soldiers were poor warriors and would be defeated easily when enough Mexican troops had arrived to "strike a blow to give the nation glory."[28]

General Mejía wholeheartedly disapproved of Paredes' decision and made this fact clear with a strongly worded missive to the minister of war, dated March 14, 1846. In it Mejía once again reminded his superiors of the need to protect the Frontón and to avoid abandoning the citizens who lived on the north bank of the river. Focusing on what he viewed as an unreasonable and ill-considered strategy, he pointed out, in lines dripping with contempt and frustration, that the Americans had set their sights not on conquering the city of Matamoros, but on occupying the left (north) bank of the Rio Grande. The new policy permitted Zachary Taylor to achieve that objective with ease. Mejía also warned that the United States ultimately intended to occupy all the Mexican states of Tamaulipas, Coahuila, and Chihuahua, as well as the New Mexico territory, and that the Army of Occupation was an important beachhead for this advance. "Every day they are applying more pressure," he wrote, "and if we do not dispute them, I have no doubt that war will not be necessary for them to achieve their goal."

The general emphasized this last point, for he believed that his countrymen had failed to absorb the lesson of Texas. Paredes and his officials viewed the situation entirely in military terms. Whether or not they believed what they said, they invariably portrayed US troops as inferior soldiers who would easily be routed by an equivalent Mexican force. Thus they considered the withdrawal of troops to Matamoros a minor concession that would buy time, permitting the arrival of more soldiers and markedly improving Mexico's odds on the battlefield. But Mejía feared that his government had missed the real threat. A veteran of years of service on the frontier, he judged that Texas had not been lost by force of arms so much as by unchecked American migration into the region. And he was convinced that conceding the delta of the Río Bravo to US occupation would make history repeat itself. He lashed out at Paredes' claim that the United States would be defeated because its soldiers lacked military skill. "If the Americans are poor warriors," he wrote, "they are good colonists. Behind their troops will come settlements; interest will increase and difficulties will multiply and will call for more sacrifice and many more troops." From this perspective, the temporary withdrawal from advanced positions became a dishonorable and permanent surrender of territory, and Mejía vowed that "as a Mexican and a general, I must do all I can to retain my honor and that of my companions in arms."[29]

Mejía may have hoped that his temporary title of general-in-chief of the 4th Division would give additional weight to his words. Just days before, Gen. Rómulo Díaz de la Vega, who had assumed the title following Arista's forced retirement, had agreed to cede it to Mejía. Díaz de la Vega gave a number of reasons for doing this, among them that Mejía was slightly older and was in a better position to assess strategy, and he referred cryptically to a need to "set aside old differences" for the greater good of national defense.[30] Whatever the reason, Mejía had been given the command and would hold it until Ampudia finally arrived with his troops. As the person now responsible for the defense of the northern frontier, his advice clearly merited consideration in Mexico City.

Still, Mejía could not push his authority too far, and he stopped short of defying orders. If a respected general like Mariano Arista could be forced from power over a dispute with Paredes, a direct challenge to the president could end Mejía's career as well. For this reason, he insisted that he recognized the authority of the central government and he vowed to obey his orders. He made clear that, despite his blunt words, he approached his superiors "on bended knee," willing to abide by their wishes but hoping that they might see the wisdom of his words before it was too late.[31]

This did not mean that Mejía intended to comply immediately. Hopeful that his superiors would reverse their decision, the loyal general left his troops in their forward positions. Mounted soldiers of the Villas del Norte, including General Canales' men atop their scavenged horses, continued to reconnoiter the US columns and set fires to obstruct their passage as much as possible. A company of troops of the La Bahia presidials, led by Lt. Ramón Falcón, captured and interrogated several deserters and even conversed with the US dragoon Fowler Hamilton, who gave them a message written in "bad Castilian." Meanwhile, Col. Rafael Quintero, with several hundred defensores, maintained the camp at a spot called Laguna Larga near the south bank of the Arroyo Colorado, ready to draw the line against the advance.[32] These troops believed they were preparing for action, for Mejía had not informed them that a shift in strategy had been ordered. When Mexican ranging parties issued dire warnings about their intent to make a stand on the arroyo, what the Americans heard was not "gasconade" and bluster as they supposed, but the heartfelt words of men committed to fight. The order to abandon the arroyo came only after these warnings had been made.[33]

Indeed, it was not until the early morning hours of March 19, 1846, that Mejía finally called his troops back across the Río Bravo to the confines of Matamoros. Shortly after 6 p.m. on March 18, the general received word that the advance party of one hundred US dragoons had arrived on the north shore of the Arroyo Colorado and camped at a point known as the Taberna pass. Not too far behind, at a point known as El Mulato, the remainder of the US force had begun to gather in preparation for crossing the waterway. Having delayed several weeks in the forlorn hope that his orders might be reversed, Mejía could wait no longer. He immediately sent a messenger to his vanguard forces, telling them to avoid a fight and allow the Americans to complete their crossing uncontested.[34]

His proclamation to the people of the northern frontier, issued shortly after this command, revealed Mejía's tortured sentiments. With fiery words, he warned of the Americans' approach, denounced their march and the policies that spawned it, and vowed that the military would fight to maintain its independence and the national honor. He also promised that the nation had not forgotten the inhabitants' plight and that a "strong, tight-fisted army was approaching rapidly to take part in the fight." He was much more cautious in offering details of this fight. He made no direct mention of his orders to pull back from the Arroyo Colorado or of the probability that reinforcements would arrive long after the US troops did. Instead, he offered cryptic hints that the shores of the Río Bravo would bear witness to the "ignominy of the prideful sons of the north" and that the citizens of the region might play a greater role in the looming conflict than they had supposed. He reminded them that they bore a sacred duty to defend their own homes, customs, and interests and expressed confidence that they would do so: "For what Mexican worthy of the name can resign himself not to fight to the death and so to see his noble race under the detestable domination of the foreigner? None: for the elevated sense of national honor dominates our heart." In light of the exchanges that Mejía had conducted in the preceding weeks, this last statement served the additional purpose of informing his readers that he himself was a Mexican worthy of his name. These words were as close as he would come to publicly airing his doubts about the wisdom of his superiors and assigning blame to them for the approaching foreign occupation.[35]

Mejía's delayed command to withdraw, coupled with his public proclamation, produced doubt and confusion that almost resulted in a battle. On the morning of March 19, Col. Rafael Quintero, in charge of the troops on the Arroyo Colorado, received orders to abandon the area immediately. Like Mejía, he was dismayed by the thought of allowing the American army to cross the arroyo without a fight. Given his commander's impassioned proclamation to the public, he was convinced that there had been some sort of mistake and requested clarification of the message. In a familiar scenario, Quintero promised to his obey his orders, if they were legitimate, but he refused to issue the call to move until he had verified them.[36]

Quintero proceeded to lead his party to the Paso Real—the primary ford on the Arroyo Colorado—where another small company of troops stood directly in the path of Taylor's army. He arrived on the morning of March 20, just as Capt. José Barrigán returned from the opposite bank, having threatened to resist any advancing American troops. Barrigán appeared determined to follow through on his vow with the handful of men at his disposal, and Quintero was inclined to support him. But the matter was decided for them. At the exact moment that General Taylor ordered his troops to begin their march across the arroyo, Lt. José María Cárdenas arrived with confirmation of the previous day's orders. With harsh words for Cardenas, but unwilling to initiate a war in the face of a direct command, Quintero reluctantly fell back, withdrawing from the southern bank of the arroyo with the enemy at his heels.[37]

As Mejía had done, Quintero viewed the decision not to fight as shameful. Upon his return to his camp at Laguna Larga, he wrote a message to the general-in-chief detailing his actions, exonerating the officers under his command, and taking full responsibility for any delay in complying with orders. He insisted that, once he found his instructions to be legitimate, he followed them without delay, though "with tears in my eyes" at the disgrace of turning his back on an offending, invading force. Mistakenly pinning the blame on a man who agreed with him entirely, he bitterly asked Mejía to relieve him of any further indignity. "If Your Excellency would deign to do so," he wrote, "I would have you order me to return to my home. It also would be better if my compatriots, who up to this moment have been full of positive patriotic love and enthusiasm for the honor of the nation, retire to their homes as well. Even though they would lose honor in an indirect way at least they will not ignore their interests."[38] Quintero had reached the same conclusion as the Americans—Mexico had allowed a golden opportunity to pass.

When Mejía received reports that the Americans had crossed the arroyo, he quickly relayed that information, "with the most profound sentiment," to his superiors in Mexico City. In doing so, he could not resist adding one more reminder that he deplored the course of action that had permitted the advance. "The usurpers will probably seize control of the Frontón de Santa Isabel tomorrow," he wrote to the Minister of War, "and the detestable banner of the Stars will wave on the left bank of the Bravo. This will happen without confrontation by virtue of the Supreme order of the 1st in which you instructed me to only defend Matamoros and gave me responsibility to strictly comply with that order."[39] His sentiments, like those of Quintero, clearly demonstrate that it was not the Mexican forces on the Río Bravo who lacked the determination to challenge the US occupation.

Unaware of the controversial Mexican order that permitted him to proceed unimpeded, General Taylor led his troops into the Rio Grande delta in a mood of cautious optimism. He recognized that he had dodged a significant danger at the arroyo but was certain of nothing else. Reports from Matamoros suggested that two thousand Mexican troops currently occupied that city and that Ampudia was expected shortly with an additional five thousand—figures that could not be confirmed and were probably inflated. More importantly, he had no knowledge of what Mejía or Ampudia intended to do with those forces. Of most immediate concern, he had no idea how many

Mexican soldiers prowled the area between the Arroyo Colorado and the Rio Grande. After the arroyo crossing, only a handful of enemy troops had been spotted—a small party led by Capt. Jean Louis Berlandier that approached the US force to turn over a dragoon who had been captured while on scout duty. Berlandier provided little insight into his army's intentions or the abortive standoff earlier in the day. When questioned, he merely responded that "all was fair in time of war," and rode off. This left open the possibility that an ambush might await in any patch of chaparral or a battle around any turn, and Taylor instituted measures to ensure the safety of his isolated force.[40]

The first order of business was to reassemble the army into a single, battle-ready force. As night fell on March 20, the US army remained dangerously stretched out, with the 3rd Brigade and many of the supply wagons still advancing toward the far side of the arroyo. Any immediate continuation of the march would leave these groups vulnerable to an attack, especially the slow-moving, lightly defended wagons, and Taylor paused to allow his trailing units to catch up. On March 21, the men of the 1st and 2nd Brigades remained in place as the 3rd Brigade crossed the arroyo and took up a position in camp. On March 22, all three brigades waited anxiously as the last of the supply wagons rolled in, unifying the force for the first time since the departure from Corpus Christi.[41]

That same evening, with the near fight at the arroyo behind him and the final stages of the advance ahead, General Taylor issued two orders that reveal his thinking about the situation he faced. The first order demonstrates that he had taken note of the Mexican emphasis on cavalry. Just as General Mejía had noted the strength of American artillery and had recommended cavalry as a deterrent, Taylor now observed the advantages that mounted troops gave the foe and concluded that cannon would be vital to him. He ordered immediate steps to increase the efficiency of that part of his army, primarily by transferring infantrymen to fill the thin ranks of the artillery corp. Each battalion of the 2nd Brigade was required to detach five men and temporarily assign them to duty with Maj. Samuel Ringgold's light artillery battery. Similar arrangements were made in the 3rd Brigade, with each battalion required to reassign ten men to the artillery companies. And those who operated the field pieces had the power to select their soldiers, apparently to insure that they received the best-qualified men.[42]

Taylor's second order reveals his conviction that conflict was on the near horizon. Although one clash had been avoided, he did not expect to have such luck again. His army would travel first to Point Isabel to secure that important port and to reunite with the troops and supplies that had moved from Corpus Christi by the Gulf route.

With the port secure, he would resume the march southward to raise the flag on the shore of the Rio Grande. Taylor did not expect to accomplish these goals peacefully. "If any faith may be placed in the professions of the enemy," he wrote, "our progress will be resisted."[43]

Consequently, Taylor abandoned the long procession of previous days in favor of a more battle-ready formation. The three brigades and the advance units would now march in four columns with dragoon forces in the lead to scout the way, "pioneers" at the forefront of each column to open a path, and skirmishers off to the sides to guard against a flank attack. The invaluable wagon trains would follow each column, supported by a rear guard to protect against an attack from behind. Such a formation would permit the US troops to form into a battle line and respond quickly if they came under attack. This order of battle was to be maintained even when the troops set up camp at night, and the men were advised to avoid letting down their guard at any time during the days ahead.[44]

When the US troops broke camp at dawn on March 23, the new rules were fully in evidence. "We presented today an imposing spectacle," wrote Capt. Ephraim Kirby-Smith, "as we moved in parallel columns across the open prairie, with our long baggage train close in our rear and our scouts far in advance and on our flanks examining every thicket." Lt. Richard Cochrane observed the columns driving across the plain, evenly spaced at four hundred yards apart, and declared, "a more beautiful sight I never witnessed than the army passing through a prairie, followed each column by its wagons, some 300 or 400 in all. And if the Mexicans saw us, I think they would have estimated our numbers at 20 or 30,000 rather than so many hundred."[45]

The soldiers felt confident that the striking appearance of their large, battle-ready force had deterred the Mexicans, for they encountered no opposition. Over the next two days, the challenges faced by the troops were all from the forces of nature. The sun blazed in the sky, sapping the soldiers' energies with its sweltering heat. The often-remarked rattlesnakes continued to slither through the ranks, with at least one massive viper attacking a man and the mule he was riding. (The soldier survived his bite; the mule succumbed.) At one point a startled skunk rushed through one of the columns, producing havoc among the troops as it sprayed those who failed to move out of its path. But the anticipated military attacks did not materialize. Concerns persisted that an ambush awaited somewhere in the brush, and rumors spread that a huge Mexican force had crossed the Rio Grande and was rapidly closing from behind. Nevertheless, the soldiers traveled the next twenty miles without any sign of armed resistance.[46]

Most of the troops welcomed this stage of the journey in spite of the oppressive heat, the snakes, and the lingering threat of violence. Since crossing the dusty, dry brushlands to the north, they had gradually advanced into a less forbidding environment. Upon fording the Arroyo Colorado, they found themselves in a region that seemed idyllic compared to the one behind them. The march now progressed across the Rio Grande delta, with its rich soil and wide prairies of tall grass and flowers. Stunted brown brush gave way to lush thickets and green trees. Ponds dotted the landscape, providing stagnant, muddy, but plentiful water for drinking. These pools served not only the soldiers, but also a variety of wildlife, including skunks, deer, rabbits, panthers, wolves, turkeys, doves, and quails; and the sight and sound of birds filled the air. Surrounded by sub-tropical color and beauty, soldiers shrugged off worries about a confrontation and grumbled that their commander had become overly cautious. But Taylor recognized that he was in a dangerous position, isolated from any source of supplies and woefully lacking in reliable information about enemy movements and intent. He continued to insist on constant vigilance and forced his troops to remain in battle formation for the duration of the march.[47]

Arriving at the primary road that linked Matamoros to the coastal port at Point Isabel, Taylor immediately initiated measures to secure his supply lines. He ordered his dragoon regiments to accompany him and the wagon trains on the ten-mile ride to the port, where he would meet the ships and the troops that had traveled down the coast from Corpus Christi, refill the supply wagons, and then return for the final push to the river. The remainder of his force he left under the command of General Worth, with instructions to continue south toward the Rio Grande until he located a suitable camping ground along the road. Once Worth selected a campsite he was to remain in position, blocking any unexpected Mexican movement along this primary corridor until Taylor returned.[48]

Worth made his march amid much alarm but little incident. After Taylor's departure, he advanced five miles along the route to Matamoros, settling his force near a pond about fourteen miles from that city. Along the way he encountered Col. José María Carvajal, one of the officers of the Defensores de las Villas del Norte. Carvajal was also a supporter of the ill-fated Republic of the Rio Grande, a close ally of General Canales, and a party to the unsuccessful attempt to strike an alliance with the US Army before its advance from Corpus Christi. Apparently still hoping to curry favor with the Americans, Carvajal informed Worth that Mexican forces were concentrating in great numbers in the city of Matamoros and that the US soldiers should move that way as quickly as possible. Shortly afterward, another passerby cautioned Worth that a force of eight hundred Mexicans was trailing him and was likely to attack from behind. These warnings prompted Worth to move the army an additional five miles on the afternoon of March 25 and to position himself at another watering hole, known as Palo Alto. He wrote to Taylor asking for permission to advance to the Rio Grande, but received strict orders to stay put until Taylor returned. Despite concerns, no opposing army approached from either direction along the roadway, and the closest the troops came to a confrontation was when they captured four Mexican boys who they believed were spying on the army.[49]

In the meantime, Taylor fielded his own series of messengers and warnings. Shortly after taking leave of the army on the twenty-fourth, he was approached by a small delegation from Matamoros under a flag of truce. It requested a parley, to which Taylor readily agreed, although he stipulated that he wanted first to move his exposed wagon train to a better stopping place. He invited the party to accompany him, and they rode together for some distance along the road to Point Isabel. The train moved slowly enough that the delegates grew frustrated with the delay, and several miles from Point Isabel, they refused to continue. Instead, they presented Taylor with a formal written protest from the prefect of the state of Tamaulipas, declaring that Taylor and his army had invaded the state and committed acts of war in spite of their protestations of peace. The note further demanded that the general explain his actions and intentions. Before Taylor could respond, a messenger arrived from Point Isabel to report that the buildings there had been set ablaze. This news infuriated Taylor, who intended to use the site as his supply depot, and he responded to the delegation by accusing the Mexicans of having committed their own act of hostility. He dispatched a group of dragoons to ride ahead and try to extinguish the fire. Before setting out after them, he dismissed the deputation, declaring it to be a tool of the military leaders in Matamoros and asserting that he "was not willing to be trifled with any longer." He did promise to answer the letter from the prefect, but only later, when he had taken up position on the Rio Grande, across from Matamoros.[50]

Hurrying on to Point Isabel, Taylor was pleased to discover that most of the area had been saved from conflagration. Even in the best of times, the settlement had consisted of little more than a collection of a dozen wooden structures perched on a low escarpment—*frontón*, in Spanish—that jutted out into the Laguna Madre, the inland waterway between the mainland and a row of barrier islands. These buildings served as storehouses and customhouses for the goods brought in by ship through the Brazos

Santiago strait—a narrow channel between the long strand of sand known as Padre Island and a smaller barrier to the south called Brazos Island. The Mexican captain of the port, seeing the US column approaching, had ignited the structures and fled the area with most of the population of the hamlet. The flames had not kindled as quickly as he had hoped, allowing the onrushing dragoons to extinguish the fires before they had consumed more than four buildings. This left a number of structures available for storing the military supplies needed to sustain the American Army of Occupation.[51]

Equally important, Taylor learned that his first shipment of supplies had already arrived. Just hours before the dragoons rode into Point Isabel to douse the flaming buildings, the steamships *Porpoise*, *Lawrence*, and *Woodbury* arrived with the baggage, heavy artillery, and troops that had not made the overland trek from Corpus Christi. "I was gratified to find that the water expedition had exactly answered to our land movement," the general wrote in his report to Washington. The rapid rendezvous enabled him to quickly begin the process of transferring supplies from the boats to his now depleted wagons. With the replenished train ready to move, on March 26 he set out in the direction of Worth's camp at Palo Alto.[52]

Before leaving, Taylor took measures to protect the port. Like General Mejía before him, he understood that Point Isabel was a lifeline to his army and the key to any success in the region. "Our great depot must be here," he wrote, "and it is very important to secure it against any enterprise of the enemy." He therefore ordered Capt. John Sanders to begin developing plans to fortify the position. Maj. John Monroe and his troops, having escorted the supplies from Corpus Christi, now stayed behind to defend the Point and to begin construction of any fieldwork. To provide mobile support, a squadron of dragoons under the command of Lt. Theodoric Porter would stay, too, until the site was less vulnerable. In all, there were only a few hundred men to hold the Point, but Taylor, again sharing the view of Mejía, apparently realized that the site, surrounded by water on three sides, could be secured with a relatively small force.[53]

With his link to the outside world suitably secured, Taylor at last turned his attention to the final stage of his long march. He arrived at Worth's camp at Palo Alto on the afternoon of March 27. The next morning the reunited force rose before daybreak and at 5 a.m. took to the road for the final nine-mile push to the Rio Grande. The advance began in the previously established four columns as the troops crossed the grassy Palo Alto prairie. Then, after about four miles, chaparral began to hem in the road on either side, forcing the soldiers to march in a single, serpentine procession between the stands of dense undergrowth. They would remain in this vulnerable formation for much of the remainder of the march, uncertain whether an ambush lurked somewhere in the thickets and concerned for the exposed, and now full, supply wagons. But their luck held; they still encountered no Mexican resistance. As the troops continued forward, the brush gave way to croplands enclosed by fences of posts and brush. The columns passed a row of houses, some constructed of logs and some of brick, and finally came to the river, 200 yards wide, with Matamoros as a distant backdrop. "Very quietly the army took up a position in the cotton fields, gardens, and pomegranate groves that stretched along the north bank of the river," recalled Lt. Arthur Tracey Lee, "and very quietly, if we except the noisy barking of hordes of Mexican dogs, and an occasional bugle blast, which brought to mind the passage of the Sal Colorado, did the dwellers and the *soldados* of the opposite bank look on."[54] The march of more than two hundred miles had come to an end.

A setback occurred at the exact moment of the army's arrival. As the US column neared the water, a group of Mexicans on horseback sprang from the brush, seized two dragoons and their mounts, and spirited them off into the thickets, along with a trumpeter's horse. Some of the American troopers said that the act had been committed by Mexican cavalry, but it was impossible to be sure, and Taylor treated the issue with caution. Unwilling to start a war on such a hazy pretext, he dashed off a message to General Mejía. "I cannot believe that these acts were committed by your orders," he wrote, and he requested that men and horses be returned as quickly as convenience allowed.[55]

Taylor also took action to cast oil upon any other rough waters stirred by his just-concluded march. After selecting a field of newly planted corn tucked into a sharp bend of the Rio Grande as the site for his camp, he drafted a message to the owner of the land, promising to pay for any damages and lost crops. He kept his promise to the Matamoros delegation that when he reached the river he would explain his intentions. He wrote letters of introduction to both civil and military authorities in the town, expressing his desire to "enter into any arrangements to secure the peace and harmony of the frontier" until the US and Mexican governments could reach an official accord, and he sent General Worth to explain the situation to General Mejía. These messages complied with the spirit of Taylor's order to avoid any sort of unnecessary provocation, especially of the civilian population. The conciliatory tone of the notes suggests that Taylor continued to harbor a personal desire to avoid conflict and to force the Polk administration to settle the Texas issues through diplomacy rather than war. It is perhaps notable that Taylor waited for Worth to make contact with the Mexicans before allowing his troops to fashion a flagstaff from the tongue of a wagon and unfurl the Stars and Stripes. Near midday on March 28, he officially established his claim to the river.[56]

The informal flag-raising ceremony proved to be a grand success, although the efforts at diplomacy did not. As a group of about two hundred Mexican soldiers and throngs of Matamoros residents gathered on the opposite shore, the US military bands saluted their flag to the tunes of "Hail Columbia," "Yankee Doodle," and "The Star-Spangled Banner." In Matamoros, the flags of France, England, and Spain suddenly appeared on rooftops as foreign consuls attempted to protect themselves from any bombardment that might follow. Meanwhile, the conferences with the Mexicans went poorly enough that General Taylor would report "no satisfactory result" and a "decidedly hostile" attitude on the part of the Mexicans.[57]

General Worth faced a difficult task even in arranging a meeting. Lacking any sort of boat to cross the river, he was obliged to wait at the nearby ferry landing, holding a flag of truce and calling for someone to send the vessel across. After a lengthy delay, a small boat carrying two cavalry officers and Capt. Jean Louis Berlandier—the familiar figure from the parley on the Arroyo Colorado—crossed the waterway to confer with Worth. Worth, speaking through his interpreter, apparently a teamster named Mitchell, delivered his letter of introduction, stated that he carried dispatches for both civil and military authorities, and requested an interview with General Mejía. The Mexican trio requested that he wait for a reply and recrossed the river to present the message to the general-in-chief. They returned a short time later to inform Worth that Mejía would not confer with an American officer of subordinate rank but that he was willing to send a subordinate officer for that purpose. Worth replied that he was not seeking to confer with Mejía but rather to provide verbal information passed on by General Taylor. Nevertheless, he agreed to meet with an appropriate officer of equivalent rank. Berlandier and the two cavalry officers returned to the far shore once again, before crossing the river for a third time to tell Worth that Gen. Rómulo Díaz de la Vega would receive him on the opposite bank. These formalities out of the way, Worth at last boarded the ferry, accompanied by Lts. Larkin Smith, John Magruder, George Deas, and Edmund Blake, this time with Lt. Miner Knowlton serving as his interpreter.[58]

The conference that followed showed little more promise than the preliminaries. Díaz greeted the Americans with appropriate courtesy and introduced his companions, who included a man named Casares, representing the civil authorities, Juan Garza, an officer of the northern militia regiments, and an unnamed interpreter—perhaps the well-traveled Berlandier. With this latest round of formalities completed, the meeting deteriorated rapidly. Díaz de la Vega received Taylor's dispatches, had his translator read them, and responded that Mexico considered the march to the Rio Grande an act of war. Worth replied that, Mexican objections notwithstanding, the US Army had been ordered to occupy the north bank of the river and that, right or wrong, the occupation would continue until the two governments had settled the matter. When Díaz de la Vega attempted to resume the discussion, Worth informed the Mexican general that he had come to report the situation, not debate it.[59]

It next became Worth's turn to complain. He inquired about the status of Americans residing in Matamoros and received Díaz de la Vega's assurance that Mexico had not declared war, no American citizens had been arrested, and the US consul continued to serve in his official function. Yet he denied Worth's demand to speak with the American diplomat. Worth denounced this refusal as a belligerent act, withdrew the dispatch he carried, and stated that it would be Mejía's responsibility to renew any contact. Díaz de la Vega brushed aside these remarks and asserted that Mexicans felt a similar sense of indignation at seeing the American flag on the Río Bravo.[60]

Neither was able to press his issue any further. General Taylor and General Mejía both remained under orders to secure their respective sides of the river and to remain on the defensive. Therefore Worth and Díaz de la Vega, acting as their representatives, might express frustration at the actions of the other army but could put no teeth into their complaints. It also appears that each of the opposing generals understood the constraints placed on the other. Beneath the surface of harsh words lay an awareness that both sides were acting out of military duty, taking required stands, and following scripts that had been written in distant capitals. The two men parted on civil terms but with a word of caution from Worth. Having already communicated Taylor's desire to avoid confrontation and his offer to allow the Mexicans to continue using the important port at Point Isabel, Worth warned that General Taylor would "regard the passage of any armed party of Mexicans in hostile array as an act of war and pursue it accordingly."[61]

At the time, the caution was unnecessary. Despite persistent rumors and reports that they prowled the area in search of a confrontation, very few Mexican troops remained north of the Rio Grande. After his last-minute recall of forces from the Arroyo Colorado, General Mejía adhered strictly to his orders and kept his troops safely within the confines of Matamoros. He had ordered the port captain at the Frontón de Santa Isabel to burn any structures that might benefit the US occupiers, but that was a purely defensive move, and only partial successful in any event. Meanwhile, General Díaz de la Vega, who had previously crossed the Río Bravo near Reynosa, had withdrawn his army as well. His troops—the mostly likely cause of the tales of an advancing Mexican force north of the river—arrived at Matamoros via the south bank just before the interview with Worth on the 28th of March. Only a few scouts and irregular troops of the Villas del Norte, often acting on their own accord and resisting control from the Army of the North, remained to patrol the lands beyond the disputed river.[62]

It is likely that one of these bands captured the two US dragoons on the morning of the twenty-eighth, and Mejía did what he could to prevent the incident from exploding into conflict. This was the only action that might have been considered a "passage of any armed party of Mexicans in hostile array," and it seems doubtful that Mejía ordered it. He had already acted rashly with his decisions regarding the arroyo and had nearly provoked combat as a result. General Ampudia was scheduled to arrive in several days, and Mejía certainly would not have wanted to hand over a newly ignited war along with his command. But neither did he wish to appear weak and reveal to the Americans his tenuous control of the Mexican "ranchero" forces along the river. Stating only that one of his "detachments of observation" had seized the American soldiers, he promised to liberate them, their horses, and their equipment. He could not return the missing horse of the bugler, for he professed no knowledge of this incident. That act, he said "was probably done by some of the citizens, who not being soldiers, had armed themselves in defense of their country."[63]

In making this conciliatory gesture, Mejía did not apologize for the captures. On the contrary, he insisted that Mexico had acted within its rights and repeated Díaz de la Vega's assertion that the US march was viewed by his command as an invasion of Mexico. He thus dismissed Taylor's claims that the march did not represent a threat and that Mexican troops should tolerate the American occupation while negotiations proceeded. If the United States had truly desired a peaceful settlement of boundary disputes, he wrote in a letter to Taylor dated March 31, it "should have forbidden an occupation in fact, because it is not easy to conceive the reason or justice of taking forcible possession of the territory in dispute, pending the negotiation." But now that the US Army had done that, he, his army, and all of the people of Mexico had little choice but to view the advance of American troops as an act of war. With hostilities already opened by the United States, Mejía explained to Taylor that his troops could, "with propriety, be made prisoners, comfortably [according] to the laws of war," and that, moreover, releasing them to Taylor was "not obligatory, whatever view may be taken [of] the circumstances of their capture."[64]

The letter served as a warning as well as a defense. In the meeting between Generals Worth and Díaz de la Vega on March 28, Worth had directly stated that a Mexican military attack across the Rio Grande would be viewed as an act of war. In his letter of the thirty-first, Mejía just as bluntly staked his own position: Mexico had been invaded and Mexico had a right to defend her territory. Implied in the message was that Mexican troops would not hesitate to pour out of Matamoros and cross the Río Bravo when circumstances permitted a favorable result. As both the month of March and the US march came to a close, the lines had been drawn and the long-developing quarrel between the United States and Mexico now centered on a small piece of territory near the banks of the disputed river.

CHAPTER 3
The Rio Grande Delta

★

WITH THE STARS and Stripes fluttering on its left bank and the Mexican tricolor on its right, the Rio Grande took center stage in the unfolding drama between Mexico and the United States. The great river, with its rushing currents, had always had an enormous impact on the delta region. It had shaped the physical environment and had distributed life-giving waters to the flora and fauna of the surrounding lands. It had also influenced human activities, providing a source of sustenance for the hardy people who had settled near its banks. In 1845 the river took on a political character as well, becoming the object of international territorial debate. Now, with American troops on one shore and Mexican troops on the other, the waterway had become a flowing line in the sand that, if crossed, would produce a fight. And when that fight erupted, this formative force of the region would define the theater of war and establish the parameters for action.

In the spring of 1846, this stream lived up to the names commonly applied to it in both the United States and Mexico. The Rio Grande was indeed grand, traveling almost nineteen hundred miles from its source in the Rocky Mountains before it pushed its way past the city of Matamoros and reached its end at the Gulf of Mexico. The river was not especially wide—it measured only two hundred yards across at Matamoros and four hundred at its mouth—but it rushed between the banks in a "mighty torrent" and emptied into the Gulf with "an immense volume of water."[1] This powerful current created a true "Río Bravo," a wild and restless river that followed a sinuous path across the landscape. The twisting of the river was less evident in mountains and foothills but became much more frequent and pronounced as the water cut across the coastal plains. "The windings of the Rio Grande are remarkable," wrote one

American observer. "There is one hacienda on its banks which a boat passes in front of seven times . . . before actually reaching it." Another noted, "The del Norte is so crooked that you often in five miles steer to all points on the compass." Others simply described the path as "tortuous" or "the most crooked river in the world." This twisting course, with its many turns and doublings back, created a series of peninsulas, like long fingers of land that pointed back and forth across the water. It also made navigation extremely difficult. The distance from the city of Matamoros to the coast was little more than twenty-two miles by the most direct road, but became a dizzying expedition of more than fifty miles by water.[2]

The river had often proved itself unwilling to remain within its serpentine banks. The Arroyo Colorado, some thirty miles to the north, had once been the path it took as it meandered across coastal flats toward the Laguna Madre—the narrow sound that separates the mainland from the even narrower spit of sand known as Padre Island. Over a period of millennia, the river had left that path behind and moved steadily southward. Sometimes the heavy current pushed its way through the sharp bends, cutting off crescent-shaped swales and leaving behind ox-bows. On other occasions, the river jumped its banks completely, slicing new routes through the earth and leaving behind long, shallow ravines; they often extended for miles. By 1846, dozens of these traces, known as *resacas* by the local residents, marked the progress of the Rio Grande like the footprints of a restless, wandering creature. No longer connected to the stream that once filled them, these channels still collected pools of water during periods of heavy rain and served as watering holes for the humans and animals that occupied the region.

This river still strained against its confines in 1846. Heedless of the politicians who claimed that it marked the definitive border between the United States and Mexico, the Rio Grande continued to sculpt and change its path. Even as troops from both countries prepared to fortify its shores, heavy rains and floods continued to slice through its banks, causing the current to shift and leaving behind new cut-offs. The river also continued to abandon its channel entirely. Although its mouth could expand to almost a thousand yards to accommodate a swollen flow, the Rio Grande regularly poured over its banks, washing away settlements and creating vast swampy areas across the coastal plain. The land to the south, guarded by a bank lower than the one on the north side, was most vulnerable to these deluges. Flood waters also tended to stand longer on the south margin, settling into additional ox-bows and forming shallow basins of stagnating water known as *esteros*. These pools were the precursors to new channels as the river followed its irresistible urge to migrate.[3]

The roaming river created an oasis of life in an otherwise harsh region. In many ways the area was no different from the vast stretches of scrubland and desert that had challenged US troops on their march from Corpus Christi. A blazing sun baked the flat earth, little rain fell to relieve the parched soil, and only the hardiest of living things could survive. But in the lands between the Arroyo Colorado and the Rio Grande, the struggle for life was easier. Hundreds of years of meandering and flooding had bathed the ground in the Rio Grande's rich brown waters, and as those waters receded, they left behind ton upon ton of mud and silt that had been carried with the current. Over the course of time, these deposits formed a thick layer of black soil, far richer than the dust and sand found just miles to the north. Lt. George Meade, who described the land north of the Arroyo Colorado as "most miserable desert" and "perfectly unfit for the habitation of man," grudgingly admitted that the Rio Grande delta "is beautiful, and fully equal in fertility to the banks of the Mississippi." Others agreed, marveling at the "exuberant soil," and suggesting that enterprising American settlers would soon make the countryside blossom with extensive fields of sugar, cotton, and other market crops.[4]

In the meantime, much of the region lay fallow: a vast expanse of open, gently undulating fields. This prairie extended from the Gulf of Mexico westward for almost a hundred miles, covered with "a luxuriant coarse grass which grows nearly waist high," and interrupted only by the occasional clump of trees, yucca, or cactus. The men of Taylor's army, undoubtedly starved for the color green after their desert trek, marveled at these surroundings. Capt. William Henry compared the prairie at Palo Alto—the point where General Worth established his camp while General Taylor moved to secure Point Isabel—favorably to a manor house lawn in old England. "Instead of being clipped close, [it] is broken into an uneven surface by the luxuriant growth of grass and flowers." But the beauty of the region was not only the result of contrast with the wastelands that surrounded it. Even a soldier fresh off the boat after a short journey from New Orleans and the rich Mississippi valley, eyed the Rio Grande delta and declared that it "contains the loveliest green plains I ever saw."[5]

These plains provided a home to fauna as well as flora. By the time General Taylor's army crossed the Arroyo Colorado, the soldiers had grown wearily familiar with the ubiquitous rattlesnakes that inhabited the arid wastelands along their route. Those vipers and other reptiles thrived in the delta as well, accompanied by tarantulas, mosquitoes, ticks, ants, centipedes, scorpions other biting and stinging creatures. But the annoyance caused by these pests was mitigated by the presence of other animals. The soldiers, most of them experienced hunters, were pleased to encounter a wide variety of game. Large herds of deer grazed on the tall grass of the prairies, often accompanied by droves of wild horses. Rabbits, javelinas, coyotes, bobcats, and other species also roamed the area in substantial numbers. The troops especially marveled at the large number and variety of birds. Turkeys, pigeons, doves, quails, and a native prairie bird called the *chachalaca* thrived. The rain-filled resacas, which served as sources of water for all the animals, also attracted migratory birds. John Henshaw of the US 7th Infantry later recalled that "immense flocks of wild geese, ducks of every species and many varieties of crane were constantly seen and they usually flew so low that a man standing could knock them down with his musket."[6]

Teeming with life, the Rio Grande plains made a lasting impression on the troops, but so did the thickets that dominated the banks of the river. Irrigated by frequent floods, the rich soil directly beside the Rio Grande's snaking path came to life with an abundance of woody plants. At a point about eight miles from the banks, low trees and brush began to hem in the broad prairies. Five miles from the waterway, the density of these coppices increased, interspersed with small, scattered clearings. Then, extending for a mile from either shore of the river, the thick tangle of shrubs, twisted trees, cactus, and subtropical undergrowth overtook the plain altogether. One traveler who encountered this chaparral called it "the densest thickets I ever saw—mesquites, huisache, ebony, nopal and a hundred other unnamed trees, shrubs and plants formed an impenetrable hedge—anything at a yard's distance from the road was out of sight." George Meade described thorny bushes that made the brush impassible and observed that they "tear your clothes to pieces in trying to get through them." Another observer, colorful if not eloquent, characterized the Rio Grande chaparral as "so thick that a rat couldn't run through hardly."[7]

Only two forces could make a significant impact on this imposing vegetation. The first was the Rio Grande itself. Its rushing current carved through the thickets, and hardy stands of cane replaced trees near the water's edge. The other influence came in the form of a small number of determined Mexican frontiersmen, who built a community and called the Río Bravo delta home.

These settlers were relative latecomers to the region. Spanish conquerors had first explored it in the 1520s, with a number of expeditions along the Gulf Coast and up the mouth of the river. Their forays revealed few signs of riches, and, coupled with increasingly hostile relations with the natives, deflected interest from the area. It was not until the mid-eighteenth century that Spanish authorities renewed efforts to develop this northeastern frontier as part of the province called Nuevo Santander. In the late 1740s and 1750s, the Spanish push resulted in the founding of a few rustic villages like Reynosa, Camargo, Revilla, Mier, and Laredo along the southern shore of the Rio Grande. These villages were far inland from the mouth of the river, close to the primary travel routes into the strategically important region of Texas, Interest did not spread to the delta region until the close of the century, when the tiny ranch of San Juan de los Esteros was rebaptized as the slightly larger hamlet of Congregación de Refugio. This settlement languished for years. Only after Mexico's war of independence did it emerge, once again renamed, as the city of Matamoros in the newly created state of Tamaulipas.[8]

The Río Bravo served as the foundation for life for these communities, including the new town of Matamoros. It provided a link to the outside world and to other isolated communities along its course. Townspeople drew from its waters for drinking and washed their clothes on its banks. The river also supported the many small farms that sprang up to provide food for the community. Despite the fertility of the soil, it proved difficult to make this land productive. The paucity of rain and the seasonal nature of the little that fell limited opportunities for agriculture on many of the plains. Close to the river, however, where primitive pumps and irrigation systems could be used to move water, farmers were able to clear small fields and produce modest crops of corn, cotton, and sugar cane. Or they could plant small orchards of figs, lemons, limes, oranges, peaches, and bananas. A patchwork quilt of fields occupied both shores, but rarely stretched more than several hundred yards from the water's edge.[9]

Ranching extended over a larger area. Early migrants had established a number of small herds of cattle in the region and beef and dairy products made up a large part of the local diet. Ranchers also eked out a living selling hides and tallow both locally and as far north as Texas. Much of the ranching activity focused on the land north of the river. South of Matamoros, the surroundings grew brushy and arid, not unlike the plains north of the Arroyo Colorado, and could not sustain equivalent herds. But the lush, green savannahs between the Río Bravo and the Arroyo beckoned for grazing. Most of the cattlemen simply allowed their mules, horses, and cattle to roam the level prairies and to drink from the many resacas until they were wanted. Then they rounded up the animals, slaughtered them, dressed them, and tanned their hides on the plains. Others carved small ranches into the impenetrable chaparral, using the brush as natural fences to contain the animals. Additions to the landscape were usually limited and rustic. One US soldier described the typical ranch or farmhouse as "mostly built by planting posts into the ground upright, close together, chinked with mud, and the roof thatched with coarse dry grass, no floor but the smooth, hard ground and no pretensions are made to cleanliness and appearance."[10]

Only the most determined farmers and *rancheros* dared to settle on the north bank. These were resilient men—accustomed to a hard life, skilled on horseback, and extremely capable of defending themselves. However, they faced equally skilled antagonists. Bands of Apaches and Comanches roamed the land in pursuit of the plentiful game and periodically lashed out against encroachment by Mexican ranches and farms. On numerous occasions armed war parties swept across the plains, killing cattle, torching buildings, and massacring residents. These attacks continued even as the tensions mounted between Mexico and the United States. American scouts reconnoitering the region in February 1846 came across scenes of several clashes between Mexican troops and Indian bands. After the occupation of the delta, other US troops encountered burned-out ranches and farms—evidence that another territorial conflict was still in progress.[11]

This warfare had several effects. The regular slaughter of the herds limited the profitability of ranching, and cattle production never exploded into the major industry that it might have become otherwise. Raiding and pillaging also prevented the physical spread of trade. Although a few scattered houses, ranches, and tanques (watering areas) could be found as far north as the Arroyo Colorado, most of the habitations lay close to the river. Places like the Ranchos de los Tomates and Rancho de San Antonio, near Matamoros, and the Rancho de Carricitos, some twenty-five miles upstream, nestled in the sharp bends of the river and used it for protection on three sides. Other ranches located at greater distances from the riverbank were more vulnerable to attack, but the occupants of these operations could still depend on the river as an escape route. In the vicinity of Matamoros, those fleeing attack could rely on three main fording points: the Anacuitas crossing several miles upriver from the city, the Paso Real crossing, on a bend in the river directly opposite Matamoros, and the Longoreño crossing, several miles downstream. Escape to the south was not an absolute guarantee of safety, but the river and its strong currents often discouraged further pursuit.[12]

Indian attacks regularly occurred south of the river as well, but the city of Matamoros was now large enough to be insulated from many of these raids. Situated on a sharp bend in the river, about a mile from its banks, the city had grown rapidly since its foundation. At the turn of the nineteenth century, Concepción had been a sleepy community of several thousand settlers. The town population grew quickly in the aftermath of Mexican independence, climbing to seven thousand souls in the 1820s and briefly passing the sixteen-thousand mark in the early 1830s. As it grew in population, the town became rather urbane for a frontier outpost. Its fringes remained as rustic as any of the ranchos across the river; wooden and cane huts, known as *jacales*, lined rutted and muddy streets. There, the only concession to city life was the presence of picket fences that enclosed some of the properties. The inner portion of town, however, had taken on a much greater air of permanence. A cathedral, a prison, and a number of other substantial buildings surrounded the broad, tree-filled plaza. Radiating out from this central square, the downtown streets had been paved with cobblestones. Along these thoroughfares, the wealthier citizens of the community had erected two-story structures of brick and wood that served as both businesses and homes. With a nod to the continuing dangers of frontier life, these houses had massive walls and barred windows, "so that one thinks they were built for defense." Nevertheless, the brick- and ironwork also took on an ornamental appearance and was, by 1846, no longer purely functional.[13]

The growth and wealth of this community was, once again, largely derived from the Río Bravo. In the final years of Spanish dominion, the river carried trade deep into the interior of the empire. Steamboats plied its current for a hundred miles, up to the town of Camargo, then entered the tributary San Juan River en route to the cities of Monterey and Saltillo. This was primarily a seller's market, with traders exchanging a variety of manufactured goods for gold and silver specie. But enterprising ship captains also carried wool and cattle hides out on the return voyage. Mexican independence caused this trade to expand significantly, because the removal of imperial trade restrictions encouraged many more merchants to test the waters of the Río Bravo. By the 1830s, dozens of merchants from many nations had ships moving up and down the winding channel.[14]

Matamoros was one of the great beneficiaries of this trade. As the town closest to the mouth of the Río Bravo, it became the primary port of entry for the ships moving up the river. Not surprisingly, residents of the community rushed to take advantage of this opportunity. Artisans, innkeepers, and others set up shop to offer support and services to steamboat operators and their ships. Landowners in the vicinity began to expand their herds in the hope of drawing income from the hide trade. Residents of the town also relied heavily on the incoming goods, purchasing lumber and manufactured items to improve their lives and surroundings.[15]

Matamoros, Mexico. *Courtesy of Library of Congress.*

Matamoros also became a base for many of those conducting this busy trade. Merchants from the United States, Great Britain, and other European nations descended upon this northeastern city, where they established trade houses to manage their Mexican affairs. Americans in particular thrived. Many came from New Orleans, which had emerged as the primary trade partner not only for Matamoros, but for all of northern Mexico. The Yankee traders also had access to river steamboats appropriate to a waterway like the Río Bravo. Not to be underestimated, they were represented by consuls who were, as described by one trader, "well versed in the peculiarities of the trade and skillful in coping with the idiosyncrasies of the Mexican bureaucracy." As early as 1829, Gen. Manuel Mier y Terán, who had been sent to investigate the growing role of American settlers in the northern province of Texas, saw a similar influence when he described the growth of Matamoros. It was with no little concern that he wrote, "The principle homes, which are beautiful and well constructed, belong to the North American merchants."[16]

This concern was shared by the government in Mexico City, which took steps to assert its influence. Authorities erected customs house in the region and attempted to collect tariffs on goods traveling up the river. As tensions with Texas increased in the

1830s and 1840s, the central government also tried to isolate that fractious province by restricting trade between it and the communities along the Río Bravo. These measures were only partly successful. Although custom receipts climbed, trade began to stagnate and towns along the river suffered. Matamoros, for example, saw its population drop from sixteen thousand to about twelve thousand over the course of a decade. Declining wealth, newly imposed regulations, and the failure of the central government to respond adequately to Comanche raids had all contributed to this general deterioration and had produced the surge of restlessness and separatist sentiment that had swept through the region. Men like Antonio Canales and José María de Jesús Carvajal had participated in rebellions against Mexico City and continued to pursue discussions with the United States even as General Taylor advanced from Corpus Christi. Others simply worked around the new restrictions. Many traders evaded the customs houses and illegally shipped imports upriver or sent hides, mules, and horses overland for sale to the growing population of Texas. This commerce continued even after Texans declared their independence, and the Mexican government was largely powerless to halt it. Even Gen. Mariano Arista, who was ultimately responsible for restricting contraband, drew a considerable amount of his livelihood from trade with Texas and was not motivated to kill off this golden goose.[17]

While many native ranchers and artisans suffered under the new regulations, outsiders tended to have the financial wherewithal to endure and overcome. By the 1840s Matamoros had become home to consuls representing Great Britain, Spain, France, Germany, and other European nations. On the eve of war with the United States, more than three hundred foreign residents had made the city their home. Once again, the US presence was the most pronounced. Ties with the port of New Orleans had strengthened and American traders were important and wealthy participants in the community. Even the buildings of the town reflected this influence. Many of the finer structures exhibited architectural features and designs that were more representative of the Crescent City than of the traditional architecture of Mexico. Despite the efforts of Mexican centralists to rein in the separatists and foreigners, the Rio Grande and its trade continued to encourage both groups to grow.[18]

Over time, it became apparent that the real limits on the towns and traders were those imposed by the river itself. In Matamoros, for example, the Río Bravo provided a livelihood for the citizens, but it could bring destruction and death as well. Although the town had been situated far back from the channel, it was by no means safe from the floods that plagued the delta. When heavy rains caused the river to rise over its banks, it inundated the community and filled streets and buildings with water and mud. The force of the torrent sometimes carried away people, animals, crops, and even houses. After several sizable floods, the river formed new cutoffs and reestablished its course closer to the city's northern limits, stirring fear that it might one day shift dramatically and overrun Matamoros entirely.[19]

This doomsday scenario never occurred, but the ebbing of the waters carried its own risk. As floods receded, some of the waters became trapped in the many *esteros* that surrounded Matamoros. In the days that followed, these stagnant pools became breeding grounds for mosquitoes and catalysts for disease. Outbreaks of yellow fever, scarlet fever, malaria, cholera, and other tropical diseases regularly swept through the city in the aftermath of heavy rains or hurricanes. These plagues could kill dozens, even hundreds, of people and often created far more misery than the initial flood or hurricane. Livestock also succumbed to sickness. Each rainy season or flood brought a variety of unknown ailments that decimated the herds of cattle and mules and set back efforts by ranchers to establish and profit from their trade.[20]

Matamoros survived these trials mainly because other places were worse. Attempts had been made to establish a settlement at the mouth of the river. In the 1820s, a community known as Bagdad had briefly thrived and competed with Matamoros for predominance in the region. But this town, which at its height boasted several thousand residents, was even more prone to flooding than its inland rival. The coastal plain also stood directly in the path of punishing storms off the Gulf. At some time in the late 1820s or early 1830s, a hurricane blasted onshore and swept Bagdad away, along with hundreds of its residents. By 1846, only a small customhouse and a settlement of about fifty rancheros remained to mark the entry to the Río Bravo. Another community, known as Burrita, sprang up on a bend in the river about ten miles from the Gulf. This hamlet sat on a relatively high rise of land on the south shore of the Bravo, which allowed it to escape the inundations that plagued both Bagdad and Matamoros. Nevertheless, while this elevation extended for several miles, it was only about two hundred yards wide, and the river frequently drowned the surrounding lowlands. By 1846 the village amounted to little more than a large rancho, with a ferry across the river and a handful of "miserably built hovels, not capable of protecting the inmates from the pelting rain."[21]

While occurrences of high water regularly troubled villages along the river, it was shallow water that most affected shipping and trade. The river was never extremely deep. Even during times of flooding the center of the channel rarely surpassed twenty or thirty feet. In general, soundings along the twisting course leading to Matamoros revealed the bed to be little more than eleven to fourteen feet down. This was low enough that ships could become stranded if they ventured too close to either shore. The mouth of the river was even shallower. As the waterway flowed out into the Gulf, its strong currents deposited a large band of thick mud on the ocean floor. Tidal action pushed and packed sand on top of these deposits, reducing the water depth to about four to six feet. The bar thus formed across the river mouth limited entry into the waterway. Many ocean-going vessels had deep hulls that prevented their pilots from even attempting to clear the obstacle. Only flat-bottomed river steamers could hope to pass over it under the best of conditions. During dry summer months, when the river ran low, even the steamers could founder in the sand. And there was always a threat of greater trouble. In 1837, a severe storm raised the sandbar to a level that temporarily closed ship access to the Río Bravo entirely and demonstrated just how unreliable river traffic could be.[22]

This situation had produced several significant impacts on trade in the delta region. Early on, it helped traders from the United States gain a competitive advantage. Americans had easier access than their European rivals to riverboats, needing only to sail them across the relatively protected waters of the Gulf to reach their market. More importantly, the obstructing bar ensured that Matamoros would never become a true port city. Although it became the site of docks and warehouse facilities and was officially designated the Puerto de Matamoros, the impediment at the mouth of the Río Bravo and its narrow, shallow, winding course inland limited the city's usefulness as a point of entry. Any attempt to dredge the channel would have been impracticable, cost prohibitive, and temporary. Residents and officials of the region were forced to seek an alternative that would make them less dependent on the unpredictable mouth of the river.[23]

In doing so, they looked northward. South of the river, the coastline offered no protected portage for at least a hundred miles. But just nine miles up from the clogged river mouth, the water of the Laguna Madre forced its way into the Gulf between Padre Island and Brazos Island. This opening, known as the Brazos Santiago strait, stretched for more than five hundred yards. More significantly, the waters had created a central channel, about sixty yards wide, through which ships could pass into the safety of the leeward side of the islands. Like the Río Bravo, the Brazos Santiago strait was guarded by a sandbar that restricted certain ship traffic. Nevertheless, the clearance in the channel ranged from seven and one-half to twelve feet, making it possible for large ships to pass. This access was also more constant than that of the river mouth, permitting year-round entry. To make use of this point officials constructed docking facilities and several wood frame storehouses on the northern end of Brazos Island, creating a humble port that would serve as the primary entry of goods into northern Mexico.[24]

Establishment of this trade depot on the strait was hardly a perfect solution. The shallow channel continued to favor the low-draught boats of Yankee merchants and enabled the Americans to maintain their stranglehold on trade. And Brazos Island was a forbidding environment, a "desolate waste." At eight miles long and three miles wide, the spit of land had none of the appeal of the long, grass-covered Padre Island just to the north. "The island is low and very level," wrote one US soldier, "and so destitute of soil that no grass or weeds grow on it." Water was hard to find, too, with wells producing only small, brackish trickles. Most observers viewed the land as little more than a glorified sandbar, "occasionally diversified by little mounds, which are moved about by the storms that visit it." Those storms struck the island with regularity, all too often washing away the homes and even the bodies of the few settlers who dared to take up residence. The site, therefore, was never considered the place for a grand port facility or a town to rival Matamoros.[25]

The island depot did provide a basic service. Throughout the 1820s, ships that arrived at the docks unloaded their goods onto waiting, mule-drawn wagons. Assembled into convoys, these carts then followed one of several tracks down the length of the island to a customhouse that occupied the southern point. After clearing the shipments, the wagons forded the narrow and shallow Boca Chica, or little mouth, of the Laguna Madre, to reach the mainland. From this point they continued toward Burrita, where a rope-drawn ferry had been set up for crossing the river. From the south shore the road continued to Matamoros, where the goods could be stored or reloaded onto boats that continued up the river. It was a long and laborious trek, but not as inefficient as it first appears. Since the road to Matamoros avoided some of the swiftest currents and sharpest bends on the river, the overland distance for a wagon was much shorter and the time involved not much longer than the trip up the Bravo by boat.[26]

Even so, Mexican officials took measures to improve the journey. By the early 1830s, the Brazos Santiago channel had demonstrated its merit, and discussions began about upgrading warehouse and customs facilities. One likely suggestion was to move the structures onto the mainland, where they might better withstand the elements. A series of damaging hurricanes and other coastal storms confirmed the wisdom of this approach. By the end of the decade, the island facility was abandoned, replaced by the Frontón de Santa Isabel depot, positioned on a mainland point, just three miles away across the Laguna Madre.[27]

Frontón possessed many benefits that compensated for its principal limitation: water depth. The route across the Laguna Madre once again turned shallow, reducing hull clearance to six feet. This meant that many of the boats that could not enter the Río Bravo were equally unable to reach the new port. On the other hand, the water level of the Laguna did not fluctuate as much as that of the river. Boats that could make the passage could expect to do so throughout the year, without unexpectedly running aground. The Frontón was also much more sheltered than the either the river mouth or the Brazos depot. With the barrier islands blocking the approach from the east, the point did not endure the same devastating winds and tides that swept across the previous portages. The higher elevation of the land, about ten feet above sea level, protected it from storm surges as well. Meanwhile, having water on the north, east, and south provided a measure of protection from attacks by marauding Comanches. Perhaps most important, the new location significantly reduced travel time to Matamoros. Goods and passengers still made the journey by wagon, but they followed a relatively direct road across the coastal plains and through the chaparral that cut the route to twenty-seven miles—about half the distance of the route from Brazos Island. Since the road crossed higher ground and stayed away from the flood-prone river, the track remained passable for more of the year as well.[28]

By 1846, the Santa Isabel-to-Matamoros route had become firmly established as the doorway to northern Mexico. More than a dozen structures formed the official port, including warehouses, customhouse, and guard facilities. These were the buildings that residents attempted to burn when US troops arrived in March. Better land and water also permitted a small community of settlers to flourish and provide a workforce for the port. The road to Matamoros remained a dirt track—wide in the places where it crossed the open prairies, narrow where it squeezed through the chaparral, and with "wet weather" spurs where travelers created detours around boggy areas in the rainy seasons. In general, however, the road was well traveled, hard-packed, and considered to be first-rate for the region—especially on the last fifteen miles to Matamoros, where it merged with the old royal road from San Patricio and Corpus Christi for the final segment of the trip. The combined road went on to the Paso Real and Anacuitas crossing points, where rope-drawn ferries had been established to carry passengers and goods across the Río Bravo into Matamoros. From there, the city continued to serve as the embarkation point for the constantly growing shipping trade up the river and into the interior.[29]

By inserting himself into the middle of this supply route in March of 1846, Zachary Taylor achieved two important results. First, he was able to seize the benefits of the port and its road for his own purposes. Point Isabel, with its reliable harbor and defensible position, stood out as the ideal place to establish a depot to receive ships carrying reinforcements and supplies. The good condition of the road made it easy to transport troops and matériel toward the Rio Grande, giving the route additional appeal. Occupation of the Point also effectively cut the primary Mexican supply line to Matamoros. Despite all the activity along the river between Matamoros and the interior, the riverside towns could provide little of the food and none of the weapons and equipment needed to sustain an army. The Rio Grande remained open, but the bar at its mouth had grown particularly high that year, severely restricting passage. Since it was primarily American-owned boats that could navigate the obstacle, Mexican military leaders could not rely on help via the river either. In keeping with his determination not to provoke a conflict, Taylor offered to allow Matamoros to continue using Point Isabel for supplies and commerce. Nevertheless, the confiscation of the port and customhouse and the severing of a vital link in northern Mexico's trade constituted a provocation that was hard for Mexican officials to stomach.[30]

When General Taylor situated his camp on a bend of the waterway near the Paso Real ferry, he intended the location to make a statement. The point of land projected south toward the heart of Matamoros, ensuring that the Stars and Stripes could be seen clearly from the center of city on the opposite shore. Even if this banner waved from a makeshift, wagon-tongue staff, no one in that city could fail to observe that the United States had claimed the territory—including some of the community's best croplands—as its own. Settlers on the north bank who occupied rustic homes on this land and tilled the rich fields responded, as they had so many times in the past, by fleeing across the water to the safety of Matamoros. This time, however, instead of razing houses, killing cattle, and moving on, the invading force settled in for an extended stay. General Taylor attempted to maintain goodwill by assuring the Mexicans that he respected individual property rights, and, as evidence of his sincerity, by negotiating a lease for the land under his camp. Such legal machinations, however, merely confirmed for residents that this was truly an occupation of their territory—one that would affect their personal possessions and livelihoods. These frontiersmen felt no strong loyalty to the distant central government, cared little about the larger political disputes swirling around them, and occasionally undermined the Mexican cause by conducting trade with their occupiers. But they did worry about the fate of their own families and community. And, as conflict mounted, it was—in the words of one US soldier— "reasonable to expect that [they would] rush in to defend their own firesides."[31]

The US troops all knew that their movements might provoke a Mexican backlash, but differed about the security of their position. Zachary Taylor felt that his riverside camp was a rather strong location. The Rio Grande wrapped around the perimeter on three sides, affording the same kind of protection it had long given the residents of Matamoros. To the north, a pair of horseshoe-shaped resacas blocked much of the base of the peninsula. This, the general believed, provided a barrier to any sort of concerted ground assault. Others saw the same features as a disadvantage. Lt. George Meade thought the multiple barriers might make the camp vulnerable to siege. Eng. Capt. John Sanders also disputed the view that the location provided protection from across the river. "I am satisfied it is a false position," he wrote to a fellow officer. "As the river men would say the army is on a point and Matamoros on a bend. A bend not only necessarily commands a point but also affords a converging fire upon it." Sanders understood that the foe was not a band of Comanches that would be deterred by the fast-flowing channel. By placing a few canon in strategic positions, the Mexican Army could bombard the US position and rain a deadly storm of metal on it.[32]

These concerns were valid, but the Mexican troops in Matamoros had their own problems to overcome. Charged with the responsibility of defending the city, Gen. Francisco Mejía and his soldiers focused their attention not on exploiting American liabilities, but on shoring up their own woefully inadequate defenses. Ironically, the security long provided by the river was responsible for one of the town's greatest vulnerabilities. For decades, the channel had served as a barrier to Indian raids, and the city had thrived in the shelter of its curving arm. Convinced that the broad expanse of water was sufficient to discourage attacks, residents had neglected the northern entry to Matamoros, concentrating instead on securing the approaches from other directions. Even during the 1830s and 1840s, when conflict between Texas and Mexico led to clashes and depredations along the river, Matamoros had escaped unscathed, giving citizens no cause to doubt the security afforded by the Río Bravo and discouraging them from erecting any battlements. As a result, when the three thousand troops of the US Army established their camp on the north bank, they looked across at a far shore that lacked even the most primitive earthworks to resist them.[33]

The river likely would have foiled efforts to build fortifications in any event. The regular floods along the Rio Grande had left the area immediately adjacent to the south bank a virtual no-man's land. While the higher north shore supported farms, ranches, and orchards, the plain leading from the river toward Matamoros remained largely barren, with a few cultivated plots giving way to a large, unoccupied stretch of grass and chaparral. If any houses ever existed along the south edge, they had long ago been washed away by raging waters accompanying heavy rains or hurricanes. Powerful currents, which regularly cut away portions of the bank as the river strained to move south, would have eroded earthen defenses as well. Even the best-designed, best-constructed structure might well have succumbed to the powerful hurricane of the early 1840s, which shifted the river in several places, swamped the town, destroyed many buildings, and even toppled the towers of the cathedral in the city center. This was especially true since any structure would have been composed of earth or brick. One of the features that made the sedimentary soil of the delta so fine for agriculture was the complete absence of rocks in the region. The only stone available for construction was quarried hundreds of miles away and transported in at great expense, or had once served as the ballast on river steamers.[34]

Mejía had not been idle in preparing a defense, but he faced a daunting task. Hurricanes, floods, and mere neglect had left much of the military infrastructure of the frontier community in ruins. Powder magazines and forts in the town were crumbling to the ground. Barracks were nonexistent or in a condition that would not permit them to shelter troops. Storehouses leaked from the roofs and walls, making them unsuitable for use. For many months before and during the US advance, the Mexican general had been so involved in tending to these basic conditions that he had little time to consider developing fortifications along the river.[35] Since he had initially intended to make a stand on the Arroyo Colorado, establishing earthworks along the Río Bravo had probably not looked crucial.

When he received the order to focus on the defense of Matamoros, General Mejía did take measures to secure the northern entry. He concentrated his efforts at Anacuitas, the primary crossing into the city. Here, on the south bank of the river, his troops built a large, round fort of earth, timbers, and brick to guard the river passage. Dubbed Fort Paredes, the structure was sturdy enough to shelter up to eight hundred troops from an assault. More importantly, it occupied one of the highest points along the right bank of the Bravo and had a commanding view of the opposite shore.[36] Any force that set up camp on the opposite point would have faced the type of fire that

Captain Sanders had feared. Unfortunately for Mejía, Taylor—who was not really planning to cross the river—instead chose to occupy the next point along the channel. At that location there were no defenses in place on the Matamoros side and the Mexican troops were in no position to confront the Americans with a converging fire.

In fact, when General Taylor's troops first established camp in the fields along the north bank, Mejía's best protection was provided by the environment. The approach of summer brought out a blazing sun that burned down on American camp. Springtime showers poured into the baked ground and threatened to turn the plowed fields and croplands into a swampy quagmire that could impede US troop operations. The rains also promised to generate hoards of mosquitoes and to spread tropical diseases and fevers. Of course these forces of nature threatened the Mexican Army as well and bode ill for Mejia's own efforts to establish fortifications to the south. Until he was able to get those defenses in place, it appeared that the only barrier to a US invasion of Matamoros was the city's longtime protector, the same ribbon of water that had defined the region and sparked the conflict—the Río Bravo.

CHAPTER 4
Final Preparations

★

"THE MEXICANS SAY they will attack us," Surgeon Madison Mills reported matter-of-factly from the Rio Grande as he ended his diary entry for March 28, 1846. Like his fellow soldiers, Mills had heard accounts of the meeting between Gen. William Jenkins Worth and General Díaz de la Vega and was aware of the warnings that had been issued. He and his peers quickly dispensed with celebrations to mark the end of a difficult march and turned their attention to preparing some sort of defense.[1]

Those on the south bank of the river also expected bloodshed. "In a very few days, perhaps moments, the blood of veteran soldiers will commence to fall," the newspaper *El Aguila del Norte* announced in an editorial. Citizens of Matamoros heeded this warning. Residents who were able to leave poured out of town toward the safety of Monterrey, to the west, and Victoria, to the south. Those who remained behind watched warily as the giant US encampment took root across the river within view of their town. "I have no doubt but that they are fearful we will attack them," Surgeon Mills reported on March 30, after several days of watching Matamoros from afar.[2]

General Mejía responded to the arrival of the US force by turning troops out of their barracks in the town and sending them to positions near the principal river crossings.[3] On the western side of the city, the troops put the finishing touches on Fort Paredes, completing a line of trenches, revetments, bombproofs, and bastions that stretched 280 yards along the shoreline at the Anacuitas crossing. He also placed several cannon in the fortifications: one high up on the bank that commanded the opposite point and a pair at water level to strike any boats that attempted to ford the site. The bend in the river across from the US camp received greater attention. When US troops arrived, only a small, low redoubt—absent any artillery pieces—covered the nearby

Paso Real crossing point. Within hours of Taylor's arrival, Ignacio Mora y Villamil, the general in charge of the fortification project, moved troops from the Fort Paredes site to strengthen the defenses. Under cover of darkness on the night of March 28, these soldiers, with "violent speed," positioned sandbags around the redoubt and placed an 8-pound cannon inside so that it commanded the opposing camp. Villamil expressed pleasure with the dedication of the soldiers, proudly announcing that "the enemy was stupefied to find well-constructed breastworks and batteries at a spot where, just eight hours before, there had not even been a line or a picket." In subsequent days, working around the clock, the Mexican soldiers added more sandbags and extended trenches, breastworks, and batteries to the east and west of the US camp. By April 7, several more batteries and trenches were finished and immediately occupied by Gen. Antonio Canales and some four hundred of his troops. General Mora y Villamil heaped praise on the men who had worked day and night to secure this line, noting that they had finished their work quickly, while the Americans had barely established a battery placement of much inferior quality.[4]

The new fortifications allowed the Mexicans to point cannon at the US camp from several directions, threatening the type of artillery crossfire that Engineer Captain Sanders had feared. But their primary purpose was defensive. In reports describing his work, Mora y Villamil assured his superior that the placements protected the most vulnerable points on the river and would thwart any American attempts to cross. The line of trenches and breastworks that crossed the chaparral and fields between the new batteries and Fort Paredes, served as a second line of defense if an invading force should manage to reach the south bank. With the US troops occupying the main supply route into the town and orders in place from Mexico City to defend Matamoros at all costs, Mora y Villamil appears to have approached Taylor's advance as a siege of the town and devised a plan to turn back an attack when it arrived.[5]

But no American attack was in the offing. True to the words of his message to Mejía, Taylor was content to remain peacefully in his new position—partly because he believed that a political solution might be reached if the armies held off on hostilities, and partly because he was still bound by Secretary of War Marcy's message of January 13 ordering him to advance to, but not beyond, the Rio Grande. Marcy had also warned that in light of certain US movements, "it is probable that Mexico will interpose resistance," but he did not give Taylor license to initiate conflict. "It is not designed, in our present relations with Mexico, that you should treat her as an enemy," wrote the secretary. But "should she assume that character by a declaration of war, or any open act of hostility toward us, you will not act merely on the defensive, if your relative means allow you to do otherwise."[6] In short, if Mexican troops crossed the Rio Grande and attacked the American camp, Taylor was expected to respond decisively.

This policy originated with Pres. James Polk, who pursued it for several reasons. It reflected his continuing belief that the presence of US troops on the Rio Grande would eventually force the weak Mexican government to the negotiating table. Despite public claims that he wanted to force his nation into war, it appears that as late as April 1846, Polk still hoped to resolve the territorial disputes without a fight. The president's orders also reflected the political climate of the United States. His election may have silenced domestic resistance to the annexation of Texas, but it did not generate automatic support either for his claims to the Rio Grande as the boundary or for armed conflict with Mexico to decide the border. While stolid expansionists were eager to engage Mexico on the battlefield in the hope of speeding the nation's inexorable push westward, most citizens hoped to avoid war. Polk's political adversaries—a loose coalition made up of Whigs, anti-expansionists, abolitionists, and Northerners—opposed him with a fervor that matched the Mexicans'. They insisted that the president had fabricated the boundary dispute in the hope of adding territory that would benefit himself, the Democratic Party, and the proslavery South. Antagonists like Congressmen Garrett Davis blasted the decision to send troops to the Rio Grande, insisting that "it was the settled purpose of Mr. Polk to have a war with Mexico," and "that he ordered the army forward to the Rio Grande, in aggressive war upon the territory, people, and authorities of Mexico, the more certainly to provoke it."[7]

Like Davis, much of the American public, even many who favored expansion, resisted the Rio Grande push. The causes of their intransigence varied. Some shared Davis's doubts about the legitimacy of the boundary claims. Some voiced concern about how armed expansion reflected upon the character of a democratic republic. At least one young man feared that an outbreak of hostilities would lead to a draft and admitted that he would find it "outrageously disagreeable to have a musket ball, or cannonball, or even an Indian rubber ball, going right through your body, leaving a red line to mark its course."[8]

Polk was aware that his vocal critics would continue to oppose him at every turn, so he devoted scant attention to them. His concern was for the broader cross section of the American public. If he simply ordered his troops to initiate a conflict, especially by invading across the Rio Grande, much of the public would reflexively resist and throw its support to the opposition camp. His only hope for war was to force Mexico to take the initiative. If properly handled, an attack by Mexico could sway public support in Polk's favor, silence the die-hard opposition, and completely change the military options. Looking back in his memoirs on this period, Ulysses S. Grant assessed the situation eloquently: "We were sent to provoke a fight," he wrote, "but it was essential that Mexico should commence it. It was very doubtful whether Congress would declare war; but if Mexico should attack our troops, the Executive could announce, 'Whereas, war exists by the acts of, etc.,' and prosecute the contest with vigor. Once initiated there were but few public men who would have the courage to oppose it."[9]

Grant, who was only a young lieutenant in the army during the spring of 1846, made this judgment based largely on the benefits of hindsight. At the time, Polk could not have been sure that Americans would support war even if Mexico did initiate the fighting. That is why he devoted real effort to achieving a favorable diplomatic settlement, even though he was certainly not opposed to war if it became the only option. But his hope for support rested entirely with his ability to cast blame on Mexico. Hence, his strict edict that Taylor remain on the north bank of the Rio Grande and avoid initiating hostilities. If and when war erupted, he wanted it to occur in territory claimed and occupied by the United States. Then, even if a large segment of the public rejected the validity of the territorial claim, Polk would seek to build support with the assertion that US troops acted in self-defense and in defense of the national borders.

Thus the initiative was thrust squarely upon Mexico, which had little choice but to seize it. Polk had miscalculated when he assumed that military pressure would lead Mariano Paredes to abandon his hardline stance on Texas. Instead, it obliged him to dig in his heels. Having used the defense of Texas as his pretext for seizing the presidency, Paredes could not simply reverse course once he held the reins of power—his fierce rhetoric and his vows to defend the national territory had inflamed passions around the country and raised expectations that he would follow through. Unless he was willing to accept ruin and political exile, Paredes was forced to interpret the Americans' march to the Rio Grande and their occupation of the port at the Frontón de Santa Isabel as an act of war. He had to respond with military force.

Even if Mexican leaders had wanted to negotiate their differences with the United States, Zachary Taylor's advance made a satisfactory outcome unlikely. With American troops stationed on the banks of the Río Bravo, any Mexican government would have found itself in the unenviable position of bargaining to reacquire territory that had already been conceded. Moreover, since Polk clearly did not intend to release his hold on the land north of the Río Bravo, the task became impossible. Formal talks would serve no purpose other than to permit the US Army to assemble more troops and strengthen its foothold along the river. Extended discussions might even allow American settlers to move in behind the protective military curtain. Mexico's only viable option, therefore, was to strike out quickly and hope that its troubled military could score a victory against the relatively small US force.

General Taylor may or may not have recognized this reality, but he understood that circumstances favored a Mexican attack in fairly short order. Although his intelligence indicated that no more than two thousand soldiers occupied Matamoros—men "of very bad description, and miserably armed"—he knew that thousands of enemy reinforcements could arrive at any moment. This would change the balance of power on the river and put teeth into the Mexican threats of an attack. Meanwhile, the unheralded soldiers in Matamoros had shown themselves capable of acting quickly in response to the US camp. After passing an uneventful first night in their new surroundings, the Americans arose on March 29 to discover that the enemy forces had used cover of darkness to erect a line of sandbag fortifications along the opposite shore. Within days, several artillery pieces pointed menacingly across the river toward the heart of the US position. Taking note, Taylor sent a dispatch to the War Department appealing for reinforcements: "I must again and urgently call your attention to the necessity of speedily sending recruits to this army."[10]

The US soldiers spent their first full day on the Rio Grande preparing for an onslaught. Many of the troops devoted their attention to improving their campsites, drawing water from the river, or gathering firewood from the brush and fence lines at the base of the peninsula they occupied. On each trip they passed through a double line of sentries who encircled the camp and watched carefully for any Mexican troop movements. Meanwhile, artillery troops under the command of Col. James Duncan responded to the Mexican entrenchments by constructing an earthen breastwork of their own. By nightfall they had two 6-pounder field cannon and two 12-pounder howitzers mounted into the defenses. One of the guns pointed directly at General Mejía's headquarters. Troops of the 1st Brigade also began building some breastworks and traverses around their position to reduce their exposure. The other brigades elected to delay similar action since General Taylor had ordered plans for a formal fieldwork to serve as his primary defense. Throughout the day, Maj. Joseph King Fenno Mansfield and his topographic engineers conducted a series of surveys, sightings, and measurements as the preliminary to designing the structure.[11]

The sense of security provided by these measures did not forestall the tense atmosphere that swept across the camp by the end of the day, when rumors of a Mexican offensive circulated among the troops. According to reports, between six hundred and seven hundred Mexican cavalrymen had forded the Rio Grande at a point about seven miles upstream from the camp. An unknown number of additional troops were supposed to have made a similar crossing at another spot downstream. No one could be sure of the destination of these soldiers, but it was assumed that the Mexicans had set their sights on the undermanned garrison at Point Isabel, the poorly protected camp on the riverbank, or both. As daylight gave way to an exceptionally dark and rainy night, General Taylor ordered Capt. Charles May and a company of dragoons to speed their horses along the twenty-seven-mile route to the coast to provide support for Captain Monroe and his forty men. Along the river, the troops increased pickets and patrols, drew up additional artillery pieces, and left horses saddled and ready for action. Soldiers slept with muskets cradled in their arms, believing they might face a fight at any moment.

The alarm came at 10 p.m. Bugles sounded from points along the opposite bank of the river and appeared to signal a Mexican attack. The US troops poured from their tents to confront the enemy, but the attack never materialized. After several hours of anxious waiting and peering into the inky blackness, most of the troops returned to their beds. They endured a fitful night, waiting expectantly for Mexican soldiers to appear. Some worried that the next alarm might cause a stampede of the hundreds of horses, cattle, and pack animals quartered in the center of camp. With morning light, they discovered that the opposing troops had increased the length and complexity of their fortifications along the river but had taken no offensive actions. Captain May and the dragoons returned to report that the Point remained peaceful as well.[12]

This night set the tone for several to follow. While the American troops took advantage of daylight to explore their surroundings and make additional preparations, the hours of darkness became periods of watchful waiting and occasional alarms. Each morning the troops arose to find that the Mexicans had constructed additional sandbag barriers and earthworks that snaked along the far shore of the river. More and more cannon pointed out from those works as well, giving them an increasingly ominous appearance. On no occasion, however, did the guns open fire, and Mexican forces never made a move against the occupying force. In a letter to his wife, Lt. George Meade described the situation as one in which the "status quo" prevailed. "They continue to work assiduously, night and day, in putting batteries all around their town,

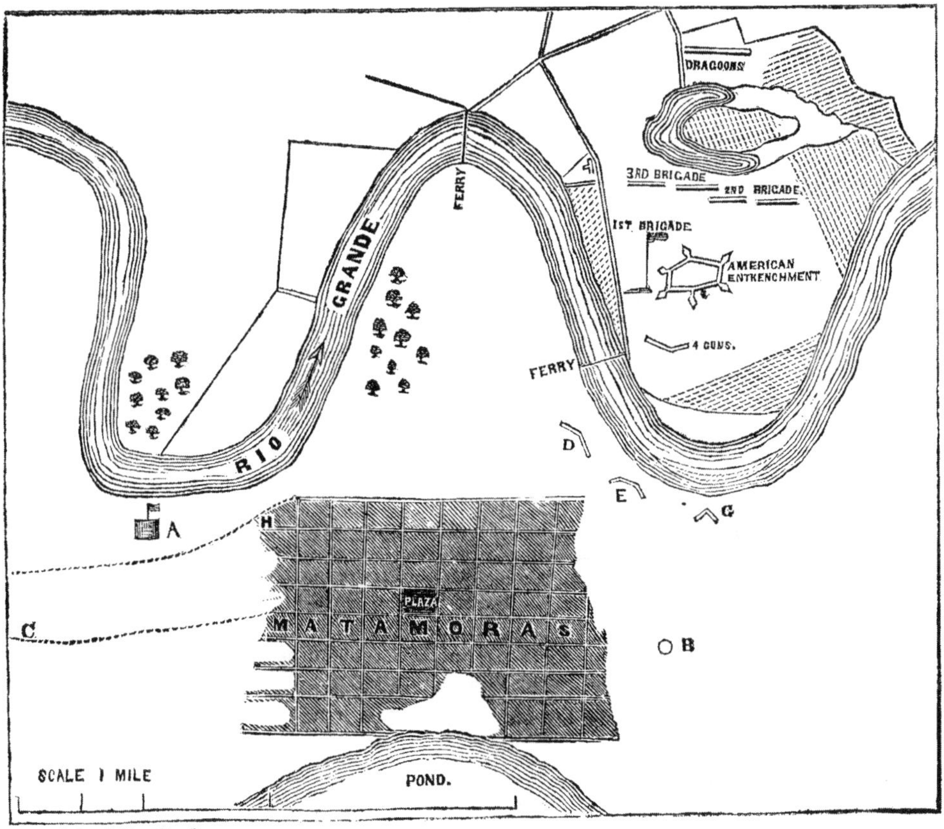

Vol. XX—Sig.3

US and Mexican positions on the Rio Grande. *Niles' National Register.*

and decline all intercourse with us," he wrote, "but they have not yet fired a gun or committed a hostile act."[13]

Many US troops welcomed this calm before the expected storm, realizing that it afforded them time to stabilize their position and improve their defenses. Mixed with relief, however, was a strong element of surprise that the Mexicans had failed to seize another golden opportunity. No soldier captured this sentiment better than Lt. William Seaton Henry, whose descriptions of life in the Army of Occupation appeared regularly in the New York *Spirit of the Times*. "Our situation here is truly extraordinary," he wrote in one article; "right in the enemy's country, occupying their corn and cotton fields, the people of the soil leaving their homes, and we, with a small handful of men, are marching with colors flying and drums beating, right under the guns of one of their principal cities, displaying the Star Spangled Banner as if in defiance under their very nose; and they, with an army twice our size at least, sit quietly down and make no resistance, not the first effort to drive us off."[14]

Mexicans also found themselves puzzled by the inactivity of their army, and military officials offered hollow excuses for the lack of action. Reports from Matamoros indicated that the troops in that city were enthusiastic for a fight, but had been forced to put their patriotic impulses on hold. Explained the *Monitor Republicano*: "With a heavily flowing river dividing them from their foe, the Mexican bayonets and lances—which are the most feared by the contemptible enemy, cannot be used to their unquestionable advantage. This leaves an exchange of cannon fire as the only option, and that would merely result in pointless bloodshed and reduce the fragile buildings of the city to rubble."[15]

Nevertheless, the accounts promised the Mexican people that the situation was well in hand. According to these narratives, all or part of the national army had already crossed the Río Bravo to challenge the enemy in hand-to-hand combat on the ground that it had occupied.[16]

These reports were fabricated tales, intended to reassure the population and to obscure the weaknesses of the Mexican force. General Mejía had no intention of opening fire on the American camp, whether with lances and bayonets or an exchange of cannon fire. Taylor had been remarkably accurate in his assessment of the low Mexican troop strength in Matamoros. When the American Army entered the Río Bravo delta, Mejía's 2nd Brigade consisted of a small professional force of 118 sappers, 250 troops of the 11th Infantry, and a 60-man artillery unit with ten artillery pieces. He also commanded two units of defensores—the frontier auxililary companies formed at the beginning of the Texas dispute in 1845—which included 100 cavalry troops and 150 infantrymen, bringing his troop total to 903. Reinforcements were coming at last. Some 200 additional infantry troops arrived about the time that Taylor's force made the crossing of the Arroyo. General Díaz de la Vega reached Matamoros on March 25 with the 360-man 2nd Light Infantry, the 250 soldiers of the 7th Cavalry, and four more cannon. On the twenty-ninth, the 6th Infantry and a company of the 8th Grenadiers provided an additional 250 men. The arrival several days later of 200 troops of the Tampico Coast Guard Regiment rounded the total out to 1913 soldiers—not quite the 2000 estimated by Taylor. Mejía, who believed that the US force numbered 4000, with as many as forty artillery pieces at their disposal, clearly understood that his force was too small to lead on the offensive. Instead, he focused on firming up the defenses along the banks of the Rio Grande and held out for the arrival of General Ampudia and his army.[17]

Ampudia came to embody both the hope and the frustration of the Mexican Army. His force, which included three thousand infantry, thirteen hundred cavalry, and ten additional artillery pieces, would provide Mexico with the numbers it needed to launch an assault against the Americans. But the column, which had been officially titled the Army of Operations, continued to move sluggishly. As Taylor pulled his troops up on the Rio Grande, Ampudia remained in Saltillo, days away under even the best of conditions.[18]

Precious time had been lost as the force confronted the same problems that had frustrated Mexican defensive efforts for months. Ampudia had put down several major rebellions among his troops and now dealt with only scattered instances of insubordination. Still, the root causes of discontent lingered. Supplies were woefully inadequate, with stocks of weapons, ammunition, uniforms, and food all low. Ampudia, the handpicked replacement for complaining generals like Arista and Mejía, quickly adopted the traits of his predecessors, bemoaning the lack of essentials for a successful march.[19]

Newspapers better captured the sense of desperation among Ampudia's troops. The *Monitor Republicano*, for example, described the cycle of activity of one of the revolts: happiness at being in action gave way minor grumblings, individual complaints evolved into general disorder, the emergence of rebellion provoked a backlash by officers, crackdown and punishment restored order, and the reassembled army marched off to beg for bread. "This," the editors noted, their tone dripping with sarcasm, "is the group destined to raise the tricolor over the Sabine."[20]

Ampudia ignored the criticism and issued a number of optimistic notices that his force would advance quickly to Matamoros, but the trials of his army had only begun.[21] As he moved further into the arid expanses of the north, the most direct route lacked grass and watering sites needed for the cavalry mounts and pack animals. Large numbers of animals died, and the general was obliged to alter his route to find suitable pasturage. This inevitably led him on a roundabout course that added days to his journey. The long, brutal march took its toll on the soldiers as well. Faced with marches of up to thirty miles a day, many deserted at the first opportunity. Others took ill from the heat of the blazing sun. Many became so sick and exhausted that they could no longer march, and Ampudia and his second-in-command, General Anastasio Torrejón, had to seek additional mules and wagons to cart the infirm to the front.[22]

Climate and terrain were not the only obstacles to this advance. Ampudia soon decided that the inhospitality of the north extended to its people as well. Like the generals who had preceded him, he bemoaned the unwillingness of the civilians to provide him with the food, supplies, and pack animals needed for the final stages of his advance. Since scrip and promissory notes had proven to be worthless in the past, the locals had practical reasons for their reluctance to trade, but Ampudia saw it as outright treason. The apparent eagerness of these same people to carry on a lively, illegal trade with the well-financed quartermasters of the US Army strengthened his opinion. Suspicion even extended to northerners who signed on to defend the frontier. Rumors abounded that Gen. Antonio Canales—well known for his past attempts to separate his home state from Mexico—had again maneuvered to break away from Mexico even as he occupied the front lines in defense of the country. Canales was apparently willing to conspire with General Taylor, possibly to the point of conceding territory, in order to achieve his objective. Tales like this may have influenced the order for auxiliary troops to abandon their defense of the Arroyo Colorado and to fall back beyond the Río Bravo. With a broad river dividing them, these separatists would have fewer opportunities to collaborate with the enemy. In any event, the new general-in-chief of the Army of the North found himself approaching his charges with a level of precaution normally reserved for the enemy.[23]

The general clearly felt frustrated by his situation. "I find the Northern Departments to be a disgrace to the Mexican family," he wrote to Secretary of War Tornel after citing some of the problems he faced. He also outlined his ideas for forcing these wayward relatives back into line. His first goal was to put a halt to the ongoing problem of contraband trade with Texas and the American troops. To accomplish this, Ampudia wanted to devote as much time and as many troops as possible to patrolling the Río Bravo from Laredo to its mouth, in order to turn back the illicit traders before they passed beyond Mexican control. He also believed that nothing short of martial law could establish order in this rebellious region, and suggested that he—as general-in-chief—should become the source of all political and military power. In exchange for these strong measures, Ampudia also recommended that the government provide an incentive in the form of free trade in tobacco. The Mexican government had maintained tight control over commerce in that product, and had for the most part restricted its cultivation and sale in the north. Ampudia believed that opening the trade would simultaneously enable the settlers to earn money and create a relationship between them and Indians that would reduce depredations by roving bands of Apaches and Comanches. He also hoped that a legitimate item for commerce would inspire residents of the separatist north to cooperate better with the central government.[24]

Officials in Mexico City gave these proposals a lukewarm reception. Minister of War Tornel rejected the proposal for tobacco cultivation outright, and offered little justification for his decision. He also rebuffed Ampudia's bid to claim supreme authority in the north. Such a move, Tornel declared, would only "produce disgust" and push frontier residents into further collaboration or a direct alliance with the enemy. For this reason, he asserted that martial law was "neither prudent nor just." Only the plan for patrolling the river had a favorable reception. Rather than dispatching additional troops for that purpose, however, Tornel suggested that Ampudia detach several units from his army and deploy presidial forces and the Batallón Activo de Zacatecas to guard the frontier between the state of Coahuila and Texas.[25] The minister's memo could have produced nothing but frustration for its recipient. Ampudia had already declared that he needed more and better troops if he hoped to wage an effective war against the United States, and his superior's solution only weakened the force that Ampudia led to confront Taylor's army.[26]

Dissatisfaction also grew in Matamoros. When Ampudia wrote to Mejía to introduce himself as the new general-in-chief, he also informed his subordinate that he had devised plans for the much-delayed assault across the Río Bravo. Aware that Mejía had long advocated action north of the river, Ampudia doubtless believed that he was delivering good news. But Mejía once again bombarded his superiors in Mexico City with complaints. "In my opinion," he wrote, "these plans are not in conformance with my orders to defend Matamoros at all costs." He made it clear that he favored a strike against Taylor's army but noted that with US forces now entrenched across the river, an attempt to advance would leave Matamoros dangerously exposed. Mejía's suggested resolution to the problem was, not unexpectedly, more men and supplies. In addition to Ampudia's troubled army, he called for thousands more troops from throughout the country. Only with this support would he achieve a much-desired victory and win laurels for the army. More importantly, this commitment of soldiers would prove that Mexico was "a nation blessed with a government that understands how to destroy the pride of the disgraceful sons of Washington."[27]

Well aware that his pleas were not likely to earn a favorable response, Mejía also sought the ear of his new commander. In a series of letters to Ampudia, he reasserted his needs. No doubt he hoped that Ampudia had greater influence over affairs in the capital and could extract additional support from his ally Paredes. Mejía also suggested more practical measures for increasing military strength, like gathering horses, supplies, and even men from the haciendas and ranches that he had passed on the march. Unlike Ampudia, who doubted the loyalty of the northerners, Mejía felt certain that they would assist with "the greatest zeal and patriotism against the detestable invaders who threaten our nation and its independence."[28]

As illness, politics, and the difficult terrain slowed Ampudia's advance, Mejía grew increasingly anxious and pleaded for the incoming general-in-chief to hurry. Like Taylor, Mejía understood that Mexico's best hope was to act quickly, before reinforcements could supplement the small US force. He was also aware of discontent within the Army of Occupation. In the days after their arrival on the Rio Grande, dozens of US soldiers had deserted Taylor's army, with at least thirty-one swimming the river for the safety of Matamoros. Mejía believed that the American ranks were now completely divided, with half of the troops effectively serving as guards to keep the other half in line. If Ampudia brought his troops and initiated an attack quickly, Mejía reasoned, Mexico could achieve victory. But if Ampudia delayed, giving Taylor time to strengthen the American ranks, victory would become much more elusive. Having made this observation, Mejía must have been dismayed that Ampudia and his army did not arrive in Matamoros until April 11.[29]

The extended wait for Ampudia created a curious interlude in the building hostilities. Throughout most of April 1846, the two armies continued to eye each other across the disputed river. Tensions remained high, with soldiers on both banks conducting their daily business as if fighting would erupt at any moment. Instead, peace reigned. Each force remained under orders to respond if attacked but to avoid initiating a conflict. Since both adhered carefully to these directives, the fever of war gave way to a lingering standoff. Days passed into weeks, during which the opposing armies bided their time and continued preparations and planning for the conflict to come.

On the left bank of the river, Taylor used the delay to push ahead with his fortifications. The first efforts of the brigades to protect themselves had resulted in a maze of shallow trenches and simple earthworks that confusingly crisscrossed the camp, and Taylor pressed for a better, more coordinated effort. He first instructed Capt. Allen Lowd and his company of artillery to see to the construction of a redoubt near the broad point of the peninsula formed by the river bend. This structure, an arrow-shaped breastwork built of bundles of sticks, or fascines, and earth, was surrounded by a deep ditch and contained an underground magazine and bombproof areas. But its most notable feature was its weaponry. On April 6, after completing construction, Lowd

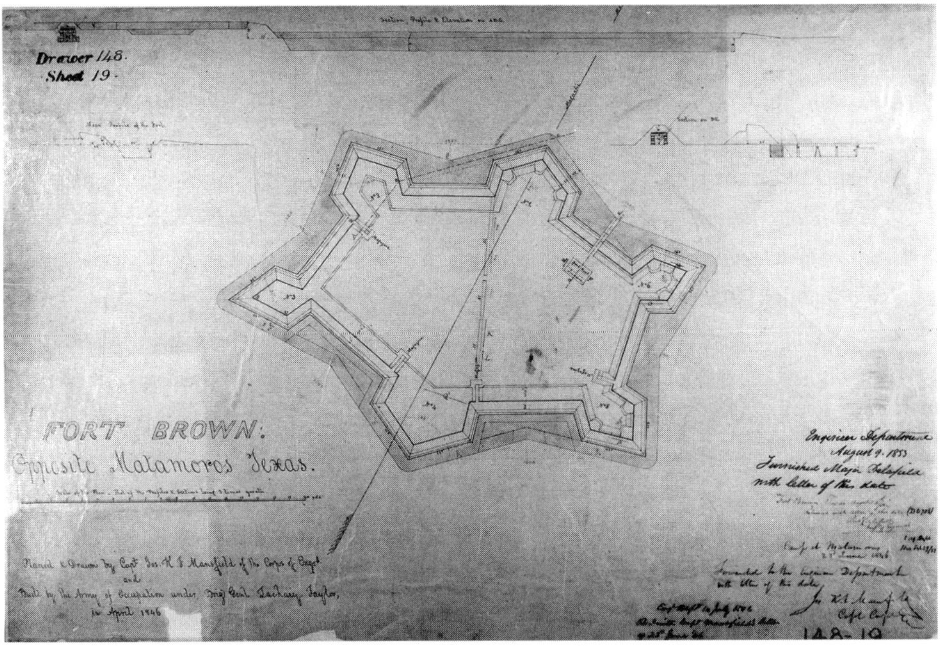

US Fortification on the Rio Grande (Fort Brown). *Courtesy of US National Archives.*

mounted his four 18-pounder artillery pieces into the walls and trained them on the Mexican city across the water. Taylor apparently believed that, at this early stage, his best defense was the ability to threaten a strong offensive. "These guns will bear directly upon the public square of Matamoros," he explained in a letter to the adjutant general of the army, "and within good range for demolishing the town. Their object cannot be mistaken by the enemy and will, I think, effectually restrain him from any enterprises on our side of the river."[30]

With this imposing structure standing as a sentinel, the troops then proceeded to begin work on a much larger stronghold just behind it. As the artillery battery came to completion, Eng. Maj. Joseph King Fenno Mansfield presented his plans for the fieldwork that Taylor had requested on March 28. It was an ambitious project. The six-sided earthen fort would have two sides at 150 yards long and the remaining four sides at 125 yards. Where these walls met, Mansfield designed arrow-shaped bastions into which artillery could be placed to counter any angle of attack. The entire complex was to be surrounded by a ditch, 20 feet wide and 8 feet deep, from which the troops would excavate the masses of earth required to build sloping walls 9 ½ feet high and

15 feet thick. Inside these ramparts, gunpowder and men could be sheltered in a series of traverses, magazines and bombproof areas, also constructed of packed earth and supported by empty food barrels and by fence posts that the soldiers scavenged from nearby farm fields.[31] The fort was large enough to hold a garrison of 500 men and designed to resist both an artillery barrage and a direct assault. Upon reviewing the plans, Taylor determined that "this work will enable a Brigade to maintain this position against any Mexican odds, and will leave me free to dispose of the other corps as considerations of health and convenience may render desirable."[32]

The US general also commanded that work commence on the project immediately. In an order issued April 6, he announced that the troops would break ground the following morning, directly after reveille. That task fell to troops of the 1st Brigade, but all would share in the construction duty. In the days that followed, the brigades took turns at the arduous task of digging and transporting tons of the dense, claylike earth and molding it into the six-pointed star that would become their fortress on the river. Week after week, from dawn until dusk, officers and enlisted men toiled side by side, as Mansfield and his engineers guided the progress. "Incessantly by day, but with alacrity, our troops plied the pick and shovel," Lt. Alexander Hays would recall, "while in view across the plains of Matamoros squadrons of gay-decked lancers and masses of infantry performed their evolutions."[33] Pressed to complete the job before the expected attack, US soldiers received no exemptions from their shifts unless they were performing other essential duties—as sentries, scouts, convoy escorts, or the like.

This resolute endeavor overshadowed another fortification project already underway at Point Isabel. Taylor had realized the need to protect the coastal depot even before he had reached the Rio Grande; it was a vital link in the supply chain that connected his army to the United States. Here, the ships that plied the Gulf waters from New Orleans could offload the supplies, ammunition, and reinforcements needed to sustain the isolated army. Likewise, quartermasters could store the supplies at Point Isabel until teamsters arrived to load them on wagons and transport them to the main camp on the river. If the Mexicans could find a way to retake the Point, the Army of Occupation would be effectively surrounded, isolated, and unable to subsist. For this reason, even before he pushed on to the Rio Grande, Taylor had charged Capt. John Sanders of the Corps of Engineers with "the establishment and construction of such defensive works as may be deemed necessary for the protection of the depot."[34]

Taylor did not give Sanders much help to fulfill this order. He recognized that the Point was vital, but he did not consider it particularly vulnerable. Since Mexican forces had withdrawn to the south bank, he concluded that the only immediate threat to the site came from armed groups of Mexican rancheros who had not fled to the opposite shore—bands that could easily be repelled by a relatively small force. An attack by the Mexican Army remained a possibility, but Taylor felt confident that an attempt to recross the river would not go unnoticed and that his troops could march quickly from their riverside camp to assist their countrymen.[35] Not all the US officers concurred with his assessment. "If they have a general worth a sixpence," Lt. George Meade wrote to his wife from the camp on the Rio Grande, "he will attack Point Isabel, help himself to our provisions, forage, and money chest, and then establish himself in our rear and oblige us to cut our way through him to get our pork and beans."[36] But Taylor remained far more concerned about a threat to the main body of the army, and left only a single company of artillery—fewer than a hundred men—to hold the Point. For Sanders, this deployment translated into a disappointingly small fourteen-man crew to begin the task of erecting defenses.

Though frustrated by lack of support, the engineer captain set to work on fortifications appropriate to his commander's expectations and his labor force. He developed modest plans for a single redoubt just to the south of the warehouse buildings on the northern tip of the point. This structure stood guard over the roadway from Matamoros, its arrow shape allowing cannon to command all approaches to the port. Constructed of earth, wagons, wood planks, barrels, and other discarded supplies provided by the Quartermaster Corps, the redoubt was not imposing. It was, however, sufficient to repel a small band of horsemen and large enough to shelter the troops of the garrison for a short time in the face of a more concerted assault.

Like Meade, Sanders doubted that this structure provided adequate protection, and he believed that the Point remained at risk. He would have preferred a much bigger fort and a correspondingly bigger force to man it. In a letter to Col. Joseph Totten of the engineering corps, he noted that the Mexican hamlet of Burrita lay a short seven miles to the south. From that point, a Mexican cavalry force numbering in the hundreds could easily cross the river, sweep up the old trade road toward Brazos Santiago, and seize the Point before Taylor could respond. With the limited crew on hand, however, he felt hard-pressed to devise anything better.[37]

Sanders was busily supervising the progress of this assignment when new information prompted him to revise his plan. In the aftermath of the less-than-cordial encounter between Generals Díaz de la Vega and Worth on the Rio Grande and as Mexican troops fortified the south bank of the river, Taylor apparently reconsidered his rather casual treatment of the Point Isabel depot. On March 30, he sent a squadron of dragoons, headed by Capt. Charles May, to inform the post commander, Major Monroe, that an attack on the site had become a real possibility. "This information," Captain Sanders noted, "changed the entire character of defenses. I at once abandoned all ideas of constructing the isolated redoubt. I endeavored to avail myself of all the natural obstructions offered by the ground, and at the same time, determined to gradually extend the line adopted so as to embrace all the ground necessary for the depots of the army."[38] The result was a plan for a large ditch and earthen embankment that extended for several hundred yards from the high shoreline of the Laguna Madre, circled around the warehouses and structures of the port, and reconnected with the Laguna bank. The serpentine structure also incorporated the incomplete redoubt as the southernmost portion of the fortification. This design—though garrison commander Monroe called it "barely large enough for the convenience of the depot but still much too extended for the defending force"—provided shelter for all the port buildings, quartermasters' facilities, and medical facilities, as well as the troops garrisoned at the depot. The layout was specifically designed to repel a cavalry charge like the one that Sanders feared might overwhelm the post.[39]

The engineer now found himself with a much larger project and a need for additional workers. Taylor's concern for the safety of the Point had grown, but not enough that he was willing to part with many of the troops based on the river. Along with his call for greater protection, he provided only two additional men. This obliged Sanders to cobble together a labor force from a variety of sources. On March 30, he recruited thirty sailors and marines from the brigantine *Lawrence*, which had arrived off Brazos Santiago. On April 7, Capt. Giles Porter and his company of artillery arrived from Saint Joseph's Island, providing thirteen more men to the detail. After another warning from Taylor on May 12, Monroe assigned his entire garrison to the work details. Sanders welcomed each of these additions, but still found them insufficient for the monumental task. "The military force applicable to the proposed end is so entirely inadequate," he wrote to General Taylor, "that, although overtaxed, their labor hardly tells in lines so extensive as ours."[40]

To meet the demands of the construction, Sanders and Monroe ultimately looked beyond the army. Initially they called on the teamsters, carpenters, and mechanics employed by the Quartermasters Department at the Point to assist. "The men work cheerfully," Sanders reported in his assessment of this group, "but without extra pay and whiskey, I doubt whether they would."[41] Still, progress on the fort lagged, and

Sanders expanded his search by contracting yet more laborers, including a group of a hundred German settlers from Matagorda, Texas.[42] By mid-April, the situation was looking up, and Sanders could report to Taylor that he had arranged contracts for the completion of palisades and blockhouses that would enable a force of 250 men to hold the Point for a period of twenty days.[43]

The structure that would emerge from this chaos and creativity bore little resemblance to its sister fort on the Rio Grande. Some sections of the defenses had carefully planned and constructed breastworks; others were little more than overturned wagons and crates. Some portions of the wall offered a straight military profile; others wandered across the landscape. In later years, critics would compare the rambling, low defenses unfavorably to the classic design of Mansfield's project, calling it "the laughing stock of the army . . . famous for the absurdity of its plans." Sanders responded by noting that field works "are the creations of an emergency to serve some transient and temporary purpose" and that the appearance depended "upon the object to be defended, the means available for constructing the defenses, and the character of the force from

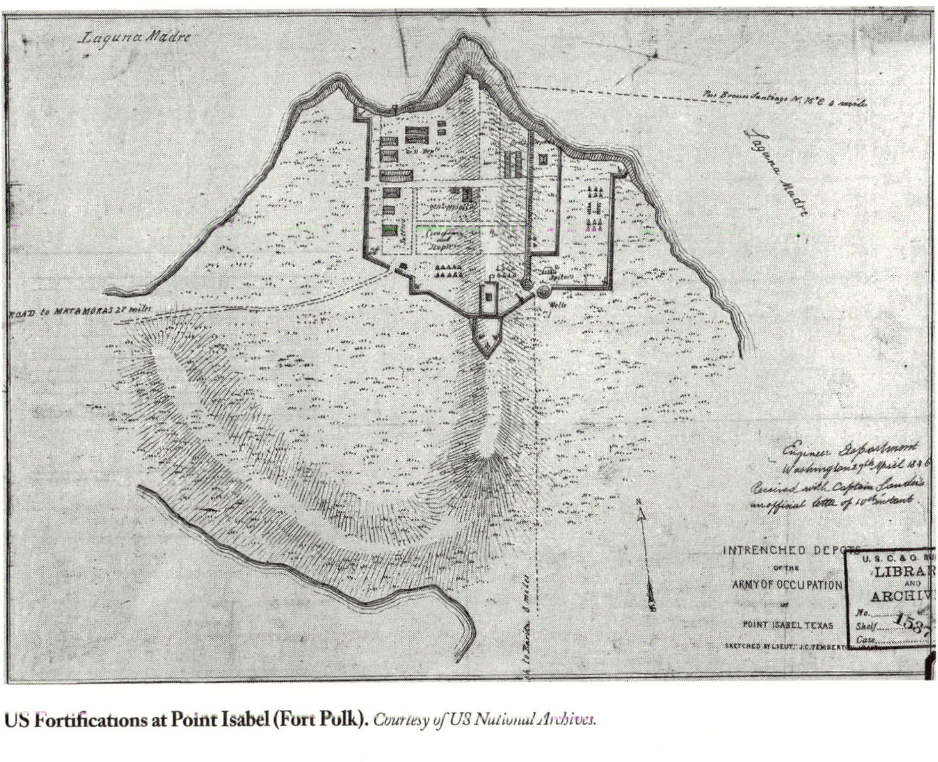

US Fortifications at Point Isabel (Fort Polk). *Courtesy of US National Archives.*

which an attack is anticipated." On at least one point, the two forts were comparable: neither received a formal name. Throughout the month of April, Mansfield's well-constructed earthwork remained known only as the "camp opposite Matamoros," and Sander's jumble of defenses was with equal informality referred to as the depot, the Point, "Frontone," or, very occasionally, "Fort Polk."[44]

The strenuous, sometimes frantic work at both sites continued for weeks to follow, but by mid-April the US troops could take stock of their situation with some assurance. Despite early misgivings, the only assaults on the troops came from the weather. Unseasonable cold left the men shivering in their tents at night. Several storms on April 7 and April 18 brought gusting winds that knocked down tents around both forts. Torrential rains mired the riverside camp in mud, temporarily halted the work on fortifications, and forced many of the soldiers to move their tents several hundred yards to drier ground. These incidents were but temporary inconveniences, however, and as bastions and breastworks began to take shape, Taylor was confident that the defenses were already good enough for his men to "hold themselves against many times their number of Mexican troops."[45]

Many of his soldiers shared his confidence. Although they maintained their vigilant watch of the river, slept with weapons close at hand, and continued to respond to nighttime warnings, much of the nervous expectation of the first days faded away. Work occupied their time and prevented them from dwelling on danger by day. The security of the rising earthen walls heartened them at night. Placement of additional heavy artillery pieces inside these walls gave added assurance. One relieved US soldier wrote with confidence that the Mexicans should now be wary, since Taylor's army was "prepared to knock [Matamoros] about their ears as soon as they fire a shot."[46] All the while, the continuing turnover of enemy commanders, which was followed closely in the camp, combined with the Mexicans' unwillingness to exploit their opportunities, convinced US troops that the enemy lacked commitment for a fight. "The Mexicans still continue to talk 'big' and threaten to attack us," Lt. Richard Cochrane wrote to his wife on April 10, "but as this has been their manner ever since our arrival I've begun to think the probability of their doing so grows less and less every day. If they have any intention of the kind, they are truly a most generous army, allowing us all the time we could possibly wish to prepare ourselves for it."[47]

As the first war alarm gave way to anxious waiting, many enlisted men chose to abandon the ranks. Reasons for their desertion were as varied as those that had led soldiers to flee Corpus Christi months before. Most deserters no doubt wanted to avoid more hard labor at the camp and the possibility of combat to follow it. Foreign enlistees may have reconsidered their commitment to their new homeland. No doubt a few deserted because they questioned the justification and morality of the war. And now that discontented soldiers had a town in their sights, many probably just responded to its lure. In the first few days after reaching the Rio Grande, several men used the cover of darkness to plunge into the river and make the swim to the far shore. Within days the trickle became a flood. On April 3 alone, more than thirty-six soldiers vanished during the night, presumably for the far shore of the river. Many officers reported the disappearance of slaves who had served as their personal servants, for with abolition laws in place in Mexico they only had to cross the river to be free. Mexican leaders encouraged this behavior, posting broadsides that called for foreign, especially Catholic, troops to avoid an unjust war or to lend their service to a nation that shared their faith. "Efforts are continually making to entice our men to desert," General Taylor reported to Washington, "and, I regret to say, have been met with considerable success." More than forty Irish soldiers fled during the first week alone. After recounting the tale to his wife, Lt. Napoleon Dana reported, "the good men are highly incensed at it."[48]

The general and the "good men" did not stand by idly. As desertions mounted, a frustrated Taylor ordered sentinels to shoot anyone who attempted to swim the river. In the ensuing days, pickets—who had been carefully selected for their loyalty—followed these orders with a vengeance. As fleeing soldiers attempted to cross the broad channel they were fired upon and allowed to sink into the current. "Those who were killed called out loudly for mercy," wrote Lieutenant Dana, "but the more they cried, the more the pickets fired."[49] This harsh response put an end to much of the problem, and the swift current of the river, which drowned several men, assisted in the process. Within days, desertions had dropped dramatically.[50]

At the same time, conflict among officers mounted. Many of the commissioned troops of the army had their doubts about the justifications for war but felt that honor required them to perform their duty if conflict arose. Col. Ethan Allan Hitchcock, for example, even as he joined the march did not fail to voice his opposition to a policy that sent troops to the Rio Grande. "My heart is not in this business," he wrote in his diary. "I am against it from the bottom of my soul as a most unholy and unrighteous proceeding; but as a military man I am bound to execute orders."[51] This sense of gentlemanly honor and propriety, however, had an unseemly side. Camp life was hard and tedious, the atmosphere was tense, and some officers, determined to use the campaign as a means to advance stagnant careers, were led to take issue with the actions of their colleagues. By mid-April affronts to honor and trivial complaints to General Taylor had become daily events. A typical exchange was that between Maj. Jacob Brown and Col. James McIntosh. McIntosh lodged a complaint against Brown for refusing to place units of the 7th Infantry on guard duty immediately after they had completed a shift on fieldwork. Brown filed a counter complaint against McIntosh for issuing the order. McIntosh replied that the order had been intended for the protection of Brown's own men and tartly asked, in the event of battle "would they also be exempted from defending themselves?"[52] This sarcasm further inflamed Brown's wounded pride, and the conflict continued. Meanwhile dozens of similar squabbles broke out over campsites, work assignments, chain of authority, and insufficient displays of respect. Some officers were involved in multiple disputes, creating a web of turmoil that threatened to ensnare the entire force.[53]

Perhaps the greatest point of discord involved the "brevet". In the US Army of the period, officers commonly received brevets—temporary field promotions—that gave them a higher rank without higher pay. In a system that had a limited number of authorized positions at various levels, these awards provided an avenue for recognizing distinguished service until an opportunity for formal promotion became available. William Jenkins Worth was officially an army colonel, but served as second-in-command under Zachary Taylor with the rank of brevet brigadier general. This became an issue in the Army of Occupation because another colonel, David Twiggs, was superior to Worth in actual rank, but did not have the brevet status. Questions arose, therefore, over which officer should be considered higher in rank. The issue festered during much of the stay in Corpus Christi and was resolved by the president only after troops reached the Rio Grande. When Twiggs came out on top in the dispute, Worth immediately submitted his resignation.[54] "His resigning at this time is considered by nearly the whole army as a false step from which he can never recover," wrote Philip Norbourne Barbour, "and, should we have an engagement will dim forever the luster he has thrown around his name."[55] Madison Mills offered a more blunt assessment. "Genl. W. acts in this matter, as in many others, like a spoiled child—like a fool—A course of sprouts would do him some good."

Mills realized that Worth's decision had an impact that extended far beyond the brevet general's own career. Worth represented a major loss in leadership. He had led the troops across the Arroyo Colorado, had served as the primary contact with the Mexicans, and would have played a significant role in any confrontation. More troublesome, others followed his example. Though none were as high ranking, several other officers subsequently tendered their resignations over the same issue. Colonel Truman Cross of the Quartermaster Corps revealed the bitterness of the sentiment aroused by this ruling when he announced that he would resign rather than abide by a decision that "exposes me to the degradation of serving in subordination to my inferiors in rank."[56] Harmony did not reign in the officer corps.

Several incidents helped prevent the disputes, desertions, and divisions from spinning out of control. Although General Mejía had abided by orders and kept his troops confined to the south side of the Río Bravo, others had seized the initiative and waged a low-level guerrilla war against the US troops. Bands of rancheros, which had long held their ground against the depredations of Comanches and Apaches, now turned their weapons on the troops of the American Army of Occupation. Unable to strike the main body of soldiers, they lurked beyond the two primary camps, waiting to fall upon any small, unsuspecting groups that happened by. Would-be deserters feared to leave the camp. Even loyal officers feared to stray far, aware that a moment of inattention, even in the vicinity of the camp, could prove to be fatal "They are just like Indians," Lt. George Meade said, "hiding in the bushes whenever a force comes after them and seizing on all single individuals they find on the road."[57]

The most notable victim of these attacks was Colonel Cross, the quartermaster general of the army. On April 10 he left the riverside camp on a solitary ride—perhaps to ponder the brevet situation—and failed to return. Hoping that Cross had merely lost his way in the chaparral, Taylor ordered signal guns fired throughout the night to guide him back to the camp. This produced no result, and an extensive search began the next morning. For days, parties combed the thickets up- and downstream of the fort. They always returned discouraged, having found no sign of the missing officer. As time passed, speculation mounted that Cross had been captured by Mexican troops and spirited across the river. Taylor went so far as to write to the newly arrived Ampudia, asking if the colonel had been taken captive. When Ampudia sent assurances that the colonel was not a prisoner of war, hope faded. The search continued, but the focus shifted to finding a corpse, a victim of the "banditti," rather than a living body.[58]

Although Ampudia professed to have no role in the Cross disappearance, he was willing to contest the Americans in other ways. On April 11, the general had arrived in Matamoros to considerable pomp, circumstance, and military display. But he quickly turned his attention to the important issues at hand and by the afternoon had reviewed the troops, surveyed the situation along the river, and issued an order to forcibly remove all American residents of Matamoros to the interior of Mexico. The following day at 2 p.m., he submitted a terse letter to Taylor in which he restated Mexico's indignation at finding the "conquering banner" of the United States on the left bank of the Río Bravo del Norte. To rectify this outrage, he demanded that Taylor break up his camp within twenty-four hours and retire to the far bank of the Nueces River. This maneuver, he stated, would create an environment in which the governments of the United States and Mexico could resolve the dispute over Texas. The alternative to such withdrawal would be dire. "If you insist in remaining upon the soil of the department of Tamaulipas, it will clearly result that arms, and arms alone, must decide the question," he warned. "And in that case I advise you that we accept the war to which, with so much injustice on your part, you provoke us."[59]

Ampudia had several reasons for issuing the ultimatum. In a way, it served as a formal announcement of his arrival in Matamoros and an indication that he had superseded Mejía as general-in-chief. The words, similar to those issued by Mejía before him, would also circulate in the Mexican streets and press, helping Ampudia establish his credentials as a firm defender of the nation. Most importantly, the general apparently had every intention of following up on his demands. Not yet aware that he had been replaced by Mariano Arista, Ampudia followed the conventional strategy of the era by offering one final opportunity for a peaceful resolution before unleashing the fury of war.

Zachary Taylor responded with the sort of understated bravado that had helped earn him the title "Old Rough and Ready." He immediately wrote a reply in which he politely acknowledged receipt of the letter, indicated that he was not the proper American authority to debate the justice of his actions, and assured his counterpart that he had carefully refrained from any acts of hostility. He also calmly, but firmly, rejected the demand to fall back, observing that "the instructions under which I am acting will not permit me to retrograde from the position I now occupy." Reiterating his intention to avoid starting the bloodshed, he also insisted that he would not shy away from a fight. "I regret the alternative which you offer," he said, "but, at the same time, wish it understood that I shall by no means avoid such an alternative."[60]

Taylor viewed Ampudia's letter as a declaration of war, expected the Mexican general to follow through on his threat, and rushed to prepare for it. He intensified his effort to finish his two forts, imposing round-the-clock shifts for the troops building the fort on the river and approving the employment of civilian laborers to complete the fort at Point Isabel. He realigned the camp, moving the 1st Brigade upriver and the 2nd downriver, out of range of the enemy batteries. In response to reports that eight hundred Mexican infantry and two hundred lancers had already crossed the Rio Grande, he sent Capt. Seth Thornton and a company of dragoons out to investigate. He also ordered two ships, the brigantine *Lawrence* and the schooner *Flirt*, to blockade the mouth of the Rio Grande, so that no military supplies would reach Ampudia up that waterway. These precautions taken, Taylor could do little more than wait for the twenty-four hours to expire.[61]

The deadline of 2 p.m. on April 13 was anticipated with a mix of anxiety and enthusiasm. "I hope, if a battle is to be fought, it may be tomorrow," wrote Capt. Phillip Barbour, who feared that any delay would cause added distress for his wife back home. Other soldiers slept in their uniforms with weapons loaded and horses saddled. Artillerymen kept their pieces charged and matches burning. As the hour approached, the troops assumed battle formation, in the expectation that the firing would commence soon after the hour passed. These precautions did not reflect a lack of confidence. "We will whip six thousand if we can catch them in the prairies," wrote Lt. John Peck, "or we will all bleach our bones."[62]

Like the expected attack at the Arroyo Colorado, however, the Mexican offensive never materialized. The deadline came and passed without incident. A wagon train of supplies traveling from Point Isabel reached the river undisturbed. Captain Thornton and his dragoons returned to camp and reported no sign of an enemy within eighteen miles. Hours passed, then days. Although Taylor suspected that they were experiencing the calm before a major storm, and spies continued to report a pending onslaught, peace continued. By April 16, tensions had dropped to the point that Mexican officers entered the American camp to once again reassure Taylor that they did not have Colonel Cross. The US troops settled back into their recent routines, but with several important changes. Newly cognizant of the dangers around them, they maintained a heightened sense of alert and continued their longer work shifts in preparation for a war that would eventually arrive. Perhaps, more importantly, they set aside their squabbles, at least until their primary mission had come to an end.[63]

The new delay in the hostilities resulted from another change in the leadership of the Mexican forces. Just days after his Army of Operations had paraded into the city to the sounds of cheers and military bands, Ampudia learned that he had been removed as general-in-chief. A letter from Minister of War Tornel, received on April 15, informed him that General Arista had been summoned from retirement and placed at the head of the Army of the North. Ampudia remained with the army, but in a role subordinate to Arista as second-in-command.[64]

The sudden change resulted from a variety of concerns about Ampudia's leadership. Born in Cuba, Ampudia had served in the army since the early days of Mexico's independence and had gained a reputation for cruelty as he moved up the military ranks. Perhaps his greatest claim to infamy occurred in the southern state of Tabasco in 1844, when he captured a party of insurgents, executed them, and boiled their heads in oil before placing them on public display. He had also served in the north of the republic, where he had aroused the animosity of the Norteños as well. Upon receiving news that Ampudia had assumed command, many residents of Matamoros and the surrounding area immediately wrote to the president demanding that he replace the undesirable general with someone more acceptable. They also questioned both Ampudia's skill in leadership and his ability to bring the campaign to a successful conclusion. The charges of incompetence struck a chord with Minister of War Tornel, who had already observed the constant rebellions within Ampudia's ranks and harbored his own concerns about the general's ability to control his force. Although President Paredes had close ties with Ampudia, he accepted Tornel's call for change. He no doubt understood that the uproar over Ampudia was an undesirable distraction as the country moved toward war. He may also have thought that Ampudia showed too much political ambition and had sought too much power in his request for supreme civil and military authority in the north.[65]

Officially, Tornel presented the transfer of power only in terms of what was best for Mexico. "The need to bring together the various military units of the northern frontier to fight the enemy," he explained, "makes it absolutely necessity to place command in the hands of a brigadier general whose circumstances and experience will bring success to the endeavor." In his view, Arista was that man. Like Ampudia, Arista had an impressive military resume that dated back to the independence era and included a long stint as commander of the northern military district. Unlike Ampudia, he had integrated himself into frontier society by taking up residence near Monterrey and was liked in the area. He had a good record as an officer, and he seemed to command the respect of his troops while avoiding discord and rebellion. Arista had clashed with Paredes over the decision to occupy Mexico City and remained doubtful of the wisdom of that move, but his desire to serve the country was clear. Even though the decision to reinstate him would delay the start of an offensive against the North Americans by another several weeks, Arista seemed capable of uniting the north against the foreign army and offered a greater hope of success.[66]

Not surprisingly, Ampudia responded to the news with resentment. Upon receiving his orders from the Minister of War, he fired back a missive that bristled with displeasure. The command had come, he claimed, just hours before he had intended to launch "the next triumph against the enemy invaders." Now, he stated, that action had been placed on hold, giving General Taylor's troops more time to prepare and delivering another blow to the goal of national defense. Ampudia made no effort to hide his belief that he was the better man for the job and that the ill-conceived elevation of Arista would ultimately prove disastrous in the days to follow. Nevertheless, he concluded with a vow that he would adhere "strictly" to military law and that "no recourse remains to me but to abide by my superior orders."[67]

The new general-in-chief wasted little time in asserting his authority over the Army of the North and his second-in-command. While still at his estate near Monterrey, he wrote a follow-up to Tornel's message, informing Ampudia that he expected to take personal control of the campaign and would arrive in Matamoros shortly. In the meantime, Ampudia was to proceed with caution. If firing had already commenced, the second-in-command could prosecute the fight with the vigor expected for the defense of Mexico. If hostilities had not yet erupted, Ampudia was to avoid the fight, focus on finishing the defenses around Matamoros, and await Arista's arrival.[68]

This command further enraged Ampudia. Had it arrived several days earlier, it would have been a disappointing blow to a career officer who had hoped to establish his credentials. Coming as it did after the ultimatum to Taylor, it made Ampudia look like a foolish blowhard. The Mexican general so resented losing the opportunity to lead the country's defense that he seriously considered acting against his orders. Immediately after learning of his demotion, Ampudia drew his officers together and proposed launching an attack despite the directive from above. He abandoned the idea and pledged his loyalty only after the others refused to join him in this "weighty responsibility."[69]

Taylor continued to forgo any military action that might justify a strong response, leaving Ampudia unable to put teeth behind his recent threat. Indeed, the humiliated Mexican general was reduced to writing a complaint to Taylor that the US blockade of the river's mouth prevented the Mexican Army from obtaining necessary supplies. Not surprisingly, Taylor showed little sympathy for this grievance and dismissed it out of hand. Like Mejía before him, Ampudia found himself powerless and waiting for the arrival of his superior officer.[70]

The true length of the delay created by Arista's order is subject to debate. Ampudia's critics scoffed at the notion that he had been prepared to cross the river on April 15. Most vocal was a group of unnamed officers of the Army of Operations. In a joint statement published in the *Monitor Republicano*, they questioned Ampudia's veracity: "We cannot believe that combat would have occurred on the day that the [Minister of War's] message arrived. This date was only two days after the arrival of Ampudia's troops. Before leading them into battle, it is essential to rest them from a long and difficult march. The army had suffered and required time for recovering and strategy before undertaking operations against the enemy position." These unnamed officers believed that the new orders had little effect and that the troops would not have been ready until Arista arrived in any event.[71]

Less debatable is the impact that the change in command had on the Mexican Army. At a time when banditry and Mexican threats of action had reunified and reenergized the US forces on the Rio Grande, the change in command created a rift between the top two officers of the Army of the North. Arista, who had so recently sent Ampudia friendly letters offering encouragement and support for the march north, now began issuing stiffly formal notes praising Ampudia's loyalty while at the same time revealing an undercurrent of distrust. For his part, Ampudia replied with messages vowing obedience and respect, all the while apparently encouraging discord among his officers. The divide became so pronounced that another group of unidentified officers wrote a letter to the *Aguila del Norte*, expressing loyalty to both officers and defending the skills of each. "We are convinced that General Ampudia has sufficient patriotism and valor to make the hated invaders bite the dust, but we also believe that the naming of General Arista is the precursor to the victory desired by all the brave troops who form the Army of the North." A force that had hoped to take advantage of divisions in the US ranks now found itself striving to overcome its own political disputes and insubordination.[72]

With the Mexican Army preoccupied with eviscerating itself from within, the Army of Occupation continued to face the more immediate threat of brigandry. On April 19, Lt. Theodoric Porter of the 4th Infantry and Lt. Stephen Dobbins of the 3rd Infantry each led a party of ten men to scour the brush for signs of Cross or his assailants. A short distance from the US camp, the two groups parted and went in separate directions. The Dobbins party completed its reconnaissance without incident;

Porter ran into trouble. On the morning of April 20, about twelve miles from the US base, he and his party came upon a horseman who fired at them and fled. Giving chase, Porter's troops stormed into the middle of a Mexican camp, scattering a group of men and capturing weapons, food, and horses. As Porter prepared to return to the fort with these prizes, a sudden rain shower deluged his party. His men advised a delay until the rain abated, but Porter was anxious to proceed and gave the order to press on. The foolhardiness of this decision became evident almost immediately. Only a short distance ahead, as Porter's party passed through a clearing, it ran afoul of a large group of assailants waiting in the thickets on either side. Porter snapped off several rounds, killing one man and wounding several others. His troops attempted to follow suit, but the rain-dampened powder rendered their weapons useless, and they scattered in the brush under heavy fire from the numerous, and evidently drier, guns of their assailants. Nine of the soldiers eventually stumbled back to the US camp. Porter and another soldier, a private named Flood, fell in the fight and became the objects of a new round of searching by the US force.[73]

This incident occurred just as the Cross mystery reached a resolution. On April 21, a Mexican man entered the US camp to report finding a body in a dense thicket just miles from the American fort. Searchers rushed to the scene and determined that it was the missing colonel. He had been taken by surprise—felled by a crushing blow to the head, robbed, and stripped of his clothing by his attackers and his flesh by the wild animals of the chaparral—an inglorious death for a seasoned military officer.[74]

Porter and Flood had died in a somewhat more soldierly fashion, downing several of their foes in traditional combat. Nevertheless, details gradually emerged from Mexican sources that the two soldiers, wounded by gunfire, had been surrounded by their attackers, who knifed them to death instead of taking them captive. Their bodies were never found. Such treatment outraged the American officers. They were willing to accept the risks of a soldier's life, but lived by a code of military chivalry that frowned on this type of cold-blooded killing. "We have vengeance to take on Mexico for more than one man's blood," Lt. Napoleon Dana wrote after learning the fate of his countrymen, "and our boys are just in the humor for the business." His words echoed the sentiments of many others in camp as they grew increasing anxious to avenge their compatriots.[75]

Still, they continued to wait. The attacks on Cross and Porter met two of the three criteria that Taylor required to justify an armed response: both incidents had been initiated by the Mexican assailants, and both had occurred on the north bank of the river. All that was lacking was confirmation that the attacks had occurred with the blessing of the Mexican government.

But such confirmation was elusive at best. Many US soldiers suspected that the military command in Matamoros had condoned if not commanded the banditry along the river. Some believed that the horsemen served under the direct orders of Gen. Antonio Canales, who, having been rebuffed in his efforts to use Taylor's army to his advantage, now sought to hasten the bloodshed. Many suspected that despite his denials to Taylor, Ampudia himself had been complicit in, if not directly responsible for, the murder of Cross. Others insisted that the culprit was Romano Falcón, whom they understood to be a sort of regional Robin Hood figure who answered only to the governor of the Mexican state of Tamaulipas. Falcón was, in fact, a lieutenant in the Bahia presidials, the auxiliary unit which had monitored the US advance from Corpus Christi and remained active on the north bank of the river. US troops were not aware of that affiliation, but they could not have drawn firm conclusions from it even if they had been. Nothing directly tied Ampudia to these incidents, and men like Canales and Falcón had already demonstrated a tendency to act on their own initiative, perhaps to the extent of contradicting direct orders. Even if it could be proven that the auxiliary troops of the Villas del Norte had committed the attacks, Taylor or Polk would have been hard-pressed to prove official blessing or to justify starting a war based on the deeds of such men.[76]

Moreover, most signs indicated that Mexican officials in Matamoros actively disapproved of this type of attack on the US forces. Like their American counterparts, the professional officers of the Mexican Army adhered to a strict code of military honor. Even before Colonel Cross had disappeared, several Mexican officers had entered the American camp under flag of truce to warn of depredations by rancheros along the river. They had admitted their inability to control these bandits and cautioned the US troops never to leave their camps alone or unarmed. When Taylor had written to Ampudia for information about Cross, the Mexican general had also exhibited courtesy in the matter, offering to seek information and promising that any American captured would be "treated with the consideration due to his rank, and according to the rules prescribed by the laws of nations and war."[77] It was, of course, possible that Ampudia was lying, as some of the American officers suspected, but his efforts to smooth over the issues may also provide the strongest evidence for his innocence. Restricted from initiating a fight, Ampudia earnestly hoped for an opportunity to engage in a clash with

Taylor's forces. Admitting to a role in the death of Cross and Porter would probably have given him what he wanted, because it would have given Taylor justification for escalating the conflict. Instead, Ampudia repeatedly denied involvement, including in a message of reassurance on April 16—the same day that he bitterly complained about the US blockade of the Río Bravo.[6] Taylor accepted Ampudia's words at face value, determined Cross's death to be a simple case of murder, and allowed the standoff to continue for another week.[78]

But the uneasy interval during which the two armies were neither entirely at peace nor officially at war was approaching an end. On April 24, Arista finally reached Matamoros, from which he immediately dispatched a letter informing Taylor of his arrival. The message came in two parts. The first was a proclamation that reiterated Mexico's grievances against the United States and declared that the time had come to respond in battle. "Pressed and forced into war," the broadside stated, "we enter a struggle that cannot be avoided without failing that which is most sacred in man."[79] The second part of the communication was a private note to Taylor. Friendly in tone, and containing none of the tirades and rhetoric of previous correspondence, Arista avowed his respect and assured the American general that "since fate has assigned us roles as opponents in the fight that our countries are entering, at the very least we as generals should conduct that warfare with all the rules and courtesy expected of civilized nations. You will always find my actions to be guided by justice, love of humanity, and other modern principles that make war less barbarous, with none of the cruel behavior that characterized the middle ages."[80]

Far more than any of the bellicose statements that preceded it, this note raised the alarm that fighting had become imminent.

The messages reached Taylor amid numerous reports that one thousand Mexican cavalry troops had already crossed the Rio Grande upstream from the US camp. While much of the army gathered around the main flagstaff to observe the solemn funeral of Colonel Cross, Taylor issued two parties of dragoons to investigate. The first, led by Capt. Crohan Ker, moved east to determine whether any movement had been directed toward Point Isabel. Ker's squadron traveled to a point on the left bank of the Rio Grande opposite Burrita before returning on April 25 to report no sign of activity. The second squadron, sixty-three men under the command of Capt. Seth Thornton, headed west and did not return. It was not until April 26 that several members of that group straggled back to the American position to report that they had been ambushed the previous morning by a large force of Mexican troops. These men could provide limited details. Many in the scout party had been killed. Most of the others had been taken prisoner. The fate of Thornton and his fellow officers remained unknown. But they provided absolute clarity on several key points. The attack was initiated by Mexican forces. The clash occurred on the north bank of the river. Most importantly, the encounter involved hundreds of troops of the Mexican Army and was by no stretch of the imagination a mere incidence of banditry. President Polk's requirement had been fulfilled and war was underway.[81]

CHAPTER 5
Escalation

★

THE APRIL 25 attack by Mexican troops provided the justification that Pres. James K. Polk needed to push for war. Upon receiving word of the ambush, Zachary Taylor informed his commander in chief that "hostilities may now be considered as commenced," and that fighting would likely escalate. Polk, who had waited for months for such an opening, pounced on the opportunity to legitimize the fighting. On Sunday, May 10, immediately after Taylor's dispatch reached Washington, the president sent a message to Congress stating that "after reiterated menaces, Mexico has passed the boundary of the United States, has invaded our territory and shed American blood upon the American soil." Asserting that "the cup of forbearance had been exhausted," the following day he delivered his address to Congress and called for a declaration of war.[1]

In the legislative chambers, insightful political pundits found their predictions proven correct. Unwilling to turn their backs on troops under fire, lawmakers from both houses of Congress—including some of the most ardent opponents of Polk and conflict with Mexico—rapidly approved a war bill. The public fell in line, too. Just over a week after the declaration of war, news arrived that additional clashes had already taken place on the Rio Grande. More importantly, American troops had emerged triumphant, a fact that thrilled a nation which had not experienced a major military victory since the battle of New Orleans in 1814. Caught up in the excitement of the moment, citizens set aside their ambivalence about the conflict and scrambled to celebrate a new generation of heroes. In the process, they silenced—or at least muffled—the recently powerful voices of opposition. Within days, a president who had previously enjoyed only tenuous and scattered support for his Texas claims found himself in possession of the legislation and funding he needed to pursue an offensive war against Mexico.[2]

The opening salvo had an equally negative impact on the Mexican forces on the Río Bravo. At the time, Mexican leaders celebrated "with trumpeting, ringing of bells, and enthusiastic demonstrations by all classes of society, the first triumph of national arms over the American forces that dared to invade our national territory."[3] But in retrospect it became clear that they had achieved only a pyrrhic victory. The action unleashed a series of battles that would leave US troops firmly in control of the lands north of the river and the Mexican Army in no condition to retake them. The unification of the United States' population in support of war also extended far beyond the political arena. In the aftermath of the opening campaign, hundreds of thousands of American men enlisted in volunteer regiments, eagerly awaiting their opportunity to join in the fight. Within weeks, the first of these units arrived in the Rio Grande delta, and in a matter of months, the tiny American Army swelled into a massive force of soldiers that would plunge into Mexico and eventually conquer its capital city.

Historians have often considered the first skirmish in the war between Mexico and the United States as the moment when the fortunes of the two nations began to diverge. But few scholars have given more than a passing nod to the series of events that culminated in those first shots. Much greater attention has gone toward demonstrating how a solitary Mexican victory served to initiate the dramatic string of American successes that ensued. In retrospect, Mexico's attack across the Río Bravo assumes the appearance of a tactical error—one that produced a fleeting rush of Mexican pride, while at the same time unleashing forces that would bring the nation to its knees. But to the Mexican soldiers, who did not know how events would play out, the opening skirmish seemed to signal a dramatic shift in control. Up to that point, Mexican generals had been in a reactionary mode, always waiting for US movements and responding accordingly. That changed on April 25, 1846, when Gen. Mariano Arista seized command of the situation and dictated the action. From then on, it would be Mexican decisions that drove the first campaign, and American troops would be forced to respond. In command of an undersized, poorly armed and trained, underfed army, Arista knew that defeat was a real possibility. After almost two years of waiting for a fight, however, he appeared determined to carry it out on his own terms.

Although he initiated this phase of the conflict just hours after arriving on the scene, Arista did not act impetuously. Long before he arrived in the Río Bravo delta, the general had taken measures to ensure that he could sustain his offensive and his troops once fighting began. "The lines of communication with an army serve the same functions as the throat for the human body," he explained to the governor of Nuevo Léon as he sought assistance. "Without this organ an entity cannot feed itself or survive." Unlike Ampudia, who was evidently surprised by the US blockade of the Río Bravo, Arista had anticipated it. Even before Taylor issued the order to seal off the river, the Mexican general suggested establishing a less-vulnerable supply route for Matamoros. An overland corridor, safely out of reach of US forces, would ensure constant contact with the orders, food, and weapons dispatched from central Mexico. "It is of the utmost importance," he wrote to the governor, "that you take great pains without delay to put such a line in practice."[4]

This was no simple task. Most of the supplies intended for the army originated in the states of Zacatecas and San Luis Potosí, requiring that they be carted several hundred miles across mountainous, unpopulated territory. A lack of adequate roads added to the difficulty of the terrain. Moreover, while this land route from central Mexico into Matamoros allowed the army to avoid interference by American forces, it did not guarantee safety from attack. As forces rushed to the northeastern corner of the republic to confront the American threat, they left behind undefended communities in the rest of the frontier region. Bands of Apaches and Comanches were quick to seize advantage from this vacuum of power, staging raids on communities like Mier and Laredo, along the Río Bravo west of Matamoros. Some presidial troops remained behind to counter the attacks, but although these forces could defend the larger towns, they could not effectively control the countryside. This permitted the Indian war parties to move south of the river, where they roamed much of the arid expanse between Monterrey and Matamoros. Largely unchecked, these bands—and groups of bandits and brigands as well—terrorized isolated hamlets and unprotected travelers on the roads. Military convoys were not exempt from the threat, and there was great danger of losing shipments of food, equipment, and money destined for the Army of the North.[5]

Arista countered this menace with an elaborate plan to ensure the security of his transports. He divided the route to Matamoros into five roughly equivalent segments. Convoys leaving the state capitols of San Luis and Zacatecas would first journey to town of Salado, San Luis Potosí, along roads that were considered relatively secure. From there, they moved northward to Rinconada, Nuevo Léon, before veering eastward to La Coma, Tamaulipas, and, finally, to Matamoros. For each leg of this voyage, the general called for a detachment of thirty troops to serve as an escort. The troops would come from garrisons that he established in the towns of Salado in the state of

San Luis Potosi, Saltillo and Encarnación in Coahuila, Monterrey and China in Nuevo León, and Santo Domingo in Tamaulipas. Troops in Matamoros served as the final garrison on this line. Only when he had this route firmly established and operating did Arista feel secure enough to initiate offensive actions against the American troops.[6]

The general's preparation included developing a thorough understanding of the goings-on inside the American ranks. He had begun covert operations during his first stint as general-in-chief, and these had persisted through the many changes in command that had followed. At first spying had been difficult; it was carried out by a few traders and scouts who braved the wastelands between the Río Bravo and the US Army at Corpus Christi. But when General Taylor settled his troops on the north bank of the river, intelligence gathering became considerably easier. Hundreds of civilians entered the US camp daily, hoping to profit from the arrival of the invading force. "The people of the country/Mexicans, are in our camp every day with vegetables, eggs, chickens, etc. and seem glad to see us here," wrote Lt. Richard Cochrane, who, like many other soldiers, welcomed the access to fresh food and stores.[7] Mexican military leaders disapproved of giving comfort to the enemy, but they also saw the opportunity to acquire information. Dozens of spies joined these commercial throngs, returning daily to Matamoros with reports about American maneuvers, plans, troop strength, and morale. "Our camp is full of spies!" Lt. James Peck complained in one of his frequent diary entries, but little could be done to stanch the flow of information. By the end of April, Arista had detailed knowledge of General Taylor's activities and even a map showing the exact location of every U.S regiment in the riverside encampment.[8]

Well aware of the advantages to be gained from spying, Arista took great care to preserve his own secrets. For months, the Mexican military leaders had strived to maintain as much secrecy as possible about the movement of troops toward Matamoros. This was intended not so much to mask the growing strength of the Army of the North as to conceal its appalling lack of weapons and supplies and the unsatisfactory state of its troops' training. The effort proved to be remarkably successful, for neither General Taylor nor the world at large recognized just how weak the Mexican Army had become. It was much more difficult to obscure the situation once the troops reached Matamoros. With Taylor's camp directly across the river, it was expected that the American general would be sending out his own scouts and spies to assess his opposition. Of greater concern were the American citizens who lived in the city. Many of these merchants had made their homes in Matamoros for years, even decades, and had developed extensive ties to the community. Nevertheless, Mexican leaders believed—

often rightly—that the expatriates' loyalty ultimately lay with the forces across the river. Fearing that the US residents would provide damaging intelligence to Taylor's troops, they developed a plan to remove the threat.

What ensued was the forced relocation of US citizens from Matamoros to the interior of the country. General Ampudia initiated the process on April 12, when he issued the expulsion order and directed the refugees to move almost 150 miles southward to Victoria, the capital of the state of Tamaulipas. The Americans initially complied. Then, on April 20, 1846, upon learning that Arista had superseded Ampudia, J. P. Schatzell, the US consul in Matamoros, and a group of prominent citizens, wrote a letter in which they denounced Ampudia and his decree. "This arbitrary order," they said, "without precedent in the history of the civilized world, was executed with such indecent promptness and precipitation that those affected were obliged to abandon their residences and monetary interests to the care of whomever luck cast in their path. They abandoned the city on foot, facing ill-treatment and threats of shackling, while being compelled to march at bayonet point." The signatories called the action illegal under international law, a violation of US-Mexican treaties, and a virtual declaration of war. They also praised Arista as a man known for his moderation and begged him to revoke the order and allow them to return to Matamoros, or at least to gather their possessions and leave the country.[9]

Arista quickly dashed any hopes of a reprieve. Although he had his differences with Ampudia, he found little substance to the arguments set forth by Schatzell and his peers. He countered that the expulsion should not be called a detention or arrest but rather a "temporary expedient." Likewise, he dismissed the assertion that this was an act of war, viewing it instead as "a precaution necessitated by repeated hostile acts on the part of a general empowered by the United States to seize Mexican territory by force." He also scoffed at the notion that he should reverse the decree. "Should we wait for the danger, allow the tempest to build which we might have dispelled at the start, permit the expansion of a neighbor and stand by peacefully while it shows a desire to enslave us?" he asked. "Will it be time to defend ourselves when there are no longer means to do so?" Having asserted the justice and reasonableness of the act, he ordered the Americans to continue to Victoria. In an effort to demonstrate his moderation, he did promise that the merchants could communicate freely with representatives in Matamoros about their business affairs. He also assured them that they were free to leave the country via the city of Tampico, though he noted that General Taylor had ordered a blockade of that port, making departures difficult.[10]

With these precautions in place, Arista saw no reason for any additional delays of his offensive. He did not even wait to reach Matamoros. Upon arriving at Camargo on April 21, he sent word to Ampudia that he wanted 400 infantry troops and a brigade of cavalry moved upriver to La Enseñada, a ranch some twenty miles west of Matamoros. The next morning, Ampudia dispatched Col. José María Carrasco with 250 men of the Batallón de Zapadores, 150 tiradores, and two companies of the 2nd Light Infantry toward this destination. On April 23, Gen. Anastasio Torrejón followed at the head of the cavalry brigade, supplemented by Gen. Antonio Canales's frontier auxiliaries, a force of 1200 men. That evening at sunset, Torrejón and Carrasco rendezvoused with Arista and his staff, who had just arrived at the ranch on their march eastward. In a conference that ensued, the general-in-chief placed General Torrejón at the head of the 1600-man force, directed him to move north to the settlement of Soliseño, and ordered him to cross the Río Bravo near there the following morning.[11]

Arista launched this advance with two principal objectives in mind. The first was to sever ties between the US riverside fort and the outside world. Arista had received intelligence that the US troops entrenched across from Matamoros were dangerously low on supplies and munitions. Even with the steady flow of Mexican merchants into the camp, the American stores had dwindled, and Arista estimated that Taylor had only enough food to last for eight to ten days. If he could prevent convoys from reaching the riverside camp and messages from traveling out, he might induce the US general to accept a quick surrender. Alternatively, he might force Taylor to launch a preemptive attack from his base before the Americans could add more troops and ammunition to their force. In either case, isolating the US camp could only benefit the Mexican effort, and Arista decided to act quickly, before the situation changed. Toward this end, he gave Torrejón careful instructions to proceed to a position north of the US fort and occupy the road linking the Frontón de Santa Isabel with Matamoros. Once in position, he was instructed to halt the passage of US supply trains along the route.[12]

Arista also charged Torrejón with the secondary responsibility of guarding the passage of the remainder of the Mexican Army. Once Torrejón had gained control of the Frontón-to-Matamoros road, he was to establish a secure beachhead along the river and ward off any attack from US forces while transport boats ferried Mexican infantry and artillery across the Río Bravo. When they were safely landed, these troops would join Torrejón's infantry in establishing an impenetrable cordon around the US base. The exact location of this crossing point had not been determined at the time of Torrejón's departure. Although the most obvious location for such a maneuver would be either the Anacuita crossing, just upriver from the US fort, or the Longoreño crossing, several miles downstream, Arista had not yet selected his best option. Torrejón would have to await additional instructions.[13]

A key step toward achieving both goals was eliminating as many American cavalry forces as possible. Taylor had a rather small complement of mounted troops in his army—several companies of dragoons and a small, recently arrived company of Texas Rangers—but the horsemen performed vital tasks like scouting the countryside, maintaining communications between the two US forts, and escorting supply convoys along the Point Isabel-to-Matamoros road. If Torrejón could crush these forces early, Taylor would find himself severely crippled in his ability to maintain links with the outside world. This, in turn, would considerably ease Mexican efforts to isolate the enemy troops. Arista therefore encouraged Torrejón to seek out US cavalry troops and "find and destroy the enemy wherever he appears."[14]

Though he felt that the US dragoons posed only a minor threat to the large Mexican cavalry brigade and were unlikely to prevail in a head-to-head confrontation, Arista did recommended a certain amount of caution. These troops, he warned, were well trained and well supplied and rode fierce, almost wild, mounts. They also often carried light artillery pieces with them to for added firepower. The plan for dealing with such foes was simple: attack in force on an open plain, strike quickly before the Americans could flee or unlimber their artillery, maneuver to avoid a head-on charge, and create commotion and confusion to drive the fiery American horses to distraction.[15]

Anticipating victory in upcoming encounters, Arista also provided strict guidelines for the treatment of enemy prisoners and wounded. Although he gave Torrejón great latitude in carrying out his orders, he demanded compassion and compliance with rules of war. Torrejón was to treat prisoners well, tend to enemy casualties if possible, and turn the severely wounded over to General Taylor for care. Such behavior, Arista hoped, might help erase past accusations of Mexican barbarity. He especially encouraged kind handling of deserters from the American Army, apparently believing that such behavior might encourage many more to abandon their posts.[16]

First, however, the Mexican troops had to successfully cross the river, and this was no easy matter. Transporting sixteen hundred troops and twelve hundred horses across the broad Río Bravo would take a considerable amount of time. It would also draw attention from the US camp. Anxious American troops maintained a constant vigil for any activity within view of their fortified position on the river, while scouts and Taylor's own cadre of Mexican spies monitored activity farther afield. If the US general learned of a concerted Mexican effort to cross the river, it seemed unlikely that he would offer Arista the same uncontested passage that had been afforded him at the Arroyo Colorado. Instead, Taylor would inevitably seize the opportunity to confront Torrejón while he battled the current. If caught at this vulnerable moment, the Mexican Army, and Arista's plan, might come to a devastating end.

This was the reason why Arista launched his campaign from Soliseño. The starting point was far upstream from the US fort, well beyond the range of American forces in their daily patrols. It was also on a narrower section of the river, which would require less time to cross. If US scouts or spies learned of the maneuver, the Mexican horsemen could probably occupy the north bank long before General Taylor could move enough troops through the dense chaparral to intercept them. Although it was certain they would be discovered at some point, with luck that would not happen until the crossing was finished. Mexican cavalry troops stationed in Matamoros regularly responded to the growing number of Indian attacks in the towns west of Matamoros, and the movement of a party in that direction could easily be disguised as an action against this other threat. It was even possible that the journey by Torrejón's troops might be seen as nothing more than a move to meet and escort the incoming general-in-chief.[17]

Not content to leave his safety to chance, Arista also engaged in a complex game of subterfuge to obscure his movements. For example, when he ordered José María Carrasco to lead his infantry companies out of Matamoros under cover of darkness on April 22, he initially directed the colonel to head downriver in the direction of Burrita. At the time of his departure, Carrasco and his troops believed that the tiny town was their destination and that they would be responsible for defending the river crossing and its customhouse against a possible American attack. But after they had been on the road an hour, Ampudia overtook the column, handed the colonel a sealed envelope from Arista, and ordered him to continue his march for an hour before opening it. Ampudia then returned to Matamoros, while Carrasco, in obedience to instructions, continued for several miles toward Burrita.[18]

When he finally opened the orders around midnight, Carrasco learned that his true objective was the Rancho La Enseñada, some twenty miles west of Matamoros. He was instructed to take pains to obscure his movements from any watching eyes on the north bank of the river, reverse his course, and rush to his destination by dawn the next morning. He complied with the orders as best he could, reversing his course and driving his troops at a rapid pace on a long, circuitous route around the southern outskirts of Matamoros, far from the prying eyes of the Americans. His efforts could not overcome weariness, poor roads, and darkness, and Carrasco's force did not reach Enseñada until 2 p.m. the following afternoon. Nevertheless, the ploy succeeded. So secret was the maneuver that a small group of soldiers traveling with Carrasco became separated from his army and reached Burrita without ever knowing that their orders had been changed.[19] US troops fell for the feint as well. When General Taylor sent out scouts to investigate possible advances across the Rio Grande, he sent one of his dragoon parties on a fruitless search in the direction of Burrita, based on reports that a crossing was occurring there.

More important for the Mexican forces, the maneuver permitted them to cross the river safely. At dawn on April 24, Torrejón and his troops gathered at a crossing point just north of Soliseño on the south bank of the river and near a point called Las Rucias on the north bank. Arista accompanied the army and conducted a final review of the men on the south bank to ensure that only the best-qualified soldiers undertook the operation. At last, around 9 a.m., he gave his approval for the mission to begin. Infantry troops went first, traversing the river in five launches that made multiple journeys back and forth across the waterway. Upon reaching the north bank, these troops took up positions to provide cover for the cavalry crossing that followed. The mounted troops came across in two discrete groups, with Col. Cayatano Montero directing the regular cavalry and Gen. Antonio Canales leading the militia forces. Despite lingering concerns about a US attack, the entire force completed the movement without interruption and, remarkably, without a single incident. By 2:30 in the afternoon, Torrejón had established a camp in a sheltered field near the river's edge. On the far side of the water, Arista hurried on toward Matamoros to take command of the troops there.[20]

The uncontested passage of Torrejón's command demonstrated the merit of Arista's subterfuge. It reinforced the widespread conviction among US soldiers that the Mexican forces did not intend to fight. The Mexican general did a laudable job of hiding his tracks. No one in the American camp even suspected a crossing until the afternoon of April 24, when a Mexican informant arrived with information that a massive maneuver across the river was underway. By that time, the operation had already been completed and the Mexican forces were resting safely on the north bank. Rather than marvel at the skillful completion of a covert crossing, Lt. George Meade chose to believe that the report was nothing but the latest in a long series of false alarms. "This has been the rumor before so often," he said in a letter to his wife, "that we are all tired of it." Surgeon Madison Mills revealed that Meade was by no means alone in this opinion. Summing up the report in his diary entry for that night, he wrote matter-of-factly, "The general believes it, though it is not believed by the officers generally."[21]

Taylor not only believed the intelligence, he sensed a significant threat and acted promptly to respond. In a display of bravado, he sent a warning to authorities in Matamoros that any crossing might oblige him to open his cannon batteries on the city. On a more practical note, he moved to protect his isolated army. He immediately wrote to the governors of Texas and Louisiana requesting militia reinforcements as quickly as possible. He also reinvigorated efforts to complete the earthworks along the river, dividing his army into morning and afternoon shifts and requiring all available officers and men to participate in the construction. He placed the troops under a state of alert, ordering them to remain in uniform at all times, to sleep with their weapons loaded and near at hand, and to be ready to respond to the slightest alarm.[22]

These preparations complete, Taylor sought next to substantiate his information and get a better understanding of the foe that was moving his way. In the late afternoon, he sent orders for two groups of dragoons to explore up- and downriver for evidence of enemy activity. Capt. Crohan Ker's party, drawn by Carrasco's feint in that direction, encountered nothing and became little more than a sidenote to the drama that unfolded. Capt. Seth Thornton, meanwhile, was charged with the responsibility of looking westward "up the river as far as 9 leagues, examining the country and river carefully to ascertain if the enemy has crossed to this side." Taylor later added verbal instructions for Thornton to attempt to determine the position, strength, and composition of the force that had crossed. He especially wanted to know if the Mexican force had transported any artillery that could be pointed at either of the two American fortifications.[23]

Stressing the need for safety, Taylor urged the dragoon captain to "move with the utmost caution, keeping out advanced or flank guards and taking the greatest care not to be drawn into an ambuscade." He placed strict time and distance limits on the expedition, presumably to prevent the squadron from straying too far from the protection of the main American force. Thornton was to turn back at the nine-league (twenty-seven-mile) mark or by noon on the following day, even if he had not encountered the enemy. The general further insisted that the captain avoid an unnecessary fight. If he came upon a small party of Mexican troops, he had the leeway to take them prisoner. If he encountered a large force, on the other hand, he was to avoid a fight and report to camp immediately—even if this meant losing a few men of his advance guard. "It would be better to sacrifice a few than the whole," Taylor reasoned. Nevertheless, if the reconnaissance party found itself surrounded and a clash became inevitable, Thornton had permission to force his way to safety. "You will hold yourself ready to cut through any armed party that may be in your way," read the final line of his instructions.[24]

Thornton was mindful of these warnings. Before leaving, he assembled a reconnaissance party that was familiar with the territory he was to examine. In addition to his own Company F of the 2nd Dragoons, he enlisted the support of the dragoons of Company C, commanded by Capt. William Hardee. Hardee was an ideal second-in-command since he had traveled the route on a previous scouting expedition. Thornton also had two Mexican guides, including José Sandoval—commonly known to the soldiers of both armies by his nickname "Chepito"—who had recently escorted the American Army from Corpus Christi. The total force amounted to sixty-three, including guides, officers, and men, as they left the American camp and headed west across the nearby farm fields at around 9 p.m.[25]

On the road, Thornton complied with the strictures for safety as best he could. He instructed his men to thread strips of cloth through their sabre belts and horse tack, hoping to muffle any jingling that might alert an enemy waiting in the dark. He also sent Sgt. George Lenz, two privates, and Chepito a quarter mile ahead to serve as the advance guard for the party. Despite General Taylor's instructions, he elected not to send out flankers. This was a practical measure. The chaparral growing along the road proved too dense for the horsemen to penetrate. Indeed, the thorny thickets crowded the route so much that Thornton found "the road in almost its entire length was a perfect *défilé* and so narrow in some places as to render it difficult for a single horseman to pass." This caused the party to become spread out over a distance of several hundred yards. The difficult route, exacerbated by the darkness of night, led Thornton to stop after a fifteen-mile ride to rest and await the light of day. Even then, he maintained pickets and required that his troops rest with their hands on their bridles, ready to mount their horses at the first alarm.[26]

The next morning the dragoon party began to investigate in earnest. The troops rose at daybreak, reestablished their order of march, and continued westward. Along the way, they carefully scoured the narrow trail and surrounding chaparral for evidence of the Mexican Army. Finding nothing, Thornton also sought information from the scattered residents of the area, stopping at several of the ranches that dotted the north bank of the river. At each, with the assistance of Chepito as interpreter, he questioned the occupants about their knowledge of military activity. Invariably he received the same response—the rancheros insisted that several thousand cavalry troops had crossed the river and waited somewhere on the road ahead. Each time, however, Thornton brushed aside concerns about the apparent danger and chose to press on.[27]

In the aftermath of the disaster that followed, the dragoon captain was forced to justify his decision, and he offered several explanations. He did not know whether the people he interviewed had the correct information. Most of the ranchers he encountered appeared to be retelling rumors, and no one stood out as a reliable eyewitness. He also suspected that those who knew the facts were not likely to give him an accurate account. He noted that recent experience with false alarms and "Mexican duplicity" gave him reason to "receive with great caution any representations of their own as to the position or strength of their force." Indeed, he was so distrustful of Mexican accounts that, like his fellow officers, he suspected the story of the crossing to be an elaborate hoax. All this speculation rested on lack of information. "I had learned nothing either of the enemy's strength or composition," Thornton explained, "and the object of my expedition had not been accomplished." Until he had something more than secondhand stories and vague descriptions of the force, he felt duty bound to continue.[28]

At least one member of Thornton's party viewed the situation differently. After talking briefly with a group of rancheros at a site about twenty-five miles west of the main US camp, Chepito reported once again that danger lay ahead and announced that he would go no farther. Thornton attempted to convince him to continue, but no argument would sway the Mexican, who turned back in the direction of the US camp. This left Thornton without his primary guide and interpreter, but he remained adamant about the need to move ahead. Mindful of the potential danger, he ordered Lt. George Mason and several others to move forward to strengthen the advance guard to twelve men. Sgt. George Lenz, who had some knowledge of Spanish, assumed the role of interpreter. Thornton also ordered all troops to remove and stow away their coats, prime their pistols, and load and ready their carbines so that they would be prepared for action if an ambush did indeed lie ahead. These preparations made, the scout party pressed onward.[29]

They traveled an additional three miles to a spot on the Rio Grande known as Las Rucias, "silver gray," probably inspired by the color of horses found in the area. At this point, the scouts had moved about twenty-eight miles from the US fort and had effectively reached the nine-league barrier imposed by General Taylor's orders. But they had not yet reached the time limit. It was only around 8 a.m., and the captain had four hours remaining before he was required to turn back to the fort. Thornton strongly believed that he should make use of that time to gather as much information as possible.[30]

The immediate object of his interest was another of the ranches that had been carved out of the thick, thorny growth that lined the river's northern bank. Rancho de Carricitos was a sizable property that included a broad field and several rustic houses, and it had enough presence that Captain Hardee, Thornton's second-in-command, referred to it as a "plantation."[31] Several men were laboring in the field, and before Thornton ended his expedition and headed back, he was determined to question them.[32]

Doing that would take some effort, because the ranch was not merely big, it was also well protected. In addition to the Rio Grande, which bounded the site to the south, there was a high, impenetrable band of compact chaparral fence surrounding the field on the remaining three sides, and the soldiers could spot no gate that permitted entrance. Thornton first attempted to hail the ranchers from the outside the enclosure, but the laborers within were either too far away to hear or unwilling to acknowledge the US troops. Thornton was therefore obliged to try approaching them more directly, and he set out in search of an opening. Having arrived at the ranch at a point about halfway along the easternmost side, he left Hardee and the main body of troops in that position, then led a small advance guard south along the fence looking for a way through. He found none, and after reaching the river several hundred feet away, he retraced his path to examine the perimeter to the north and west.[33]

In that short time, Hardee and the main body of dragoons had been driven into a state of excitement. Shortly after Thornton had left, one of the US soldiers spotted a Mexican horseman riding into view from a spur path in the brush. Seeing the dragoons, he quickly wheeled about, plunged back into the chaparral, and disappeared from sight. Moments later, when Thornton returned and heard the specifics of the incident, he at once ordered a pursuit. The dragoons followed the narrow trail for almost a mile before they turned back without having seen any additional horsemen. But they did see tracks indicating that a large party of cavalry troops had passed along the way. This, along with the sighting of the lone enemy soldier, erased any lingering doubts that a crossing had occurred. It also convinced Thornton that the enemy troops had taken up a position behind him and that he would have to cut his way back to the US camp.[34]

Rather than confront that unpleasant prospect immediately, Thornton once again elected to seek out information at Rancho de Carricitos. "I determined to return and endeavored to gain information from the persons seen in the field if it could be done with safety," he later explained. This time, he felt that the survival of his scout party depended on an accurate knowledge of the force that awaited him. But the decision also led him to continue much father westward. Having failed to find an opening in the chaparral fence on the northern boundary of the ranch, he was forced to ride almost a mile before he finally found one—a series of horizontal bars that served as a gate—on the western edge of the ranch. It was around 10 a.m. when Thornton pushed aside the bars and led his troops single file into the ranch.[35]

A flurry of activity ensued. When the dragoons passed through the bars and entered the field, the Mexican workers near the ranch structures responded by scattering and taking flight. Fearing he would lose the opportunity to secure valuable information, Thornton spurred his horse forward in pursuit and quickly crossed the two hundred yards between the gate and the houses. As he rode away, he gestured for the advance guard to follow without taking his eyes off his quarry. He was, therefore, unaware that his entire command had joined the charge. The series of marches and countermarches in search of a gate and on the trail of Mexican troops had gradually shortened the separation between the advance guard and the main body of dragoons. By the time the soldiers located the bars, the gap that had been maintained for so much of the march had been closed altogether. When Captain Thornton signaled, men who should not have been in view of the gesture interpreted it as a call to action, and the entire scout party rushed forward in pursuit of the fleeing Mexicans. Such was the fervor for the chase that Captain Hardee, who was responsible for the main body of troops but unaware that Thornton now suspected the enemy of being nearby, failed to post a single sentry. The dragoons dashed off in a southeasterly direction across the ranch, paying no heed to the entryway they left behind them.[36]

The resulting situation might be remembered as a comedy of errors if not for the grim results. As Thornton reached the houses, he saw that he had been joined by additional troops and admonished them, saying "I did not want you all to come in here." Nevertheless he did not order them back to the gate and continued searching in and around the huts for signs of the vanished occupants. Meanwhile, his troops, who had maintained a state of high alert for hours, seemed to drop their guard entirely. Some soldiers joined the hunt, weaving their horses among the structures and poking their heads into doorways and open windows in search of the hiding ranchers. The remainder of the party seized the opportunity for a moment of rest. About half the troops dismounted, casually milling about as they lit their pipes and replenished their water supply. When Thornton finally turned up an elderly man and began questioning him, a small group gathered to watch the proceedings. It was only by chance that, after five minutes of this inattention, Sergeant Javier Tredo glanced westward and spotted a line of Mexican infantrymen pouring through the narrow entry to the ranch.

His shout of "There are the Mexicans!" roused the dragoons. Those on foot scrambled to regain their mounts. Those still on horseback rushed to regroup. Thornton abandoned the now-pointless questioning of the ranchero and assessed the situation at hand. With the river at his back and high fences on all sides, there was little hope for escape. Judging that most of his men were in the saddle, he believed that his best hope lay in rushing the gate before the Mexican troops firmly established a foothold. "I ordered and executed a charge upon the enemy at the bars, the only opening," he later explained, "determined to fall in the attempt or in the words of my instructions to cut my way through the enemy." His squadron, or as many of its members as he could muster, drew sabres and charged forward even as they struggled to come together in formation. Thornton sprang to the lead, apparently trying to spur his mount into the state of fiery frenzy commented upon by General Arista. He reached a thundering gallop, "expecting that the squadron might effect a passage through an opening I hoped to make by the superior power of my horse."[37]

Aware that he needed to act before the Mexicans fully secured the entry, Thornton had made this rash charge without pausing to assess the strength of the force arrayed against him. As he hurtled toward the gate, however, he could not fail "to observe the immense strength of the enemy," and he found it a daunting sight. Several hundred Mexican infantrymen had already cleared the bars, effectively sealing the tiny gap in the chaparral. Beyond the brush, more than a thousand cavalrymen waited on their mounts, ready to swarm in the unlikely event that any US soldier succeeded in breaking through. The Mexican troops opened a murderous musket volley that threatened to cut down the entire dragoon force. Convinced of the futility of seeking escape by that quarter, Thornton broke off the charge. Just a hundred feet from the Mexican line, he suddenly swerved to the right, leading his men eastward along the northern boundary of the ranch in search of any manageable break in the brush.[38]

This strategy was as fruitless as the charge. The frantic race along the northern edge of the clearing moved the dragoons out of range of the enemy troops occupying the western part of the ranch, but exposed them to a blistering fire from the Mexican cavalry positioned around the exterior of the brush fence. Meanwhile, the desperate ride failed to reveal any previously unseen breaches in the brush fence—hardly surprising since the Americans already had examined it closely from the other side on their

Skirmish at Rancho Carricitos. *From Edward S. Ellis,* Library of American History.

way in. As musket balls rained down on them, Thornton and Hardee both realized that their ensnarement was virtually complete. In a brief, breathless exchange as they raced forward on their horses, the two agreed that their only hope lay in hacking a path through the thorny fence "in the face of the enemy." Thornton issued the order, but he could make neither his troops nor his horse comply. The men ignored the order and fled the fire in a state of pandemonium. The horse raced along fence at full speed within close range of the Mexican gunfire. When a shot struck the terrified animal, it stumbled and then crashed to the ground atop a stunned Thornton, who could not drag himself from underneath his dying mount.[39]

Captain Hardee, who thought Thornton would perish in his lone charge into enemy fire, now found himself in command of the chaos. Recognizing that he could not force his men to approach the fence line, he immediately belayed Thornton's last order and shepherded his desperate party southward, away from the line of Mexican troops and toward the Rio Grande. There he hoped to swim the river to safety, or, barring that, to establish a defense along its bank. The first option was impossible. The shoreline at that point consisted of a broad coastal flat, punctuated by pools of stagnant water and stands of river cane. A soldier sent ahead to navigate a path to the distant central channel returned almost immediately without having found a way across the boggy terrain. Confronted with this disheartening news, Hardee pursued his final option. Rallying his surviving men, he formed a line of battle just out of reach of the Mexican musket fire and prepared to meet the advancing foe.[40]

Hardee declared that he and his troops intended to "fight to the last extremity," but a final review of the situation convinced him to reverse that decision. Only twenty-five of the US soldiers remained with the group and "almost everyone had lost a sabre, pistol, or carbine." Less than a hundred yards away, more than a thousand Mexican troops had taken position around them and closed in to settle the issue. The result of the pending clash was certain, and having already left fourteen men, including Lieutenant Mason, dead on the field, the captain saw no glory or purpose in continuing resistance to its inevitable end. Leaving his men in their defensive formation and vowing "to sell our lives as dearly as possible if I could not secure good treatment," he advanced under a flag of truce to seek terms of surrender. In a brief parlay, he was pleased to learn that General Torrejón shared his belief in "the rules of civilized warfare." The Mexican commander, in keeping with his orders and his own sense of honor, had already shown kindness to a number of who had fallen prisoner and he vowed give Hardee's entire force fair treatment in the event of a surrender. Hardee gratefully accepted the terms and, little more than ten minutes after the first shot had been fired, he and forty-six survivors entered custody as prisoners of war.[41]

The Americans found Torrejón to be true to his promise. Immediately after the firing ended, Mexican surgeons tended to a number of the dragoons who had been injured in the fight. Two of them, seriously wounded in the fray, received first aid before being escorted back to Taylor's camp. The Mexican general also dispatched a note to Taylor in which he explained that he lacked adequate hospital facilities to treat the men. Shortly afterwards, he sent the rest of the dragoons east as well, this time across the Rio Grande and on the road to Matamoros. Upon arriving there, on the afternoon of April 26, the captives continued to experience "uniform kindness and attention." Captain Hardee and Lieutenant Kane enjoyed especially good treatment. As the only two officers among the prisoners, the men became the guests of General Ampudia, sharing his quarters and dining with him at his table. Ampudia played the role of gracious host well. Hardee reported that "his frank, agreeable manner and generous hospitality almost make us forget our captivity."[42]

He included these words of praise in a report to General Taylor. In that document, he provided a brief description of the Carricitos incident and reported the deaths of Sgts. Tredo and Smith, Lieutenant Mason, and the squadron leader, Captain Thornton. He also placed the blame for the debacle squarely on the shoulders of the fallen leader. Omitting details of his own errors, Hardee informed Taylor that the "gallant" commander "was prepossessed with the idea that the Mexicans had not crossed; and if they had they would not fight," and implied that Thornton's disbelief led them into the disastrous ambush.[43]

Hardee was unaware that Thornton had survived the debacle near Las Rusias and had provided his own version of events. Late in the day on April 26, Torrejón's forces discovered the captain hiding in the dense brush near the Carricitos fence. He had survived his jarring fall but was "almost dead from thirst and hunger." They provided for his needs, then quickly bound him off to Matamoros to join the rest of his squadron. Granted the same courtesies as Hardee, Thornton took time after his arrival to write a short report to his commander. In it he provided a clinical description of the misfortunes that had befallen his squadron, commended his troops for their gallantry under fire, and echoed Hardee's praise for the kind treatment he had received at the hands of his Mexican captors.[44]

Unaware of Hardee's imputation that he had underestimated the Mexican threat, Thornton in his initial communication did not address that claim. In later defenses of his actions, however, he insisted that the charge was far from true. Not only did Thornton understand the potential danger when he entered the Carricitos ranch, he had come to believe that he had been lured into it. Although he was unable to understand conversations between Chepito Sandoval and the Mexicans they encountered on the expedition, Thornton suspected that something was amiss. A final, hushed exchange, just before Chepito abandoned the squadron, convinced the captain that the Mexicans had contrived to lead him into an ambush and had, by means of the guide's duplicity, successfully gained his rear. "Here the suspicious conduct of my guide caused me to doubt his fidelity," Thornton noted weeks later, "and subsequent events have but confirmed my suspicions." His Mexican captors later claimed that they had tracked his movement from the moment he left the US camp. At the time of Chepito's abrupt departure, they had managed to move 500 cavalry and 150 "Indians" (probably members of Mexico's Carrizo tribe who served as troops of the Defensores de las

Villas del Norte) to the rear of the dragoon party. They also noted that Chepito had been congratulated by General Arista and pardoned for past service to the Americans, apparently lending support to Thornton's accusations of treachery by his guide.[45]

There is little doubt that Chepito acted against Thornton, but probably as a matter of survival. The guide had a long history in the frontier. He had served Mexican commanders in their efforts to spy on Taylor's camp at Corpus Christi, yet he had maintained close ties with Colonel Kinney at his settlement there. His assistance to Zachary Taylor in his march to the Rio Grande tested his ability to balance these opposing interests. While the Americans welcomed his guidance and knowledge of the area, Arista had called his behavior treasonous and vowed punishment. The threat of death hovered over him, and Chepito probably seized the opportunity to regain favor in the Mexican ranks. His decision paid off. In the aftermath of the Carricitos clash, a number of Mexican officers credited him with leading Thornton to Torrejón and praised him for his service. Arista, in a more practical expression of gratitude, permitted his wayward countryman to live.[46]

It is more difficult to ascertain Chepito's exact part in the Carricitos affair. Since Thornton was determined to locate the Mexican forces with or without help, it is difficult to believe that his guide had to coax him westward. None of the American accounts of the march portray Chepito as a force in driving the squadron forward. On the contrary, many of the US soldiers doubted that he was a spy precisely because he continually advised Thornton to turn back. It is more plausible that the guide provided Torrejón with information about the advancing dragoons by sending a message at the outset of the mission and through contacts made along the march. Even so, Torrejón did not learn of Thornton's approach until scouts sent from his own camp returned to report that the dragoons were headed in his direction. Whether Chepito tried to lure the Americans onward is unclear. His behavior as a guide was either an elaborate ploy to trick the dragoons into trusting him or a sign of reluctant acceptance of his role as a betrayer.

Whether or not Chepito played a role in revealing Thornton's advance, Torrejón certainly sought and intended to capitalize on intelligence about it. Shortly after completing his crossing of the Río Bravo on the afternoon of April 24, he sent Lt. Ramón Falcón and four of his presidial troops to scout the road in the direction of the US fort. Falcón returned in the early hours of the twenty-fifth with a report that a small body of enemy troops was approaching along the same route. Torrejón, who had already commenced his march eastward, welcomed this news. Sensing that he had been granted a golden opportunity to eliminate a significant portion of the American dragoon force and quickly accomplish one of the primary directives of his mission, he immediately doubled the pace of his advance to close the gap between himself and his quarry. He also sent Falcón back out to monitor the progress of the US force and to ensure that he did not lose contact.[47]

Despite Captain Thornton's assertion that he had been lured into an elaborate trap and cut off from his base camp, Torrejón appears to have had neither the time nor the inclination for such subterfuge. Only half an hour after Falcón left on his reconnaissance, he retraced his steps and announced that the enemy had advanced to within half a league (one and a half miles) of the Mexican position. Torrejón responded by assembling his troops into an attack column with a rifle company from the Villas del Norte at the vanguard, followed by the 2nd Infantry, the Sapper Battalion, a rifle company, and the cavalry as a rearguard. Certain that this army would overwhelm the smaller enemy force, he rushed onward toward a direct confrontation with the dragoons.[48]

Although he made little effort to establish an ambush, Torrejón willingly seized the opportunity when it provided itself. He arrived at Rancho de Carricitos several minutes after the US dragoons, and discovered that the Americans had foolishly entered the clearing without securing or even guarding the only exit. He immediately directed troops of the cavalry and militia forces from the Villas del Norte to move around the outside of the field and cut off any escape routes to the north or east. These were, presumably, the 500 cavalry and 150 Indians that the Mexicans later proclaimed had gained Thornton's rear. Next he positioned his infantry units on either side of the bars set in the western end of the field. Having successfully surrounded the area without attracting the notice of the enemy force at the far end of the ranch, he then ordered these foot soldiers to rush through the opening, form a line, and confront the trapped dragoons.[49]

For all this preparation and their vast numerical advantage, the Mexican troops were not completely in control of the situation. "The enemy presented himself," Torrejón noted, "and when our infantry opened fire, he responded by bravely coming onward with sabre in hand." This movement toward the gate posed problems. As the Mexican troops pushed into the field, they had left a gap in the cordon around the ranch, in the area just north of the bars. When Thornton led his dragoons onward and then to his right, it appeared possible that he might charge past the still-forming Mexican line and successfully break through the brush in that area. To prevent that move, Torrejón sent a company of his auxiliary troops into the void. Supported by a company of the

7th Cavalry, these flankers successfully cut off the escape route. In a matter of minutes, they corralled the American dragoons, who "despite defending themselves by force of arms, were completely defeated." Torrejón's force suffered few casualties, with one soldier killed and Lieutenant Falcón suffering an injury to his hand.[50]

The Mexican leaders—those on the scene and those watching from afar—applauded this triumph of arms. Gen. Antonio Canales, commander of the forces of the Villas del Norte, took the opportunity to write a letter to Minister of War Tornel in which he proclaimed not only that Mexican forces had defeated the best US cavalry company, but that the invading force showed little stomach for the fight. "The truth is," he noted, "they didn't even defend themselves. They stuck with their horses and tried to run." He believed that Mexican forces, on the other hand, had demonstrated their mettle. "Even when we were not at full strength, we knew how to seal off the escape routes and seize them." Gen. Anastasio Parrodi, from his base in Victoria, Tamaulipas, welcomed the news and assured Tornel that local residents had received it with trumpet calls, gun salutes, and other demonstrations of support. For his part, the minister of war offered assurances that the nation owed a debt of gratitude to the troops. He also passed on words from President Paredes, expressing admiration for "the brave comportment of the proud defenders of national independence, who spare no effort in punishing our gratuitous enemies and making them understand the justice with which we protect the integrity of the republic."[51]

These men had real reason to celebrate the outcome of the Carricitos skirmish, but not necessarily because they believed the clash demonstrated their ability to effectively punish the enemy. The officers were not foolish enough to believe that success in this mismatched encounter set the stage for a sweeping victory over the US forces. All remained painfully aware that their underpaid, underfed, poorly armed, and poorly trained troops would eventually have to confront the well-stocked, well-practiced American Army under much less advantageous conditions. Even the brash, outspoken Canales admitted in his letter to the secretary of war that his news would come as an "agreeable surprise" and that the victory was strategically "insignificant."[52] Much more important was the composition of the force that accomplished this feat. Both Canales and General Torrejón were careful to point out that that the auxiliary regiments of the Villas del Norte had played a significant role in the fight. Although these frontier units contributed to what was only a minor triumph in the field, they represented a major advance in the effort to present a unified front against the invading Americans. "Just days ago," Arista noted in his official report of the action, "the auxiliary troops of the northern frontier were accused of treason, charged with seeking an accord that would assist the enemy general with his conquest in return for independence of the northern departments. But their positive actions have put the lie to such talk."[53] The active support of these roughhewn frontier regiments added little to Arista's firepower and offered no guarantee of future success in combat. Nevertheless, their demonstration of loyalty diminished Arista's worries about treachery from that quadrant and allowed the Mexican general-in-chief to focus his attention on his primary objective: confronting Taylor's army.

With hostilities underway, Mexican forces rushed to capitalize on their victory as quickly as possible. The delay occasioned by the clash at Carricitos was brief, and on April 26, Torrejón resumed his march eastward. Pushing his troops along the narrow trails through the brush, he reached the Resaca de San Antonio, not far from the American fortifications under construction at the Frontón de Santa Isabel. In command of the road to Matamoros, he immediately began efforts to disrupt communications and convoys between the two US posts.[54]

Meanwhile, Arista prepared to push additional troops across the river. On April 31, he sent General Ampudia with a brigade of infantry troops downstream from Matamoros to the Longoreño crossing point. Ampudia had orders to take advantage of the distraction caused by Torrejón's brigade and quickly cross the Río Bravo before the Americans could contest the move. Once on the other side, he would support the passage of Arista himself, at the head of another brigade and with twelve pieces of artillery. General Mejía remained in Matamoros with twelve hundred troops to man the fortifications along the left bank of the river. Arista expected to have the enemy fort surrounded by midday on May 1. With cannon in place to fire upon the earthworks, infantry troops positioned to prevent an escape, and Torrejón's brigade guarding against the arrival of reinforcements, he believed he might be able to force an American surrender.[55] More likely was the possibility of an armed response. In a letter to the minister of war, Arista conceded that the cornered Americans might respond by bombarding the buildings and people of Matamoros, but he expressed hope that Taylor would instead turn his attention to confronting the Mexican troops who had ensnared him. "I wish to find more fruitful results in the open field," he wrote. "This is the best means of reducing bloodshed and ensuring that the proud Americans will come to know the valor of our soldiers."[56]

At the very least, the Americans finally knew that the Mexicans intended to fight. News of the fate of Thornton's dragoons slowly trickled into Taylor's camp. The first report of the incident came from Chepito Sandoval, who appeared in the early hours of April 26. In advance of the multiple accounts to follow, he provided his version of the events of the morning: he had received word of a force ahead, he advised Thornton to turn back, Thornton pressed on without him. He also explained that he soon heard shots in the distance, hid in the brush, and short time later observed a large body of Mexican lancers sweep past, apparently in search of any dragoons who might have escaped. Though he had seen none of the fight, the Mexican guide expressed his certainty that the Americans had been defeated. The sight, several hours later, of a Mexican soldier escorting a US dragoon along the south bank of the river served to reinforce his judgment. When at 2 p.m. Mexican surgeons arrived with several wounded men and a message of explanation from Torrejón, there was no longer any room for doubt. Captain Hardee's report, received on April 27, and Thornton's own version of events, received on April 28, merely filled in the details of the incident.[57]

The realization that war had finally arrived provoked a range of reactions among the US troops. Some felt that the small US force on the Rio Grande was ill-prepared for the threat that now confronted it. "My only regret," wrote Lt. George Meade, "is the Government did not send a large force in the first instance, and overawe the Mexicans. If we were determined to take the country from them, it should have been done in such a manner as to crush at once all hopes of resistance on the part of the Mexicans."[58]

Others, like Captain Hawkins of the 7th Infantry, believed the army had been adequate up to that point, but that Arista's bold move across the river now called for their own commander to be "reinforced with troops sufficient to render his success beyond a doubt." Hawkins was not alone in that opinion, and he noted "a disposition in the army of General Taylor to see some few battalions of New Orleans and Western sharp shooters arriving ... ready for action to help the regulars." Nevertheless, there were some troops that wanted to confront the Mexicans right away. Many in the regular army had seen their organization maligned by an American public that prized the ideal of the citizen-soldier and viewed professional military men as elitist and unnecessary. These soldiers were eager to demonstrate the value of their institution and believed that General Taylor would "disgrace the Army if he [did] not beat back the enemy across the Rio Grande before [the volunteers] arrived."[59]

Those who wanted to "beat back the enemy" faced a significant obstacle; they had no idea where that enemy could be found. The Americans assumed that Torrejón had continued eastward from Carricitos and that he was preparing for some sort of follow-up to his victory, but US scouts could not determine with any certainty his exact location or his objective. Late in the evening of April 28, Taylor sent Capt. George McCall and seventy-seven men up the road toward Point Isabel in search of the enemy. The party rode all night and followed a circuitous twenty-mile route through fields, resacas, and areas of dense chaparral, but eventually returned without locating the Mexican camp. A small party of Texans rode into Taylor's camp on the twenty-ninth and reported having seen signs that troops had marched through an area eighteen miles to the north, but they too failed to spot the Mexican force. Without solid facts, the Americans could only guess where Torrejón had gone and could make no plans for a decisive strike.[60]

This uncertainty also reminded the US troops of their isolation in a hostile territory. Although the fortifications on the river and at Point Isabel now provided safe haven for the soldiers and boosted their sense of security, these remained small islands in a dangerous sea. The untimely deaths of Colonel Cross and Lieutenant Porter and the capture of Thornton's dragoons had already demonstrated that security extended a very short distance beyond the fort walls. "General Taylor's efforts were entirely confined to maintaining his own forces, his depots and lines of communication," Capt. William Montgomery of the 8th Infantry later recalled. "Beyond that, he was wholly unable to give protection to the western frontier five miles from his own camp; nay, I might say, for a much less direction." Now, with a large force massed somewhere near on the north bank of the river, that zone of protection shrank even further, and the troops grew warier of moving beyond their two strongholds.[61]

Many even expected an attack on one of those forts and viewed the lightly defended supply depot at Point Isabel as the most likely target. Their opinion seemed to be validated when on April 29 a scout arrived from the coast and reported that the attack had already been attempted. The witness, a nephew of Chepito's, said that two regiments of Mexican infantry, supported by cavalry, had attacked the depot and been cut to shreds by Major Monroe's artillery. Shortly afterwards the troops would learn that the assault had never occurred. Even so, the alarm left a lingering concern that Arista might capture the coastal fort and effectively sever the connection to supplies coming from New Orleans and the rest of the United States.[62]

A more immediate fear was that the Mexican forces might already be in control of the Point Isabel-to-Matamoros road. This twenty-seven-mile-long road connecting the two American forts had been a point of concern long before the Mexicans crossed the river. Where the route crossed the open prairie near the coast, a mounted force of moderate size could quickly surround and overtake wagons. As the trail squeezed into the chaparral, travelers became vulnerable to foes lying in ambush in the dense growth. In the preceding weeks, Taylor had taken steps to guard against attacks. He moved his supplies in large convoys of wagons under the watchful eyes of heavily armed teamsters and escorted by companies of dragoons. He also ordered labor crews to systematically harvest trees that grew within ten feet of the roadway, a practical step that provided wood for the camps, widened the road to the Point, and removed brush that might hide ambushes. He had even recruited a party of twenty-six Texas Rangers, under the command of Capt. Samuel Walker, to set up a small camp midway along the route and conduct daily scouting missions to ensure that the way was clear. But these measures were clearly insufficient to meet the threat of the large, organized army that now occupied a position near that route. With General Torrejón somewhere in the vicinity, convoys came to a halt and the riverside fort across from Matamoros was largely cut off.[63]

Supplies became an immediate issue. General Taylor had a number of artillery pieces at the fort—four 18-pounder siege guns and two batteries of four 6-pounder field pieces—but believed he needed additional guns to ward off attack. He also had limited ammunition on hand and needed to supplement his arsenal with matériel recently off-loaded at the Point. Food was an even greater concern. The force of more than three thousand troops consumed an immense quantity of provisions, in the form of both government requisitions and purchases from local ranchers. Now that war had begun, the local market for meat, milk, and eggs disappeared, and the Point Isabel road was the only supply line for food. With this route blocked, men who had enjoyed several months of abundance suddenly found themselves with enough rations for only a few days.[64]

And there was no question that the route was closed. On the morning of April 28, a party of more than two hundred Mexican horsemen swept into the camp of the Texas Rangers near the Resaca San Antonio, surprising the fifteen men at their small stockade. The rangers' captain, Samuel Walker, was not present, and the fifteen novice recruits holding the stockade were completely dumbfounded by the attack. In a brief exchange of fire, at least five were killed. The others fled into the chaparral, some without clothes or shoes. Walker reported the incident to Taylor later that day. Taylor was disappointed by the poor showing of the rangers, but the incident did at least confirm that a substantial Mexican force occupied the road between the river and the Point. If the US general and his troops hoped to gain access to the supplies stored at their depot, they would have to fight their way past this army. With supplies dwindling, Taylor resolved to do that as soon as possible.[65]

The general announced his intentions on May 1. Although his riverside fort was by no means complete, even after days of reminding work crews of the "great importance of bringing the field work into a state of defense," he determined that the post was secure enough to leave in the charge of a small garrison. He selected Maj. Jacob Brown and the 7th Infantry to hold the post, supported by Company F of the 2nd Artillery and Company E of the 3rd Artillery. Captain Mansfield of the Corps of Engineers also remained behind to oversee final touches to the structure. All other units and the teamsters with their wagons were ordered to prepare to march for the Point "as soon as practicable" after 2 p.m. They would march forward in a column with companies of dragoons occupying the front, rear, and middle and infantry and artillery regiments interspersed in between. The supply wagons, several hundred in number, were distributed along the length of the procession to afford them the greatest amount of protection in the event of a fight. Capt. George McCall and his scout party would depart in advance, scouring the brush along the route for signs of enemy troops.[66]

Taylor believed that an ambush awaited. He took precautions to speed the march through the brush as much as possible. All women, servants, and nonessential support personnel remained in the relative safety of the earthwork, and the soldiers left their excess baggage behind, carrying only their weapons and ammunition. The general also issued specific orders for response to an attack, including that "the alternate companies of the battalions near the point of attack will face to the right and left and enter the chaparral deployed as skirmishers, driving back any force they may meet."[67]

With these words firmly implanted in their minds, the troops completed their final shifts working on the fort walls and gathered at the appointed hour. At 3 p.m. they marched past their earthworks—where the men of the 7th Infantry continued to labor on one unfinished wall—and set out toward Point Isabel and the anticipated encounter with the Mexican Army.[68]

The Mexicans had intended to offer that fight. After reaching the Matamoros-to-Santa Isabel road on April 27, Torrejón had proceeded with plans to establish control of the route. As a first step, on the morning of May 28 the general dispatched some of Antonio Canales' auxiliars to attack a small Texas Ranger corral in near the Resaca San Antonio. Capt. Rafael Quintero led the assault, quickly killing and dispersing the Texans. The man who had so loudly protested the orders to fall back from the Arroyo Colorado in March was the only Mexican casualty, receiving a wound to his arm in the melee. Having removed the only obvious threat, Torrejón then proceeded to the watering hole at Palo Alto, about two miles to the southwest, and established camp. This point, roughly halfway between the two US outposts, was an ideal location from which to keep watch over both American forts and intercept any American wagon trains that ventured along the roadway.[69]

Next Arista moved into action. Upon receiving notification that Torrejón had occupied the roadway, the general-in-chief sent additional troops from Matamoros to the Rancho Longoreño, about eight miles downstream. On April 30 he ordered the 1st Brigade, consisting of the Sapper Company, 2nd Light Infantry, 1st and 6th Infantries, 10th Battalion, and Tampico Coast Guard Battalion and including four pieces of artillery, to ford the waterway at the nearby crossing. Once these units had secured the opposite bank, the remaining brigade, composed of the 4th Infantry, the Puebla Battalion, and the 8th Artillery would follow. These two brigades would then unite with Torrejón to engage the ill-provisioned and lightly armed US troops as they made their march toward the Frontón.[70]

The plan started to go awry as the troops began their passage at Longoreño. In an effort to prevent the Americans from discovering this activity, the Mexicans had elected not to send troop boats to the site via the river, but instead to load them on wagons in Matamoros and carry them to the crossing overland. By following a long, roundabout course, they prevented the Americans from spotting the movement, but the jostling on rutted paths caused considerable damage to the launches. When they were placed on the river on the morning of May 30, they immediately filled with water and began to sink. The troops devoted the next several hours to caulking and tarring the boats to make them seaworthy, and it was not until late afternoon that the first passengers made their way across the Bravo. With only three small boats available for the operation, the ferrying of the 1st Brigade continued late into the night.[71]

Problems continued the following day, May 1. General Ampudia and his brigade had planned to move to the left bank of the river at 7:30 a.m., but lingering issues with the boats delayed the start of the crossing until almost midday. Frustrated by the slow progress, Ampudia wrote to Arista asking for another boat to be sent down the river to Longoreño. He also requested that the general-in-chief himself make an appearance to help speed the process along. The boat never arrived, but Arista did and found his troops in complete disarray, with cargo and supplies strewn along the left bank and many troops and much of the artillery still stranded along the right. He and his officers eventually established order, but it still took until midafternoon for all the soldiers and equipment to complete the crossing. At about that time a party of scouts, commanded by Rafael Quintero, arrived to pass on news from Chepito that the Americans were preparing to march toward the coast. The Mexicans hurried to intercept, but by the time the two brigades were ready to move, Taylor and his troops had already taken up their march and had a three-hour head start along the road to the Frontón.[72]

The Americans had not only escaped Arista, they eluded General Torrejón and his troops as well. On April 29, Arista had ordered the troops positioned at Palo Alto to relocate to the river opposite Longoreño in advance of the crossing. Activity in the US riverside fort raised concerns that the Americans had discovered the Mexican movement and planned to contest the river crossing. The general-in-chief wanted Torrejón to provide protection against a possible attack. He expected the cavalry brigade to remain only long enough to protect the early stages of the passage, when the Mexican troops were most vulnerable, then quickly resume its vigil on the roadway. But the chaotic situation on the riverbanks stymied this plan and forced Torrejón to offer protection for the duration of the crossing. As Taylor left his earthworks, Torrejón remained at Longoreño with the rest of Arista's army.[73]

Unaware that the route lay open before them, the US soldiers marched cautiously down the narrow roadway. They entered the thick chaparral to the north of their fort with the expectation that shots might be fired at any moment, but eight hours later, at about 2 a.m., they reached the broad coastal prairie without interference. With no sign of enemy troops in the vicinity, General Taylor allowed the soldiers to pause near the Palo Alto watering hole, just a short distance from the point where Torrejón would have waited if he had not been called away to Longoreño. Exhausted from a twelve-mile march on the heels of a day of hard labor on the earthworks, all without pausing to eat, the exhausted men seized the opportunity to sleep. "I never was so fatigued before," Lt. John Peck wrote in his diary. "When we stopped men would drop down and fall asleep in the road. I slept in the road and without anything over me, forgetting Mexicans and snakes." Neither attacked, and after three hours of rest the army was on the move again. Four hours later, on the morning of May 2, the entire US Army and its train of wagons entered the walls of the Point Isabel depot without encountering a single Mexican soldier.[74]

Arista's force had tried to head off the march. As soon as he learned that the Americans had left their post, the Mexican general rushed his troops to the Frontón road to try to catch up with the rear units of the US column. But the Mexican Army was too far behind; the path before it remained empty. As night fell, Arista hoped that darkness might slow Taylor's march and allow his own troops to gain ground. Toward this end, he ordered a party of one hundred lancers and the mounted riflemen of the Villas del Norte to press ahead along secondary trails in an effort to reach Palo Alto ahead of the American force. These men would "entertain the enemy and keep them in reach" long enough for the main Mexican force to catch up the next morning.[75] The troops sped to the appointed site and arrived before daybreak, but were just minutes too slow. The US troops had already aroused themselves from their uneasy slumber and moved on.

This unfortunate timing ended any chance of halting Taylor's drive to the Frontón. By the time Arista's troops reached Palo Alto, the Americans were near their coastal base. The Mexican general-in-chief abandoned his pursuit and established his camp at last near the watering hole. Unable to use their weapons of choice, the Mexicans launched a verbal assault. The American "fugitives," claimed the Matamoros newspaper *Boletín del Norte*, had escaped the Mexican force only because they had flung themselves toward the Frontón in "complete flight and terror . . . in order to close themselves off and avoid an encounter." Arista had hoped for an honorable fight, but "since fear has wings," General Taylor had chosen instead to flee.[76] These words were an effort to reclaim some dignity in the aftermath of a strategic debacle, but they rang hollow. Arista and every officer in his army knew that Taylor had achieved a victory simply by avoiding combat. And in its failure to contain the Americans in their riverside camp, the Army of the North had squandered an important opportunity to gain the upper hand in the early stage of hostilities.

CHAPTER 6
Strategy

★

WHEN THEY REACHED Point Isabel at midday on May 2, the US soldiers reacted variously to reaching the end of their tense but uneventful race to the coast. Capt. William S. Henry welcomed the end of a march that he viewed as "one of the most fatiguing I have ever endured." Surgeon Madison Mills expressed outrage that he and the others were forced to undertake such a "harassing" and "unnecessary" maneuver. Lt. Samuel French welcomed the opportunity to rest again near the shores of the Gulf, but he recognized that by leaving six hundred men behind, Taylor had guaranteed the need for a return trip along the dangerous Matamoros road. For his part, Lt. George Meade revealed a touch of frustration that the inevitable battle had been delayed once again, "without seeing a soul. But . . . the war has commenced and cannot now be finished without fighting." Underlying all these statements was a prevailing sense that the march had served little purpose and that only the venue had changed.[1]

But in reality, the move created a dramatic transformation of the standoff in the Rio Grande delta. For weeks, the United States and Mexico had been engaged in a confrontation of bluster and posturing, their actions guided by politics, passion, and necessity, but very little by real military strategy. Now, as Meade had noted, war was underway and the armies were, at last, assembled in force and in proximity and on the same side of the river. The American and Mexican troops alike understood that the approaching confrontation would test both sides. But the period of inaction and delay had not completely ended. In the brief lull afforded by the near miss of May 1, Generals Arista and Taylor both had several days to ponder their strengths and weaknesses, consider their next moves, and decide how best to employ the manpower and armaments of their respective forces.

The most commonly remarked difference between the two armies was size. Arista never received more than a small fraction of the troops he had requested for his mission, but he nevertheless commanded an appreciably larger army than his American counterpart. When the last companies of soldiers arrived on April 24, about fifty-six hundred men filled the ranks of Mexico's Army of the North. Of that number, about two thousand remained on the south bank of the Río Bravo, guarding the various river crossings and manning the defenses of Matamoros as ordered by Mexico City. Some forty-two hundred had crossed or were just crossing the river. A few hundred, mostly from units of the Villas del Norte, served as scouts or occupied approaches to river crossings along the north bank. The rest would be available for a fight when it came. General Taylor on the other hand had a rather small force. Having arrived on the Rio Grande with fewer than four thousand troops, he endured a month of desertions, illnesses, expirations of service, and officer resignations that had reduced his force to around three thousand men. Of those, about six hundred now found themselves bottled up inside the riverside fort and an additional one hundred formed the garrison on the Point, leaving around twenty-three hundred for operations between the two posts.[2]

Nevertheless, the Mexican troop advantage was far less marked than has often been stated in historical accounts. Following the campaign, US soldiers reveled in their success, claiming that they had vanquished an army of six to eight thousand men. No doubt some soldiers deliberately inflated these numbers, but many genuinely believed them, and Arista appears to have been their source. While Mexican leaders enjoyed a steady stream of spy reports from the Mexican merchants who infiltrated the US camp, Taylor found the flow of information to be decidedly one directional. "With all of the General's effort to obtain information," wrote Lt. George Deas, "[the enemy's] exact numbers and their strength in artillery could not be arrived at."[3] Lack of facts led to calculations based on rumor and, frequently, on trickery perpetrated by Arista. In autumn of 1845, for example, traders working for Arista warned the Army of Occupation that thousands of Mexican troops were converging on Matamoros—this as the general-in-chief was begging Mexico City for reinforcements. After the Americans established their camp on the Rio Grande, Mexican troops repeatedly marched through the streets of Matamoros in long circular parades to create the impression that a massive force had mobilized in the city. Even crossing the Río Bravo on April 24 involved an elaborate feint to the east of Matamoros, designed to convince Taylor that this phantom army had moved north of the river. Arista undoubtedly sought a psychological edge by convincing the Americans that they would be far outnumbered. And he

General Mariano Arista. *From Albert C. Ramsey,* The Other Side, *1850.*

was successful in his deception. On the eve of battle, Taylor and his troops believed that they were about to face a force two times larger than the one that actually awaited them.

Not only did General Arista lack an overpowering edge in manpower, he also feared that troop numbers might shift quickly and dramatically in Taylor's favor. The reinforcements that Taylor requested in the immediate aftermath of the Carricitos skirmish had not yet arrived, but some four thousand Louisiana volunteers were converging on New Orleans and were prepared to ship out toward Point Isabel. Though these troops would probably include many raw recruits, they would nevertheless provide a vital boost to American manpower. They would arrive quickly, something that could not be said of Mexican troops. Officials in Mexico City continued to offer vague promises of additional soldiers and supplies, but it had become abundantly clear that few reinforcements were actually available. Moreover, even if a force set out immediately, it could not hope to reach Matamoros in time to influence any opening battles. With US naval ships controlling the Gulf coast and the mouth of the Rio Grande, the only options for reinforcements involved grueling overland marches across Mexico's rugged highlands or steamy, tropical lowlands. "Arista is positioned on an immense field confronting the Army of the United States and the entire strength of that republic," warned the editor of Mexico City's *Monitor Republicano.* "With a force that is inferior in equipment and perhaps in numbers, and that must wait up to two months to receive aid from the capital, he is trying to draw into battle an army that can be supplied or protected in 50 hours."[4] Though somewhat overstated—the Mexican Army was not so small and travel from New Orleans required five to seven days—the point highlighted an essential truth: to make the most of his limited advantage in numbers, Arista needed to act decisively and quickly.

As he proceeded, however, Arista could not fail to note the other point made in the *Monitor.* In all categories except numbers, the Army of the North was indeed inferior to the Army of Occupation. Tales of the Mexican Army's strength were as fictional as the inflated troop figures. Weaknesses riddled all parts of the operation.

The problems started at the top echelons of the military. Although the Mexican Army of the mid-nineteenth century had adopted the elaborate uniforms and colorful trappings of the European martial tradition, its leaders had never established the same level of professionalism and *esprit de corps* as their Old World counterparts. Instead, Mexican generals all too frequently viewed the forces under their command as tools that could be used to press forward their preferred political ideologies—often by fighting the troops of fellow generals with opposing ideologies. Centralists, who favored a strong national government, frequently marched to the periphery of the country to combat federalist troops, who fought to retain autonomy at the state or regional level. Liberals, often but not always federalists, were willing to use military forces to fight for free speech, democratic reform, and freedom of religion, while conservatives used them to defend the traditional powers of the aristocracy and the Catholic church. After winning in battle or seizing power, generals and civil authorities generously doled out commissions and promotions to the soldiers who had supported them, a process which further politicized the military and created a system that valued personal loyalty over rank, experience, and the national interest. The shortcomings of such a system were manifest when the conservative, monarchist general Mariano Paredes easily persuaded other officers to lead their troops against the moderate Pres. José Joaquín Herrera instead of marching northward to bolster Arista's efforts at national defense.[5]

As he waited on the field of Palo Alto, Arista was concerned about the political differences and divided loyalties of the leaders in his command. The Army of the North was fortunate in having a number of highly qualified officers, many with military experience dating back to the War of Independence. But it also included leaders from across the spectrum of political views. At one extreme, Pedro de Ampudia, Anastacio Torrejón, Rómulo Díaz de la Vega, and Tómas Requena supported conservative centralists, with Torrejón and Ampudia even backing attempts to install a monarch in Mexico City. At the other, Antonio Canales of the Villas del Norte was a lawyer from the northern state of Tamaulipas who first entered military service by leading an effort to split northern states from Mexico and create an independent Republic of the Rio Grande. In the middle were Francisco Mejía and Arista himself. Both were moderate liberals who supported central control but had spent much of their careers on the northern frontier, where they had learned to sympathize with federalists who believed that Mexico City was unresponsive to their needs. It was now Arista's duty to insure that this collection of officers could work together against the US forces.[6]

There were some positive signs that this could happen. Many of those in Arista's command had a history of discord and conflict of interest, but had found ways to overcome their disputes. Generals Mejía and Díaz de la Vega admitted to personal disputes over some unspecified issue in their past, but when the US Army began its advance in 1845, they quickly patched up their differences and came to an agreement on leadership. Ampudia, who had been actively engaged in the campaigns against the Texas rebellion, frowned on Canales and his federalism, especially the frontier leader's efforts to enlist the support of Texans in the separatist movement of 1840. Nevertheless, the general had welcomed Canales' assistance when the two combined forces to defeat a Texan expedition at Mier in 1842. Arista also had personal experience with reconciliation. In 1839, he had commanded the centralist forces arrayed against the Republic of the Rio Grande and had personally delivered a crushing blow to rebel forces fighting under Canales' command in a battle not far from Palo Alto. But the two leaders had quickly set aside personal disagreements to fight a common enemy in the form of marauding Comanches. In 1841, just months after the Republic of the

Rio Grande collapsed, they had already joined forces in a campaign against the Indian attacks. These examples of setting aside differences to face a common enemy offered some promise for the struggle to come.[7]

Nevertheless, there was also some cause for unease. Although the leaders of the Army of the North spoke publicly about cooperation and harmony, an undercurrent of discord existed between the officers of the original units of that force and those of the new regiments that had recently arrived as reinforcements. Part of the problem appears to have been the unified stand of Arista, Díaz de la Vega, Mejía, and Canales in their refusal to endorse Paredes' move to seize the presidency. It was a decision of principle and an effort to stress the importance of sending troops to the frontier, but men like Generals Ampudia and Torrejón, loyal supporters of Paredes, viewed it only as a rejection of the new regime. They arrived in Matamoros with subtle doubts about the reliability and loyalty of their northern peers—sentiments that spread to the subaltern officers of their commands.

This doubt developed into a larger schism when the secretary of war suddenly selected Arista to supersede Ampudia as general-in-chief. Ampudia might have been willing to forgive past political differences, but he viewed his demotion as a personal affront. Although he had served without incident in the northern army under the command of Arista for extended periods after the Texas Revolution, he now gave in to resentment. He was unwilling defer to his fellow officer and protested bitterly to his superiors in Mexico City. When his complaints went unanswered, he encouraged the officers loyal to him to rise up and resist the transfer of power. They did not, probably for fear of raising doubts about their own dedication to Paredes. Ampudia at last accepted his role as second-in-command, but did so gracelessly, continuously reminding others that he remained the better man to lead the Army of the North. In addition to constantly questioning Arista's strategy and planning, Ampudia impugned the general's patriotism and revived tales of his treachery. These actions are hard to document; the charges were not stated openly or formally until after the campaign had come to its tragic conclusion, but damage was being done. Subaltern officers in Ampudia's and Torrejón's commands, already aware of Arista's differences with President Paredes, were willing to believe rumors of treason. In response, Mejía, Díaz de la Vega, and Canales, who had become integrally associated with Arista through their unwillingness to endorse Paredes, were obliged to defend their general-in-chief to preserve their own honor.[8]

It was the botched attempt to trap General Taylor's troops in their riverside fort that first openly revealed the split between the Arista and Ampudia factions. The slow

General Pedro de Ampudia. *From Albert C. Ramsey,* The Other Side, *1850.*

and confused river crossing that afforded the Americans time to escape to the coast became the source of finger- pointing and criticism. Ampudia and his supporters denounced Arista for a failure of planning, arguing that the general-in-chief should have focused his efforts on capturing the Frontón. They also faulted him for logistical problems that had left them without the proper resources to cross the Río Bravo quickly. Arista and his defenders responded by pointing out the disorganization of the troops on the riverbanks and denounced Ampudia, the man who had directed the crossing, for a failure of execution. The difficulties had not produced disastrous results and the divide in the ranks was not yet irreparable. Nevertheless, as Arista plotted battle with the United States, he must have harbored doubts about the reliability of a good part of his command. Indeed, he likely recognized that some of his most dangerous resistance might be found on his own side of the battle lines.[9]

By comparison, divisions within the US ranks were little more than petty squabbles. General Taylor had endured challenges to his leadership, but the angry departure of William Worth and the murder of Colonel Cross effectively removed the two highest-profile malcontents from the Army of Occupation. As the only remaining general officer in the Army of Occupation, whether by brevet or formal commission, Taylor had no real challengers for command of the army and faced none of the intrigue that ran rampant in the Mexican ranks. What dissention there was, was mild. Taylor's junior officers regularly pointed out that "he knew little of tactics, rarely put any military evolution in practice, and had not the confidence of the army like [Generals] Worth and Scott." In their letters to friends and family, some were quick to criticize his limitations and his orders. But the grievances remained private matters, and none of Taylor's subordinates actively broadcast their disagreement or sought to undermine his authority.[10]

Actually, most of Taylor's subordinates appeared to like and respect him. This was in part because the officers of the line appreciated their commander's style. The aging, unaffected general projected an image of simplicity, calm, and confidence that earned him the nickname "Old Rough and Ready" and endeared him to even his severest critics. At the same time, he benefitted from the brilliance and support of Capt. William Wallace Smith Bliss, his adjutant and future son-in-law, who deftly translated Taylor's words into carefully crafted letters and ably managed relations with other officers. Bliss's military bearing and efficiency lent an air of authority to the homespun leader and helped inspire confidence at all levels. It was sometimes at the urging of Bliss that Taylor so willingly listened to the advice of his subordinates. While the old backwoods fighter had his own ideas and ways of doing things, he was never intransigent and showed respect for the informed opinions of knowledgeable juniors. Taylor consequently inspired a startling level of loyalty. Critics like the young lieutenant George Meade described the general as lacking in judgment, "irritable and deficient in command," with "prominent defects" and showing "utter ignorance" of basic military strategy. But in almost the same breath, he described the commander as a "gallant, brave

General Zachary Taylor. *From Edward S. Ellis,* Library of American History, *1919.*

old man" and "the best general I have yet served under and as good as any I know of at present in our service."[11]

Taylor, for his part, put great trust in his officers. Many in the higher echelons of the Army of Occupation, like Taylor himself, were closing out long careers in the army. Some, like Capt. Martin Scott of the 5th Infantry, had fought in the War of 1812 and then toiled for decades in remote posts on the frontier. Others, like Maj. Samuel Ringgold of the light artillery, had devoted years to studying their craft, developing new techniques and perfecting training in preparation for some future conflict. Those conflicts had never arrived, and men who might otherwise have become generals and colonels found themselves mired in the middle ranks of the service. Behind this old guard, a new generation of highly trained US Military Academy graduates crowded the lower ranks. The US Congress had established the school at West Point, New York, in 1802, to fill a void in military knowledge and provide the leadership lacking in the early army. The school had been training officers since that time, but really reached its stride in the 1830s and 1840s, producing lieutenants with a thorough background in military history, engineering, and tactics. All they lacked was the experience that was so plentiful in the older generation. "A better army, man for man, probably never faced an enemy than the one commanded by General Taylor," wrote Ulysses S. Grant, looking back on the army that he had served as a newly commissioned second lieutenant. Taylor recognized the quality of the young officers' training and therefore sought their counsel and gave fair consideration to their opinions.[12]

The American public did not unequivocally share Taylor's admiration of his officers, who, as they prepared for a conflict with Mexico, also found themselves under assault on the home front. "Our military service was then at the lowest ebb of popular favor," recalled Alexander Hays, "for former services had been forgotten, and congressional demagogues had lately thundered forth to the nation their ignorance of 'epauletted loafers.'" West Point became a focus of this assault. Critics of the Military Academy viewed it not as a training ground for talented officers but as an elitist haven for the sons of the rich and powerful. Cadets were granted little more respect when they graduated into the army. In a nation that treasured the image of the citizen-soldier—the common man who took up arms to defend his country in times of need—the troops of a regular army were viewed with suspicion. Professional officers of that force could almost be classified as un-American. The generation of peace that had followed the war of 1812 had merely reinforced the image of the military and its training ground as unnecessary features of an American republic. Consequently, while dozens of West Point graduates took up positions near the Rio Grande, legislators in Washington debated a bill to shutter the academy after the graduation of its current crop of cadets.[13]

These attacks strengthened the resolve of the army officers on the Rio Grande. Bonds forged at West Point and isolated frontier posts created a degree of camaraderie and mutual respect, but a shared sense of under-appreciation inspired a much stronger esprit de corps. Like the Mexican Army, that of the United States had its share of factions and fissures. Officers differed in their political outlooks. Some supported the war with Mexico while others vehemently opposed it. Many nurtured personal grudges against their peers and superiors. Dozens of formal complaints lodged during and after the march from Corpus Christi remained unresolved. Nevertheless, the men shared a desire to prove their value to the country. When it came time for a fight, they were prepared to set aside differences and petty squabbles and present a solid front against the Mexicans. In part, of course, their motives were selfish: most recognized that cooperation improved their odds of success and created opportunities for the personal laurels and advancement that had eluded some of them for so long. But they were also determined to bring honor to the two institutions that had shaped their lives. By uniting their efforts, they hoped to emerge victorious, win public approval, and bring glory to the endangered Military Academy and the much-maligned regular army.[14]

To accomplish these goals, Taylor and his officers looked with some hesitation toward the thousands of common soldiers who filled the lower ranks. If West Point graduates were children of privilege, soldiers of the line occupied the opposite end of the social hierarchy. In the mid-nineteenth century, the United States had no military draft or legislation that compelled men to serve in its army. Officially, military service was entirely voluntary. In reality, many of the private soldiers of the army had been forced into service by circumstance and necessity. Military officials screened out known felons, drunkards, and miscreants in the recruiting process but still ended up with a force filled with petty criminals evading prosecution, debtors avoiding creditors, and social outcasts with nowhere else to go. Rushing off to distant duty, often under false names and one step ahead of their troubles, these men were frequently scorned, sometimes justifiably, by civilians and officers alike.[15] When soldiers like Grant spoke in glowing terms of their army, they commonly referred to themselves and their fellow commissioned officers who formed the backbone of the force, not the motley humanity that made up its body.

Despite the obvious drawbacks involved in leading such troops, the officers of the Army of Occupation also had reasons to be optimistic about the men under their command. The soldiers of the US Army were no worse and often far better than those of any other national military of the day. Moreover, the regimentation and rigor of military life forged true soldiers of many of these men. Although many never adapted and sought escape through alcohol or desertion, others thrived in the disciplined environment and meant to use the experience as a stepping-stone to success in other trades. Some viewed the army as their calling and found themselves enlisting for multiple five-year terms. Often they were joined by experienced veterans of wars in Europe, career professionals who sought to ply their trade in the United States now that their former homelands had entered an era of relative peace. Through constant drilling, service, and discipline, this collection of individuals developed into a skilled and reliable fighting force. When these troops moved into Texas in 1845, longtime veterans insisted that "the soldiers of the 'Army of Occupation,' in discipline, military skill, and martial bearing, were not inferior to the choicest troops that rallied around the eagles of Napoleon."[16]

Some doubts remained. US soldiers had honed their experience mainly by skirmishing against Seminoles in the swamps of Florida or defending border outposts in the forests and thickets of the western frontier. Except for a few of the foreign veterans, they were much less familiar with large-scale army maneuvers and the European open-field tactics that they were likely to face when confronting Mexican troops. The winter sojourn at Corpus Christi had provided some reassurance. After months of drilling on the plains adjoining the Nueces River, the men had mastered the basics of operating in brigades, and their progress provided General Taylor with a degree of confidence as he prepared to put their skills to the test.

It was no secret that the foot soldiers of the Mexican Army assembled on the Río Bravo could not match this level of skill. "The Mexicans have it in their power to concentrate a large number of men at Matamoros," noted the editors of the *Richmond Whig* in early May, "but they ought by no means to be called soldiers. They have neither the equipment, the discipline, nor the moral force of well-organized troops." The problems with the Mexican Army began with the system used to fill the ranks. For years, Mexico relied on the *leva*—a type of conscription that involved emptying prisons of criminals or simply rounding up vagrants on the streets. Citizens of the lower classes unlucky enough to be caught in a sweep, suddenly found themselves facing ten years of military service. "There is scarcely a day that droves of these miserable and more than half naked wretches are not seen thus chained together and marching through the streets to the barracks," wrote Waddy Thompson, who observed the process during his tenure as a US envoy to Mexico. Efforts to replace this oppressive system with an annual draft lottery among eligible males largely failed. Loopholes in the law permitted wealthy draftees to buy their way out of the obligation, and the dreaded sweeps continued. The result was an army filled with unwanted and unwilling soldiers who resisted commands, rebelled or, more commonly, deserted when the first opportunity presented itself.[17]

Many of these troops were also Indians, a situation that added another dimension to the personnel problem. The large, insular native population had never been incorporated into the Spanish system except as cheap, tractable labor. This exclusion of Indians continued in independent Mexico, where they served as laborers on *haciendas* or toiled in the mines but otherwise had no role in the social order. Often, their only real interaction with the Mexican state began when military impressment gangs swept into highland villages to haul off eligible men. Unable to speak Spanish and completely unfamiliar with their surroundings or the nation they served, these victims nonetheless became the backbone of the Mexican Army. Despite their origins, many eventually earned praise for their comportment. "As soldiers they are really quite good, because—aside from not being cowards—they have great endurance in the campaign," wrote politician Manuel Otero. "They have shown that they can cross hundreds of leagues over bad roads, barefoot, badly clothed and worse fed, and this without complaining or committing any notable act of insubordination." Nevertheless, Otero questioned the limits of their loyalty. "These Indians have little or no conception of nationality, and no interest whatever in maintaining an order of things in which they figure only as beasts of burden," he added. He therefore found it difficult to trust that they would willingly lay their lives on the line to defend that order. General Arista undoubtedly shared this concern as he made final preparations for battle.[18]

With proper preparation in arms and discipline, these Mexican troops might have overcome the doubts that surrounded them, but many soldiers received only the most rudimentary training. Mexico had no formal program for preparing its conscripts. Moreover, the officer corps, filled with political appointees, generally had neither the knowledge nor the inclination to develop advanced skills in the ranks. "Drilling consists mainly in teaching them to march in column through the streets," wrote Waddy Thompson, who also described the limits of this approach to preparation. "Their military bands are good, and the men learn to march indifferently well—but only indifferently well—they put their feet down as if they were feeling for the place, and do not step with that jaunty, erect and graceful air which is so beautiful in well drilled troops. As to the wheelings of well-trained troops, like the opening and shutting of a gate, or the prompt and exact execution of other evolutions, they know nothing about them."

The inadequate training seen on the parade ground frequently revealed itself on the battlefield as well, and soldiers struggled with basic maneuvers while under fire. Unimpressed by what he saw, Thompson closed his scathing assessment with the observation, "I do not think that any commander could perform a tactical evolution with five thousand Mexican troops." General Arista, encamped on the prairie near the Río Bravo, now faced a situation where he would put that opinion to the test.[19]

Arista could not have full confidence in the training and loyalty of his men, but he and his fellow officers consoled themselves with the observation that the US Army also harbored its share of reluctant troops. They had seen throughout the early weeks of the American occupation the dozens of enlisted men who had fled the US camp, crossed the river, and sought refuge in Matamoros. Although Taylor had checked the drain on his troop strength by ordering his pickets to fire on deserters, the initial flood of refugees had left an impression in Matamoros. The deserters, with their varied tales of woe, complaints of mistreatment, and insistence that they had no quarrel with Mexico, convinced the leaders of Mexico's Army of the North that the American Army was on the verge of mutiny and that opportunities existed to exploit this supposed widespread discontent in the ranks.

Of particular interest were the foreign-born troops of General Taylor's force. In the years before the dispute with Mexico, thousands of Europeans had fled the famines, oppression, and political turmoil in their homelands, and sought a new start in the United States. But all too often, new starts proved hard to come by. Unable to find work or a place in American society, many men turned to the one institution that would accept them: the military. By 1846, immigrant soldiers made up more than half of all enlistments and a high percentage of almost every company. George Ballentine, himself an English-born soldier, noted that the typical military company of the era "consisted of 60 men, including non-commissioned officers and privates; of these 2 were English, 4 Scotch, 7 Germans, 16 Americans, and the remainder Irish." The Irish and Germans in particular were relatively content during peacetime, but as they marched toward an increasingly certain war, some balked at risking their lives for their newly adopted country. The deserters who swam the Rio Grande to escape service included a sizeable number of these foreign-born troops, and Mexican officials in Matamoros believed that their discontent was characteristic of the immigrant soldiers in the Army of Occupation.[20]

Not surprisingly, the Mexican leadership targeted the immigrants in its efforts to encourage dissention and instability in the US force. In the aftermath of the initial wave of American desertions, and while still on the road toward Matamoros, Gen. Pedro de Ampudia issued a proclamation "to the English and Irish under the orders of the American General Taylor," encouraging them to cross the Rio Grande in greater numbers. The message, also directed at the "Germans, French, Poles and individuals of other nations," exhorted the soldiers to "separate yourselves from the Yankees, and do not contribute to defend a robbery and usurpation, which, be assured, the civilized nations of Europe look upon with the utmost indignation."[21] After replacing Ampudia as general-in-chief, Mariano Arista offered a similar plea. He warned the Europeans in the US ranks that "North Americans are ambitious, overbearing, and insolent as a nation, and they will only make use of you as vile tools to carry out their abominable plans of pillage and rapine." He also offered substantial incentives for deserters, including 320 acres of land for any man who left the ranks and adopted the life of a peaceful Mexican citizen.[22]

Few soldiers responded to these calls, but the Mexicans attributed that to fear of being shot while crossing the Rio Grande. General Ampudia in particular believed that if a suitable opportunity arose, a majority of the foreign-born troops would "place their caps on the points of their bayonets as proof that they are our friends" and refuse to fight.[23] He informed the newly arrived General Arista that in the event of a battle, the Mexican troops need only wave a flag toward the American lines and fifteen hundred immigrant soldiers would lay down their weapons and abandon their ranks, leaving the US Army in disarray.[24]

Such scenarios undoubtedly appealed to the Mexicans, but they revealed a lack of understanding of United States enlisted men, both native and foreign-born. Although deserters from the American force probably portrayed themselves as representative of the men they left behind, they were not. Many soldiers did suffer abuses and arbitrary punishments at the hands of officers, and many immigrants did find themselves on the fringe of American society and bore little animus toward Mexico. Nevertheless, this was not necessarily a recipe for mass defections. Enlisted soldiers often found a home in the ranks, and their sense of belonging gave them a surprising capacity to endure the outrages and hardships of army life. And soldiers often understood that faithful military service offered a path toward acceptance and success; they did not wish to abandon this course for the uncertain fate of a deserter.[25] Perhaps equally important, many soldiers saw little south of the Rio Grande to convince them that their lives would become dramatically better by casting their lot with Mexico. On the contrary, as the fear they had felt on first arriving at the river faded, they became increasingly confident that they were better off staying with their regiments and weathering the coming storm. When battle finally came, no soldiers threw down their guns and allied themselves with Mexico.

Even if they did contemplate desertion, the US troops had good reason to hold tight to their weapons, because they were far better than those of their Mexican foes. Both armies relied on the smoothbore musket—a gun that was severely limited in both range and accuracy. Ulysses S. Grant, who wielded one as a young lieutenant in Taylor's force, later summed up the deficiencies of the weapon when he observed that "at the distance of a few hundred yards a man might fire at you all day without your finding it out." Efficiency was further decreased by the complicated and time-consuming steps required to load the guns and prepare their flintlock mechanisms for firing. These limitations dictated that both armies would rely heavily on the battle-line formations and coordinated volleys that increased the effectiveness of their guns.[26]

If the muskets used by Zachary Taylor's army were inefficient, they were at least in good condition—and plentiful. Since the time of independence the United States government had emphasized developing a reliable source of weapons for its military. By the 1840s, two armories—the venerable factory at Springfield, Massachusetts, and a newly established one at Harpers Ferry, Virginia—served this goal, churning out many thousands of firearms each year. Interestingly, starting in 1844 these centers shifted to production of percussion muskets, a new model that used a more efficient cap to spark the firing process. But military officials balked at sending troops to the Rio Grande and a potential war with unfamiliar equipment, and instead furnished them with 1822 and 1835 flintlock models. Dated in technology, these guns were nonetheless in good condition, and there were plentiful interchangeable replacement parts for them. As General Taylor and his soldiers looked toward battle, they could do so with confidence that their weapons were well made and reliable.[27]

Mexican soldiers had no such faith in their firearms. Mexico lacked the industrial capacity to produce guns for its army and turned to Britain to meet its needs. In the decades leading up to the war, Mexico phased out aging Spanish muskets left over from independence wars and replaced them with British "India Pattern" muskets, so named because originally they had been developed for use by the British East India Company. This weapon was reasonably reliable and effective when maintained in good condition, but few guns reached Mexico in that state. The debt-ridden Mexican government could not afford new weapons, opting instead to buy lower-priced guns that had been used previously by the British military. Unfortunately for the Mexican soldiers, Britain had cast off these muskets for good reason. The Mexican soldiers lucky enough to be given a gun at all usually found themselves holding weapons that one US soldier described as "old and worn out, having evidently been condemned as unserviceable in the British Army."[28]

Mexico lacked the parts and technology to repair these guns, so soldiers devised ways to compensate, which often merely compounded the problem. A prime example was the attempt to increase the range of the muskets. Well aware that newer US muskets fired farther than their own worn-out ones, Mexican soldiers often used double charges of gunpowder with each shot loaded. The larger detonations propelled musket balls a greater distance, but often at the cost of decreased accuracy. More significantly, these large charges had an effect on the soldier firing the gun. In the best of circumstances, the heavy load of powder produced a powerful, bruising recoil that would drive the soldier backward with each shot. In more unfortunate cases, igniting the powder might make the weakened barrels of defective guns fail, creating an explosion that might burn or blind the man pulling the trigger. To avoid such problems, Mexican foot soldiers generally fired their guns from hip level, often holding their muskets well away from the body as well. Thus they reduced serious injuries, but they also further reduced the accuracy of their already questionable weapons.[29]

If the muskets in the hands of Mexican infantrymen were old, the cannon used by artillery crews were truly antique. Relics left over from the Spanish colonial era, many of the guns had been produced in Spanish foundries in the 1760s and 1770s and became the property of Mexico when the country achieved independence. These guns had seen heavy service in the wars of independence and in the civil strife that engulfed Mexico in its early national years, and their effectiveness inevitably deteriorated over the decades. These aging tubes also sat on bulky eighteenth-century-style carriages that were troublesome to transport and even more difficult to reposition once placed on a field of battle. Despite these disadvantages, the artillery pieces remained sound weapons and, unlike the muskets, provided reliable service during the course of a fight.[30]

A greater issue for General Arista and his army was the caliber of his cannon. Mexico City had responded to pleas for weaponry by sending several dozen artillery pieces to the theater of war. Transporting these heavy guns across the country's mountainous terrain was an arduous task, however, and only smaller pieces could be carried on the long march from central Mexico. When the troops occupied their camp near the watering hole at Palo Alto, they had no guns larger than 8-pounders—cannons that could fire a projectile of that weight—and far more of their weapons were smaller 4-pounders. Artillery commander Ignacio de Mora y Villareal viewed this situation with concern and dispatched a letter to the secretary of war pleading for a ship loaded with heavy artillery to bolster his armaments. "With a large bombardment cannon (up to 80 pounds) and four 24-pounders we would have a superiority in our position," he wrote, and he expressed confidence that he could pound the Americans into submission within their fortifications. The letter would not reach the capital in advance of the next round of fighting, and that it would have the desired effect was a forlorn hope in any event. With US naval ships in control of the Gulf of Mexico, the Frontón, and the mouth of the Río Bravo, the Ministry of War had no means to get siege guns to Matamoros. Arista could expect no new shipments of artillery and was obliged to develop plans based on the guns already in his arsenal, that is to say, cannons with limited power against earthworks and limited range on a field of battle.[31]

Poor quality gunpowder compounded the shortcomings of the Mexican weapons, especially the cannons. Months before, Mejía had lamented the poor facilities in Matamoros for storing gunpowder, noting that the storage areas were poorly secured and the powder was exposed to the high humidity. This further compromised the powder, which was already notoriously unreliable. For years, the Mexican Army had searched in vain for a favorable source of saltpeter—the potassium nitrate that gives gunpowder its explosive punch. During the Texas Revolution, a bad saltpeter mix had substantially reduced the firing range of Mexican guns in battle, and the problem had not been resolved a decade later. Mexican cannoneers typically addressed this deficiency by doubling the standard powder charge in their guns to extend the distance of their shots. The gains in range, however, came at the expense of accuracy, and Mexican artillerists who generally struggled to reach their targets also found it difficult to aim their shots with any precision.[32]

These deficiencies became all the more significant when Mexican artillerists confronted an efficient and thoroughly modern American cannon corps. For years, US artillery had also languished, its capabilities little better than those of Mexican artillery, until a proactive push for improvement and modernization transformed the stagnant service. In 1835, the War Department announced plans to phase out aging cast-iron cannon barrels and to equip the artillery with newer, bronze tubes. The next year, the army decided to abandon traditional French-style cannon carriages, which had been in use since the War of 1812, in favor of a more modern and mobile English design. By 1840, the nation had committed to a whole new system of field artillery that dictated specific designs for all guns, carriages, and equipment and oversaw the production of that matériel. These Model 1840 guns went into production shortly afterwards, and many of the freshly forged 6-, 12-, and 18-pounder guns found their way to the Rio

Grande in 1846. Charged with reliable powder produced exclusively by the E. I. du Pont de Nemours Company and loaded with an array of solid shot, canister shot, and exploding shell, these guns had an enormous destructive force. Under the command of a dedicated corps of officers who had been trained in the nation's artillery school at Fortress Monroe, Virginia, the cannon were the equal of any artillery in the world.[33]

The portion of this artillery that fell under Taylor's command allowed for a range of military tactics and options. A collection of 18-pounder heavy guns provided him with substantial firepower. Fixed onto the ramparts of his riverside earthworks, these siege guns could hammer the Mexican defenses on the far shore and even reach the distant structures of Matamoros. In a trade of fire, the opposing Mexican guns would have little impact, matching up to these powerful pieces "as a humming bird does with an eagle."[34] The heavy guns could also be fixed onto sturdy carriages to provide service on a field of battle. There, the advantage of destructive force was tempered only by the immobility of the pieces. Once drawn into position by a team of up to twenty oxen, these cumbersome pieces were almost impossible to reposition and had to remain in place for the course of any confrontation. The presence of 6-pounder, horse-drawn light artillery helped to mask this limitation. Not only were these guns significantly more powerful than the smallest of Mexican cannon, they sat on the new, English style, single-stock carriages that enabled cannoneers to change position and location quickly in the course of battle.

The light artillery also benefitted from the detailed instruction and dedicated tutelage of its US founding father, Major Samuel Ringgold. In 1836, while recuperating from illness contracted during the Seminole Wars in Florida, Ringgold crossed the Atlantic and studied European field artillery techniques under experts at the École Polytechnique in Paris and Sandhurst Royal Military College in London. He returned to an army that was in the middle of an artillery renaissance, and in 1838, his expertise made him the natural choice to rewrite the US Army field artillery manual. He also was given the responsibility for organizing a light artillery corps and devoted years of effort to that task, perfecting the European methods he had observed, developing advances in equipment, and honing the skills of his select companies. By 1845, his corps had become so refined in its precise, rapid-movement and rapid-firing techniques that it earned the moniker "Flying Artillery." Deployment to the Rio Grande presented the opportunity for Ringgold and his elite group to finally put their new manual and their years of practice to the test.[35]

A longtime infantry officer, Zachary Taylor may not have had a thorough appreciation of the quality of his cannon corps, but his Mexican counterparts undoubtedly did. Taylor occasionally spoke of the importance of artillery and had taken steps to bolster that wing of his service upon reaching the Río Grande delta, but he continued to put great emphasis on the foot regiments with which he was far more familiar. But Arista and his officers focused on the American artillery as their greatest challenge. As the US cannoneers endured the winter in Corpus Christi, Mexican spies observed their every move, and relayed detailed descriptions of precision drills, rapid maneuvers, and efficient firing. After comparing these skilled men to his own ranks, Mejía concluded that "the artillery that I have at my disposal cannot rival that of the enemy."[36] Two months later, with the US force entrenched on the Río Bravo, Artillery Commander Mora y Villamil noted a disparity in equipment as well. In a letter to the secretary of war in which he detailed the formidable collection of cannons transported by the US troops, he cautioned that "we have the disadvantage in number and caliber of artillery." As general-in-chief, Arista was aware of the assessments of his subordinates and well understood that the powerful enemy artillery made it nearly impossible for him to dislodge the Americans from their fortifications. At the same time, he realized that it could be extremely dangerous to confront the US Army in an open field engagement where the enemy artillerists would have the space and opportunity to put their cannon drills into full execution.[37]

If Arista was to counter this threat, his best course of action was to rely on his mounted troops. The Mexican military had long cultivated horse soldiery, and the Army of the North, with more than a thousand men in saddle, was no exception. The majority of these troops formed Torrejón's cavalry brigade, which included some of the best soldiers in the Mexican Army. Most of them were trained as lancers in the European tradition. Bent low to the shoulders of their mounts with six-foot-long spears pointed forward, they relied on speed and fearless determination to drive like a wedge into enemy lines, creating disorder and destruction in the opposing ranks. The remaining horsemen—mounted presidial troops and several hundred volunteers of the Auxiliares de las Villas del Norte—lacked any formal training or military experience. Nevertheless, these rugged frontiersmen had spent much of their lives in the saddle and had developed into "bold and dexterous riders" with equestrian skills that matched those of the best cavalrymen in the world. They were also natives of the northern frontier, willing to fight fiercely in defense of their homeland. Most importantly, their knowledge of the region and its terrain made them useful, not only in battle but also as couriers and scouts for the army.

Both groups of horsemen had some drawbacks. The volunteer forces in particular presented problems for Arista. Having qualified for service primarily by their willingness to volunteer and their ability to provide their own horses, the Auxiliares de las Villas Nortes were a somewhat unknown quantity. General Arista, who had more experience fighting against many of these men than leading them, knew that they could be brave, determined, and even ruthless in battle. He was well aware of their tenacity in resisting roving bands of Comanches, but he could not have complete confidence in their ability to perform under fire from the imposing force now arrayed against him. These independent-minded men of the frontier also remained suspect in their loyalties because of their willingness to rebel against the central government. Their apparent determination to turn back the American incursion could not entirely erase doubts about their commitment to reestablishing Mexican control.

It is also questionable how much control Arista actually exerted over the willful horsemen from the frontier. At a time when the general-in-chief was writing to officials in Mexico City assuring them of the patriotism and cooperation of the Auxiliares, an incident unfolded along the Arroyo Colorado that belied his trust. Following the initial skirmish at Rancho de Carricitos, a small party of Reynosa Scouts under the command of Juan Antonio Ballí Cavazos continued northward, investigating reports that an American supply train was arriving from Corpus Christi. Just north of the Arroyo, they located the Americans and six wagons moving along the Camino Real toward the Frontón. Ballí and his scouts attacked and proudly reported that they had defeated the enemy and confiscated valuable supplies, all with the loss of only a single man. They portrayed the clash as a glorious follow-up to the Carricitos skirmish and additional "evidence of the triumph of the Mexican arms over the rapacious invaders." Pleased to have another victory under his belt, Arista passed the report on to the minister of war as additional evidence of the service of his auxiliary cavalry.[38]

Unfortunately, Ballí's report distorted the incident and omitted important details. Ballí had captured supplies headed for the Americans at Point Isabel, but this was no reprise of the military action at Rancho de Carricitos. The American force was, in fact, a party of teamsters headed by Patterson Rogers, and included his two adult sons, nine other men, and a number of women and children. The lightly armed party quickly surrendered to Ballí's fifty-man force after receiving a promise that they would be treated as prisoners of war. Instead, the scout commander shot two of the men, slit the throats of the others, and tossed their bodies into the Arroyo Colorado. One man, William L. Rogers, survived and lingered for days until a group of Mexican ranchers discovered him and took him to US surgeons for treatment.[39]

The incident revealed Arista's imperfect command of his frontier horsemen. Throughout the ordeal on the Río Bravo, he had worked not only to protect Mexico's territory, but also to restore its image, which had suffered from outrages committed by the Mexican Army during the Texas Revolution. Thus Arista strived to maintain the moral high ground in the conflict. His attention to the good treatment of the prisoners and wounded from the first skirmish demonstrate the value in which he held "civilized" warfare. The butchery along the Arroyo Colorado sent a message contrary to everything he had preached to the troops of his command. When Arista learned of it he denounced it as "repugnant to humanity" and in disregard of "our effort to make war in a manner that respects human rights" and demanded prosecution. Nevertheless, the truth did not emerge until almost a month after the event. Until that time, Arista gave his mounted auxiliary units the benefit of the doubt, prizing their skill as scouts, guides, and support staff and assuming that he could control their tendencies to exercise frontier justice and engage in brigandry.[40]

The general had more immediate concerns about his lancer battalion, particularly the tactical limitations of that arm. Since the lancers thrived on lightning-fast strikes, he had to be wary of rough terrain and difficult vegetation that could slow the speed of their charges. Because the horsemen relied on small, speedy mustangs, he had to avoid situations in which they could be overwhelmed by the larger, stronger mounts favored by the US troops. In short, Arista had to ensure that his troops could make good use of the lance. This was especially true since the cavalrymen had little else at their disposal for the fight. Often their only other weapon was the *escopeta*, less than glowingly described as "a short bell-mouth, bull-doggish looking musket, carrying a very heavy ball, which is 'death by law' when it hits, but that is seldom, for they shoot with little accuracy."[41] These notoriously unreliable carbines made the lancers almost useless if they could not mount a charge and virtually defenseless if unhorsed. Thus if he did not take care in the deployment of his cavalry, Arista could easily nullify his greatest asset.

Despite these worries—both apparent and hidden—the Mexican cavalry remained a powerful force, one made all the more so by General Taylor's lack of a comparable body of men. The mounted troops of the Army of Occupation were, however, more versatile than the Mexican lancers. The US dragoons relied on tactics that were a hybrid of infantry and traditional cavalry methods, and these soldiers could charge on horseback with sabers drawn or with pistols aimed along the necks of their mounts if they wanted additional range. They were also comfortable on foot and were willing to dismount and rely on their carbines like infantrymen. During the occupation of the Rio Grande delta, the dragoons had consistently demonstrated their merit by carrying communications between the two US posts, escorting supplies along the dangerous roads, and conducting scout expeditions in search of Mexican forces. Their great weakness was their lack of numbers. They had never amounted to more than three hundred, about a quarter part of the cavalry force arrayed against them. The capture of Captain Thornton's force at Carricitos further depleted their strength.

Samuel Walker's small group of mounted Texans provided only a limited amount of extra support. Taylor had welcomed Walker's offer to organize a company of Texas Rangers as a support unit for the army and quickly signed the men up for a short, quite possibly illegal, three-month enlistment. Walker had years of experience in operations against Mexico and a broad knowledge of the Rio Grande frontier that made him valuable as a scout and a spy. His group of horsemen could also be used as escorts for supply trains, filling some of the void created by the loss of Thornton's troops. But these potential advantages were offset by the small size of the unit and the relative inexperience of the men. Walker filled his twenty-six-man company from among the settlers who had gravitated to Point Isabel and the US depot over the recent weeks. Many were unfamiliar with the region and inexperienced as fighters. Although they were heavily armed, and carried weaponry like the newly developed Colt revolver, they were not as reliable as Taylor had hoped. Their limitations had become strikingly obvious on April 28 when they were routed by Mexican troops at the Resaca San Antonio. Taylor took the incident in stride, noting that the men "have spirit enough, but lack prudence, which a little active service will soon teach them." Until he was convinced that they had acquired that experience, however, he could not have high expectations of them.[42]

Well aware of all the disparities between his forces and the enemy's, General Arista sought to maximize the advantage provided by his cavalry and devised his strategy accordingly. His preference was to eliminate Taylor's main body of troops at the Frontón, but he quickly determined that this would be a poor use of his resources. Although the fortifications around the Point were poor, the location of the depot and the terrain surrounding it made it "one of the most secure points of the coast" and a difficult position to attack. The waters of the Laguna Madre provided protection on three sides, while the fourth, western front faced out onto a broad, open prairie, devoid of trees for miles. This plain presented the lancers with an opportunity to assemble an impressive charge on the barricades, but it afforded them no cover or protection from the defenders within. Approaching horsemen could be seen from a great distance and would face intense cannon and musket fire as they advanced. Arista believed that he might eventually breach the defenses, but only after losing a significant number, perhaps even a majority, of his cavalrymen and infantry. It would be a pyrrhic victory, leaving his army weakened and almost defenseless at a time when thousands of American reinforcements were expected via the Gulf of Mexico.[43]

The Mexican general also saw little benefit in a full-scale assault on the riverside fort across from Matamoros. Like the defenses at the Frontón, these earthworks were well positioned to frustrate an assault. Tucked deep into a bend in the Río Bravo, the fort received additional protection from a water-filled resaca that blocked much of the approach to the peninsula. These natural barriers promised to slow any attack; the strong manmade structure threatened to halt it entirely. High sturdy walls and the deep surrounding moat made the earthwork almost impervious to an advance by either infantry or cavalry. This left Arista with the option of besieging the fort and starving its occupants into submission. Doing this would involve a considerable investment of troops and equipment over an extended number of days. It would also afford the Americans ample time to transport reinforcements across the Gulf to Point Isabel. From there, the expanded enemy force could march over land and threaten the preoccupied Mexican troops from the rear.[44]

Determined to strike while numbers were still in his favor, Arista sought to force the Americans into the open, where his cavalry might have an impact. General Taylor showed no sign of accommodating this desire. He sent out several scouting expeditions to survey the landscape. On their return these observers could not provide exact troop strengths but reported that the Mexicans had blocked the Matamoros road with a significant force. Instead of rushing out to face this challenge, Taylor remained ensconced at the Point. "I propose remaining here, if not necessarily called back to the river," he wrote in a dispatch to Washington on May 3, "until the arrival of some ordnance supplies, and perhaps recruits from New Orleans."[45]

This delay seemed unlikely to hurt and very likely to benefit Taylor's cause. Like Arista, he recognized the security provided by his fortifications and believed the Mexicans would be foolish to attack. He was especially confident of his riverside base. "I do not believe that even with 4000 men [Arista] would make an attempt upon my camp opposite Matamoros," he announced in a letter to Washington. This did not mean that the sites could not be improved, and he viewed the lull in activity as an opportunity to strengthen the barricades around the depot. Taylor also saw advantages in waiting for more troops. Newcomers could be pressed into service in the defense of the supply base, freeing several hundred additional troops for battle. Other reinforcements could march with the army, swelling the numbers when a confrontation came. Time was on his side, and unless the situation changed dramatically, Taylor planned to stay put.[46]

Arista hoped to make Taylor move. "I have resolved to push to see if I can force a battle with the large body of the enemy's troops," the general explained to his minister of war, and he outlined a simple strategy. He would launch an assault on the US fort on the Río Bravo, not with the goal of seizing the site but with that of luring General Taylor's main force out of its secure quarters and into the open. If the Americans could be convinced that their countrymen were in danger, it seemed likely that they would retrace their steps along the road to Matamoros to help. When they tried to do that, the Mexican Army would block the roadway and halt the enemy advance. As US troops prepared to engage, Mexican cavalry forces could sweep down on the American columns and crush resistance before the men in the opposing ranks could deploy themselves for battle.[47]

The success of this strategy would depend on finding the best spot to confront Taylor's army, and Arista believed that he had found it right where he had camped. The Palo Alto watering hole lay at about the halfway point of the Santa Isabel-to-Matamoros road, at a spot where the route broke out of a stand of dense chaparral and crossed into the wide prairie that lay just to the south. The Mexican general hoped to deploy infantrymen in the brush on either side of the road, so that they could fire on Taylor's forces as they marched into view. The Mexican cavalrymen, arrayed across the road where it entered the prairie, would halt the American advance, using the open field to maneuver and bear down on the enemy soldiers as they tried to escape the gantlet of Mexicans positioned in the woods. Bottled up in the narrow corridor through the brush, the Americans would have little cover and less room to deploy their artillery. The cannon, which would be deadly if arrayed on the open plain, would become ineffective. Meanwhile, the Mexican fire would take its toll, producing heavy casualties in the US ranks. It seemed to be a scenario that capitalized on Mexican strengths while negating those of the US force, and Arista was determined not to let the opportunity slip away. "I will have probabilities in my favor," he assured the minister of war as he detailed his plan, "and I am decided to attempt it."[48]

He also revealed his proposal to his second-in-command, who reluctantly accepted the course of action. Pedro de Ampudia had none of the caution of the general-in-chief and was filled with optimism about the possibility of success, no matter the venue. In a letter to Arista, he detailed six reasons while he believed that the Army of the North would crush the invading troops. Taylor, he said, was nothing more than a "garden variety" general. US troops were too demoralized to fight. Many of the enemy soldiers were untrained and lacked experience. Immigrant soldiers would not raise their guns against the Mexicans. The American cavalry was "absolutely null" when compared to their Mexican counterparts. Most importantly, Ampudia cited the enthusiasm of the Mexican forces and the people of Matamoros that would undoubtedly result in a day of glory for the nation. Based on this confidence, much of it completely unfounded, Ampudia wanted to take a more direct approach and simply drive the Americans from their fortifications. He chafed at restrictions posed by Arista's more methodical approach. Nevertheless, he was pleased that the general-in-chief had decided on some form of action and vowed that "the greatest harmony rules between us" and that he would "march intimately united with [Arista] for the sacred cause of saving the honor and integrity of the nation."[49]

Having received this vow of support, Arista moved swiftly to follow through on his decision. On May 2, he sent Ampudia with troops of the 4th Infantry and the auxiliars of the Villas del Norte toward the American fort on the Río Bravo to cut off any routes of escape for the occupants. He also sent a letter to Gen. Francisco Mejía in Matamoros, outlining his plan and calling for him to initiate a bombardment of the US earthworks the following morning. The cannon positioned in Matamoros, he believed, would make a sound loud enough to be heard in the other fortification at the Frontón and would force General Taylor to take some sort of action. Arista believed strongly that he knew what measures Taylor would pursue. "If the enemy general resolves to liberate his subordinates as honor demands," he wrote to the minister of war, " I will have achieved what I anxiously seek—a battle that will decide the fortunes of the campaign, the end of which is that in a single day the country will achieve the advantages of enthusiasm, the enemy will be destroyed and the national arms will shine as the justice that we seek triumphs."[50] All he had to do now was wait.

CHAPTER 7
Battle

★

AT DAYBREAK ON May 3, 1846, Arista's plan roared into action. As the first rays of light broke over Matamoros, Mexican artillery pieces positioned in the sandbag fort on the south bank of the river opened fire on the American earthworks across the river. These first shots, carefully aimed and coordinated, were quickly followed up with dozens of additional rounds, and in moments the town was alive with excitement. "The thunder of Mexican cannon was saluted with bugle calls from the barracks and at all points along the line, with bells from the church and cheers from the residents of Matamoros," reported the *Boletin del Norte*. "They filled the streets in an instant, delighted that the hour had come to give a terrible lesson to the American camp, whose odious presence could be tolerated no longer."[1]

The commencement of shooting also spurred activity within the US fortifications. Reveille had just sounded when the first rounds came whizzing across the parapet. Infantrymen, who had been busy preparing for the day, tossed aside their cooking and washing and rushed to their tents for muskets to fend off a possible advance on the fort. Artillerymen hurried to their pieces, which were already positioned in the bastions of their earthworks. In that short interval, the initial shots had given way to a torrent of incoming rounds from a group of seven cannon. Despite the surprise and the continual shower of metal, the US cannoneers quickly recovered. Within fifteen minutes, Capt. Allen Lowd with the four 18-pounders at his disposal and Capt. Braxton Bragg with his battery of field artillery began to respond. They quickly transformed the one-sided barrage into a general exchange between the two sides of the river.[2]

The two forces used different strategies. Operating with the primary goal of attracting Taylor's attention at the Frontón, the Mexican artillerists showered the American post with their fire. Some shots were directed specifically at the US artillery pieces in their bastions, but most were simply lobbed into the interior of the earthwork as the Mexicans "fired away powder and copper balls as if they cost nothing and they had plenty of ammunition."[3]

The American response was far more selective. One of the reasons Taylor had marched to the coast was to gather ordnance for the artillery. Until his return with the new supplies the post defenders had only about four hundred rounds on hand to cast back across the river. Initially, the gunners expended some of these shells with shots into the northern suburb of Matamoros. "Captain Lowd occasionally delivered an iron messenger from his guns crashing into the city," wrote Capt. Daniel Whiting, "which we could distinctly hear tearing its course through the houses and streets." Seeking to make the best use of their limited supply, however, Lowd and Bragg directed their guns primarily on a single Mexican piece and concentrated firing on that point. The strategy produced almost immediate results. After just fifteen minutes of firing, a direct hit unseated one of the Mexican cannons and silenced the others as the Mexican artillerists relocated from the sandbags battery to a more secure position. A short time later, however, the Mexican fire resumed, first from a downstream position that the US troops referred to as the lower fort and then from an upstream mortar battery.[4]

Maj. Jacob Brown, whom Taylor had left in charge of the riverside fort, answered by calling for increased activity from his own works. He ordered a "deliberate fire" on the repositioned Mexican guns and also directed his artillery to target the center of Matamoros, presumably hoping that the opposing forces would back down from this escalation. Neither tactic produced results. The Mexican mortars had been sunk deeply into the ground and were well protected at the front. After almost an hour of firing, the Americans failed to replicate their early accomplishment by upending another gun and succeeded only in drawing more concentrated return fire. Their efforts to wreak havoc on the city proved even more futile. The cannon crews attempted to hit the distant buildings with hot shot, but could not heat their cannonballs to a temperature that would ignite the wooden structures. Having expended almost half of his ammunition, Brown decided to conserve his remaining supplies for the possibility of an assault on the earthwork. By eleven in the morning, about six hours after the start of the cannonade, the US guns went silent. The Mexican guns continued to fire.[5]

Unable to strike back at their assailants, the troops inside the fort turned their attention to self-protection. Immediately after the first shots, Major Brown rushed the soldiers of the 7th Infantry to the north end of the earthwork to complete construction

Siege of Fort Brown. *Courtesy of Library of Congress.*

of the enclosure. The troops had continued to work on the fort since the departure of Taylor and his troops on May 1, but despite their best efforts, one face of the structure remained open with a road passing through it. Fearing that the Mexican forces intended to mount a charge along this route, the soldiers labored feverishly with pick and shovel to complete a ditch and seal off the opening. After ordering a ceasefire, Brown also sent several field artillery pieces to guard the roadway in case an attack came during the construction. Meanwhile other troops scrambled to create shelter from the incessant firing by assembling a series of structures out of pork barrels, fence posts, and boards, then covering them with six feet of earth to make them bombproof.[6]

As the troops rushed to shield themselves from attack, it appeared unlikely that any would escape unscathed from the steady rain of Mexican cannonballs. "I had hardly left my tent before a shot riddled it," wrote Joseph King Fenno Mansfield, "and in the course of the day it received several shots." Another unnamed soldier watched from just inches away as one of the first cannonballs bounded into his tent, tore through his recently vacated bed, then skipped on toward others in his camp. "I'm glad I was not 'caught napping,'" he later assured his family. Shortly afterwards, Horace Weigart became the first casualty of the bombardment. An incoming shell struck the sergeant of the 7th Infantry in the head as he stood on one of the fort ramparts and killed him instantly. The men of his unit moved his body to a nearby hospital area, but he was to have no peace even in death. Another round landed on that tent, striking the unfortunate soldier once again and completely severing his head from his body. Some observers noted that it appeared as if the Mexican gunners "had a special spite against that particular man."[7] Others observed his unhappy death and feared they would soon meet their own.

Nevertheless, as the day progressed, confidence began to rise. Shots and shells continued to bound past or explode nearby, but no other US soldiers suffered serious injury. This was mainly good luck, but the troops also quickly learned measures to improve their chances of survival. Each time they saw smoke belch forth from a gun across the river, soldiers dove from the parapets, dropped to the ground, and covered themselves as well as possible. The incoming shells tended to explode upward on impact, causing much commotion but little injury to the figures prone in the dirt. "The Mexicans thought they had killed nearly all of us," wrote one of those who endured the long day, "as they were under the impression that all who fell were shot."[8]

The optimism in the American fort was absent from the Mexican trenches. The cheers, bells and trumpeting that had accompanied the first shots from the Mexican cannons had barely faded away when an incoming round struck one of the 8-pounders and knocked it out of its seating. The shell also killed three of the soldiers manning the gun, Capts. Clemente Castro and Carlos Mora, and Lt. Andres de León. A short time later, two more men suffered serious injuries from burning gunpowder and six others sustained undisclosed wounds. The difficulties continued as one of the aging Mexican howitzers cracked while firing and had to be retired. This collection of problems and the accurate incoming fire from across the river forced the cannoneers to abandon their forward position and gave the Americans the advantage in the opening round.[9]

The situation for the Mexicans improved considerably when they resumed their barrage from the upriver mortar battery. Although General Mejía remained apprehensive, the troops now found themselves better protected from the US shots and suffered no additional casualties before firing from the US fort stopped. Nevertheless, the brief burst of American cannon shots had produced serious effects. Much of the sandbag fortification along the river had been destroyed by startlingly accurate fire. Mejía expressed disappointment at the degree of damage and lamented that his troops had evidently been so contemptuous of US construction over the preceding weeks that they had become complacent about their own. He vowed to repair the breastworks immediately, but he could do little to fix another problem. Three of his guns had been knocked out of commission, possibly beyond repair, and he despaired of replacing them.[10]

On a more positive note for Mejía, the fire into the US fort appeared to have taken a significant toll as well. Although the Mexicans were not really so naive as to think that all who fell were dead, their observations of men throwing themselves onto the ground led them to believe that they had "impressed" the Americans by dismounting two of their cannon and killing at least fifty men. American efforts to throw hot shot and grapeshot into the heart of Matamoros merely reinforced this misperception, as the Mexicans interpreted targeting a "defenseless city" as an act of desperation. When the firing stopped completely, it appeared that the besieged US troops were themselves defenseless. In that case Gen. Taylor would be forced to leave his covered position and march to the rescue.[11]

But Taylor did not come. The troops at Point Isabel awoke on May 3 to the rumbling of distant artillery and knew at once that their countrymen had come under fire. "The camp was wild with excitement," wrote Capt. William Seaton Henry. "We knew our gallant fellows were resisting a bombardment, and all were anxious to fly to their rescue."[12] General Taylor shared the sentiment. After receiving a reconnaissance report from Capt. Samuel Walker, who apprised him that the Mexicans had gathered en masse at Palo Alto, he straightaway issued orders for a march at 1 p.m. A short time later, however, he rescinded the order, after deciding that a headlong rush toward battle would leave the fort at the depot undermanned and vulnerable. He wanted to gather more information about conditions at the riverside fort before acting. Accordingly, he accepted an offer from Walker, who vowed that he could evade the Mexican force and establish communications with Maj. Brown and his beleaguered command. Capt. Charles May and a company of dragoons accompanied the Texas Ranger as far as the chaparral just to the north of Palo Alto. There, in compliance with his orders, he was to wait until 8 a.m. for Walker's return. The rest of Taylor's command remained at Point Isabel and continued the work of fortifying the position.[13]

The wait for Walker occasioned much anxiety there. The distant thunder of cannon from the direction of Matamoros continued until almost midnight on May 3 and resumed early in the morning on May 4, raising concerns for those who were enduring the fire. "It is painful to be so far from our men who are fighting under the Stars and Stripes," wrote Lt. John James Peck. "Our hope is that they will hold on."[14] Tension turned to alarm later in the morning when sentries spotted a mounted party approaching the Point across the prairie to the west. Troops rushed out to confront the attack, but it was only Captain May and his horsemen returning from their mission. The dragoon captain reported that the Mexicans remained in camp near Palo Alto. Walker and his men had skirted that force in the direction of the river, but had not reported back by the designated time. The US troops at the Point would have to wait another agonizing day before learning the fate of the rangers and of the men under attack at the riverside fort.[15]

Taylor's stubborn refusal to move also frustrated Arista. He maintained his bombardment of the fort, but as hours gave way to days of waiting, he still could not draw the Americans out of their shelter and lure them into the desired battle. "We have not been able to achieve this end," he wrote to General Ampudia, "despite the fact that the enemy has sufficient forces and supplies and the provocation of opening fire on their base across from Matamoros."[16] In the meantime, he saw his soldiers growing complacent from the wait. When spies reported on the morning of May 4 that the American cavalry was advancing on their camp, troops guarding the roadway failed to heed the warning. The auxiliaries of the Villas del Norte and the presidial troops of the Bahia Regiment remained idle in their camp until the enemy charged into their midst. The surprised men were fortunate that the attacker was only Charles May's small company of dragoons—which raced forward, fired on them several times, and then withdrew.[17]

Later the Mexicans would discover that the charge had merely been a diversion and that another maneuver was afoot. While the Mexican soldiers scrambled to confront the US dragoons, Captain Walker and six men used the uproar and cover of darkness to slip around Arista's camp. This ploy allowed the rangers to escape notice by the huge Mexican encampment, but several miles closer to Matamoros they blundered onto a sentry post in the black of night and were ordered to identify themselves. With the main Mexican force to their rear, retreat was not an option. Instead, Walker responded that he was an "amigo" and was given permission to approach. Without hesitation he and his men drew their Colt revolvers, spurred their horses forward, and fired wildly to the right and left as they galloped past the outpost.[18]

A combination of luck and stealth got the rangers through. Helped by sentry fires that both illuminated and blinded the Mexican troops, Walker and his men rushed past the guards virtually unseen. Their shots wounded or killed five or six of the sentinels, while they themselves suffered no injuries. Forging ahead, they outdistanced any pursuit, evaded additional outposts, and arrived at the earthworks in the early morning hours after the first day of the bombardment.[19]

The rangers did not linger at the fort. Pausing only long enough to gather news and to rest their tired horses, they left at around 4 a.m. on May 4 and set out on a return journey no less eventful than the trek in. Ten miles from the fort, on the expansive prairie just south of Palo Alto, Walker and his Texas Rangers encountered a large unit of Mexican cavalry. It tried and failed to encircle them as they beat a hasty retreat toward the river. They soon outdistanced the enemy, only to discover that a group of about thirty of the riders had cut them off by taking another trail through the brush. The rangers forced their way through and managed once again to reach the confines of the fort just after reveille and just ahead of their pursuers.[20]

As a result, Walker endured day two of the bombardment at the fort and was able to see for himself how the garrison dealt with the ongoing exchange. At daybreak both armies resumed firing across the river. Once again, Major Brown ceased fire quickly while the Mexicans maintained a steady barrage throughout the day. But the urgency and alarm of the previous day had faded. The garrison of the fort had worked throughout the night, and by morning had bombproofs soundly erected, giving the men secure places to shelter themselves. The north walls of the fort had been closed enough to limit the danger of assault from that quarter. And the men had grown accustomed to the hail of cannonballs. Many of these fell short of the works or passed harmlessly over the far side. Explosive rounds that reached the fort often thudded into the ground without igniting or had long fuses that allowed the soldiers to escape before an explosion. Despite having endured more than twelve hundred incoming rounds, Brown and his men had suffered no additional casualties. "All their firing which has been very expensive to them has as yet done nothing but annoy us," Lt. Napoleon Dana wrote to his wife as he summed up two days of the salvo. "We think that the general will immediately march to this place and fight General Arista on the road." Others shared his optimism. Spirits were high.[21]

Captain Walker carried news of this good morale when, at dusk, he set out once more. In addition to his personal observations, he carried a letter that Jacob Brown had written to Taylor earlier in the day, in which he detailed events since the start of hostilities and praised the comportment of his officers and men. The message also indicated that the troops were prepared to wait out their situation until Taylor felt able to come to their assistance. This time, Walker succeeded in his mission. Even though troops of Mexico's Morelia and Puebla Battalions had taken up positions on the north side of the American fort earlier that day, the rangers passed through them unnoticed.

At 8 a.m.. on May 5, Walker finally arrived at the Point Isabel depot and delivered his messages to the eager audience within.[22]

The news from the riverside fort considerably brightened the mood of the army at the depot, in part because of the exploits of the bearer and his success in completing his difficult task. Within hours of his return, officers of Taylor's army had raised money to buy the ranger a new horse and signed a petition recommending him as an officer in the US Army. More importantly, his personal account and the message that he carried from Major Brown reassured the men at the Point that their compatriots had fared well and were not in desperate peril. General Taylor was especially pleased and felt confident that he could wait for additional recruits to arrive from New Orleans before setting out to confront Arista.[23]

Walker's successful maneuver provoked a much different reaction in the Mexican camp. General Arista had wanted to prevent all contact between Taylor and his force, in the hope that lack of information about his men might make the general to speed to their rescue. Although Arista could not be entirely certain that Walker had successfully navigated his way back to the Frontón, it appeared that he had. And he was likely to pass on good news. Mexican scouts got their first closeup view of the riverside fort during their efforts to trap Walker in it, and they realized that their prolonged bombardment had been far less devastating than they had thought. Arista undoubtedly understood that if Taylor knew his troops were secure, he would be unlikely to abandon his conservative course.[24]

His solution was to ramp up his assault on the fort to force Taylor out of his inactivity. On May 5, he placed Pedro de Ampudia in charge of 497 men of the Villas del Norte, 701 infantrymen, and 32 artillerymen with two 8-pounder guns and two howitzers and sent him to besiege the enemy fortification from the left bank of the river. He also assigned the 1367 troops still in Matamoros to provide support, as required, from the opposite bank. In his instructions he called for Ampudia to engage the enemy whenever the opportunity arose, halt the entry of resources and supplies to the fort, and cut off access to water if possible. Most importantly, he demanded that the troops sever all mail between the Americans in the earthwork and the rest of their army. "In effect," he wrote, "I give you complete liberty of action. I only warn that you abstain from attacking without awaiting my orders." Reasoning that siege would be more efficient, Arista remained determined to avoid a bloody assault on the riverside fort or the Frontón. He believed that when Taylor became aware of the renewed pressure on the fort and of his inability to establish communications with it, he would at last prepare for a "decisive strike." If he did not, the undersupplied troops in the earthwork would be forced to surrender in a matter of days, and Mexico would emerge from the episode with some level of success.[25]

Meanwhile, the extended wait produced a number of concerns for Arista, still camped at the Palo Alto. During the search for Walker and his men, reconnaissance parties had discovered another narrow road through the brush near Loma Alta, a small rise of land about three miles to the southeast. The Texas Rangers had passed in that direction during their foray around the Mexican forces, and it was possible that they had discovered this previously unmapped road from the Frontón to Matamoros. At the same time, a report that a large party of US dragoons had been spotted on Brazos Island near the mouth of the river led Arista to consider that the US troops might ignore the fort altogether and instead launch an assault up the Río Bravo toward Burrita and Matamoros. Walker and the dragoons' ability to slip out of the Frontón unnoticed made Arista doubt the reliability of his own spies. He worried that Taylor might leave the Frontón unseen and reach his destination—whatever it might be—without being detected.[26]

Arista's concern may have been overblown, as the Americans gave no sign that they knew about or were interested in the newly discovered route, but Arista felt compelled to act. First, he increased troop strength at the garrisons guarding the most important river crossings to ensure that any attempt to pass would be contested. In the early daylight hours of May 5, he ordered his troops to break camp at Palo Alto and relocate to the Tanques de Ramireño, another collection of ponds in the vicinity of Loma Alta. There he positioned his force at a point equidistant between the two roads. This, he believed, would permit better monitoring of both and would allow quick movement in either direction to intercept Taylor's troops if they showed up. The Tanques provided the added benefit of abundant water and grasslands. Five days' heavy use by some four thousand men and additional thousands of animals had depleted these resources at the Palo Alto camp and may have contributed to Arista's decision.[27]

Resources were also scarce in the American earthworks as the Mexicans imposed their siege. Less than an hour after Walker made his final departure from the riverside fort, Arista's troops closed in on the north side and opened a sustained musket fire on the works. Additional units appeared to the east and west from across the river, effectively sealing off the peninsula of land. The US artillery fired a few times in response but again ceased quickly. The supply of cannon rounds had dwindled to about two hundred, and they would all be necessary to repel the charge on the works that now seemed inevitable. Perhaps more disconcerting was the limited store of food and water. This situation became all the more critical when troops of Antonio Canales' auxiliaries of the Villas del Norte occupied a nearby ranch structure that the US troops had used as a bakery and seized a large supply of bread that had just been pulled from the oven.[28]

When not huddled for shelter in their bombproofs, the soldiers filled their hours by devising defenses against the new threat so visible all around them. As the Mexican troops closed in, Jacob Brown turned his attention to a dozen ranch huts several hundred feet from the fort walls, which had served the camp as officers' quarters, hospital, and support facilities. He saw that Ampudia's men had taken refuge in the buildings, including the one so recently used as a bakery, and he ordered the use of some of his small store of cannonballs to knock the structures to the ground. Captain Mansfield continued to devote all his energy to improving the fort. He kept a watchful eye on the enemy soldiers as he instructed the men to widen the exterior ditches, augment the earthen walls, and expand the growing network of bombproofs. Under cover of darkness other troops ventured out of the enclosure and piled branches around the far edge of the moat, providing an additional obstacle to an enemy cavalry charge.[29]

Tensions grew along with the fort. As the bombardment wore on with no sign that their general planned to return, the men could only hope that Jacob Brown had not been "a bit too positive" in his report to Taylor. The exhausted soldiers began to doubt whether they could hold out much longer without any hint of rescue and with a charge on the walls imminent. "Sleep was out of the question in the day for no one could tell where a bomb would strike or burst," John Henshaw, a captain of the 7th Infantry recalled of the fretful wait in the fort. "At night it was equally so, for we at all moments expected an assault."[30]

General Ampudia yearned to launch the expected attack. On the morning of May 6, he resumed the shelling of the fort at daybreak, then wrote a brief and friendly message to his superior stating that he was in position and that he felt confident that he could easily take the earthwork if given permission to do so. Arista remained reluctant to accede to this request. He expected Taylor to advance at any moment and believed that he needed the help of Ampudia's brigade to check him. He had also ordered measures to ensure that his second-in-command would arrive quickly. A cannon would fire at the first sign of an American advance, alerting the distant troops to the danger. In case the boom of that signal could not be heard, Arista posted a series of messengers on the route between the Tanques and the Río Bravo. These men, each riding at "horse-killing speed," could relay a message between the two positions in less than a half hour, still affording Ampudia plenty of time to gather his troops and march to join the main force. Having devised these extraordinary precautions, Arista had no wish to signal for help only to find that a good part of his army was tied down in another fight.[31] He was also afraid that a charge on the fort walls would result in enough casualties to cripple his force just as US reinforcements showed up.[32] Much as he wanted to remove the Americans from their position within sight of Matamoros, he insisted that Ampudia allow the bombardment and siege take its course.

Ampudia responded with a series of messages in which he deconstructed Arista's plan and offered his own as an alternative. In one he explained that although he had isolated the fort, the Americans still had access to water from a well inside their walls. Additionally, they had a plentiful supply of food and could not be starved into submission in fewer than five to seven days. In a subsequent dispatch he added that closer inspection had revealed the enemy earthwork to be unbreechable by the Mexican cannon.[33] This was not a concession to Arista's perspective. Although Ampudia declared that he had settled in for a long siege, he also hinted that with more troops from some of the better-trained units, he could seize the site as he had suggested earlier.

Any additional troops would have to be drawn from Arista's army, weakening the general-in-chief at the Tanques. But Ampudia argued his case by raising doubts about Arista's strategy. He cited the distance between Arista's force and his own on the river as a significant challenge. Despite the precautions taken to monitor Taylor's army and the arrangements made to summon reinforcements quickly, Ampudia doubted that he could assemble his scattered troops and move them fast enough to be of use to Arista. "In the event that you are attacked by a superior force," he warned, "it is not certain that I would be able to arrive on time." And trying to would require him to abandon his siege and surrender any gains made over the previous days. With so many doubts, it seemed better to abandon the uncertain wait for Taylor at the Tanques and fall back toward the river. This would shorten communication lines, allow for better protection of river crossings, and still permit a confrontation with Taylor on the open plain near the US fort, if a march ever materialized. In the meantime it would also enable the Mexicans to focus all their attention on the certainty of eliminating the offensive riverside fort. With that victory complete, it would then be possible to concentrate fully on the main body of US troops.[34]

Arista did not reject this logic outright, but he countered with his own arguments. He still suspected that the Americans would march soon, and he could not risk falling back at this late hour. He continued to believe that the confrontation should occur near Palo Alto, where his army had room to maneuver and did not risk becoming trapped between Taylor's advancing troops and the garrison at the fort. He conceded the desirability of capturing the fort but offered one more reason to delay a full-scale assault—benevolence. Still concerned that Mexico's reputation had been tarnished by tactics used during the Texas Revolution—especially the brutal assault on the Alamo and the massacre of prisoners at Goliad—Arista did not want his siege to be similarly remembered for its inhumanity. Although he too was weary of the wait and wanted to conclude the standoff at the fort, Arista extended an olive branch before committing to a course that would result in immense bloodshed. He wrote a letter to Major Brown in which he explained that he had enough troops to seize the earthworks and was prepared do so, but that he would rather avert the carnage of war by offering an opportunity for peaceful surrender. He forwarded this note to Ampudia, asking him to deliver it to the US fort and assuring him that such a step was necessary to the honor of the nation: "Civilization and love of humanity," he wrote, "which are the symbols of this century, demand gentle measures to obtain the results we desire before we resort to the extremes of an assault." If this attempt failed to sway the fort's defenders, he promised Ampudia that more direct action would be considered.[35]

Although he doubted the value of these "gentle measures," Ampudia complied with his orders. The general, who had participated in the assault on the Alamo and other brutal campaigns, had no compunction against using harsh tactics against an invading force. But around 4:30 p.m. on May 6, he ordered a lull in the shelling of the fort and sent Colonel José López Uraga and Camilo Mauro under flag of truce to deliver the letter. Two Americans ventured out to meet them and accepted the message. Mauro, who had been selected for his ability to speak English, translated the note and informed the Americans that they had one hour to consider and respond to the offer.[36]

The answer came within the allotted time, but not from Jacob Brown. Just before midday on May 5, a Mexican artillery shot had struck the fort commander in the leg as he patrolled the ramparts. The wound required amputation, which went well, but the only safe place to convalesce was in the cover of one of the newly constructed bombproofs. In that oppressively hot, closed space, gangrene set in, and it became evident that Brown could not survive long. Since Brown was incapacitated, Capt. E. S. Hawkins had assumed charge of the garrison, and it was the captain who would reply to Arista.[37]

Hawkins gathered the commanders of all the companies of the garrison to consult their opinions. No one at the meeting fully understood Spanish, and the message that Arista hoped to convey was largely lost on them. Still, the choice he offered was clear, and the group unanimously rejected the opportunity to surrender. In spite of all their difficulties, the officers believed that their earthwork had become relatively impregnable and that they could fight off any attack. Buoyed by this show of support, Hawkins wrote an official response in which he simply said, "Your humane communication has just been received and after the consideration due to its importance, I must respectfully decline to surrender my forces to you." Couriers once again delivered the communication under flag of truce. As soon as the content of the message became clear, the Mexicans resumed bombardment of the fort.[38]

The Americans again anticipated an assault on the morning of May 7, but day broke at the Fort Brown with no change in the Mexican strategy. Once more, Mexican artillerists started the morning with a fierce volley of shells that lasted for an hour and a half, then periodically resumed fire for the remainder of the day. Infantry troops also approached the walls from time to time but fired randomly toward the fort, showing no sign of an organized advance. Some of the US troops also forayed out of their confinement to remove several mesquite trees and destroy an old traverse structure that provided the Mexicans with cover. They met no organized opposition. Over the course of the day the artillery barrage did take a toll. One soldier lost his arm to a cannon shot, four horses died, a caisson was damaged, and one well-placed shell destroyed all the instruments of the 7th Infantry band, but no attempt had been made to breach the walls or take the fort.[39]

This preservation of the status quo revealed Arista's reluctance to abandon his present plan. Although the sound of resumed artillery fire probably indicated a refusal to his request for surrender, the general did not receive an official account of the response until 8 p.m. on May 6. As he waited for that news, Arista mulled over Ampudia's correspondence and concluded that the US fort would be too difficult to infiltrate. He reconsidered an attack on the Frontón, which he believed would be a more effective tactic, but decided that the time for that option had passed. Rumors abounded that Taylor would commence his long-awaited advance at any moment, and it seemed unwise to modify plans that had been in place for days. Rather than committing himself to an attack on either fort, Arista held his ground. He also once again ordered Ampudia to prepare his troops for a quick response should the tales of US activity prove true.[40]

Ampudia was not happy with the decision but accepted his orders. He devoted much of the day on May 7 to preparing the 4th Infantry and the volunteer companies so that they would be ready to march at a moment's notice. Nevertheless, he was loath to abandon the siege. He continued to fire artillery toward the fort's interior and directed occasional sorties against its walls. To all appearances, he was still planning an assault. He also called for Gen. Joaquín Morlet to bring troops from the Puebla Regiment and the Grenadier Company of Mexico to supplement his own. When Arista's signal came, these troops would remain behind and attempt to keep the US soldiers bottled up in their post. To that end, he requested that General Mejía, still in Matamoros, cooperate with Morlet in any way possible to create the appearance that the fort remained surrounded by a large force.[41]

Arista was correct about the pending march. On the afternoon of May 6, a ship arrived at Point Isabel with additional supplies and several hundred new recruits for the US Army. Another boat, loaded with four companies of more seasoned soldiers of the 1st Infantry, was slated to arrive the following morning. With these troops on hand and with the promise that volunteers from Louisiana would arrive shortly, Taylor finally felt confident of his ability to march to the rescue of his fort on the river. He incorporated the experienced troops into his army and assigned the raw enlistees to Maj. John Monroe of the 4th Artillery to serve as a garrison for the supply depot. On the morning of May 7 he ordered the army to prepare to march that afternoon. "It is known the enemy has recently occupied the route in force," the decree stated. "If still in possession, the general will give him battle." He also sent a dispatch back on the departing troop ship notifying his superiors of his action and stating simply, "If the enemy oppose my march, in whatever force, I shall fight him."[42]

The order generated considerable excitement among the troops. Even though the sound of continuing cannon fire from the direction of Matamoros now heartened the soldiers, assuring them that their countrymen still held their ground, the men were eager to render aid. They greeted the announcement with cheers, even when solemnly warned to expect a fight en route. And when the army, consisting of 2228 men, eight field pieces, and two 18-pounder siege guns, headed out of the Point at 3 p.m. on May 7, its soldiers carried with them a sense of great purpose. "We had understood that we should have a fight on the way to the Rio Grande and all felt that we must do our best," recalled John Hatch. "We had not only the reputation of the army but of the country to maintain." This duty did not undermine the high spirit of the force, which set out for the Rio Grande "without a question or doubt of getting there."[43]

Indeed, in the first stage of the march, the only hindrance was a train of about three hundred wagons that followed behind the troops. Taylor elected to carry all his supplies with him rather than push through to the fort and then have to escort them later. This ensured that if he reached the river without destroying the Mexicans or pushing them back to Matamoros, they could not block the road behind him and again separate him from his ordnance and provisions. A drawback to this strategy was that the line of wagons extended for miles along the narrow road and presented an inviting target. In the event of an attack, Taylor would have to focus his attention on defense of his supplies or face a real chance of losing them. The train, pulled by hundreds of mules and oxen and tended by dozens upon dozens of teamsters, also moved at a glacial pace. For all the enthusiasm of the troops to move forward, by nightfall the American column had advanced only seven miles along the road toward the Rio Grande.[44]

The mood of the men darkened considerably as the sun set. They established camp near several ponds of potable water, and the wagon train carried an abundance of food, but the position on the coastal flats seemed dangerously exposed. The men remained in a state of watchful alert, knowing that Arista's troops might wait just a few miles ahead. But it was not a fear of Mexicans that made the hours pass so slowly. "The night was awful," recalled Lt. James Longstreet years later: "The mosquitoes seemed as thick as the blades of grass on the prairie, and swarmed and buzzed in clouds, and packs of half-famished wolves prowled and howled about us. There was no need for the sound of reveille. The wolves and mosquitoes, and perhaps some solemn thoughts, kept us on the qui vive."[45]

Even though they awoke to temperatures that were "excessively hot" and knew that battle likely awaited them, when they rose on the morning of May 8 many of the troops eagerly marched forward merely to separate themselves from the site of their night's misery.[46]

For all his precautions to monitor the US advance, Arista did not learn until the morning of May 8 that Taylor had set out on his march. All through the day on May 7, Arista's spies rode into camp with reports of no unusual activity at the Frontón. Convinced that all was well, Arista devoted much of the day to scouting areas for a campsite with quicker access to the Palo Alto. During this reconnaissance, his troops encountered an American horse and a donkey wandering along the recently discovered road to the coast. Arista suspected that the stray animals might have escaped as the US Army left the Frontón, and at 10 p.m. he sent out additional scouts to make certain that nothing momentous was in the offing. Those men returned at 7 a.m.. and again reported that all was quiet. Relieved by this news, Arista began organizing his troops for a move to the eastern edge of the plain that extended unbroken from the Loma Alta to the Palo Alto.[47] Just an hour later, however, a presidial soldier named Vasquez rushed into camp and breathlessly reported that the Americans were not only on the march along the primary road, but were well on their way to Palo Alto. Apparently the spies sent out previously had been too frightened to make a close approach to the Frontón and failed to spot Taylor leaving.[48]

This revelation sparked a frantic change in plans. Arista immediately signaled for Ampudia and dispatched a message calling for him to advance with the 4th Infantry and Canales' troops in the direction of the Palo Alto. He also sent additional scouts to investigate the progress of Taylor's army. The rest of the troops, busily involved with breakfast preparations and breaking down the camp, were ordered to set those tasks aside and make ready for combat. In short order, officers were assembling their companies, distributing weapons and ammunition, and organizing the supplies needed for a fight. In less than two and a half hours, units that formed an army of 3339 men were lined up and ready to march.[49]

The rapid response was not fast enough. As Arista prepared to move, he received another piece of troublesome news. Lt. Inés García, one of the scouts sent out earlier in the day, returned with confirmation that Taylor's troops were indeed on the road. And this army had already advanced to a point just a few miles north of Palo Alto, having made far more progress than previously suspected. The General immediately put his troops to march across the broad plain, but he knew that he faced a difficult challenge to arrive at Palo Alto in advance of the enemy.[50]

At midday, it became apparent that the Mexican Army had lost the race. As the troops marched through a small area of chaparral that bordered the southern edge of the prairie—about one and a half miles south of Palo Alto—a group of scouts reported that the advanced units of the Taylor's army had already reached the watering hole. Moments later, Arista observed the situation for himself through a telescope. A squadron of American horsemen patrolled the northern end of the field and at least half of the US force had already emerged from the distant brush onto the plain. Despite the rapid march, the Mexican force had arrived too late to contain the Americans in the chaparral and had no hope of gaining control of the strategically important watering hole.[51]

Out of position and unprepared for the situation that he faced, Arista had to reassess his options quickly. They were few and largely unfavorable. It would be foolhardy to continue toward the US force. His troops would be exposed on the open plain and an easy target for the American artillery. Nor was it practical to head south on the road to Matamoros in search of a better location. The dense chaparral that bounded the route afforded few good positions for deploying troops with Taylor's army close on their heels. Any thought of seizing the US earthwork had long since faded. With Ampudia already called forward to assist, Arista could not even be certain that the American troops within were still contained. This left Arista with a choice to retreat, and possibly abandon his last reasonable opportunity to check Taylor's army, or to stage a defense where he now stood. He elected to fight.[52]

Several points justified this decision. For all the bad luck and miscues that had befallen it, the Army of the North remained between Taylor's troops and the riverside earthworks. This put pressure on the Americans to push their way through, while Arista merely had to hold his ground. The Mexicans also found themselves in a reasonably defensible position. To the west, just past the Matamoros-to-Frontón road, a long, shallow resaca cut across the plain. Beyond that, heavy chaparral hemmed in the prairie. The combination of uneven ground and dense thickets ensured that the Americans, burdened with their wagons, could not cast off in that direction. To the east there was nothing but grassland for miles, and any movement in that direction would leave Taylor's army extremely vulnerable as it passed in front of Arista's force. The only route was south on the road, where Arista waited. The southern edge of the prairie lacked a water source as reliable as the deep pond at Palo Alto, but a shallow resaca some distance to the rear of the Mexican position held water enough to support the troops for at least two days. A series of shallow pools also dotted the ground near the Mexican line. Although the water within appeared stagnant and dirty, it could be resorted to if the need were dire. The area was by no means an ideal location to make a stand, but neither was it an impossible one.[53]

Arista moved quickly to secure this position. Since his forces were already marching westward across the prairie, he let them continue. Gen. Anastasio Torrejón's cavalry troops at the head of his column proceeded across the field until they reached the roadway about three quarters of a mile south of the Americans. There, in a boggy area between the road and the chaparral to the west, they established a barrier to the US advance. The rest of the troops stretched out behind, with the rear guard resting on a low, brush-covered rise more than a mile to the east. Turning northward to face the Americans, the troops quickly, "with perfection as if it was a day on the parade ground," turned their line of march into a line of battle. By about

2 p.m. the force had created a reasonably daunting barrier across the southern end of the prairie.[54]

For their part, the US troops approached the prairie cautiously, not knowing exactly what awaited them. During the previous days, scouting parties had repeatedly patrolled the roads but found find no sign of the Mexican Army once positioned at Palo Alto. When reveille sounded at daybreak on May 8, the soldiers broke their miserable camp, formed their columns, and headed southward with no idea when or where they might encounter Arista's force. They relied on the eyes of Capt. Charles May's dragoons, who rode in advance, scouring the countryside for any sign of a waiting foe. As the army reached the north side of the band of chaparral that formed the Palo Alto, one of these scouts returned, reporting that the enemy had been sighted ahead. This brought the army to a halt. Men rushed to secure the wagons and formed into a battle line in case the Mexicans were hidden in the brush. Moments later, word came that what May had encountered was actually just a company of Mexican scouts, which had fallen back. The main body of Arista's army was still some distance away. Thereupon the troops resumed their march for another mile and safely cleared the brush near the Palo Alto pond.[55]

The panorama from this spot immediately convinced them that a battle was at hand. "In front, about the three miles distant, we saw the forest of mesquite that extends nine miles out from the Rio Grande," Lt. Phillip Barbour wrote in a letter home, "and between our position and that forest the enemy had formed his line of battle." General Taylor also took in the scene, noted that that Mexican cavalry were "occupying the road in force," and prepared for a fight. His first order of business was to help the troops to recover from the morning march by allowing them to drink from the pond, one regiment at a time. Next he brought his train fully out of the brush and secured it in an area near the pond. Only then did he pull his men out of their columns and begin to deploy them in battle formation.[56]

The forces divided into two large sections. Troops of the 5th Infantry occupied the far western end of the line, followed by Maj. Samuel Ringgold's battery of four light artillery pieces, the 3rd Infantry, two 18-pounder siege guns, and the 4th Infantry. This wing merged the former 2nd Brigade (minus the infantry now garrisoned at the riverside fort) and the 3rd Brigade (which had left portions of the 4th Infantry to garrison Point Isabel) into a single unit under command of Lt. Col. David Twiggs. To the west of the road, Colonel William Belknap continued to oversee the 1st Brigade, which included Lt. Col. Thomas Child's light artillery battalion, with its soldiers serving as

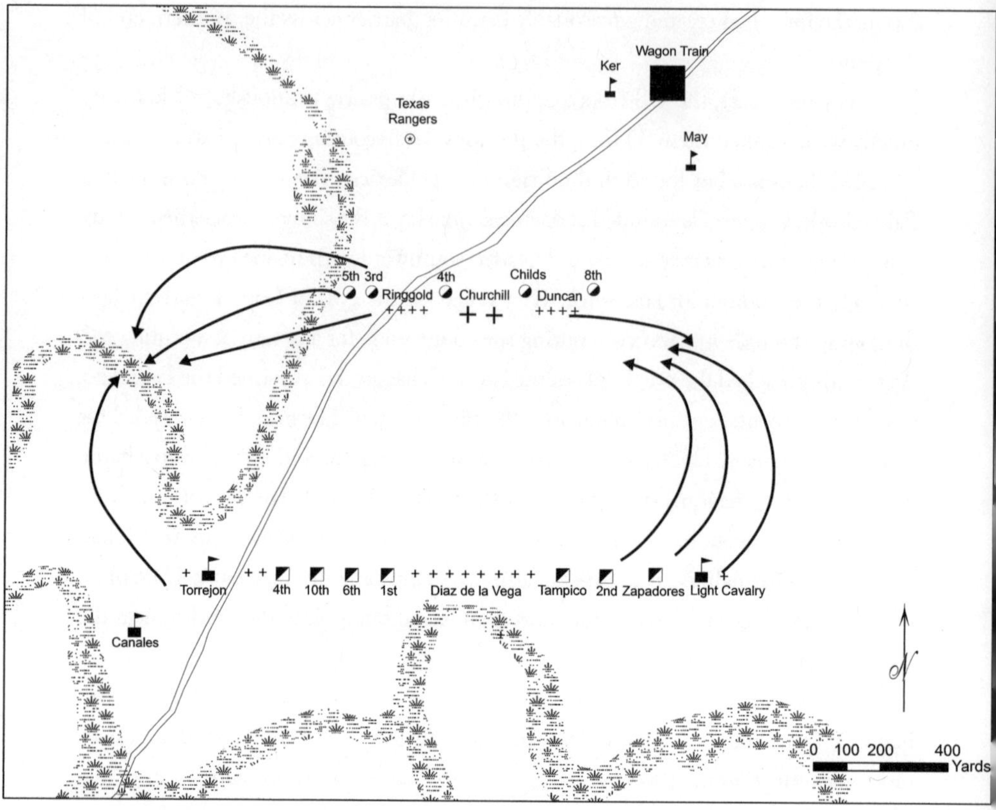

Battle positions at Palo Alto.

infantrymen, Capt. James Duncan with four more 6-pounder guns, and troops of the 8th Infantry to the far left. Dragoon companies commanded by Capts. Charles May and Croghan Ker were also assigned to Colonel Twiggs on the right wing and initially placed to the rear to cover the US supply wagons. Once established in this formation, a far more compact line than that displayed by the Mexicans across the field, the troops methodically pushed forward toward the waiting foe.[57]

The advance unfolded slowly. Lt. George Deas later gave a glowing description of the field as "a beautiful level prairie, covered with luxuriant grass and flowers,"[58] but in reality it was a slow, difficult march through dense coastal plants and stands of tall, stiff cord grass, "pointed at the top, and hard and almost as sharp as a darning-needle."[59] Movement of the artillery was even more cumbersome. Although the companies of light artillery were able to position their guns quickly to the fore of the line, the two

18-pounders, under the command of Lt. William Churchill, were more troublesome. The huge cannons and accompanying ammunition wagons were each pulled by teams of twelve oxen. Considerable maneuvering was required to drag the guns forward, swing them around in a wide, arcing turn, and place them, muzzles forward, to command the Mexican line. By the time U.S troops reached a position about eight hundred yards north of the enemy position and declared themselves ready to fight, it was already after 2 p.m.[60]

Many of the soldiers expressed astonishment that the Mexican force did not strike out as they deployed. This wonder increased when Lt. Jacob Blake of the engineers rode forward to within one hundred yards of the opposing line and methodically surveyed artillery placements without receiving a single shot in challenge. "Arista must have thought he had performed his whole duty when he barred the road with his troops to prevent Taylor from advancing," recalled Lt. Samuel French. "He had been in line of battle all the morning awaiting our coming, yet he permitted us to deploy undisturbed, although we were in easy range of his guns. Instead of assuming the offensive as he should have done."[61] This inactivity appeared all the more curious as the US troops judged that the enemy formation contained from five thousand to eight thousand troops and could have easily overwhelmed them as they deployed.

The scene that French and his companions interpreted as a display of confident strength in fact demonstrated the very weakness of Arista's position. The long, menacing-looking Mexican line was, in fact, a dangerously overextended formation caused by the rapid march from the Tanques with no opportunity to close the ranks adequately. The patient, almost courtly wait by the Army of the North as Taylor's force deployed was equally illusory. The Mexican troops had rushed to the field without a chance to pause for water or rest and had barely moved into position when the U.S soldiers began to advance. As Lieutenant Blake made his notable foray along the Mexican front, Arista was still surveying his ranks, rectifying his formation where possible, and exhorting the men and officers "to maintain order and bring victory to the Nation."[62] It was not until 2:30 p.m., when messengers brought word that Ampudia was approaching from the south, that Arista felt prepared to engage in battle. Ampudia had been very nearly right about being unable to reach the field of battle in time to fight. His imminent arrival, at the head of the 4th Infantry, a sapper company, and two additional artillery pieces, and accompanied by Gen. Antonio Canales with two hundred additional cavalry from the Villas del Norte, gave Arista the confidence at last to roll his cannon forward and commence firing on the Americans.[63]

Even then, Arista did not complete his order of battle until his second-in-command actually arrived on the field. The eastern portion of the line had been set for some time. Col. Luis Noriega and several squadrons of the light cavalry brigade held the rise on the right, supported by a single 4-pounder cannon. Moving to the left, Arista had positioned the Sapper Battalion, the 2nd Light Infantry Regiments, the Tampico Coast Guard Battalion and the Tampico Veterans Company. Continuing from right to left, the center of the line consisted of a battery of eight cannon from Gen. Rómulo Díaz de la Vega's artillery brigade, the 1st, 6th and 10th Infantry Regiments. The important left flank of the line did not take its final shape until the very last moment. When General Canales arrived from Matamoros, his force fell into line to the west of the road, just to the right of General Torrejón's cavalry regiment, which was made up of the presidial companies, most of the 2nd Light Cavalry and the 7th and 8th Cavalries, and a single light artillery piece. Canales and the troops of the Villas del Norte were separate from this group, assigned to watch the road and brush to ensure that no surprise attack would come out of the chaparral or from the direction of Matamoros. Last to arrive was Ampudia, with 4th Infantry, sappers, and two additional artillery pieces, which settled onto a point on the roadway between the cavalry and the 10th Infantry. With this force in place, the end result was a long line of alternating infantry and artillery units. The all-important cavalry units occupied each flank.[64]

Having adopted this formation, Arista now hoped to use the broad prairie to his advantage. He was well familiar with his American adversary and believed that he could lure the old infantry commander into a bayonet charge across the coastal plain. He intended to meet this charge with his infantry and artillery, mowing down as many US soldiers as possible as they advanced and confronting the rest with organized volleys from his lines. Once the two lines engaged, he could also bring his cavalry units into action, directing the horsemen to sweep around the flanks and engulf the US troops in a classic pincer maneuver.[65]

In the process, he would also separate the American soldiers from their wagons to the rear, depriving them of supplies and ammunition. If fighting progressed as Arista hoped, the strategy would nullify the effectiveness of the American artillery. As the lines closed on each other and the US and Mexican ranks mingled, the well-trained American artillerists would have to hold their fire to avoid hitting their own countrymen. Meanwhile, the Mexican cavalry would still be free to operate, and Arista hoped that fast-moving lancers could sweep across the field to silence these guns permanently. It was a risky strategy, but Arista had reason to be hopeful. During his crossing of the

Arroyo Colorado in March, Taylor had already demonstrated his willingness to thrust infantry forward at the expense of artillery effectiveness. Then, against a small force that had withdrawn, the move had had no ill effects. Now, with his force of more than thirty-nine hundred men, Arista hoped to make him suffer.[66]

In both word and deed leading up to the battle, Zachary Taylor had demonstrated that he fully intended to make an infantry charge as Arista envisioned. Despite earlier statements about the importance of artillery, as he prepared to leave Point Isabel he had little to say about that arm of his forces. Instead, when the general emphasized the probability of battle, he wanted "to enjoin upon the battalions of infantry that their main dependence must be in the bayonet." He reiterated this goal on the prairie south of Palo Alto. As he rode the length of his line, he paused before each infantry regiment and exhorted his foot soldiers with the reminder, "The bayonet, and my hearty cocks. The bayonet is the thing." Once finished with the revue, and after inspiring enthusiastic cheers from the brigades, he ordered them forward in a slow, precise, and deliberate advance toward the center of the Mexican line. When he halted the men at a point about eight hundred yards from the opposing forces, most believed that the order to charge would come at any moment.[67]

Instead, artillery took over. As the Americans moved within range, a cannon on the right of the Mexican line opened fire on the approaching US 8th Infantry. James Longstreet, a lieutenant in that regiment, recalled the shot as a puff of smoke and a ball that bounded across the field and over the heads of the troops before striking a teamster well to their rear. Other pieces on the Mexican line followed suit, sending a salvo toward the US ranks. Taylor responded by rolling his own guns to the fore and returning fire from the two light artillery batteries and the two massive 18-pounders. Within minutes the fighting escalated into a thunderous exchange of cannon fire on a grand scale. "The roar of so many pieces of artillery was truly appalling," wrote Pvt. Styles Hawley, "while round, grape, and canister shot hurled through the air in metallic showers of death dealing missiles." The infantry troops, in the meantime, remained to the rear, some standing, some prone, but all "anxious for the order to rush in and participate actively in the affair."[68]

Taylor never issued the awaited order. From the first shots in the exchange it became apparent to the troops that their artillery had exacted a significant toll in the opposing lines. The US batteries, Capt. Phillip N. Barbour recalled, "fired incessantly and with such dreadful effect that at each discharge we could see their ranks thrown into confusion and gaps made in them which it required some moments to close up." Despite his avowed determination to press forward with bayonets, Taylor appears to have acceded to the advice of his two brigade commanders, Colonels Twiggs and Belknap, who recommended that he continue to concentrate on artillery. The US general could not fail to recognize the effectiveness of his cannon and saw no reason to revert to his original plan. He also appears to have assessed the situation and decided that a charge would leave his wagon train vulnerable to a counterattack by Mexican cavalry. Placing high value on the security of his supplies, he permitted the artillerists to continue the fight while the infantry remained at the rear.[69]

For much of the afternoon, the foot soldiers would remain spectators to this display of artillery power. As observers they had little doubt that the exchange of fire favored the American Army. "The physical effect, acting reversely on the two armies, was distinctly manifest," wrote Alexander Hays, a lieutenant in the 4th Infantry. "Rapidly the heavy guns continued to deliver their iron shower, greeted each round by the almost frantic cheers from our line, while confusion and consternation appeared fast demoralizing our opponents." This did not mean, however, that the US troops were completely out of danger. "The balls were constantly hissing over our heads or mowing their way through the tall grass," wrote Pvt. Barna Upton of the 3rd Infantry, "and it was astonishing how few struck our ranks. I noticed one ball spinning its way through the grass close to the ground with the swiftness of the swiftest car. It passed about six feet from me. The men who were in its path dodged it in safety."

Similar scenes unfolded along the entire US line to surprisingly little effect, for, as Ulysses S Grant of the 5th Infantry noted, the Mexican rounds "would strike the ground long before they reached our line, and ricocheted through the tall grass so slowly that the men would see them and open ranks and let them pass."[70]

Taylor's decision to rely on artillery yielded dire consequences in the Mexican ranks. Despite their rush to the battlefield, which had forced them to forego their breakfast, the soldiers of the Army of the North prepared for battle with pomp, enthusiasm, and energy. Regimental flags fluttered in the breeze, military bands guided the movements of the units, and the troops greeted the opening blasts from the cannons with patriotic cheers. This spirit soon faded. Troops of the 4th Infantry were still stepping into line when their movement drew the fire of Samuel Ringgold's light battery. Casualties mounted even as the men rushed to complete the line. At the same time, the two massive 18-pounder guns unleashed a shower of balls, canister shot, and exploding shell that targeted the bands of the 2nd Light Battalion, the 1st Infantry, and the cavalry regiments. "The enemy batteries . . . pounded our left," recalled one participant in the fight, "and our brave soldiers flew through the air without firing their weapons. They remained in formation, like an immobile wall, and responding to the balls and hail that pounded our line only with cries of Viva Mexico and Viva la Independencia. The battle calls along the line sounded over the cannon fire, but the regimental bands ceased as if by enchantment, because they were all destroyed at once by the heavy artillery of the enemy."[71] Within moments all portions of the line were receiving heavy fire and experiencing similar devastating results.[72]

Arista's artillery crews could not replicate the intensity or effect of this fire. The smaller- caliber Mexican cannon lacked the range of the American artillery, and many shots struck well short of their targets and bounced harmlessly through the US lines. Lacking a selection of exploding projectiles to match the Americans' and unable to effectively shower Taylor's infantry with shrapnel, the artillerists instead directed their guns at the opposing cannons, hoping to silence one of the offending weapons with a direct hit. The inaccuracy of their guns made this an unlikely proposition, and the shots consistently missed their marks, though they occasionally took a toll as they bounded into the infantry troops positioned to the rear. But these lucky shots did nothing to arrest the steady stream of incoming rounds as they pounded the ranks of Mexican infantry and cavalry. The enemy artillery "shed death all along our line without having the slightest fear of our guns," lamented Gen. Antonio Jauregui of the 7th Cavalry. "Our soldiers rested on their weapons, able to do nothing but thrust themselves into the gaps that the enemy balls constantly made in our lines."[73]

Confronted by the overwhelming power of the US artillery, Arista tried to salvage a portion of his plan. From his position on the extreme right of the Mexican line, he sent orders to Gen. Anastasio Torrejón, who anchored the far left, to initiate a sweeping charge around the western edge of the field to engage the US right flank. He intended for this cavalry—especially the well-trained lancers—to use their blazing speed to take the Americans by surprise. Then, at the moment the two forces engaged, he planned to send José María Carrasco's light infantry and Luis Noriega's light cavalry around the American left flank as the second point of the pincer. These charges were made more difficult by the refusal of the American force to advance across the field, but with speed—and a little bit of luck—the Mexican horsemen could skirt around the enemy artillery and engage the infantry that waited at the rear. The best possible outcome would be that the lancers might cut off or destroy the American supply train. Failing that, the charge might, at least, produce a lull in the withering cannon fire.[74]

Like so many other plans of the day, however, this one did not proceed smoothly. After issuing his command to charge, Arista waited patiently for his distant lancers to spur into action, but Torrejón showed no sign of advancing. Questions later arose as to whether Torrejón had simply refused to charge, or whether Ampudia, seeking an opportunity to disgrace the men who had replaced him in command, neglected to pass the order down the line. Whatever the cause, Arista had to send out the call four more times before the cavalry began to respond. This delayed the maneuver by almost an hour, during which time the length of the Mexican line continued to take deadly fire.[75]

The charge itself was equally ill-fated. In his hurry to establish position on the prairie, Arista never reached the far western segment of his line and had not adequately scouted the terrain in that area. He did not realize that the course he had charted for his cavalry led through areas of dense brush and across the marshy bed of a long resaca. Torrejón formed his troops in a broad column and blundered into this swampy area, causing one third of his horsemen and a 4-pounder artillery piece that he carried with him to became mired in the mud. The remainder of his force continued forward but slowed to a trot to avoid the same fate. As it approached the US flank, the troubled charge also suffered from the indecision and hesitation of the vanguard troops. For reasons that he never explained, Torrejón placed presidial troops at the fore of his ranks and had them lead the charge. These men had considerable experience fighting Comanches along the northern frontier but little practice with this type of maneuver. As a result, they failed to drive their horses to the necessary "violent charge" as they came into contact with the US troops.[76]

The delay and confusion ensured that Torrejón's charge did not take Taylor's force by surprise. The troops on the US right flank clearly saw the Mexican cavalry move off into the trees in a long, loping arc that would carry them toward the American supply train. Colonel Twiggs responded by sending much of his infantry and two guns from Ringgold's light battery to counter the move. The Mexican horsemen advanced so slowly that Col. James McIntosh and the 5th Infantry were able to move four hundred yards to the west and form a defensive square, partly protected by the low bank of a resaca. The troops then waited as the body of about eight hundred horsemen approached, "expecting, by the show of such superior numbers, to be entirely enveloped by an aggressive charge." But the presidials at the head of this mass relied instead on frontier Indian-fighting tactics. As the cavalry slowly advanced, a small party of troops would rush forward, deliver a fusillade from their *escopetas,* then wheel back toward the main body and out of range of the US guns. The US infantrymen waited patiently for several cycles of this maneuver, reserving fire even as several soldiers were struck by Mexican shot. Then, as the enemy approached to within fifty yards, an entire face of the square opened fire, "giving them a glorious volley of buck and ball cartridges" which unseated more than thirty men and forced the horsemen to withdraw.[77]

The action had not yet ended. Mexican cavalrymen regrouped out of musket range, rolled forward the cannon they carried with them, and prepared to force their way around the US troops. At that moment, the US 3rd Infantry rushed in and formed another square to the right and rear of the 5th to block the way. Simultaneously, Randolph Ridgely and his troops charged forward and planted their two 6-pounders between the two squares. In the rapid fashion that had earned their corps the title of "flying artillery," they unlimbered and loaded their guns and fired several rounds of canister shot before their foes could muster a single artillery round. Thwarted by this fire, the Mexicans finally withdrew toward their original position, hastened and scattered by additional rounds from Ridgely's guns.[78]

The US troops not only repelled this maneuver, they pursued Torrejón as he fell back. While other units had rushed to confront the advancing cavalry, Maj. Samuel Ringgold continued to rake the opposing line with his remaining two field pieces. The Mexican 4th Infantry reeled from his withering fire and Ringgold methodically pressed forward down the roadway with each shot. He eventually reached the position held by Torrejón at the start of the battle and opened fire on the retreating cavalry as it attempted to return to this spot. Confronted once again with a deadly mixture of exploding shot, Mexican riders were forced to continue southward to reassemble to the rear of the 4th Infantry.[79]

The failure of Torrejón's charge was compounded for the Mexicans by their inability to launch the accompanying attack from the far end of the field. Col. José María Carrasco's 2nd Light Infantry and the troops of the 2nd Light Cavalry endured prolonged fire from Capt. James Duncan's light artillery battery as they waited for the distant cavalry forces to initiate the charge. Torrejón finally advanced, and they watched intently for the contact that would serve as their signal to advance. But the view was soon shrouded. Wadding from one of Duncan's cannon set the grass on fire, and a steady northeast wind carried the flames and a dense grey smoke across the field. When the smoke cleared, the scene from the western part of the field revealed that Torrejón had been turned back, and Carrasco "remained firm in the line."[80]

General Arista and his fellow officers thought that Taylor's troops had intentionally set the grass ablaze. Movement behind the wall of smoke appeared to support that opinion. Just as the haze had begun to blow across the field, Samuel Ringgold's artillery started moving toward the Mexican left. When the smoke had all but cut off sight of the US line, the Mexican officers caught glimpses of other units advancing down the roadway behind the artillery. Even the units on the eastern end of the American line where the fire had begun appeared to be using the smoke screen to position themselves for a push toward the weakened part of the Mexican line far across the field. Arista responded by matching his line to the new US orientation: his troops turned from the north to face in a more northwesterly direction. In this position Arista felt that he was better situated to maintain a front against the Americans if they tried to push down the road toward the riverside fort.[81]

Despite Mexican concerns, the combination of dense smoke and the reorientation of the American line was not a scheme by Taylor to hide preparations for an attack against the Mexican left. The US troops did make substantial adjustments to their line, but they were responding to Torrejón's failed assault, not plotting a charge of their own. The movement of infantry and light artillery to confront the Mexican cavalry had left Lt. Churchill and his 18-pounders unsupported on the roadway. Their isolation became even more conspicuous when Ringgold rolled his pieces forward to pursue the retreating horsemen, leaving the heavy artillery far to his rear. Fearing that the cavalry troops might circle around and attack these deadly guns, Taylor ordered the 4th Infantry and Child's artillery battalion to advance down the road in support. It was this movement that changed the face of the US line from the south to the southeast and prompted the Mexican concern. As a wall of fire and smoke forced a lull in the firing—and at some points along the lines a complete halt in it—the 5th Infantry returned from intercepting Torrejón and took a place in the newly constituted formation as well. Moreover, troops on the US left shifted to protect that flank from the Mexican horsemen, who could be seen assembling nearby.

All these movements coincided with the grass fire, but the US troops hardly saw the flames as an advantage. Many thought that the Mexican cavalry's retreat would have allowed them to overrun the Mexican line if the wall of smoke had not blocked their way. "We should soon have been at them horse, foot and dragoons," wrote George McCall, remembering the incident. Instead, he found himself sitting with his regiment in defensive square formation for more than an hour as they waited for the smoke to clear.[82]

The Mexicans were, however, correct in their assumption that Taylor had not given up on reaching his besieged fort. As the flames burned down to embers and firing resumed, the American general vowed that he would reach Matamoros and that he would drive the Mexicans out of the way in the process. He ordered Charles May to lead his squadron of dragoons against the Mexican left, to see if he could turn the weakened Mexican cavalry. Troops with the US 4th Infantry, now clustered near the 18-pounder guns, were sent to offer support. May advanced about four hundred yards toward the Mexican forces still positioned on the road, but his small party of riders drew heavy fire from several artillery pieces. Five of his men were wounded and six of his horses killed, and he fell back, realizing the futility of persisting.

The troops of the 4th, meanwhile, got a hint of what might have happened had the US Army opened the battle with an infantry charge. As they approached the opposing line, Mexican cannon opened upon them fiercely, wounding one man, killing another, and striking Capt. John Page in the face with a blow that removed his jaw. Although the death of Pvt. Lee was equally ghastly—he had his entire head carried away by a cannonball—it was the sight of the bloody and writhing Captain Page that truly captured the attention of the troops around him. "He presented such a ghastly spectacle that a sickly, fainting sensation came over me," recalled C. M. Reeves years later, "and the memory of that sight I will carry with me to my dying day." Reeves and the rest of the 4th, who had suffered no other injuries up to that point, quickly moved out of range. Like most of the other US regiments, they would remain out of reach of the Mexican fire for the duration of the battle.[83]

As the artillery exchange resumed, the Mexican forces again suffered badly. Once more the American guns mowed down men, horses, and anything else within their substantial range. Even those well to the rear of the action were not safe. Artillery rounds bounded into a supply area more than seven hundred yards behind the line, striking a hospital tent well to the east of the battle. An unfortunate soldier who was having his wounded left arm amputated suddenly had the right removed by an errant round. It was a devastating experience in which "the soldiers succumbed not while engaged in a combat that permitted them to return the death that they received and not while performing daring acts in the heat of the fray, but in a fatal situation where they died without recourse, decimated in cold blood."[84]

Surrounded by the bodies of their fallen comrades, the Mexican troops pleaded to be allowed to either charge the enemy with bayonets or fall back out of reach of their guns. Arista refused both requests. He knew that a retreat would effectively result in the surrender of the land north of the Río Bravo to the United States. And he believed that an advance would create an outcome like that of the 1832 Mexican civil war battle of Gallinero, in which an ill-fated charge produced more than two thousand casualties. Uncertain how to proceed, he continued to keep his troops in formation, perhaps hoping to hold out for the approach of nightfall. His response to the demands of his infantry for a general charge was to move his line forward about twenty yards, so that men would no longer have to stand among the dead or hear the moans of the wounded who lay on the ground at the previous position.[85]

The Mexican cannoneers, meanwhile, redoubled their efforts to silence the damaging US guns. Gen. Rómulo Díaz de la Vega, in charge of the Mexican artillery, concentrated all his attention on silencing the two 18-pounders and Samuel Ringgold's foremost guns. He was unable to do that. One well-directed shot did strike Ringgold in both legs as he directed the firing of his battery, but this success for the Mexican gunners was minor. Medical personnel rushed the major away to tend to his grievous wound, but his efficient corps never slackened the pace of their firing.[86]

With the sun beginning to slant low in the western sky, Arista finally decided to try another offensive maneuver. Once again, he called for a two-pronged cavalry charge against the American flanks, hoping to sweep around a line that had become constricted in the course of the fight. As before, General Torrejón set out on the left, this time avoiding the marshy resaca and driving his cavalry directly toward the muzzles of the giant siege cannons. The charge proceeded much more quickly than the previous one had, but it was no more successful. As the riders approached, they once again met a defensive square formation, this time made by the troops of General Taylor's artillery brigade, which effectively checked their advance. Next, the huge 18-pounders erupted with several rounds of canister shot that created disorder in the ranks and threw the Mexican horsemen into such disarray that they were obliged to fall back to the relative safety of the Mexican line.[87]

On the eastern end of the field, the charge fared little better. Arista had noted that James Duncan's light artillery battery and the US 8th Infantry Regiment had been left somewhat isolated by the shift of the US line, and he sent the light cavalry, the Sapper Battalion and the 2nd Light Infantry to turn that flank. But the advance soon demonstrated that Arista had been correct to avoid a full-scale advance. The foot soldiers became entangled in the tall, sharp grass that covered the field and their units fell into disarray as they attempted to rush forward. By the time the scattered troops reconstituted themselves into an organized fighting force, they found themselves directly in front of the US 8th Infantry, which halted them with a volley of musket fire. The cavalry troops had also been slowed by the grass

Battle of Palo Alto. *Courtesy of H. R. Hudson Collection.*

and by the disjointed advance of the infantry. As they finally burst from the haze of smoke that still shrouded the area, they encountered heavy fire from two of Duncan's guns. Driven westward across the front of the US lines, they faced a barrage of musketry and canister shot as they herded the infantry before them back to the Mexican line.[88]

This action, when viewed from the US line, provided proof that that scattered units thrown together in Corpus Christi nine months before had emerged as a unified fighting force. From the instant the Mexican troops began their advance, the diverse elements of the 1st Brigade responded in unison like a well-oiled machine. The 8th Infantry, which had remained idle but under heavy fire for much of the afternoon, hurried to intercept the advancing Mexican infantry, quickly formed another defensive square, and calmly met their foes with well-directed, organized fire. Capt. Crohan Ker provided cavalry support. When Cayetano Montero, who had replaced the wounded Luis Noriega at the head of the light cavalry, tried to lead his horsemen in a sweeping arc around the 8th Infantry square, Ker and his Dragoons rushed forward from their position near the American wagon train and blocked the path.[89]

But it was James Duncan and the light artillery that really stood out. Observing the two-pronged attack of cavalry and infantry, the captain divided his battery to respond to both. He repositioned two of his guns to the extreme left of the American line, unleashing a deadly fire as Ker forced the Mexican cavalry in his direction. He then used his guns to drive the enemy across the face of the infantry square, which responded with its own fire. The other two cannons, in the meantime, were moved to the right of the 8th Infantry, punishing the Mexican foot soldiers as they advanced and showering the enemy cavalry and infantry alike as they fled back across the field. "The impression made by Duncan's battery on the extreme right of the enemy line contributed largely to the result of the day," General Taylor noted impassively in his official report of the battle.[90] John Porter Hatch was somewhat more enthusiastic in his recollection of the incident. "It was really terrible in its effect," he wrote in a letter to his sister, "entirely breaking their ranks and throwing them into the utmost confusion. . . . If the General had only have let the infantry charge we should have put on the finishing stroke, but the general is a very cautious man and would not leave his train."[91]

The lieutenant of the 3rd Artillery Regiment was not entirely correct in this assessment. Although his general undoubtedly did not want to invite unnecessary risks, it was the lateness of the hour rather than caution that prevented him from following up on the effects of Duncan's guns. As the Mexican horsemen returned to their lines under fire, it was close to 7 p.m. With twilight setting in and the field illuminated only by the glowing embers of the dying fires, the general realized the futility of attempting to advance into the shadows that obscured the enemy. Arista had reached the same conclusion, and was already pulling his troops back toward the shelter of the chaparral on the southern edge of the field. Allowing nature to dictate events, Taylor called for a cessation of firing and pulled his troops back into a defensive formation around his wagon train. After five hours, the battle of Palo Alto had come to a halt.[92]

CHAPTER 8
Decision

★

IN HIS INITIAL report of the recently completed battle near Palo Alto, Mariano Arista presented a fairly positive assessment of the day's events to Mexico's minister of war and interim president. He described a fierce battle in which the Americans had attempted to break through the Mexican lines but were repeatedly turned back by determined Mexican troops. "The national arms shone forth," he wrote, "since they did not yield a hand's breadth of ground." He did add details that considerably tempered these positive words. It had been primarily an artillery clash and the enemy had been superior in that arm, launching about 3000 rounds into his lines while his return fire had amounted to only about 850 rounds. Although he assured his superiors that the enemy had "suffered much damage," he offered no specific numbers of American dead and wounded. By contrast, he provided somewhat alarming figures for his own casualties. "Our troops have to lament the loss of 252 men dispersed, wounded, and killed, the last worthy of national recollection and gratitude for the intrepidity with which they died fighting for the most sacred of causes." But the casualty figures—probably significantly lower than the actual tally—could not be ignored no matter how glorious the cause. Although Arista tried to accentuate the positive, these numbers indicated that the Army of the North clearly had a problem.[1]

The army's troubles, though, went far beyond what Arista revealed. It was true that the Mexicans had stayed on the battlefield, but this was due to good luck more than to the "shining" of the national arms. Gen. Antonio Canales later observed that many of the soldiers were preparing to abandon the field just as the sun set. "If the night had not covered this shameful flight," he wrote, "our defeat would have been complete in that moment."[2] Casualties also soared far above the levels Arista reported.

Even as the general wrote his report, crews of soldiers continued to locate more bodies that had fallen in the blackened shrub and become obscured by the darkness. The dead they buried in shallow graves, with little fanfare or concern for an accurate count. The wounded, more easily located by their piteous moans, were carried to the field hospital for treatment, usually the amputation of one or more limbs. This sad work exacted a toll on the soldiers who had survived the horrific cannonade. As the evening wore on, officers noted a steady and unsurprising drop in the spirits of their troops.

Demoralization led to anger, and rumors spread through the ranks that Arista had sold out his army and his nation for some unspecified personal reward from the Americans. These charges had begun flying during the heat of battle and appeared to have originated in the part of the line under the direct command of Pedro de Ampudia. In his headquarters the general-in-chief sensed the collapse in morale and the insubordination of his second-in-command. As the night deepened, he plotted strategy for the following morning. All the while, he grew increasingly doubtful of his ability to rely on his downhearted troops and disloyal officers when the fighting resumed at daybreak.[3]

The battle was far less damaging to the US force. In his initial report, General Taylor briefly recounted the events of the clash, praised the performance of his artillery, and listed losses at four men killed, three officers and thirty-nine enlisted men wounded. Maj. Samuel Ringgold, Capt. John Page, and others would eventually succumb to their injuries, raising the mortality count to thirteen. Nevertheless, the relieved troops generally agreed with Taylor that these casualties were "comparatively trifling" and passed the evening with none of the infighting that afflicted the Mexican force.[4]

Confidence also climbed as the Americans saw the effects of their cannonade on the enemy. From their position along the Matamoros road and the western edge of the field, the American soldiers could hear the cries of the Mexican wounded. Flames still flickering across the charred prairie illuminated the movement of the Mexican search parties as they scoured the field for their fallen comrades.[5] Lt. Arthur Tracy Lee described the scene in the poem "The Night of Palo Alto," written by the light of a campfire that evening.

> Let us rest on the sod, whilst the moon shines bright;
> We have nothing to fear from our foes to-night:
> On the battle-stained field, where their dead are strewn,
> They have plenty of work, 'neath the midnight moon.
> Hark! 'tis the sound of the mattock and spade,

Breaking the ground by the chaparral shade,
God! whilst thy zephyrs are over us sighing,
Grant peace to the dead, send hope to the dying.[6]

Awareness of their success and a degree of sympathy for their fallen foes did not lead the Americans into complacency or overconfidence. Although the soldiers knew that they had caused substantial damage to the Mexican force, they remained unaware of the degree of its impact. They also continued to overestimate the size of Arista's army, believing that he still had some fifty-five hundred troops who were not only in fighting condition, but also anxious to turn the tables when battle resumed. With visions of this potent fighting force driving their imaginations and the knowledge that the Mexicans rested just a few hundred yards away, sentries kept a careful watch through the night. The remaining troops tried to sleep, however fitfully, on the bare ground, with weapons close at hand—for, as Lieutenant Lee went on to write,

When the morning light breaks over yesterday's slain,
Each arm must be strong for the conflict again.

Soldiers throughout the American ranks agreed and expected the battle to resume at dawn.[7]

For much of the night, Arista proceeded as if he intended to give them that battle on the same field. At around 9 p.m. he sent a dispatch to his officers near the river, detailing the bloody clash that had occurred and indicating that he expected another encounter in the morning. He instructed General Mejía in Matamoros to send five hundred 4-pounder cannonballs and one hundred 8-pounders across the river to the Villa de Ampudia, a small settlement on the north bank of the Río Bravo about five miles upstream from Matamoros. From there, Lt. Gen. Joaquín Morlet, who now commanded the small compliment of Mexican troops that still kept watch over the fort, was to send this matériel by cart to Palo Alto. Arista was dangerously low on ammunition following the cannonade of that afternoon and desperately needed the supplies before daybreak.[8]

As the night wore on, however, Arista's troops became increasingly reluctant to stay near Palo Alto for another day. The soldiers had interred as many of their dead as possible and shipped most of the wounded by wagon to Matamoros, but images of the damage done by the US cannons was not so easily erased from their memories.

Exhaustion, hunger, and darkness contributed to the general lack of confidence, and the men began to express doubts about their chances during another day of artillery fire. Moreover, the charges made against Arista, presumably by Ampudia, helped whip soldiers' fears for life and limb into a mood of rebelliousness verging on outright mutiny. "I have not been able to understand the goal of the authors of this infamy," Colonel Antonio Jauregui would write of the defamation of Arista, "and I am persuaded that they failed to calculate the degree of damage that they were doing to the fatherland when they thought that all they were doing was discrediting and robbing glory from our general-in-chief." Whatever the motive, the murmuring in the ranks indicated an increasing unwillingness among the troops to resume fighting on the same spot. As General Canales more succinctly put it, "The fortunes of the battle were very much in doubt if it was to continue on the same field."[9]

Hope that the light of day would dissipate some of the gloom and rebelliousness faded quickly. As the first rays of sunlight streamed onto the field, the soldiers realized that the shallow pools on the battlefield that had been their source of drinking water as they labored in the darkness were stained red with the blood of their fallen companions. Relief at seeing the end of a bad night gave way to revulsion and further eroded the will of the soldiers to fight.[10]

Although he was determined to engage the Americans again, Arista had already decided to abandon the field at Palo Alto. In a strategy session with his chiefs, he outlined the reasons for a move. He was afraid that Taylor's troops had discovered another route to the river and could use it to bypass his force without a fight. If fighting did resume, his artillerists had expended most of their ammunition and had only a few rounds of grapeshot left with which to fend off an advance. But the overriding motive for a change of venue was the deteriorating spirits of his men and the realization that they lacked the will to undergo another day of artillery fire on the prairie. "Following the battle of Palo Alto the troops were generally frightened and had lost morale," he announced to the minister of war. "This obliged me to seek another way to challenge the enemy and I proposed to place the troops under cover from the fire of cannon, where they might make use of muskets and bayonets." Although he had no clear idea where he would reestablish his line, Arista ordered the army to fall back along the road to Matamoros to seek refuge and a new line of defense in the chaparral to the south.[11]

The dim light of the sunrise found US soldiers watching the motion across the field and assuming that the Mexicans were reestablishing their battle line near the

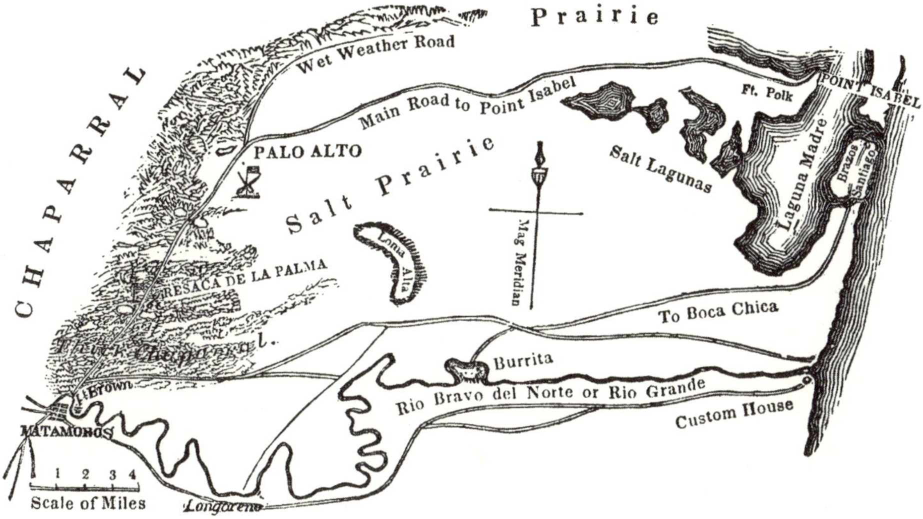

Military Sites of the Rio Grande Delta. *Courtesy of Library of Congress.*

brush on the southern edge of the prairie. Taylor responded by positioning the supply train where the troops could build low entrenchments to protect it. Once these rudimentary fortifications were completed, the army would reestablish its battle line and advance to meet the enemy once more. As these preparations got underway, however, Colonel Twiggs informed the general that many officers in the ranks opposed the idea of reengaging the Mexicans. Despite the obvious success of the previous day, rumors had spread that thousands of additional Mexican troops had arrived under cover of darkness and that Arista now had the strength to annihilate the small US force. Some officers consequently advised extending the entrenchments to protect the entire army, and then awaiting reinforcements. Taylor hastily convened a council of war, at which seven of the ten officers involved voted to hold their ground. But the general had already made the decision to proceed and was not to be dissuaded. He ignored their recommendation and directed his troops to deploy in a battle formation largely identical to that of the previous day.[12]

At about 7:30 a.m. the US troops once again found themselves methodically marching their battle line forward to engage their foe. This time, however, there was no opposing line waiting to fire at them. As the sun rose higher in the east and they closed on the position where the Mexicans had been, they realized that Arista's troops were nowhere in sight. Unsure whether they had retreated or just hidden themselves in the brush beyond, Taylor halted his line and sent scouts forward to reconnoiter the area. An hour later, at about 9 a.m., the scouts reported that they could find no Mexican forces in the brush at the south end of the field and that Arista had evidently continued southward on the road toward Matamoros.[13]

As the soldiers waited for the scouts to return, they began to better appreciate the devastation they had brought. They found several mass graves hastily dug near where the bodies had fallen on the Mexican line, and estimated that their foes had buried about 150 of their men. Additional bodies remained strewn across the field, most of them bearing signs of wounds from the American cannon fire of the previous day. "What havoc and what horrid wounds our artillery made," noted Surgeon Madison Mills. "I saw heads and limbs severed from their bodies and trunks strewed about in awful confusion. Many a body I saw that had been cut in twain by our 18 pounders and such ghastly spectacles I hope never to behold again." Others who also recorded the appalling scene were struck by scattered, broken weapons, abandoned supplies and ammunition, and other evidence of a hasty departure. Quickly the men fanned across the field, some gathering trophies of the fight, others tending to several wounded Mexican soldiers who had been left behind in the darkness and confusion.[14]

The scene boosted the American troops' confidence. Officers who just hours before had questioned the wisdom of a second confrontation now appeared eager for one. Taylor had never wavered in his determination to reengage the Mexicans, but now it was his turn to act with restraint. Aware that the most dangerous stretch of road lay ahead, he decided to leave his wagons at the Palo Alto battlefield, permitting a faster advance with less risk to his supplies. His troops took up shovels and devoted the next several hours to improving the fortifications that had already been constructed around the train earlier in the day. Lieutenant Churchill's 18-pounders, so effective in battle, were left behind to command the position. Two 12-pounders, not used the day before, were off-loaded from one of the carts and installed on heavy four-wheeled truck carriages and placed in the remaining corners of the defenses. When the rough structure finally was deemed sufficient to protect against a sudden cavalry assault, Taylor assigned fifty men from Churchill's artillery company and three hundred teamsters armed with muskets to stay behind to guard the supplies. The remainder of the troops gathered together what they needed and prepared to march.[15]

An advance party under Capt. George McCall set out first. Taylor had summoned McCall earlier that morning and put him in command of four light infantry companies, Capt. Charles Ferguson Smith's company of the 2nd Artillery, Captain

Walker and the Texas Rangers, and a small party of dragoons. This mixed force, numbering about two hundred, was to push ahead of the main army, scour the chaparral on either side of the road for evidence of an ambush, and verify that Arista's force had headed toward Matamoros. If he failed to encounter the enemy, McCall had instructions to wait at a small area known as "Jackass Prairie," about three miles along the road. If he encountered any Mexican detachments before that point, he had authorization to fight, as long as he did not risk his command. That was, as McCall later remembered, "a thing easier said than done in a country where you cannot always tell whether you are about to attack fifty men or five thousand." As it turned out, he encountered no enemy forces and reached the northern edge of Jackass Prairie without incident. He sent notice to Taylor that despite signs of Arista's troops' having passed through, the first stage of the route remained clear. That message reached Taylor about midday, and the general finally urged his army forward.[16]

The resumed advance began under the shadow of tragedy. As the troops waited for a report from McCall, another group of scouts returned from a long night of patrol duty. One of the men was Jacob Blake, who had distinguished himself with his reconnaissance in advance of the Palo Alto battle. Blake had been in the saddle for almost twenty-four hours and seized on the delay as an opportunity to take a brief rest. He dismounted his horse, unbuckled his holsters, and expressing relief for the respite, let his heavy gun belt drop to the ground. The impact caused one of the pistols to fire and the ball struck him in the femoral artery at close range. It was immediately apparent that Major Brown would not survive the wound, and he was left behind with the wagons. Although Samuel Ringgold would soon gain national attention as the first American officer to die in the war, Blake actually preceded him in death. His body would become the responsibility of Churchill's troops, who had already occupied themselves with the burial of the remaining Mexican dead.[17]

Despite this rather ominous start to the day's march, the advance proceeded without further mishap, quickly covering the first three miles to the prairie where they were to meet McCall. But only a small party waited for them there. The captain and his troops had gone on, hoping to locate the exact position of the Mexican force. Taylor and the rest of the army paused briefly for water at a resaca near the northern edge of the clearing, then resumed their march. During this stop, there was a brief moment of excitement at the discovery of the body of a Mexican woman, apparently murdered, that had been left by the side of the road. She was dressed in the clothes of the upper class and had features "singularly regular and beautiful." In the aftermath of the previous day's bloodshed, her unexplained death had a disproportional impact on the men. The poetic Lieutenant Lee even paused to write an ode to the unfortunate "maiden fair and lovely, midst the tangled chaparral." But the mysterious victim was the only Mexican living or dead that they spotted along the route. As they continue forward no threats emerged from the dense chaparral that flanked both sides of the narrow road.[18]

McCall and his advance party had experienced a more eventful march. After sending a message to Taylor that the route was clear, the party pushed ahead into the prairie to wait. There they encountered two stragglers from Arista's force, and after a brief pursuit, Walker's rangers killed one of them. The other surrendered and became a prisoner. This survivor informed McCall that Arista's army had lost five hundred men and was in full retreat. Encouraged by this information, McCall, who felt that he had accomplished little with his mission, decided to push ahead, against orders, and attempt to pinpoint the position of the foe. "I felt a strong desire to take a peep at the other Resaca [Resaca de la Palma]," he wrote, "for if the Mexican were not there no time should be lost in the pursuit." With this in mind, he continued on the road across the prairie to the chaparral on the far side. There he divided his command. He left the horsemen on the road and sent Captain Smith with four companies of the 1st Brigade to the right, while he and a hundred men entered the brush on the left. Both McCall and Smith immediately encountered small groups of Mexican horsemen hidden in the brush and came under increasingly heavy fire as they crept forward through the thickets. By the time they had moved within 150 yards of the resaca, a barrage of cannon fire, which killed one of his men and wounded two more, assured McCall that Arista was hidden in the dense foliage of the ravine ahead. He dispatched a message to Taylor to inform him of the situation, then fell back out of firing range to wait.[19]

Arista's own journey to that spot had been plagued with troubles and challenges, the first arising even before he began his march. Throughout the night, a number of his army's pack animals and carts had been commandeered for the duty of transporting the numerous wounded soldiers to Matamoros. At sunrise many of these carts were still on the road, and Arista discovered that he did not have enough wagons to carry his cache of supplies and ammunition. Eager to get on his way and locate a new defensive position, he loaded all the supplies that he could carry, then sequestered the remaining items in the woods to the south of the battlefield, at a point known as Resaca de Mesquite. He placed himself at the head of the 1st Battalion Artillery and his supply train, and set off in search of a new location. He had assigned General Ampudia charge of the 4th and 6th Infantries and the sappers and ordered his him to remain behind with these troops as a rearguard. Ampudia's party of about a thousand men was supposed to wait for wagons to return from Matamoros, assist with the loading, then hurry on to reunite with the rest of the army and the remaining matériel.[20]

Ampudia wanted no part of this plan. He estimated a two-hour wait for the wagons, with additional time required for loading. Then he would have to escort the wagons on the slow march to their new location, all the while guarding against an approach by the US Army that was expected at any moment. Ampudia doubted that he could successfully hold back Taylor's advance with only a thousand men, and he feared that a delay might endanger his chances of establishing a strong position farther down the road. He decided therefore to simply leave the extra supplies hidden. After waiting briefly to allow Arista time to travel some distance down the road, he sent a message to the general-in-chief announcing that the defense was impractical and that he was marching to rejoin the army. Arista twice sent aides back to repeat his demand that Ampudia wait, but each time the second-in-command refused to comply. It was only after Gen. Antonio Jauregui himself delivered the order that Ampudia paused and gave grudging support to the undertaking.[21]

Arista might have dealt with the insubordination more forcefully if he had not been busy searching for a suitable place to establish his new position. When he left the scene of the Palo Alto battle, he was evidently looking for the first defensible point along the road. He traveled only about three miles, to the open plain known to the US troops as "Jackass Prairie." There he began deploying his troops in the brush on the northern edge of the field, so as to trap the US forces on the narrow roadway and force them to fight an army hidden by brush. This was essentially the same strategy that he had intended but failed to employ at Palo Alto twenty-four hours earlier. As Arista organized his troops, however, Capt. Jean Louis Berlandier indicated that a more defensible position lay about three miles farther to the south, at the Resaca de Guerrero. Berlandier had an unrivaled knowledge of the region and Arista willingly heeded his advice. He reassembled his order of march, and at about midday set off for this new destination. An hour later, he redeployed his forces at the new site.[22]

The move was of mixed benefit. The Resaca de Guerrero did stand out as a superior defensive site. Here the roadway, cut through an area of particularly dense chaparral, narrowed the route to about twenty feet across. The path also passed over the resaca, a dry river bed about fifty yards wide, that snaked through the brush in a long, curving path. Long pools several feet deep dotted the channel, creating a ready supply of water for troops positioned along the banks. More significantly, the high, brush-covered banks of the ravine provided natural breastworks that afforded added protection. But the shift to this spot also cost the Mexicans valuable time and ensured that many soldiers could not eat or rest before battle. This did little to lighten the dark mood that continued to envelop them. The move also provided General Ampudia with another reason to denounce his commander, and he pointed to the shift of position as evidence that Arista "did not know the terrain or had not developed a fixed plan of operations."[23]

That assessment was not entirely true. Although Arista lacked an elaborate plan, he had determined that it was vital to maintain the isolation of the US troops in their fort on the banks of the Río Bravo. At the start, bombarding the fort had been an expedient to draw Taylor into the open. Now, preventing him from reaching it had become necessary. As long as Arista could stay between Taylor and the riverside fort, he could continue to control the action. Unlikely as it appeared, he might even still pull out a victory over the Americans. But if the Americans pushed past Arista's army, they could hold out in their earthworks indefinitely, bombard Matamoros, and continue to frustrate Mexican efforts to oust them. If the issue was not settled before additional American troops and supplies arrived at the Frontón, the undersupplied and undermanned Mexican force would have would little hope of reclaiming the lands north of the Bravo.[24]

Arista's deployment of troops at his new position demonstrated a rather detailed awareness of his location, its strengths and its weaknesses. He used his artillery to block the roadway, placing two 8-pounder and two 4-pounder guns on the north side of the resaca, and two additional pieces in the middle of the road to the south. To the right of the road, he stationed the 6th and 10th Infantries and the sappers. The 1st Infantry occupied the extreme right of the line, where the swale made a sharp bend to the north. A smaller route from the Tanques del Ramireño also passed through this area, cut across the resaca, and turned west to meet the main road. Here Arista positioned two more cannon to prevent passage along this only other known route toward the riverside fort. To the left, or west, of the road, the Tampico Coast Guard and Veterans Battalion and the 4th Infantry guarded the resaca with additional sappers on the extreme flank where the resaca turned shallow and nearly disappeared. Behind them, the Defensores de las Villas del Norte, supported by additional artillery, watched a narrow trail that led to a pool in the resaca, known as the Charco de la Palma, far to the west. His vanguard was the 2nd Light Infantry, which held a position on either side of the road several hundred yards ahead of the resaca. At the rear, his cavalry troops occupied a small opening in the chaparral about five hundred yards south of the resaca.[25]

Arista believed that this disposition would force the Americans to engage in a battle that would play to his strength. The brush and resaca banks would shelter his men from artillery fire, forcing Taylor to rely on an infantry charge. When that occurred, Arista's own artillery would be waiting on the roadway to frustrate the advance and push the attackers into the brush. There his infantry could engage them, at last enjoying the benefit of greater numbers and a sheltered position. He believed that if he could will his soldiers to put up a strong fight, he could repay some of the damage that Taylor had inflicted the previous day.[26]

Motivating his own troops was the great challenge. Arista had hoped that a withdrawal from the prairie at Palo Alto would improve spirits within the ranks, but the long march and a morning of toil without food had only worsened their dark mood. Given the troops' frame of mind, the general-in-chief prepared for battle with a relatively simple aim: to have the infantry lines successfully fire five volleys at the advancing enemy. This would not be enough to win the battle, but it would slow and disrupt the American advance companies. More importantly, he believed that a show of strength—and a corresponding display of weakness and confusion on the part of the US troops—would give encouragement to his men and help restore some of their lost confidence. If he could revive even a fraction of the enthusiasm that had prevailed in the ranks before the battle at Palo Alto, he felt certain that he could reverse the fortunes of that earlier clash.[27]

Simple as it was, Arista's strategy for a defensive stand was far better developed than Taylor's plan of attack. The US general received Captain McCall's report of the Mexican position at 3 p.m., while his army paused near Jackass Prairie. He immediately put his troops back on the road and arrived at McCall's location at 4 p.m., at the head of the troops that had formed his right wing at Palo Alto. Pausing just long enough to listen to McCall's description of the force mobilized ahead, he initiated his attack without hesitation. As the lead units arrived on the roadway, he immediately pushed them forward with little more than an exhortation to break the Mexican position.[28]

The general now reposed great confidence in his light artillery. Although he had had limited experience with cannons before the battle on the previous afternoon, their performance on the prairie had convinced him that he could replicate his success elsewhere. "Because the artillery had rendered such signal service on the field yesterday," wrote Lt. Samuel French of Ringgold's artillery company, "Gen. Taylor was impressed with the idea that it was available for pursuit of cavalry in mountain passes, for storming entrenchments, or charging a line of battle." The resaca was his first test of that confidence. When this light company emerged along a bend in the road, he hurried it forward, supported by McCall's advance party.[29]

Ringgold was no longer with the troops, having been taking to the hospital facilities at the Point, but Lt. Randolph Ridgely, who now led the unit, demonstrated that Taylor's trust had been well placed. He pushed his four pieces forward to within four hundred years of the batteries guarding the road, then waited briefly as some of McCall's men rode forward to draw the opposing fire. Using this ploy to pinpoint the location of the Mexican cannon in the brush, he opened up on them with a heavy shower of grapeshot. Giving the Mexicans no time to recover, he then moved up another hundred yards and entered into a fierce exchange with the opposing cannon. Each time the enemy artillery slackened its fire, Ridgely edged closer, firing and advancing until he occupied a position less than one hundred yards from the Mexican pieces.[30]

At the same time, infantry regiments moved into the brush on either side of the roadway. On the left the 5th Infantry, supplemented by a portion of the 4th, deployed as skirmishers and picked their way through the thorny brush toward the Mexicans fortified in the resaca bed. The 3rd Infantry deployed in a similar manner to the right, with the assistance of the remaining troops of the 4th. Any organization, however, broke down quickly in the dense thickets. It was impossible to hold the regiments together; as Lt. James Longstreet noted, "The companies were obliged to break files to get along." Lt. George Deas saw an even greater breakdown: "Formations became impossible," he wrote. "It was all pell-mell in a very short time." Lt. Ulysses Grant agreed. "The fight was a pel mel affair," he wrote to a friend, "everybody for himself." Within minutes Grant and a handful of men under his command had become entirely isolated from the rest of the army, with little awareness of what occurred beyond their line of vision. In all directions around him, others shared that experience as men of different units gathered around the closest available officer and advanced.[31]

Arista would soon discover that his defensive position at Resaca de Guerrero had serious weaknesses. The chaparral provided the shelter he desired, but it also hid the American attack. Along sections of the Mexican line, soldiers did not even realize that the battle was underway when the US troops suddenly appeared among them. Mexican cannon directed toward the distant point where the Americans were thought to be, fired high, and with little effect, over the heads of the nearby foe. And Arista's troops had trouble keeping in contact with each other as well. "The brushy forest that

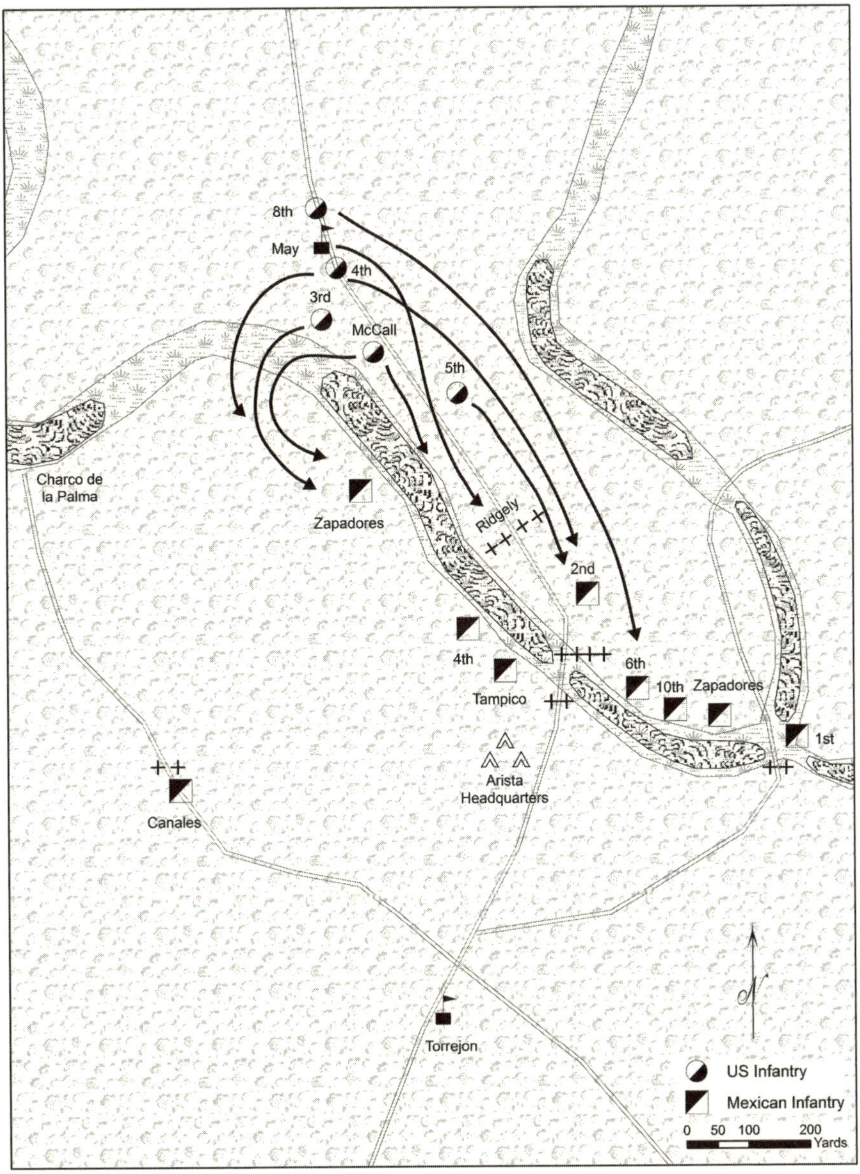

Battle Positions at Resaca de la Palma.

forms this battlefield is so dense that the soldiers had to use shovels simply to clear a big enough area to stand," wrote one official. "Our own officers couldn't even see the ranks and in the companies, men could only see those who touched shoulders with them." Most of the troops had never been in such a situation. As the shooting began, they felt isolated and afraid, uncertain whether friend or foe approached.[32]

Arista also discovered that his own position was not as impervious to cannon fire as he had hoped. The road running from the Frontón did not approach the Resaca de Guerrero on a straight, north-to-south orientation. Instead it came at an angle from the northwest, before bending sharply southward at the crossing point. The advancing US artillery began firing well before it reached that bend, with their shots following the same southeasterly direction followed by the road. The initial rounds had limited impact on the troops guarding the path across the swale, but poured almost directly along the length of the resaca in an unintended enfilade action. The infantrymen in the ravine, facing forward into the brush, found themselves under fire from the left flank. These rounds of cannister shot had limited impact, or at least far less than at Palo Alto, but they nonetheless contributed to the disorientation and anxiety of the Mexican troops.[33]

Overtaken by fear, many of Arista's troops simply would not put up a fight. The two companies of 2nd Light Infantry offered some firm resistance as the fighting began, but they soon fell back after suffering heavy losses. As the survivors fled for safety, the troops behind them became disconcerted and lost the will to hold their ground. Arista had hoped for five volleys from each unit, but in many instances he was lucky to get a single wildly inaccurate shot before the men dropped their muskets and ran. At many points along the line officers struggled mightily to restrain their soldiers, but often to little effect. Gen. Mariano García of the infantry brigade exhorted the troops of the 1st, 6th, and 10th Infantry Regiments to hold their ground, but he soon stood alone. Col. José Uraga confronted similar defections. His 4th Infantry troops had endured some of the heaviest fire at Palo Alto without breaking, but they could not sustain that courage at the resaca. Uraga started the battle with 450 men, but soon could rally only 15 or 16 around the regimental flag. Even officers of high rank fled. Following the initial shots, a colonel of the 2nd Light Infantry Regiment threw aside his coat, hat, and sword, seized the first horse he could find, and rode away—abandoning his men. Gen. Antonio Jauregui lamented that such behavior was all too common, noting that "most retreated almost without seeing the enemy and very few cartridges were fired that afternoon."[34]

The advance took Arista by surprise. He had just completed his deployment of troops around 3 p.m., when Captain McCall and his scouts stumbled upon the advance skirmishers of his army. The sound of sporadic gunfire continued for almost a quarter of an hour at some distance from the resaca before the woods once again fell silent. Several minutes later, a captain of the 2nd Infantry approached Arista to inform him that a party of about a hundred US infantrymen had discovered the Mexican position but had been driven back and dispersed. No additional forces had been spotted for some distance on the road. This report, and the lateness of the hour, led Arista to assume that Taylor would not have enough daylight to arrive, deploy, and fight a battle, and he announced that the Americans apparently had decided not to attack that afternoon. After instructing his second-in-command to maintain a sharp watch for any evidence to the contrary, he retired to his tent—at a point about two hundred yards behind the lines—to write reports and letters. He would not be on the battle line when the US troops rushed in a short time later.[35]

The general had good reason to tend to his correspondence. Ampudia would later blast his commanding officer for his absence, avowing that Arista was so preoccupied with dictating reports of the battle on the 8th that "he didn't even want to know that the action had recommenced." In reality, the general-in-chief was writing two memoranda to General Mejía in Matamoros: one calling for a shipment of additional cannonballs, "since we are almost out," and the other to request rations, "since the troops have nothing to eat." Time was of the essence, if he hoped to have these items in advance of a US attack the following morning.[36]

Arista's attempt to complete these letters showed just how fast the battle progressed. He had reached his tent and completed only about three sentences of dictation when he heard shooting coming from the left end of his line. He and his staff rushed outside and spotted a handful of troops from the 4th Infantry rushing through the small clearing. They had no sooner moved to ask what had happened, than suddenly hundreds of men—officers and soldiers alike—poured through the clearing as they fled. Troops of the US 3rd Infantry had found a pathway between the Resaca de Guerrero and the Charco de la Palma and had unexpectedly flanked the left position of the Mexican line. Stunned by the sudden appearance of enemy forces behind them, many troops of Canales' defensores did not know where to direct their fire and were dismayed by their plight. "A panicked terror took over everyone," wrote Canales, "and no one wanted to be the last to reach the Río Bravo." The troops of the 4th Infantry put up more of a fight, but, left isolated by the flight of the volunteers, they soon broke and scattered as well. Arista tried to halt the torrent of frightened men, appealing to their sense of honor and assuring them that the US troops were cowardly and lacked the will to fight. Few listened, and within moments most of his infantry had disappeared.[37]

On the road to the North of the resaca, General Taylor was unaware that his troops had gained ground so quickly. After the regiments had scattered into the chaparral, he waited at the center of the roadway with his reserves, able to track the action only by the sounds that emanated from the brush. "After he had once given his orders to advance, fighting," wrote Lt. George Deas, "he could do no more; for he could not possibly see his troops." This inaction frustrated the old soldier particularly because, from his perspective, the battle did not appear to be proceeding smoothly. Despite the heavy fire from Duncan's cannon, the guns seemed to have little effect on the Mexican artillery blocking the road. Instead, the Mexican pieces, from their protected positions in the brush, poured a heavy shower of grape and canister shot into the areas where the US infantry had moved. Fearing that his men were suffering from the fire and unable to take any other measures to halt it, Taylor summoned Capt. Charles May and two companies of dragoons forward from the reserve and ordered them to charge down the roadway and drive the Mexican cannoneers from their guns. He also sent troops of the 8th Regiment forward to help with the maneuver.[38]

Randolph Ridgely welcomed this decision. The lieutenant and his light artillery corps had been at the fore of the fighting for about half an hour and had managed to drive several of the Mexican guns from the road into the ravine. From that point he could push the cannon no farther, and he sent a messenger to Taylor requesting infantry support for a direct assault. Taylor had assured him that troops were on their way, and the brush soon filled with men, but no units appeared to be focusing attention on the Mexican artillery. Ridgely again sent word that he could carry the guns with some direct support, but the general seemed to brush off the message, apparently preoccupied with other matters. It was therefore a source of considerable relief for the artillerymen when May, with his company of horsemen, rounded a bend in the road and announced cheerfully, "Hello! Ridgely, where is that battery? I am ordered to charge it."[39]

The artilleryman answered this display of bravado with a bit of his own. Telling May, "Hold on, Charley, till I drawn their fire, and you will soon see where they are," he rolled all his guns forward and fired them simultaneously. The Mexican pieces responded, each sending up a puff of smoke to reveal its location in the brush, and May was on his way. Advancing in a column four horses across—a formation that filled the entire width of the road—the dragoons galloped toward the Mexican batteries. Behind them, Ridgely limbered his guns to his horses and advanced as well.[40]

The charge was rapid, dramatic, and heroic, but only partly effective. The captain and his party of about fifty men rode directly into the muzzles of the Mexican guns. May led the advance against the guns on the right side of the road, while Capt. Lawrence Pike Graham directed his half of the column to the left. Both sections swept into the ravine under heavy fire and scattered the crews manning the guns. The swiftness of the charge carried the horsemen all the way through the batteries and across the resaca. The confrontation was also costly, with Lt. Zebulon Inge, seven privates, and eighteen horses killed and an additional ten men and ten horses wounded. When he attempted to regroup his unit on the far bank of the ravine, May could assemble only six men to make a second charge. In the meantime, the Mexican artillerymen regained their pieces and resumed firing.[41]

The final capture of these guns would not be as easy as the action on other parts of the field. Arista had positioned his very best troops at the point where the resaca crossed the road, and these troops stood their ground even as the rest of the defense crumbled around them. The artillery brigade, under the command of Gen. Rómulo Díaz de la Vega, remained stalwart. The general was probably unaware of the fate of the units to the far right and left, but he knew that loss of control of the road would spell disaster for the Mexican Army. If the US troops cleared his cannon from their positions, nothing remained to prevent Taylor's own artillery brigade, currently waiting in reserve, from racing across the resaca. So the Mexican general continually rallied his troops to fight at their guns or with bayonet when necessary. The soldiers of the Tampico Coast Guard Battalion and the Veterans Company of Tampico also stood their ground on the west side of the road and showed every indication that they would fight to the last man to defend the crossing. General Ampudia distinguished himself as well, drawing together remnants of other regiments to assist in the defense.[42]

It required the coordinated effort of many US regiments and units to overcome this resistance. Ridgely's battery followed up its advance with several blasts at the Mexican cannon from close range. Troops of the 5th and 8th Infantries took advantage of the lull created by May's charge to swarm in from the east and engage the defenders at close quarters. A scattering of other units, including McCall's skirmishers, also pushed into the area to provide additional support from the west. Rounding out the onslaught, May, and the handful of his men still able to fight, wheeled their horses around on the road across the resaca and rejoined the fray from the south. All converged upon the

Mexican guns with a determination to capture them, open the road, and force an end to the extended siege of their fort, now just several miles distant.[43]

Attackers and defenders came together in chaotic close-quarter fighting in the dense chaparral. Men on both sides fired their muskets frantically, often at targets unseen or greatly obscured by the brush. "The air was full of balls, each whistling its own tune," Lt. George Wainwright recalled of his experience as he rushed in with the 8th Infantry. The soldiers of the 5th likewise found themselves in a position "where the balls fell thick and fast, as if *bushels of hickory nuts* had been shot at them." As the two armies intermingled, the troops resorted to hand-to-hand combat with bayonets and swords. On at least one occasion, an officer who tired from the exertion of swinging his sabre simply brought down his Mexican opponent with his fist.[44]

The amount of bloodshed matched the fury of the fight. Lieutenant Wainwright narrowly avoided injury from a ball that grazed his neck, and Grant had his men throw themselves to the ground to evade shots that clipped branches all around. Many others were not so fortunate. Lt. Col. James McIntosh of the 5th Infantry took a bayonet wound through his mouth and neck. Capt. Alexander Hooe of the same regiment received a severe wound to his right arm that would require amputation. Lt. Charles Jordan of the 8th suffered both a gunshot wound and a bayonet wound to the side. Dozens of men died in the exchange, including Lts. Theodore Chadbourne of the 8th Regiment, who was shot in the heart, and Richard Cochrane of the 4th, who fell with five lance wounds. And the casualties could easily have been much higher. Capt. George McCall recalled that "their grape and canister mowed the tops of the bushes like a scythe." By moving in so close, the Americans had forced the Mexican cannoneers to overshoot their targets. "They fired too high," he wrote, "or they would have swept us from the earth like chaff."[45]

The US forces prevailed in this struggle. Squeezed in on all sides, the Mexican defenders dwindled in numbers and began to give way. The Tampico Battalion, reduced to a handful of men, finally waivered and broke. The standard bearer for the unit secured its flag to his body in an attempt to save it from capture, but failed in his purpose. He was shot as he rushed for shelter in the brush, and the beloved banner became a trophy of the fight. Troops of the US 5th and 8th Infantries won even greater prizes. They surged ahead with bayonets pointed forward, driving away the crews and capturing the Mexican cannon one after another. May and his dragoons administered the coup de grace. On their return charge across the resaca, they bore down on the last of the artillery pieces and confronted General Díaz de la Vega as he directed its

Battle of Resaca de la Palma, Capture of General Vega by Captain May. *Courtesy of H. R. Hudson Collection.*

fire. The artillery commander had held his ground even after most of his corps had fled. Only after the dragoons had trapped him inside the wheel of his cannon, did he finally tender his sword and accept defeat. "The conflict when it became general was too deadly to last long," Lt. Samuel French recalled of the heated clash at the crossing. He was correct; the fiercest of the fighting had lasted less than an hour.[46]

General Arista had not remained idle during this phase of the engagement, but instead of fighting the enemy, he had once again found himself involved in a battle of wills with one of his own officers. Realizing that much of his infantry was lost and having received a report from General Ampudia that the remainder of his defense was rapidly failing, he turned to his rearguard for support. He sent an aide to General Torrejón, calling for him to bring the cavalry brigade forward to join the fray. Torrejón received the order, but he questioned the command, saying that it was unheard of to attempt a cavalry charge through a forest and expressing doubts about the chances of success. Instead of advancing, he delayed and obliged Arista to send several additional messengers to repeat his directive. None of these couriers elicited the desired result, and after several minutes of impatient waiting, the general-in-chief rode to the rear to gather the horsemen and direct a charge himself. Boldly riding at the head of his cavalry, the general exhorted his troops to follow him down the roadway.

Arista hoped to drive the enemy from his artillery and enable his remaining defenders to regroup, but the charge was ill-fated from the start. As he spurred his mount forward, he soon saw the reason for Torrejón's reluctance. The brush tightly hemmed in the narrow road and his riders could establish a column no more than four abreast. This was the same formation that Charles May had used when he and his dragoons had charged in the opposite direction, but Arista's large force was much less successful. Bottled up along the narrow road, Arista's 350 cavalrymen became strung out in a long parade that prevented the general from bringing his full force to bear. It was also difficult for the lancers to advance with spears forward in these tight quarters, which further reduced the effectiveness of the charge. These problems probably would have thwarted the advance even if it had been carried out in time, but delay had been fatal. By the time the charging column of horsemen arrived at the crossing point of the resaca, the Mexican artillery had been silenced and US cannon had pushed across the ravine. Heavy American fire mowed down a number of Arista's troops, bringing the charge to a halt and forcing the general-in-chief "to cede the field and the glory to the enemies of his country." With his troops pausing only long enough to lance a few stragglers of the US dragoons, Arista joined the general retreat from the field.[47]

For the Americans, the end of the battle quickly turned into a chase. With the Mexican artillery securely in the hands of the US infantry, Randolph Ridgely rolled two of his own guns across the resaca and had just begun to inch forward along the road when Arista approached with his cavalry. A single, well placed barrage of canister sent the closely packed horsemen staggering backward, and a deafening cheer from US troops in the brush helped scatter the Mexicans in all directions. Ridgely paused, having no orders to advance any farther than his present position. At that moment, however, James Duncan's light artillery, Croghan Ker's dragoons, the artillery battalion, and companies of the 3rd Infantry moved forward and commenced a heavy fire on the fleeing troops. These units had not been involved in the battle to that point, and Taylor had ordered the fresh troops to harass the enemy in his retreat. Ridgely joined the rush forward, and caught up in the enthusiasm of the moment, horse, foot, and artillery soldiers alike chased the Mexicans in the direction of the Rio Grande.[48]

Taylor might have delivered a crushing blow at this point had he committed all his forces to the pursuit. Soldiers in the units that joined it overcame all resistance. "They marched through," wrote Lt. Raphael Smead, "sweeping all before them. . . .

It was a perfect rout. The enemy throwing their arms away that they might run the faster." But Taylor remained cautious. Darkness was falling, he lacked an adequate cavalry, and he continued to worry about the security of the wagon train left behind at Palo Alto. Instead of calling for a concerted effort to hunt down the Mexican forces, he ordered his men to establish camp on the battlefield and settled in for the night. The units at the forefront of the chase continued and some reached the Rio Grande, but most were more interested in reestablishing communications with their fort. When the unencumbered Mexicans outpaced them on the race to the river, they pulled back and allowed their foes to escape.[49]

After permitting the Mexicans to retreat, the US soldiers took possession of a bounty of trophies as they swept across the field of battle. At the road crossing, they captured eight of the enemy artillery pieces, along with the equipment, ammunition, and accouterments associated with them. On the right side of the route, the infantrymen who poured across the resaca broke out of the brush and suddenly found themselves in the clearing that housed Arista's field headquarters. Arista himself had rushed off to lead the final, futile cavalry charge, leaving no one to defend the area, and the Americans seized his grand tent, stacks of guns, and surplus ammunition. Continuing onward, they finally reached the main Mexican camp area, well to the rear of the lines. There they took possession of additional supplies, most notably pots filled with food for a long-awaited meal that the Mexican soldiers never had the opportunity to eat. The official catalog of items captured included 393 muskets, more than 155,000 rounds of ammunition, almost 500 mules with pack saddles, 20 horses, and a number of ox-drawn carts, as well as swords, shovels, band instruments, more food, and the personal baggage of Arista and his staff. The troops also captured hundreds of prisoners—mostly the wounded left behind—and an array of discarded personal weapons and uniform parts.[50]

Taylor's troops were proud, almost in awe of their accomplishment at the resaca, and did not hesitate to congratulate themselves on the victory—often on confiscated stationery that bore Arista's letterhead. "We immediately went to work and gave them the best thrashing that they ever got," Lt. Robert Hazlitt wrote to his sister about the battle, after providing his own tally of the spoils. Lt. George Meade agreed. "We have whipped them in the open plain and we have done so in the bushes," he said in a letter to his wife, "and I now believe the war will soon be ended." In his letter home, Lt. Styles Hawley suggested that victory would have even greater impact. He described Palo Alto as a "well contested action" but touted the battle at Resaca de la Palma as one that "will live forever in the annals of American history and for long ages to come for the crowning glory of its brightest page."[51]

Others also praised the bravery of the American soldiers, who became "perfect demons" as they "rushed through showers of grape, round and canister to the very mouth of the enemies' pieces." Many even pointed to the statements of General Díaz de la Vega as confirmation of their valor. The captured Mexican general reportedly declared that he had fought against a variety of foes, including Texans, Spaniards and Englishmen, but that he had never before encountered men willing to charge directly into the muzzles of cannon. The dashing enemy officer also assured his triumphant captors that by doing so the Americans had conquered an almost impregnable position. "If I had with me $100,000 in silver," Díaz de la Vega was quoted as saying, "I would have bet the whole of it that no ten thousand men could have driven us from our position." The Americans were pleased to point out that they had done so with a force of only about nineteen hundred men—after leaving behind a portion of their army at Palo Alto—and that some of these troops had remained in reserve without entering the fight. The number of Mexican troops engaged in the battle had not been substantially larger than the American force, but the US Soldiers continued to estimate that they had faced a force of between five thousand and eight thousand Mexican troops, a figure that made their victory seem all the more impressive.[52]

Although the soldiers emphasized their valor and actions on the battlefield, the real significance of the clash at Resaca de la Palma was that it brought an end to the prolonged siege of the riverside fort across from Matamoros. As they pushed the fleeing Mexican forces toward the Rio Grande, the US troops moved directly down the road toward their comrades ensconced inside the earthworks. At first, they had some concern that another line of enemy troops awaited near that camp and that they would meet with a stronger defense. As they neared the river, however, it became apparent that the enemy had scattered and that no one stood between them and their countrymen. The only obstacle was incoming fire from along the opposite riverbank that sent cannonballs crashing perilously close to some of the soldiers as they raced forward. General Mejía had maintained the bombardment of the outpost until the very end, still hoping to force the surrender of the fort. Only when it he realized that the north bank of the river was filled with retreating men from his own army did he order a halt to the firing. That cannonade never resumed. It was about sunset on May 9 that the first of General Taylor's troops reached the walls of their fort without molestation and were welcomed by the weary troops within.[53]

While battles raged at Palo Alto and Resaca de la Palma, the troops stationed in the earthworks continued to endure another two full days of bombardment. After five days of dodging incoming rounds, some of the troops held out hope that the Mexicans were nearing the end of their ammunition supply. Daybreak of the 8th proved otherwise as shots once again poured in at a brisk pace. Indeed, during the night the Mexican troops had moved one of their mortars across the river and placed it near the roadway to the northwest of the earthwork. Throughout the day, rounds now came from three different directions, with the Mexicans holding their fire at intervals only long enough to let their guns cool. The shooting also became more accurate when a Mexican soldier climbed a tree across the river and guided the artillery batteries until their rounds regularly fell within the American fort. The extensive series of bombproofs and protective shelters within the earthworks provided protection from this fire but was not entirely secure. One private of the 7th Infantry had his arm taken off by a cannonball, and several others were wounded by splinters when a round struck the wooden support of a bombproof.[54]

Outside the earthworks, the camp remained an extremely dangerous place. At no time was this more apparent than when Lt. Earl Van Dorn left the works to attempt to raise the Stars and Stripes after it tumbled from its flagpole. Throughout the bombardment, the flag had remained in a prominent position, several hundred feet in advance of the fort, near the original arrow-shaped earthwork. Mexicans in Matamoros continued to see the banner as an outrageous affront by foreign occupiers of their territory. The US troops under siege viewed it as a symbol of their defiance under fire. When the halyard that held the flag aloft broke on the evening of May 7, the troops were determined to see it rise again. On the morning of the 8th, Van Dorn accepted the task of restoring it and ventured out to lower the top mast of the pole, repair the rigging, and lash the staff back into place. It took only about a quarter of an hour to complete the job, but in that interval the lieutenant became the target of dozens of rounds from the enemy batteries. "I dodged several bomb-shells which threatened to fall on my head," he recalled. "I skipped out of the way of a rolling howitzer ball; and stooping . . . accidentally, a cannonball passed over my head which would have cut me in two. . . . The only wound I received was a scratch on the ankle in dodging a shell."

Other forays beyond the walls attracted similar fire and became increasingly scarce. Except for a few missions aimed at destroying structures and brush that sheltered enemy sharpshooters, the men remained under cover and in a tedious but dangerous routine.[55]

During this time, the troops penned in at the fort knew very little about events beyond its walls. After Samuel Walker left the site on the morning of May 4, they received no news of the movements of the remainder of Taylor's army. "We didn't know where General Taylor was. We didn't know what was happening," Robert Pruyn, a drummer boy at the time, recalled years after the siege. "All we did know was that we were left to hold the fort." As each ensuing day dragged past, many of the troops of the 7th Infantry began to question the fate of their companions and to ponder what had occurred to prevent the army from coming to their assistance. "We had now settled down," wrote Lt. John Henshaw, "completely at a loss for even a moderate conjecture of the causes that delayed General Taylor in returning to our succor." They were equally unaware of Mexican actions beyond their line of vision. Busy evading the shots and shells from the heavy barrage on the morning of the 8th, the soldiers did not know that the majority of enemy troops surrounding their position were departing to join Arista at Palo Alto. It was only that afternoon, when they heard the far off boom of cannon, that they become aware that a battle had started that would determine their fate.[56]

The possibility of rescue put the troops on a rollercoaster of emotions. Once they realized that the rumbling came from artillery rather than thunder, troops, teamsters, and other denizens of the earthwork rushed from their shelters in a spontaneous celebration. These high spirits gradually ebbed with the realization that the sound and the army behind it seemed to be advancing no closer toward the river. When the cannonade ended at sundown, the final reverberations remained far in the distance, causing weary men like Lieutenant Henshaw to despair of the fate of their comrades and themselves. "The cannon have ceased firing," he wrote in his diary, "but no appearance of Taylor yet. We cannot tell whether he has been forced to retreat or whether he has conquered and is collecting his wounded and burying his dead. The suspense is terrible; for if he has been defeated from hints that have been thrown out, I fear that this Fort will be surrendered."

But the timely arrival of a Mexican soldier bearing a flag of truce offered some encouragement as the day came to a close. The man reported that he had been with Arista's army in the clash with the Americans and had fled as his fellows had fallen *en masse* around him. This revelation, combined with the sight of Mexican reinforcements rushing past the fort in the direction of the battle, led the soldiers to believe that Taylor had fared well and might reach them early the following morning.[57]

Sunrise on May 9 ushered in another day of suspenseful waiting. The Americans arose hopeful that they would soon hear the sounds of battle moving closer to them along the Point Isabel road. Instead, they received a new round of fire from the Mexican artillery surrounding the post and faced hour after hour of an almost continuous barrage. Once again the fort defenders could do little in response. With their ammunition almost exhausted, they resumed a now-familiar regimen: seeking cover from Mexican cannonballs and "giving them now and then a 'crowder' to let them know that the 'degenerate sons of Washington' were not all dead yet."[58]

As midday approached, however, some of these sons began to consider that death might not be far off. They had still heard nothing from their would-be rescuers, and the naysayers began to murmur, suggesting that General Taylor had been defeated or forced to return to the Point. These words of doom grew more pronounced at about 2 p.m., when the troops learned that Maj. Jacob Brown had finally succumbed to his wounds. Then, shortly after 3 p.m., the sound of cannons, much closer than the day before, dispelled the gloomy rumors and signaled that Taylor had renewed his advance. Once more the fort defenders listened intently, striving to discern the fate of their comrades from the sounds of the invisible battle. This time, the news was good. After 5 p.m. the popping of musket fire began to move closer in their direction. Shortly afterwards, they spotted masses of Mexican troops passing the fort to the east and west as they rushed for the safety of the Rio Grande. "Our men thronged the adjacent rampart, regardless of the fierce missives from the city batteries," recalled Captain Whiting. "They eagerly watched the progress of their redemption."[59]

Despite these promising indications, the enforced idleness of the fort defenders had not ended. Their first impulse was to join the fight. After six days of being holed up inside their works, passively enduring thousands of incoming rounds, the men eagerly responded when Captain Hawkins called for them to return the favor against the fleeing Mexicans. But they quickly came to the three-fold realization that their quarry remained well out of range, the result of the latest battle remained undetermined, and they might later have need for their carefully hoarded ammunition. Hawkins ordered the firing to halt and the men resumed their wait, attentively listening to the din of battle to the north. The rolling volleys of musketry gradually subsided and finally stopped. Another evening approached without a sign of Taylor's force.[60]

It was just before nightfall that the men inside the fort finally learned their fate. In the gathering darkness, a lone, unidentified soldier on horseback raced from the Point Isabel road and galloped across the field toward them. Uncertain of the man's motives, Hawkins sent several cannon shells in his direction, narrowly missing with at least one round. The rider continued toward them, frantically waving his hat and sword until he was recognized as one of Samuel Walker's Texas Rangers. Hearing his joyful shout of "We've licked them, we've licked them all to smash," the fort defenders rushed to lay down a drawbridge that would let him enter the fort. As they gathered to hear his account of the battle and his dramatic ride through Mexican lines, additional troops began to appear, offering further proof that enemy forces had been pushed back. Even then, those in the fort garrison remained wary that the bombardment might resume. But as the night progressed and the Mexican cannon across the river remained silent, the men gradually allowed themselves to believe that their trials had truly come to an end. [61]

As order and calm returned to the US earthwork, the troops of the Mexican Army anxiously sought their own respite from battle. "With the assistance of Second-in-Command Ampudia, Gen. Tómas Requena, Anastasio Torrejón and other officers," Arista wrote in his official account of the battle, "I was able to organize a respectable force to sustain a retreat."[62] General Canales presented a much bleaker scenario, in which "the entire division fled for the Bravo at different points."[63] This portrayal more accurately described a situation in which the officers separated and followed numerous paths to the river, each gathering as many stray troops as he could find along the way. Arista took the main road toward Matamoros and halted his troops at Villanueva, several miles upriver from the city. Canales and his horsemen managed to salvage two of the Mexican cannon from the left of the line and to gather a substantial number of scattered infantrymen as they headed for Tahuachal, a point even farther upstream. Generals Ampudia and Requena directed their troops to the Ramireño crossing, just downriver from the fort. Soldiers from the far right of the Mexican line at the resaca proceeded to Longoreño, well downriver from Matamoros. Meanwhile, the only troops that truly made an orderly retreat were those that had surrounded the US earthworks, under the command of Joaquín Morlet. Arista had warned Morlet on the evening of May 8 to be prepared to retreat if US forces broke through the Mexican line, and Morlet complied by leading his men to Villa de Ampudia and the Anacuita crossing, directly across from Fort Paredes.[64]

These efforts merely provided a veneer of order to the chaotic escape from the Resaca. Most of the Mexican troops had fled the battlefield with no objective other than to escape the deadly onslaught of the US forces. Many rushed for the shelter of the thickets extending for miles in all directions, never to rejoin the ranks. Some undoubtedly became hopelessly lost in the dense brush and may well have perished before finding their way out. Others found their way southward on narrow tracks through the chaparral, crossed the Río Bravo, and continued south, seeking refuge in the Mexican interior. In the days and weeks that followed, the progress of these men could be measured as they spread their woeful accounts of the battles in the towns and villages of northern Mexico. Many soldiers of the Defensores de las Villas del Norte also seized upon the occasion as an opportunity to escape the ruins of Arista's army. "They knew the land in all directions," Jauregui noted as he lamented the large numbers of deserters, "and they simply marched for their homes."

Even the soldiers who reassembled under the leadership of various officers rushed with an almost blind panic for the safety of Matamoros. Some men fled with US troops directly at their heels. Others heard the firing of cannon in the American earthworks and became convinced that they were being pursued. In both instances men became so terrified that they refused to stop their flight even when they reached Río Bravo. "They threw themselves into the water carrying with them their weapons and without even knowing how to swim," recalled General Jauregui. "Others tried to cross the river on horseback." Some managed to complete their escape, but dozens were caught in the swift flow of the river and were swept to a watery death.[65]

Despite the danger of trying to swim the river, many of the panic-stricken troops viewed that as their best chance of survival, for there were few boats to carry them. General Mejía in Matamoros had been forewarned by Arista's gloomy reports on the evening of May 8 and had taken it upon himself to send reinforcements and boats to the primary crossing points on the river. He also sent a detachment of soldiers to the north shore of the river to collect the deserters and dispersed troops expected after any major battle.[66] He was completely unprepared, however, for the mobs of men that gathered on the riverbank on the evening of the 9th. Even after he sent every available boat across the river, there were far too few to quickly evacuate the north shore. Each craft had to make multiple, laborious journeys back and forth, slowly carrying the army to safety.

The panicked soldiers were in no mood to wait patiently for a place on the transports. At Anacuitas, where the largest complement of troops gathered, soldiers found only two boats and began to fight among themselves for the right to cross the river. Similar quarrels erupted at other crossings and accomplished little but to delay the passage of the launches. Soldiers left behind during the initial crossings began to spread rumors that American soldiers had been spotted putting the bayonet to any Mexican stragglers found in their path. This story added to the mayhem, and growing numbers chose to forego the wait for transport and take their chances in the murky waters. Although Arista and his officers would make no official determination of the number of troops to drown, it is likely that far greater numbers perished in their battle with the deadly currents of the Río Bravo than in the two clashes with US forces.[67]

Losses in this crossing could have been much higher if not for some displays of support and bravery by soldiers and civilians alike. Despite their failure in battle and the simmering differences among them, most of the generals of the Army of the North acted efficiently to restore calm in the ranks. Rancheros who lived on both banks of the river turned out in numbers, producing additional boats for the crossing, fishing waterlogged soldiers out of the Río Bravo, and rendering assistance to those who reached the far shore. Ferrymen also proved their worth, rowing for hours back and forth across the waterway until all the troops were evacuated. Perhaps most important were the contributions of some hundred soldiers of the Puebla and Morelia Battalions. As other units remained in disarray, these troops obeyed Arista's command to serve as a rearguard for the retreat. They took up positions at the point where the Matamoros road forked between the two primary ferries—very near the US fort—and gallantly waited to turn back any assault by Taylor's troops. Darkness slowed the enemy forces and the attack never occurred, but this stand was important nonetheless. Reassured that some defenders stood between them and the advancing threat, the remainder of the soldiers managed to overcome their initial terror and reach the right bank of the Bravo in a much more orderly fashion.[68]

Even so, it was a dreary and broken army that reentered Matamoros under the darkness of night. First to arrive were officers who fled the battle and rushed to present their tales of disaster and ensure that blame fell on the shoulders of others. Shortly afterwards, scattered groupings of enlisted men began to wander in. Dazed and frightened by what had befallen them, they milled about in the streets without guidance or direction. As the evening wore on, the trickle became a torrent, with troops pouring in from all the scattered crossing points along the river. Last to appear were the generals, including Arista, who had seen the evacuation through to completion. He returned to a town full of ragged soldiers without uniforms, troops without weapons, and men without hope. When he mustered the troops that night he could account for only about two thousand men, fifteen hundred in fighting condition.

At least one of Arista's officers tried to offer reassurance in the bleak hours immediately after the haphazard flight from the resaca. In his report on Resaca de Guerrero, Gen. Tómas Requena admitted that the losses were unfortunate, but suggested that his commander deserved credit for a gallant effort. "This sort of thing arises often in war," he wrote of the defeat. "Do not allow it to draw your attention away from the valor and calmness of the generals, officers, and troops who redoubled their efforts to triumph, despite the absolute improbability of doing so."[69]

But the defeated general-in-chief was in no mood to be consoled. Immediately upon reaching the safety of Matamoros, he had written a report to his superiors in Mexico City in which he attempted to soften the news of the defeat by offering assurances that the troops had fought hard and that he had fulfilled his duties. Several hours later, however, as the clock neared the stroke of midnight, his disillusion became evident in a separate message to the commander of Mexican forces in Tampico. "Disgracefully my troops were deluded because of the strafing of the enemy artillery from the previous day," he wrote. "Today in a position that was sufficiently strong they ceded the way without turning back the enemy, even when I personally took charge of the cavalry." He brought his sad account and a sad day to an end with the simple statement, "I am pained to have to inform you of these results."[70]

CHAPTER 9
Advance and Retreat

★

AS THE SUN came up on the morning of May 10, the Mexican Army, still dazed by the crushing defeat at Resaca de Guerrero, arose with the expectation of a new tragedy. "The greatest consternation reigned among the inhabitants of Matamoros," wrote Capt. Jean Louis Berlandier. Soldiers and civilians alike expected the US Army to follow up on its successes on the left bank of the river with a rapid assault on the wounded army holed up in the town on the right. Town residents took cover in their homes, believing that they would soon be at the center of the fighting. Fearful and exhausted soldiers anxiously awaited word that they would be required to make another defensive stand. Even the generals, who had so recently scoffed at the notion that the US forces wanted to take Matamoros, now saw a fight for the city as a certainty. As military leaders, they understood that Zachary Taylor would be foolish not to press his advantage and try to roust a damaged foe from its stronghold. They no longer questioned whether the Americans would launch an assault; instead, they wondered when it would come and what form it would take. [1]

The anticipation of the attack weighed heavily on General Arista. Despite his determination to strike a blow against the Americans on the left bank of the Río Bravo, he had never forgotten his oft-repeated orders from Mexico City to defend Matamoros at all costs. Undoubtedly he, like Mejía before him, had questioned the wisdom of that order when it seemed more important to prevent the US troops from solidifying their hold on the opposite shore. But he had accepted the command. Now, the outbreak of fighting and the accompanying Mexican defeats made preservation of the city a matter of paramount importance. With US troops firmly in control of the north bank of the Bravo, Matamoros would play a key role in the course of warfare south of the river. If the Americans seized the town, Taylor would have a secure base from which to mobilize troops and supplies for assaults on places like Monterrey, Tampico, Victoria, and Saltillo. If he did attempt assaults on those cities, Mexican troops would have to fall back to them, thereby conceding thousands of square miles of territory to an invading force. Moreover, the capture of Matamoros would be of vast symbolic importance. Losing battles could be dismissed as misfortune. Losing control of a city and the surrounding region would be a tragedy that would damage morale throughout the republic and undermine efforts to fight back. Arista understood the importance of Matamoros and the need to defend it. He also understood that after the events of May 8 and 9, his army lacked the means and the will to make this vital stand.[2]

It appeared likeliest that Taylor would initiate any attack with an artillery bombardment. One of the primary goals of the US march to the Frontón had been to collect heavy guns and ammunition that could pummel Matamoros from the opposite shore. Taylor's troops had demonstrated the deadly potential of 18-pounders at Palo Alto, and these guns had now been advanced and placed in position to fire across the river. Gen. Tómas Requena, commander of the Mexican artillery, had limited resources with which to respond to such a barrage. Although he still had cannons and mortars in place along the right bank of the Bravo, they were of a much smaller caliber than the US weapons. Additionally, he had shipped most of the ammunition for these guns across the Bravo to replace the rounds fired at Palo Alto on May 8. Almost all those rounds, as well as the cannons intended to fire them, had been left behind in the flight from the resaca. These losses not only weakened the Mexican ability to respond to an assault, they also raised the disturbing possibility that US troops might turn the captured weaponry against the walls and ramparts of its former owners. "Everyone," wrote Captain Berlandier, "saw the consequence of losing a battle that augmented the enemy's already strong artillery while depriving us of eight guns, all the mules, and the ammunition."[3]

Arista realized, however, that US troops really had little need to resort to this type of salvo to get access to the city. Despite the concerted construction efforts during March and April, the fortifications around Matamoros remained woefully inadequate. Fort Paredes at the Anaquitas crossing and the serpentine breastworks near the Paso Real guarded the northern approach to the town, but these defenses covered only a small part of the riverbank. US troops could easily march to the Longoreño or Ramireño crossings, traverse the river beyond the range of Mexican guns, and enter Matamoros from three undefended points of the compass. Even the direct approach from the north was vulnerable. The sandbag batteries along the eastern bend in the river had been hastily constructed and probably would not stand up to a concerted attack by Taylor's troops. Fort Paredes was suspect as well. Arista, who had not seen any of the defenses before he initiated the crossing of the Río Bravo on April 24, considered this fort the only reasonably strong one—and even so he thought it needed four days of additional work and a considerable investment in supplies to be serviceable in the event of attack.[4]

Finding troops willing and able to man the works presented the next hurdle. Arista estimated that a proper defense of Matamoros would demand a force of at least seven thousand soldiers, properly fitted and armed—more than he had commanded before the disastrous battles at Palo Alto and Resaca de Guerrero. In the aftermath of those engagements, he could assemble only a fraction of that number. He could take some solace in the fact that his dispersed soldiers, many previously presumed dead, continued to limp into town throughout the night of the 9th and the morning of the 10th, gradually increasing the garrison of the city. The arrival of General Canales near midday, with five hundred defensores and two cannon, restored the Army of the North to about thirty-seven hundred men. A significant number of these, however, had been wounded and could not turn out for the defense. Far more simply lacked the spirit to fight, and Arista doubted that he could muster them to man the barricades. "It is clear that we can maintain only a weak defense," he wrote to his superiors. "And the situation will become worse since the enemy felt pressured to call for reinforcements. Those troops are now arriving and, upon seeing the outcome of the 9th, their morale is soaring."[5] Arista questioned whether any of his troops on the front line would hold their ground if these confidant US forces attacked.[6]

A strong, unified front presented by the officers might have restored morale and order, but the leadership of the army was irreparably splintered. Tensions among the top chiefs had increased daily during the operations north of the Bravo, and only a shared desire to defend their country prevented them from openly turning against each other. The appalling bloodshed at Palo Alto and the crushing defeat at Resaca de Guerrero shattered the fragile shell of unity. As the troops fled for the safety of Matamoros, officers of the Ampudia faction dropped their earlier insinuations of treason in favor of open condemnation of Arista. Those allied with the general-in-chief lashed back. Antonio Jauregui, for instance, a staunch defender of Arista's, put responsibility for the defeat at the resaca squarely on the shoulders of the critics. "Many of the general's gratuitous enemies reached Matamoros by five o'clock in the afternoon," he wrote, "while [Arista] remained until vespers, risking his life on the battlefield in an effort to restore national honor." Both sides turned on General Canales, "who by some extraordinary instinct had entered in neither battle" and who "undertook his retreat without firing a shot." The stinging rebukes from all quarters accomplished little except to undermine the authority of all the leaders. As May 10 wore on, both Arista and Ampudia found their reputations tarnished in the eyes of the troops. With the one accused of betrayal and the other of cowardice, neither was in a good position to inspire the soldiers or lead the army out of its malaise.[7]

Arista addressed these concerns and others as well when he called a meeting of his command staff at his quarters on the morning of May 10. He greeted his generals and brigade commanders with a broad tirade against their disruptive and divisive behavior and ordered them to halt the spread of rumors and insidious commentary. This, he informed them, they should do not only as a sign of respect for his authority, but also as a step toward restoring discipline in the troubled army. Although he hoped that his critics and detractors would comply with his order willingly, he assured them that he was ready to confront anyone of any rank who continued to stir up trouble.[8]

But Arista was decidedly less enthusiastic about fighting to maintain his position in Matamoros. Having completed his harangue, he went on to spell out a list of ills facing his officers and their army: the devastating decline in manpower, the disorganization in the ranks, and a state of morale so low that there was not a single unit that the rest of the army could rally around. Other issues were the poor condition of the fortifications, the loss of transports and weaponry, and the limited supply of ammunition. On this last topic, General Requena spoke up to add that he had only enough cannonballs and shells to sustain his artillery for a four-hour period. Any of these issues would have made it difficult to fight—and there was, in addition, the lack of food. Arista pointed out that the Army of the North currently had only fourteen days of rations and lacked the means to procure more. He stopped short of ordering an evacuation of the city. Instead, he asked the others to corroborate his assessment, encouraged them to undertake all possible efforts to induce the troops to fight, and advised them to prepare for the possibility of leaving the city if conditions failed to improve.[9]

If Arista had expected the assembly to resolve any of the issues he cited, he would have been sorely disappointed. The officers patiently bore their commander's harangue, readily approved the propositions he brought forward, and then moved back out among the troops, where his detractors promptly incited more discord. Charges that Arista had betrayed the army were now supplemented with details about the effects of his treachery. Within hours of the gathering, rumors had spread far and wide that the army possessed only enough ammunition to last three hours, that nothing could be done to improve the city's defenses, and that food would run out on May 14. Coming on the heels of the previous day's tragedy, the troops readily accepted these stories, and their alarm grew. Arista had hoped that the officers would answer his call and help raise spirits. He saw that instead they had resigned themselves to meeting one of two equally disagreeable fates: "die of hunger or be defeated again." Predictions that they were doomed to do one or the other threatened to become self-fulfilling. Already convinced of their defeat, few were willing to stand and fight when Taylor brought on his inevitable attack.[10]

As the Mexican troops waited fearfully for the next battle, the US Army remained at Resaca de la Palma, addressing the aftermath of the last clash. Late into the night on May 9th and resuming at daybreak on the 10th, teams of men fanned out across the area, collecting the casualties of both armies—mostly fallen Mexican soldiers—scattered amidst the dense brush. In at least one instance, this process created some comic relief. Lt. Samuel French found a fallen Mexican officer in the brush and attempted to use his rudimentary knowledge of Spanish to ascertain the man's rank. To his surprise, when he posed his question, the soldier responded by reaching into a pocket and handing over a biscuit. It was a fellow American soldier, who pointed out gleefully that French's attempt to ask, "Teniente o capitán?" ("Lieutenant or captain?") had actually come out as "Tiene usted pan?" ("Do you have any bread?").[11]

That incident aside, it was the US troops who adopted the role of providers, offering food and water to friend and foe alike before transporting them for medical treatment. Although eighty-nine US soldiers suffered injuries, some of them very serious, a far greater number of Mexican casualties littered the field. The wounded of both armies were deposited at a hastily established field hospital near the resaca, the men lying in long rows in a small clearing near the bank. There a handful of surgeons practiced rudimentary, often brutal procedures to tend the victims of the fight. "Oh, what a sight I witnessed that night and the next morning!" Private Barna Upton wrote after observing the scene, where "the wounded, both friend and foe, were collected on the bank of the pond. Their groans were heartrending as the dreadful and rapid progress of amputation was going on. The dead lay in a heap beside. So much misery on account of a disputed and uninhabited piece of land." The dead—those who had died on the field and those who succumbed during the efforts to save them—were placed in two mounds, one composed of US troops, and a much larger one of Mexican dead.[12]

As the collection progressed and the rows of wounded and piles of dead continued to grow, Taylor turned to his foes for assistance. He pressed some of the able-bodied Mexican captives into service excavating pits, each large enough to hold fifty to a hundred bodies, and in these pits the captive enemies placed the bodies of their fallen comrades. This permitted the Americans, who counted only thirty-three deaths within their ranks, to concentrate on burying their own. The fallen officers, Lts. Zebulon Inge, Richard Cochrane, and Theodore Chadbourne, were each given an individual grave alongside the Matamoros-to-Point Isabel road, while enlisted men were placed in a large, shared grave nearby. Realizing that his small complement of surgeons could not provide adequate care for the injured, many of whom had suffered grievous wounds, Taylor sent a message to Matamoros requesting assistance on the field of battle. General Arista responded by dispatching two men from his own medical staff to work side-by-side with US doctors to treat the Mexican wounded. An additional crew of men arrived to assist with the burials as well.[13]

This spirit of goodwill continued the next day with an exchange of captives. Having taken a substantial number of prisoners at Resaca de la Palma, Taylor believed he had leverage to secure the release of Thornton's dragoons, who remained confined in Matamoros. On the evening of May 10 he sent an envoy to the city to gauge Arista's willingness to negotiate. The response was positive. Indeed the Mexican general had already dispatched his own emissary to carry a similar proposal to Taylor. The two leaders quickly reached an agreement in principle and in the afternoon, in a driving rainstorm, the two groups of prisoners were assembled on the left bank of the river, near the Paso Real ferry, for the swap.[14]

Taylor's representatives were generous in their dealings. The transfer commenced under established codes of war, with the US officers Thornton, Hardee, and Kane exchanged for Mexican officers, and enlisted men offered up on an equal basis. There were far more Mexican than American prisoners on hand, however, and in the end, a one-to-one trade became impossible, and the Americans simply handed over an additional twenty-two men. They also turned over a number of wounded without an exchange, requiring only that the officers in the group swear an oath not to take up arms again. This humanitarian gesture was also a practical one, as the US troops lacked facilities and supplies to adequately tend to these captives.

Only three men did not gain their freedom. Gen. Rómulo Díaz de la Vega, Lt. Silverio Vélez of the 4th Light Regiment, and Lt. Alejandro Prado of the Presidials could not be exchanged because the Mexicans held no other officers for a trade. Under rules of war, Díaz de la Vega presented a particular obstacle, since his elevated status demanded an equally high-ranking prisoner in return, and there were none to offer. The members of this trio also refused parole, which would require them to lay down their guns for the duration of the war. With the charismatic Díaz de la Vega acting as their spokesman, the Mexican officers declared that they had taken vows to defend their country against all enemies and remained duty bound to fulfill those vows if they were released. If Taylor did not want them to fight, he would have to continue to hold them captive. Suitably impressed by this display of Mexican honor, the Americans praised them, then transported them back to Point Isabel. Once there, the trio boarded a steamboat and sailed for New Orleans, to be held until the war ended or a suitable exchange could be arranged.[15]

The prisoner exchange effectively closed the door on activities at the Palo Alto and Resaca de la Palma battlefields. When the captives assembled for their march to the Rio Grande for transfer, US troops also left both scenes of conflict. Medical personnel and the American wounded headed for Point Isabel, which would serve as a hospital facility, a burial ground, and an embarkation point for the injured who were able to tolerate the sea voyage to New Orleans and home. The rest of the regiments, along with the teamsters, wagons, and guards once left behind at Palo Alto, joined the long convoy—now more of a parade—as it completed the final leg of the journey toward the river that had started five days before. As the Mexicans continued to the Paso Real for the formal swap, most of the Americans turned toward the battered walls of their fort and set up tents on the ground that they had occupied at the beginning of the month.[16]

The site had changed in that time. On May 1 the Americans had marched away from an efficient camp situated inside well-designed and well-built walls. Those earthworks had held up adequately during the six days of siege, limiting the number of casualties within the fort and testifying to the quality of its construction. But there was no doubt that the outpost had been at the center of a maelstrom. Gone were the smooth walls, neatly stacked baggage, and orderly rows of tents. In their place was a scene of wreckage. "The whole interior," wrote Capt. Daniel Whiting, "was plowed and furrowed by exploding bombs, dug up and piled in heaps and ridges, amid spattered rubbish and bursting baggage. Tents riddled by shots and shell were in tattered ruin, while the torn parapets and ragged embankments testified to the vindictiveness of the siege." So impressive was the scene of wreckage that soldiers who had fought in two bloody battles thought the defenders of the fort had undergone the worse ordeal.

William S. Henry found it hard to believe that anyone in the garrison could have survived—he concluded that "a special Providence seems to have preserved them from destruction." Returning soldiers were dismayed to find their possessions scattered or destroyed and their tents and bedding transformed into walls and bombproofs. But the reunion was a cause for celebration. The goal of the march had been achieved. Taylor and his troops had broken through the blockade and were now supplied with enough provisions, ammunition, and weaponry to sustain a lengthy battle with the Mexicans or a prolonged siege of their base.[17]

Few soldiers, however, believed that the supplies were still necessary for those purposes. The possibility of a renewed Mexican attack appeared remote. "This has broken them up for the present," Lt. Raphael Smead wrote in a letter to a friend. "It will be a long time before they can get such an army together again, if they ever do." Lt. George Meade sounded even more confident. "So certain are we of the great impression we have made on them," he wrote to his wife, "that I feel sure, were our little force to show themselves before the town, it would be immediately abandoned, and we should have nothing to do but to march in." Even General Taylor shared in the optimism. "The Mexican forces are almost disorganized," he announced in a dispatch to Washington, "and I shall lose no time in investing Matamoros, and opening the navigation of the river."[18]

To achieve this aim—especially the navigation of the river—Taylor required naval assistance, and he turned to David Conner, commander of the US fleet that patrolled the Gulf of Mexico. Conner had arrived at Point Isabel on May 8, and upon hearing the sound of cannon fire in the distance, had ferried several hundred of his men ashore to provide assistance. Although he was tempted to rush these troops to battle, he recognized that his sailors lacked skill at fighting on land and instead remained at the depot to bolster that garrison in the event of attack. Eager to make better use of the commodore and his ships now that the immediate peril had passed, Taylor directed Col. David Twiggs to lead the army onward to the riverside camp, while he returned to the coast to coordinate with Conner on operations on the Rio Grande.[19]

The meeting of the two officers on May 12 had a slightly comic edge. General Taylor, known for his unaffected demeanor and plain garb, decided to show his respect for the commodore by equipping himself in full-dress uniform. Meanwhile, Conner, usually very formal in manner and appearance, chose to wear the simplest uniform available in deference to Taylor's habits—plain sailor's whites. The two men, both distinctly uncomfortable in their chosen attire, were taken aback at each other's appearance. Nevertheless, they set aside their awkward first impressions and developed a joint plan of operations. As Taylor headed back to his riverside camp and prepared to attack Matamoros, Conner would sail to the mouth of the Rio Grande and move some of his vessels across the sandbar that covered the entry. Once he had boats on the river, the commodore would ferry troops upstream and establish garrisons at several strategic points between the Gulf and Matamoros. This movement would serve a threefold purpose of distracting the Mexicans as Taylor moved his main force, guarding the general's flank as he crossed the river, and preparing the way for shipping once Matamoros fell under American control.[20]

The plan took on greater urgency the next day. Taylor and his escort of dragoons had just left the depot, which he had formally named Fort Polk "as a mark of respect to the Chief Magistrate of the Republic," and turned down the road toward the riverside fort when a courier caught up with them. He passed on a message from Col. David Twiggs saying that hundreds of additional Mexican horsemen had arrived in the area and planned to cross the Rio Grande at Burrita, downstream from Matamoros. Unsure of the accuracy of the rumor but concerned by the potential threat, Taylor rushed back to Fort Polk to check its defenses and to start the advance of troops along the river as quickly as possible.[21]

Taylor's return coincided with the arrival of ships carrying reinforcements—both regular troops and several companies of volunteers from Mobile and New Orleans—and he promptly put them to use. This force of 440, under the command of Lt. Col. Henry Wilson, set out for Burrita on the morning of May 15, expecting support and supplies from ships in Conner's fleet. High seas, the poor condition of the boats, and the shallow bar that spanned the river mouth frustrated this joint exercise. It was not until May 17 that a single boat, the steamer *Neva*, finally overcame these obstacles and moved up the winding waterway. A short time later, the *Neva* reached Wilson at a point near Burrita and helped move him and his force safely to the right bank. The rumors had been unfounded; no Mexican troops were entrenched in the small settlement. Wilson's troops occupied the town without firing a shot or even seeing a Mexican soldier.[22]

It was a milestone event—occupying land that even the United States acknowledged to be Mexican territory. As it occurred, Taylor bided his time at his riverside fort. He had left Point Isabel on the afternoon of May 14 and reunited with his army that evening, still with the intention of crossing the Rio Grande and seizing the city at the first possible opportunity. The only thing holding him back was the two-hundred-yard-wide river. Even before he had left Corpus Christi, Taylor had written to his superiors in the War Department pointing out that he might need to cross the Rio Grande or some other body of water and requesting equipment to do that. His pleas had fallen on deaf ears. Now his troops idled on the north shore of the river while Matamoros lay before them, tantalizingly close but still out of reach. "If, now, we only had the means of crossing the river," wrote Lt. George Meade, expressing the mood of the entire camp, "Matamoros would be ours; but, alas, General Taylor's repeated demands on the Government . . . to send us a pontoon train, for bridges, have not been answered up to this date, and the enemy having carefully guarded and taken on their own side all the boats for many miles up and down the river, we are unable to cross."[23]

Taylor shared this frustration and turned his attention to rectifying the problem. He began by positioning his available artillery along the river so that, if necessary, he could assail the town from the left bank. He gave greater attention to finding a way to reach the opposite shore. Without the long-awaited pontoons, bridging the river was out of the question. Most of the ocean-going steamboats were too large for service on the river, and the *Neva* was needed to provide support for Lt. Col. Wilson's small force. The aging ship was also found to be so worm-eaten it could not be relied upon for much additional service. This obliged Taylor to scour his surroundings for dories and skiffs to carry his regiments. He assigned some men to build boats out of any materials deemed seaworthy. Others he dispatched to comb the banks of the Rio Grande upstream and down from Matamoros for craft of any size that might be commandeered for military use. These forays produced mixed success. On May 15, a team led by Capt. William Montrose Graham swam the river, scared off several sentinels, and cut loose a number of boats that had been secured to the opposite bank. The next day, Graham set out once again with the aim of capturing boats that had been spotted about four miles downstream, but this time the soldiers arrived to discover them spirited away, and they returned to camp empty-handed. Nevertheless, Taylor apparently believed that he had gathered enough boats to proceed. On the evening of May 16, he notified his troops that they would prepare to move on Matamoros the following day.[24]

That advance would be delayed once again. Taylor intended to march his army upriver from his fort, newly christened "Fort Brown" in honor of the fallen Jacob Brown, and ford the river at the Anacuita crossing near Fort Paredes. That movement was to occur in conjunction with Wilson's advance on Burrita. Taylor believed that Arista had about three thousand men available to defend Matamoros, and he hoped that the activity downstream would divert some of those troops and ease his efforts to capture Fort

Paredes. At 1 p.m., he had just issued the order to move out, when Mexican general Tomás Requena approached under a flag of truce, requesting an armistice and suggesting that the military men allow politicians to settle the differences between the two countries. Taylor refused this request, noting that he had made a similar offer a month earlier only to have it rejected by General Ampudia. He said that he would not revisit the topic now that circumstances had changed dramatically in his favor. He said also that the capture of Matamoros was now a certainty and that the process was already underway. He did concede that the occupation need not be a violent one and insisted that bloodshed could be avoided if Arista would withdraw and leave behind all public property, including his artillery and ammunition. Requena offered to take this proposal to Arista and promised a response latter in the afternoon. Taylor suspected that this was little more than a ploy by the Mexican to buy time for some sort of maneuver, but he nonetheless agreed to wait on the reply. By sundown no answer had arrived, and Taylor would accept no more postponements. With Colonel Wilson already in position in Burrita and his own force now waiting near Anacuitas, Taylor rode out of Fort Brown with the intention of finally crossing the river at dawn the next day.[25]

While the week of forced idleness frustrated soldiers of the Army of Occupation, Mariano Arista welcomed it. Following the confrontational meeting with his command staff on May 10, some officers continued to sow seeds of discord, but Arista and others used the time to impose some degree of order in the city. Medical staff established six hospitals and set about the task of tending the many wounded. Guards watched the roads leading south of Matamoros; they collected any dispersed troops found fleeing to the interior and returned them to their units. Negotiators secured the return of the prisoners captured at Resaca de Guerrero, a move that restored a number of foot soldiers and officers to the depleted ranks. Meanwhile, Arista and his loyal commanders made the rounds of the barracks and regiments, attempting to rearm the troops and restore discipline in the ranks. "With great fatigue and continued effort we work to reestablish the strained morale of the division," Arista wrote to the Minister of War José María Tornel. And as each day dawned, still with no sign of an American assault, the Mexican general gained some hope that he might be able to rebuild the morale and fighting ability of his force.[26]

This glimmer of optimism did not blind Arista to the many lingering problems around him. Although doctors conscientiously tended to their charges, they could do little to cure either battle wounds or the fevers that commonly followed them, and the hospitals became little more than overcrowded containment areas where the injured went to die. The return of prisoners added to this misery. Dozens of wounded soldiers accompanied the healthy returnees. Upon arrival in Matamoros, these forlorn casualties traveled from hospital to hospital, unable to find a place for treatment. Many eventually took refuge in the barracks alongside the rest of the soldiers. Their ghastly wounds served as a constant reminder of the recent battles and counteracted efforts to restore confidence to the troops. Two days after their return to Matamoros, the troops remained frightened, skittish, and unpredictable in their reliability.[27]

This became all too evident on the evening of May 11. Earlier in the afternoon, US troops had advanced to the Río Bravo to trade Mexican captives for Americans held in Matamoros. That exchange proceeded smoothly, but news spread that the US force had advanced along with the prisoners. Shortly afterwards the Mexican barracks buzzed with speculation that General Taylor intended to follow up with an immediate invasion of the city. The source of the rumor was unclear. Some claimed that one of the participants in the prisoner exchange had relayed news gleaned while meeting with the US negotiators. Others insisted that General Ampudia was the source. More likely, the story was a spontaneous reaction to the close proximity of enemy forces. But whatever its cause, it had an immediate impact. The troops in several of the barracks panicked and began to agitate for immediate withdrawal from Matamoros. A number of the men, and even a few of the officers, refused to await an official order and fled. Arista noted the growing "effervescence" for retreat and feared that his entire force would soon become caught up in the alarm.[28]

He reluctantly gave in to the demands. Realizing that many of the troops were incapable of fighting, Arista ordered Ampudia to take charge of those most affected by panic and march them out of reach of cannon fire. This would allow for an orderly retreat if an attack was pending and would prevent fear from spreading to any troops still willing to fight. Subsequently, at 3 a.m. on the twelfth, Ampudia led the 1st Brigade and most of the cavalry out of the city and established a camp in the fields to the south of town. The 2nd Brigade remained in position along the river, to serve as a rearguard in the event of a full retreat. The entire maneuver was unnecessary. Late in the afternoon, an American soldier involved in the prisoner exchange revealed that Taylor had not even considered crossing the river. In the morning light of May 12, Arista confirmed that the enemy forces remained idle with no apparent intention of advancing. By mid-morning he recalled his troops, telling them that the activities of the previous night had been nothing more than a practice exercise to prepare the troops in the event of an actual attack.[29]

Although he struck a positive tone with his troops, the incident weighed heavily on the general-in-chief. In a letter to the Minister of War Tornel, Arista described his "unceasing efforts to pull together the dispersed troops" and vowed to continue trying as long as possible. But, in light of the recent events, he also confessed, "With all due frankness, the magnitude of the task suggests that the troops are not capable of fighting either as a part or as a whole." He once again lamented the lack of supplies and troops that had constantly hindered his efforts to defend the homeland. This was especially troublesome now that he faced a rejuvenated and reinforced enemy. If he finally received additional forces and matériel for his own command, he vowed that he could still defend Matamoros as he had been ordered. Otherwise, he could only promise to hold the city as long as US forces remained on the opposite side of the Bravo.[30]

Still, Arista had not succumbed entirely to despair. Although little could be done to reverse the effects of two devastating battles, these events finally generated some resolve among Mexico's political and military leaders to support the troops on the Río Bravo. In reply to a plea made by Arista on the eve of the battle at Palo Alto, Minister of War Tornel had responded that supplies, artillery, and money were headed north via the port of Veracruz, while companies of infantry and cavalry had begun an overland march to provide relief.[31] Commanders of forces around the country also responded, offering words of support and vowing to send their own troops and supplies to supplement the wounded Army of the North. Many of their letters, as well as the resources they promised, would arrive far too late to benefit Arista, but as early as May 14 and 15 he received word that help was on the way and that he was not entirely alone. If he could stand his ground in Matamoros for even a few weeks, he might get enough reinforcements to solidify his hold on the city.[32]

Taylor appeared willing to cooperate. Although the occupants of Matamoros continued to anticipate his advance, the American commander showed little enthusiasm for the attack. Hours gave way to days; and then a week passed after the battle at the resaca, and the US troops remained stalled in their camp on the far bank of the Río Bravo. Unaware of the cause for this delay, Arista and his officers had reason to hope they had misjudged their foe. Taylor had shown an unwillingness to pass beyond the Bravo before to the recent battles and had repeatedly expressed a preference to allow politicians to resolve dispute. His silence in the aftermath of Resaca de Guerrero suggested that he might be content to secure his riverside fort and call once again for negotiation—this time from a newly earned position of strength. If so, the events of the 8th and 9th remained setbacks, but were not necessarily a disaster for Mexico. "With the Americans on one bank and us on the other," wrote one Mexican officer, "we were free of our past actions and as good as new."[33] An influx of reinforcements and supplies would reestablish the stalemate that had existed during the month of April. Although the country would have lost a number of valiant men and have little to show for their sacrifice, Mexico, at least, would be in no worse condition than before.

In the months that followed, Arista would be criticized for failing to use these peaceful days to either complete a withdrawal from Matamoros or develop a plan to defend the city, but neither course was a legitimate option. The general-in-chief probably would have abandoned the city during the scare of May 12 if he had been able to do so. The loss of so many wagons and mules at Resaca de Guerrero, however, left the army without the transports needed to move men, weaponry and supplies to safety. At the same time, Arista could make little headway in improving defenses, because he was devoting so much effort to rebuilding morale and deflecting demands for an immediate retreat. "No man has the power to do miracles," General Jauregui wrote in defense of his commander, "and the general-in-chief would have had to do them." Instead, Arista embraced the ephemeral hope that the Americans would spare Matamoros while he was preparing himself for the moment when he would have to abandon the city to them.[34]

That occasion arrived on May 17. In the early morning hours, Mexican observers along the river noted movement in the US camp and reported to Arista that Taylor's troops appeared to be mobilizing to cross the Río Bravo. Arista immediately summoned his officers to another 6 a.m. strategy session in his quarters. In addition to himself and Ampudia, as his second-in-chief, the group included commanders, or their representatives, for each of his five brigades: Gen. Mariano García of the infantry, Gen. Anastasio Torrejón of the cavalry, Gen. Tómas Requena, replacing the captured Díaz de la Vega, at the head of the 1st Brigade, Col. José Uraga, representing Ampudia's 2nd Brigade, and Col. José Morlet of the 3rd Brigade serving as proxy for Gen. Francisco Mejia, who had been seriously ill for much of the preceding month and was unable to attend. Gen. Antonio Canales may or may not have been in attendance. He claimed to have participated in the gathering, while others did not recall his being in the room and said that he had already left the city with the troops of the Villas del Norte.[35]

Arista painted the assembly as an opportunity to discuss the military options for dealing with the imminent threat, but he clearly sought endorsement of a decision to abandon Matamoros. He initiated the session by briefly recalling the conditions of the army and the city—both substantially the same as they had been in the meeting of May 10—and then encouraged his subordinates to offer their opinions on how best to proceed. The officers agreed that the city could not be held, and most of the older officers endorsed the option of retreating. Colonel Uraga offered a different view. Although he conceded the difficulty of defending Matamoros, he insisted that the army should nonetheless make a stand. The loss of this city, he argued, would have a significant impact on Mexico's ability to continue the war against the United States, and he maintained that they should spare no effort to save it. He suggested fortifying several likely crossing points along the Río Bravo and confronting the Americans wherever they attempted to cross the river. Once one unit engaged the foe, others could rush to lend support at the point of attack. In this manner, Uraga stated, the Army of the North could guard a significant expanse of the river and try one more time to turn back the invading force.[36]

The other officers commended Uraga for his passion and several of his younger peers agreed with his plan in principle, but in the end the group showed no enthusiasm to put it into practice. After leaving most of their artillery, transports, and mules behind at the resaca on the ninth, they could not take on the logistical challenge of moving forces to multiple points on the river, much less carry out a strategy of rushing units to any point of contact. The scheme also assumed that the troops had the will to leave the protection of the city, take up defensive positions, and fight. To a man, Arista's command staff agreed that this was not the case.[37]

They also saw little benefit to making a stand in the streets of Matamoros. They believed that Taylor had already increased his numbers to about thirteen thousand troops and that their small army could not resist such a force. Not that Taylor had any real need to attack. With a huge advantage in artillery strength, he could simply surround the town with his heavy guns and pound the occupants into submission. If he did that, the Mexican post Fort Paredes suddenly became a liability rather than a benefit. The Mexican leaders had once touted it as the keystone to their defenses, but they now believed that their soldiers would not defend the site and that the Americans would capture it easily. Once inside, the enemy troops could quickly refit the stronghold with their own cannon and use the position to bombard the city at close quarters. "Apparently," wrote Capt. Jean Louis Berlandier, acknowledging the irony of the situation, "the intention of the designer was quite hostile to the city." The expected barrage from this secure location would destroy buildings, decimate the remaining army, and bring profound misery to the residents of the city. Concern for the civilian population proved to be the deciding issue, and the command staff reached a consensus to withdraw their forces from Matamoros and allow an embarrassing but peaceful occupation.[38]

Even after making their decision, the generals allowed themselves one final plan to save the city. It was General Requena who recalled that Taylor had requested a ceasefire in advance of the recent battles, and he suggested that the American general might grant one in the aftermath. He proposed requesting a stay in the fighting on humanitarian grounds and asking for enough time to remove the wounded and noncombatants from the city. If granted, this delay at the very least would allow the Army of the North to begin a more organized withdrawal from the city. With luck the cessation of hostilities might last long enough to let the Mexican Army better secure the town. Perhaps there would even be time to bring in reinforcements to help defend it when the armistice expired. Eager to take any step to save themselves from the ignominy of abandoning the town charged to their care, the assembled officers decided to request a month-long delay. On the advice of Ampudia, they also selected Requena as the negotiator to meet with the Americans.

Requena accepted the responsibility and set off at about 11 a.m. on May 17. After ferrying across the Río Bravo under a flag of truce, he met with Taylor at the American earthworks and presented a written request for the suspension of hostilities. Taylor responded with an "absolute negative," announced that his troops would cross the river shortly, and quickly dismissed the Mexican negotiator. In less than an hour, Requena had rejoined the command staff to report the rejection. Still, the mission had not been completely useless. Requena's observations of the active preparations inside the US camp verified that Taylor was not simply making idle threats. And Requena had also pledged to relay Taylor's request for a formal surrender of Matamoros and all Mexican military supplies and to report back with Arista's response. Requena had no intention of returning with another communication, but he offered the promise as means to gain a few hours for the Army of the North to respond to this news.[39]

General Requena's report erased any doubt of the course of action to follow. Upon hearing the news, Arista decided forthwith that the time had come to abandon the city, and he ordered preparations to move out of Matamoros beginning at 4 P.M. The maneuver would follow the template of the aborted withdrawal several days previous. This time troops of the cavalry and the 2nd Brigade would gather at the Llano la Laguna, an open plain on the outskirts of town, then march southward under the command of General Ampudia. Meanwhile, the soldiers of the 1st Brigade would stay in position along the riverfront. They would maintain the pretense that they intended to defend the city, while they were actually covering the departure of the rest of the army in the event of a sudden attack. Only after darkness fell and obscured their movements would these troops withdraw from their fortifications and join the exodus, with General Arista at their head.[40]

The paucity of transports turned preparations for this movement into an ordeal. Although Arista had devoted great effort over the past week to acquiring pack animals and teams for a possible withdrawal, when the moment finally arrived he had only twenty-one mules and twenty carts to carry the supplies of his three-thousand-man army. This obliged officers and men to abandon all personal supplies that they could not carry on their backs and to cull the public stores and matériel down to absolute necessities. Chiefs of individual regiments scattered throughout the town, hiding papers in private homes and burying equipment or dropping it down wells in the hope that it would not fall into the hands of the conquering enemy. General Requena did locate enough teams of oxen to transport most of his artillery, but still had to leave several smaller pieces behind. The artillerymen disabled their guns to the best of their ability and tossed them into the Río Bravo along with all the ammunition that could not be carried. This became one of the more difficult projects of the day. Not only did the men charged with this duty have to escape notice of the American troops mobilized nearby, they had to find a way to move the ordnance to the river. All the trained beasts of burden were occupied elsewhere, and the soldiers resorted to yoking together teams of cattle to drag the heavy load to the water's edge.[41]

Disposition of the many wounded required more careful thought. Hundreds of soldiers injured in the recent battles lay in makeshift hospitals set up in various quarters of the city. Hundreds more, infirm or simply incapable of marching, remained with their units but cloistered in the barracks. Leaving these troops behind would be perceived as abandonment. The soldiers would undoubtedly be labeled prisoners of war, an embarrassment for all involved and a particular disgrace for those who had gained their freedom in the exchange of captives just days before. Nevertheless, Arista had no real hope of taking them along. Even if he filled every cart with these wounded, dozens would be left behind, along with the food and supplies needed to sustain a long march toward Monterrey.

Instead, Arista took measures to provide for his men as best he could. He ordered a rearrangement of accommodations for the invalids, with all rank-and-file soldiers moved to the hospitals and all officers conducted to private homes for their care. He also instructed Capt. Jean Louis Berlandier to remain behind in the city to oversee the hospitals and direct the care of the injured after the army had left. A longtime resident of Matamoros, Berlandier had ties to the local population that would help soothe their feelings of abandonment and encourage them to look after the ailing soldiers. Arista also hoped that the Frenchman could serve as an advocate for the wounded when the American troops eventually seized control of the town. Toward this end, he left Berlandier with a message for Taylor requesting that the enemy general offer the same display of humanity to the stricken Mexican soldiers that the Army of the North had previously given to their American captives. As an additional incentive, he left assurances that the Mexican Republic would honorably pay all expenses for the treatment of its invalids.[42]

These arrangements made, the army at last began its withdrawal. At five o'clock in the afternoon, Arista arrived at the Llano la Laguna and reviewed the troops gathered there. After tending to some final issues involving the disposal of documents, the general-in-chief set the 2nd Brigade on its march out of town. About two hours later, the sound of their movement obscured by the noise of the Americans hastily assembling additional boats across the river, troops of the 1st Brigade began pulling back from the defenses on the north side of the city. By eight o'clock they too had assembled on the plain in preparation for a march. Even at this point there was some degree of confusion in the ranks, with soldiers unsure whether they were moving to challenge an advancing US force or preparing to evacuate. The answer came quickly. Within moments they moved southward, away from any possible fight. An hour later, the entire army had left Matamoros behind. "Everything was silent," wrote Captain Berlandier as he tended to the wounded. "The formerly agitated streets were now deserted. You could only hear the barking of the dogs."[43]

The US troops were not entirely unaware of the activity taking place in Matamoros. In the darkness, the soldiers heard sounds that they believed to be artillery in motion, and they suspected that the Mexican force had fled Matamoros. Several Mexican ranchers who had crossed the river to return to their lands on the north bank reported seeing Arista's force on the move. Taylor was inclined to believe the reports, but remained wary. There was always danger that the informants sought to mislead him or had misinterpreted a move by Arista to intercept the American force.

Taylor therefore proceeded with the caution that had become his hallmark and prepared for the next day as if he would confront the strength of the entire Mexican Army. He selected a crossing point about five miles upstream from Anacuitas and Fort Paredes, far enough from Matamoros to discourage a Mexican resistance, but at a point

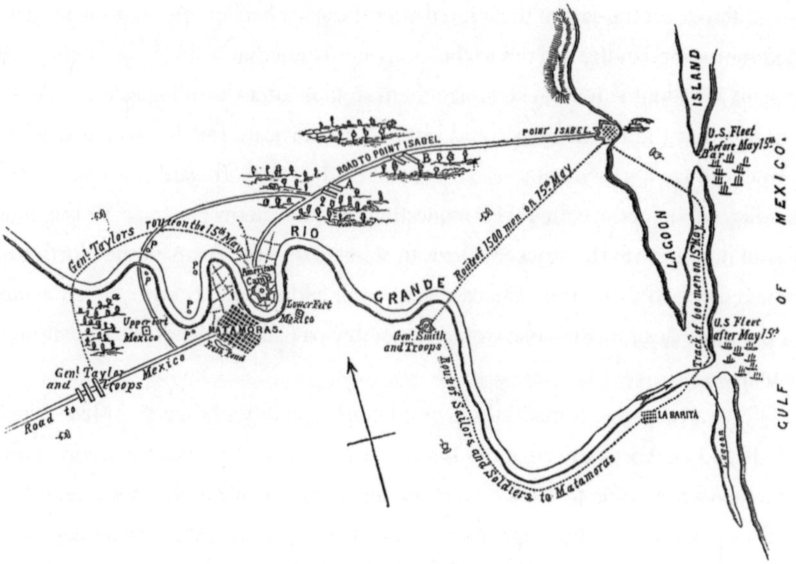

Movements and Positions on the Rio Grande, May 1846. *New York Herald.*

where boats and men on horseback could cross with relative ease. Here he planned to transport an advance force of light infantry companies, several field artillery pieces, and all of his mounted troops. The rest of his army stretched out along the left shore of the Rio Grande, ready to follow once a bridgehead had been established.

The crossing began just after dawn on May 18. At first light, the American artillerists positioned two 18-pounder siege guns and two batteries of field artillery at the river's edge and prepared to fire at the first appearance of any enemy troops on the far shore. Under the commanding protection of these guns, the first boats filled with infantrymen pushed off from the left bank. The dragoons and rangers followed close behind, swimming their horses through the murky waters. These troops arrived safety on the far shore without any challenge from Mexican troops, but the crossing was not without mishap. The strong currents beneath the placid surface of the river swept Lt. George Stephens and another soldier of the 2nd Dragoons from their mounts as they reached the center of the river, and the two men were dragged under by the weight of their accouterments and drowned. This disheartening accident tempered the jubilant mood of the soldiers, who had come to think that their crossing would be easy. In the days that followed, several excoriated the War Department for its failure to provide pontoon bridges, which would have eased the crossing and saved the lives of two of their own.[44]

General Taylor shared their displeasure at the lack of pontoon bridges and would make that clear in his report to Washington later in the day, but his immediate concern was to determine the location of the Mexican Army. He therefore ordered a small group of dragoons to follow the opposite bank of the river toward Matamoros and assess the truth behind rumors that Arista had abandoned the town. The answer came quickly and from a different source. The scouts had just left, and the general had begun shuttling his light artillery across the river, when a group of civil authorities from Matamoros arrived on the right bank and requested a conference. Taylor ferried them across to his base on the north shore, where they delivered a detailed account of Arista's flight from the city, the destruction of weaponry and ammunition, and the abandonment of the sick and wounded. Asserting that they were defenseless, they offered to turn their city over to the US Army and requested terms for surrender. The impassioned plea convinced Taylor of the sincerity of the deputation. In response, he assured the party that he would indeed take possession of Matamoros, but that he "would respect persons and private property, and permit their civil laws to go on as usual, at any rate for the present."[45]

Convinced that he faced no armed opposition, Taylor saw no need to continue the slow, difficult process of crossing the Rio Grande so far upstream. The units that had already crossed the river—including the artillery, which was crossing during the conference—remained on the right bank. Taylor assigned Col. David Twiggs to take charge of that battalion and lead it eastward to Matamoros. But the remainder of the troops made an about-face and retraced their steps for five miles toward the established crossing points opposite the city. They arrived just in time to witness the symbolic capture of Matamoros. The mounted troops of Twigg's command had hurried along the far shore of the river and seized control of Fort Paredes without firing a shot. By the time Taylor's slower-moving column returned to Anaquitas, by way of the north bank, Capt. Crohan Ker of the 2nd Dragoons had already removed the Mexican tricolor from its staff. In its place he raised the Stars and Stripes until they "floated gracefully in the breeze, and proudly waved over Mexico." The thousands of American observers viewed this moment as the final triumph of the campaign. "As it went up our regiment gave three deafening cheers," wrote Lt. Phillip Barbour, "which were taken up successively by those in the rear until the air was fairly rent with the glorious shout." The enthusiastic troops then raced to the water's edge, eager to join their compatriots and to share in the thrill of conquest.[46]

Transportation of that main body of soldiers began shortly afterward and took on a character entirely different from that of the carefully guarded advance just hours before. "We had the felicity of being ferried across by the enemy," Captain Henry noted in his description of the event. Using three large boats that had been secured on the far shore and a length of rope that extended from bank to bank, Mexican boatmen conveyed the army, company by company, to the Matamoros side of the waterway. One after another the different regiments made the journey, re-formed on the opposite shore of the river, then marched off to the sounds of "Yankee Doodle" or "Hail Columbia" as a growing crowd of Matamoros residents gathered to watch the display. By early afternoon, the entire army had crossed the Rio Grande with the exception of a token force of troops from the 7th Infantry that remained in possession of the Fort Brown earthworks.[47]

With his troops safely on the right shore of the Rio Grande, General Taylor acted to ensure that the actual occupation of Matamoros would occur in an orderly and peaceful fashion. Rather than marching immediately into the city streets, he established his camp on the open plains and fields that filled the interval between the Mexican defenses along the river and the houses of Matamoros, about half a mile to the south. He also appointed David Twiggs to serve as the governor of the occupied city. As a first order of business in this role, the US colonel established a police system to maintain order among the troops and to prevent conflicts between soldiers and civilians when the troops moved into the center of town. This precautionary force would face challenges in the weeks to follow as units of undisciplined and occasionally unmanageable volunteers poured into the town. In the first hours of occupation, however, intervention was largely unnecessary. After scouts swept through the city streets and verified that Arista had indeed fled, Taylor and Twiggs lifted restrictions on entering the town. By nightfall, small groups of officers mingled peaceably with local residents, enjoying coffee and bread in local cafés. On the morning of May 19, hundreds of soldiers wandered the streets, exploring the town they had viewed for so long from afar and enjoying meals in restaurants as if they were tourists and not members of an occupying army.[48]

The ease with which they had captured of Matamoros intrigued these men. "Citizens in crowds came down to see us," wrote Captain Henry of the reception. "Many of them, who ten days ago would have cut our throats, were now apparently our warmest friends, shook our hands heartily and cried lustily 'amigo.'" This type of greeting from war-weary civilians was understandable, but the actions of Arista and his generals created a certain amount of puzzlement. Despite having seen the hundreds of wounded Mexican troops in hospitals and having trumpeted the substantial enemy losses in battle, many US soldiers continued to believe that the Army of the North had well over five thousand troops in fighting condition. This force, they believed, could have presented a significant challenge had it chosen to defend the streets and houses of the city. "The Mexican General must have had good reasons for thus permitting the American Army to seize Matamoros as it did," Lt. George Deas reflected later. "What they were must ever remain a mystery to us." Others, however, had a much clearer understanding of the circumstances that forced Arista to abandon the town. "I wrote to you yesterday . . . that Matamoros had fallen," Lt. Napoleon Dana wrote in a letter to his wife. "In fact she may be said to have fallen on the day of Resaca de la Palma."[49]

Although there was no longer any threat from Arista, some fighting continued. On May 19, Taylor sent Col. John Garland and all the cavalry troops to pursue the Mexican Army, with instructions to harass the rear units, capture any prisoners and supplies possible, and generally make the enemy uncomfortable in their retreat. Garland performed this task efficiently, chasing the army for about sixty miles toward Monterrey and engaging the rear guard in at least one skirmish. When he returned to Matamoros on May 22, forced back by a scarcity of water and the deteriorating condition of his horses, he reported the death of one Mexican soldier and brought back twenty prisoners and a wagonload of Mexican weapons and supplies. This news, which would have generated considerable excitement just weeks before, was largely accepted without remark. While Garland and his troops were absent, the remaining soldiers had been occupied with official duties like uncovering hidden document, supply, and ammunition caches, retrieving Mexican cannon from the Rio Grande, tending to the many Mexican wounded, and locating campsites for the volunteer troops that had started to arrive. By the time the cavalry returned, the focus of activity had shifted dramatically, with US officers involved in leisurely pursuits like parceling out cigars left behind by the Mexican Army, introducing themselves to the señoritas of the community, and planning fandangos.[50]

Reports that Mexican forces were regrouping and would return for a fight were generally dismissed as unfounded gossip. "There are rumors in town of the advance of a force of five thousand men, under Bustamante, to support Arista," Lt. George Meade announced in a letter to his wife after one of these tales had circulated. "But I very much fear there no such good luck in store for us as the reappearance of a Mexican Army in this neighborhood or anywhere this side of the Sierra Madre." Meade and his peers agreed: the first campaign of the war had come to an end.[51]

The Mexican Army experienced a much longer, considerably more difficult close to the campaign. As the American troops prepared to cross the Río Bravo on the morning of May 18, the soldiers of the Army of the North rose at their camp at Venado, reorganized their supplies for greater efficiency of movement, and set off once again. The object of their march was Linares, a town about midway between the northern Mexican cities of Monterrey and Victoria and a strategic location that would allow Arista to march to the defense of either city if necessary. His troops initially viewed the retreat as a blessing and gratefully placed additional distance between themselves and the US forces near Matamoros. But they soon began to realize that hard trials lay ahead. The heavily laden men and beasts of burden trudged slowly across a dry, desolate landscape under the heat of a blistering sun, and managed to cover only about fifteen miles before making camp for the evening. At nightfall, while US officers sat down to dine in the restaurants of Matamoros, Mexican soldiers parceled out their limited water and indulged in rice, beans, and meat—the last regular rations they would receive during their journey.[52]

The situation grew considerably worse the next day. Marching once again in the blazing heat over ground without water, troops and animals alike suffered the effects of sun, thirst, and hunger. As the sun climbed higher into the sky many of the horses could no longer carry their riders, forcing cavalrymen to lead them on foot, or, in many cases, shoot the animals that could no longer carry on. Soldiers also began to lag and grow restless, and Arista called for careful policing of the regiments to prevent disorder. It was anxiety, however, that kept the army moving. In the afternoon, the Mexicans became aware that a group of about five hundred mounted US troops were pursuing them from Matamoros. As the Mexican rearguard paused to fend off an attack by the enemy, at the cost of some men, animals, and supplies, the rest of the units hurried onward, fearing that the entire enemy force was about to descend upon them. They covered almost twenty-five miles by day's end and settled into camp at a spot called Ebanito, without any semblance of military order, and with only small portions of meat and water to sustain them.[53]

Nevertheless, on May 20 the weary soldiers took up a line of march once again, pushed by fear and pulled by the hope of finding water. With the American cavalry close on their heels, Arista and his officers drove their units forward at a frantic pace that left many lagging far behind. Over the course of an eight-hour march they traversed more than twenty-seven miles of desert scrublands and arrived at last at a promising location known as La Nutria, "The Otter." Here was a large, shallow pond that might well have been home to such an animal and certainly promised to ease the thirst of the parched, weary troops. To their dismay, however, as the men rushed to establish their camp, a number of horses and cattle broke loose from their tethers and trampled through the pool, roiling the water and making it too muddy to drink. Straggling troops who arrived at the site eager to quench their thirst at last, were forced to wait hours before the water was fit for consumption.[54]

During those hours of waiting, Arista was able to reestablish some order in the ranks. Aware that his pursuers also suffered from the arid environment, and realizing that the water hole was a strategic location, he took measures to secure it. He deployed his cavalry units around the pond in a defensive circle and placed one of his few remaining artillery pieces and ammunition in a forward position to confront the enemy horsemen if they approached. Soldiers who had fled their Americans pursuers for two days exhibited signs of resolve that had been absent since the fight at Palo Alto. Fear of death from thirst outweighed any fear of defeat in battle, and the troops firmly held their position, expecting an attack at any moment. They were rewarded with a night free of violence. In the early morning hours, scouts sent out to determine the location of Colonel Garland and his cavalry discovered that he had broken off his pursuit and gone back in the direction of Ebanito.[55]

Although he had eluded the threat from the American cavalry, Arista could not escape the cruel twists of fate that plagued his army. On the morning of May 21, he let his troops move forward at a more measured pace for about ten miles. Having put additional distance between himself and the enemy, he then paused to give his men some much-needed rest and to let them eat. But when he ordered the slaughter of some livestock to provide fresh meat, the cattle stampeded and disappeared, leaving the men with empty stomachs as they resumed their march in the evening. The troops prayed for clean water to replace what they had put in their canteens at the muddy pond that morning, and after midnight a long-awaited rain began. But it turned into a torrential downpour that disoriented them and brought their march to a halt.[56]

The deluge was a final blow to the weary Army of the North. Soldiers became scattered in all directions in the darkness and confusion, and hours passed before the column could be reassembled. When the march resumed at first light on May 22, a number of men were still missing, some never to be located again. The storm also took a toll on the animals. Cavalry horses, already been weakened by overexertion, dehydration, and lack of forage, now succumbed to the storm by the dozens. Oxen and pack animals also died, leaving few beasts to pull the overfilled supply wagons. This forced the equally exhausted and underfed troops to lighten the loads by burying most of their ammunition under the trees that lined the road or by putting supplies on their own backs. Most burdensome were the few remaining artillery pieces. Arista refused to leave these important weapons behind and assigned troops of the infantry regiments the arduous task of transporting them more than a hundred miles using their own failing strength.[57]

The remains of this once proud army finally reached its destination at Linares six days later, on May 28. The bedraggled force that wandered into the town was only a shadow of the already-ragged column that had left Matamoros ten days earlier. "You can guess the suffering," wrote General Jauregui, "on this trek through the desert without any type of provisions except for a few wagons of corn that had been sent in our direction and for which we were extremely grateful." General García collapsed just as the army reached Linares. Dozens of men had died en route from thirst, hunger, sunstroke, and apoplexy. Some had committed suicide when they could no longer carry on and were buried where they fell. Hundreds more suffered from fevers, chills, and exhaustion and arrived at their destination too weak or ill to function.[58]

Some two hundred miles away, US soldiers in Matamoros had moved on from the recent hardships of warfare. "We are now resting out and do not feel equal to any exertion," Lt. Raphael Smead wrote to his wife. "We have been now since the 20th May in a state of perfect repose—no work, no enemy, no alarms at night, can sleep well every night except when on guard and really we have enjoyed it."

During that same period, the Mexican soldiers had experienced only trials and suffering, and they expected more to follow. But for a brief time they paused to breathe a sigh of relief that their tragic campaign had finally come to a close.[59]

EPILOGUE

IN THE EARLY afternoon of May 18, 1846, at about the time US troops were making their entry into the city of Matamoros, a steamship out of Point Isabel moored at the wharves of New Orleans. A gathering crowd cheered as the passengers disembarked and related tales of decisive action on the Rio Grande. For the first time, American citizens heard of the powerful artillery at Palo Alto and the frantic fighting in the dense chaparral of Resaca de la Palma. They eagerly listened to tales about Samuel Ringgold and the success of his "Flying Artillery" in the first battle. They marveled at the gallantry of Charles May and his dramatic charge in the second. They even had an opportunity to gawk at one of the grandest trophies of the war when Gen. Rómulo Díaz de la Vega himself descended the gangway and headed off for a pleasant imprisonment at one of the town's finest hotels. Within hours, the news had made the special edition of every one of the Crescent City's many tabloids. By nightfall, few New Orleanians could have failed to hear that the United States Army had emerged victorious in its combat with Mexico.[1]

Within days, the word spread around the country as ships, railroads, and riverboats carried accounts of the battles to every major city. In many communities, proclamations of victory arrived almost as soon as the revelation that war had been declared, and residents eagerly praised the quick success of American arms. That success appeared all the more impressive as excited tabloid editors accepted virtually all reports at face value and further exaggerated information that had already been distorted by the soldiers involved. By the end of the month, in an article reprinted by many other papers, the New York *Courier* was reporting that a mere two thousand brave US troops had taken on seventy-five hundred seasoned veterans of one of the most powerful armies in the world. Similarly, the Philadelphia *Public Ledger* portrayed an army at the pinnacle of its strength and asserted that General Taylor "has gained a glorious victory over the best appointed army that Mexico ever sent into the field, confident of success, in a position selected by themselves, and with an overwhelming force, at odds more than 3 to 1. . . . They were veterans of twenty successful battles, and in their own country, upon whichever side they fought, victory perched. Everything was in their favor—position, numbers, and confidence, and yet with all these they were badly beaten."[2]

Small wonder then that soldiers who fought these battles—from Ringgold, May, Zachary Taylor, and Jacob Brown down to even the lowliest of enlisted men—emerged as heroic figures. By the end of the summer, many of the battle participants had become national celebrities, their deeds honored in patriotic music, artworks, books, dramas, and poems.[3]

This excitement of the bravely fought and well-won campaign helped draw the country together in a unified effort to see the conflict to its conclusion. Although Congress had overwhelmingly supported a declaration of war just weeks before, the decision had been made against a backdrop of strong public debate. Many legislators had cast their votes as a show of solidarity with Zachary Taylor's imperiled army, rather than as an endorsement of claims against Mexico. Now the danger seemed to have passed, and voices of protest were lost as newspaper columns filled with accounts of the "Heroes of the Rio Grande." Excited citizens clamored to volunteer to join the adventure. Even those of a more moderate bent reluctantly cast their lot with finishing the task that had been started at Palo Alto and Resaca de la Palma. "The die is cast, the sword is drawn," wrote the editor of the Cincinnati *Catholic Messenger*, and "and every man must enter with all of his heart into the conflict. Until peace be restored, our great object must be to defend by every means in our power the national cause. . . . Any other feeling than this would be contrary to the allegiance which we owe the Constitution and which the government has a right to demand."[4]

Had the Army of Occupation not succeeded in its clashes with Mexican troops, opinion might well have shifted dramatically in another direction. Victory created confidence that Mexico would crumble quickly. With varying degrees of enthusiasm, Americans set aside differences and agreed to press on.

The successful military campaign created an even greater sense of unity for those who had participated in the fighting. The army that had squabbled its way from Corpus Christi to the Rio Grande delta in March 1846 concluded the month of May as a cohesive force. Victory in battle created a sense of shared accomplishment. Graduates of the Military Academy banded together to laud their embattled alma mater and to make certain that Americans understood how West Point-trained minds had positively influenced the engagements. "Our Alma Mater may be proud of her sons," crowed Lt. William Seaton Henry; "conspicuously have they shown themselves soldiers upon the field of battle. Away hereafter, with opposition to an institution which sends forth, for the country's service, yearly, a class of young gentlemen fitted for any walk in life."[5]

The praise extended to the much-maligned army as a whole and in fact to all who had chosen soldiering as a profession. "We all feel proud that these conquests have been effected by the army proper," Lieutenant Henry said. "We only asked for an opportunity, few as we were, to prove to our country she had a safe anchor in our small but gallant force." Lt. Napoleon Dana agreed. "You don't know . . . how much we rejoice that all this has happened before the volunteers arrived," he wrote to his wife. "The country will see that it is the regulars which can do their business, and had the volunteers have been here they would probably have gotten all the credit for our hard fighting." Raphael Smead shared the sentiments of his peers, but with less lofty expectations. "I hope," he said to his wife, "that they will stop abusing the army after this and allow them at least the credit of being brave."[6]

This type of sentiment was widespread in the ranks and encouraged many to set aside petty differences in favor of jointly promoting their treasured institutions. Officers dropped complaints against each other. Soldiers heaped praise on longtime rivals. Even William J. Worth joined in this spirit of reconciliation, despite having missed the battles. Worth, who had angrily left the Rio Grande after Zachary Taylor had made David Twiggs second-in-command of the army, had barely reached Washington to plead his case when news of the war-opening skirmish at Carricitos reached him. He abandoned his complaints, withdrew the resignation of his commission, and rushed back to Matamoros, where he meekly took his place in the town that Twiggs now commanded as military governor. In time, such displays of solidarity would give way to a new round of rivalries and jealousies over who should receive credit and promotions for the heroics of battle. But for the moment, the soldiers basked in the glow of victory and proudly stood together. "No matter what our internal dissentions," Lt. William Henry asserted, "when the foe appears, *united* we will meet him."[7]

They also would meet that foe with confidence. Long gone was the collection of frightened soldiers who had suffered from doubts and desertions in the initial days of the Army of Occupation. In their place was a collection of men who had convinced themselves that they had defeated a force of as many as eight thousand of the finest troops Mexico had to offer. A change in name accompanied this change in attitude. Upon reaching the southern shore of the Rio Grande, the troops shed the somewhat ambivalent title of Army of Occupation in favor of the more decisive "Army of Invasion" and anxiously awaited orders to extend their conquest deeper into the heart of Mexico.

Most doubted that the command would ever come. Mexico, they believed, was too thoroughly defeated to continue the conflict for any length of time and would quickly come to the bargaining table for a settlement. Nevertheless, should the southern republic foolishly attempt to carry on a resistance, Americans harbored few doubts who would triumph. Even if the fight carried them across vast deserts, far from supplies, deep into enemy territory, and into confrontation with massive and skilled armies, the US troops believed that they would prevail. "Still, I have no fears for the result," wrote Lt. George Meade after enumerating the many challenges that he and his comrades-in-arms would face. "We shall beat them wherever we meet them, and in whatever numbers."[8]

Those numbers had dwindled. The Mexican force that entered Linares on May 29 after suffering the ravages of battle and nature included only 2638 soldiers. Hundreds more were in no condition to fight again even if they had the weapons and supplies to do so, further reducing the effective strength of the army. In some cases, companies that had included up to thirty or forty soldiers before the start of fighting on the Río Bravo could muster only three or four able-bodied men on arriving at Linares. This depletion in the ranks forced officers to combine and eliminate units, sometimes even entire regiments, in an effort to reestablish a workable command structure. Perhaps the most notable loss to the Army of the North, however, was the departure of its top leader. Shortly after quartering his dispirited troops in the northern city, General Arista received a summons to Mexico City to face charges that he had betrayed Mexico with his conduct in battle and disobeyed orders by abandoning Matamoros. On June 4 he surrendered his command, leaving behind the defense of the country for the equally challenging task of defending his reputation.[9]

Arista's departure was the final stage of the fractious relationship between him and Pedro de Ampudia. Although both the general-in-chief and his second-in-command passionately believed in the importance and justice of the Mexican cause, their inability to cooperate as professionals had undermined their military effort against the United States. Ampudia bore much of the responsibility. After being stripped of command in favor of the more popular Arista, he had refused to set aside personal ambitions and jealousy for the benefit of the republic. Instead, he had resisted orders, created divisions in the ranks, and constantly sought ways to restore himself to power, even if his efforts came at the expense of the Army of the North and the national interest. His maneuvering had continued during the final days in Matamoros as well as on the long march to Linares. He had sent a series of reports to the minister of war detailing the shortcomings of the campaign, deriding the decision to abandon Matamoros, and carefully placing responsibility for the failures at the feet of Arista. These letters, and messages from others in Ampudia's faction of the army, left officials in Mexico City with little choice but to recall Arista and put him on trial for undefined violations of orders and offenses against the nation.[10]

Arista fought back against the slanderous campaign to bring him down. In his own messages to the capital, he expressed frustration that he had not been presented with a clear explanation of the accusations against him. "How can I clarify the necessary points," he wrote in an exasperated note to Minister of War José María Tornel, "except by hearing them first, understanding the accusations against me, and responding?" He also objected to the anonymous nature of the charges. "I should not have to seek out who accuses me from among my subordinates," he complained, "to find out which charges I should deny. Instead I should hear those charges in court and have the opportunity to demonstrate whether my actions were correct based on the circumstances as they stood during my time as commander of the Army of the North. Only in this manner can I form my defense."

The general admitted that he might have made some errors during the course of the failed campaign, but he believed that he should be given a fair chance to defend his actions. His subordinates, he argued, did not share all the information that he used to devise strategy and were therefore not the appropriate persons to judge its correctness. And since these unnamed accusers had themselves contributed to the demise of the Army of the North, he demanded that they also be investigated and held responsible for their actions during the campaign.[11]

Despite these protestations, Arista was certain that Ampudia had levied the complaints against him, and he and his loyal lieutenants took several parting shots at the troublesome second-in-command. When called upon to step down, Arista did so willingly, but instead of naming Ampudia as his successor, he once again placed Gen. Francisco Mejía in charge of the Army of the North. There were legitimate reasons for choosing Mejía over Ampudia. Mejía had held the position before, had loyally assisted Arista, and was respected by the troops and the residents of Northern Mexico, while Ampudia was disliked by a large segment within the army and by a vast majority outside the ranks. Nevertheless, it was an obvious snub of a man who had been removed from power and longed to return. Although Mejía gamely attempted to fulfill the duties of general-in-chief, he suffered from a debilitating but unnamed illness that had limited his role in the Río Bravo campaign. In July, he too was obliged to surrender command. Like Arista before him, Mejía rejected the ambition of Ampudia and selected Gen. Tómas Requena as his successor. An outraged Ampudia pressed his case with supporters in the capital, but it was not until August—at a time when Zachary Taylor's rejuvenated army had already commenced a push toward Monterrey—that the one-time second-in-chief finally reclaimed his title as head of the army.[12]

The former general-in-chief also found some powerful support outside of the Army of the North. As Arista prepared to face questioning about whether he had dishonored his country with his conduct in battle, Vicente García Torres, the editor of Mexico City's *Monitor Republicano*, analyzed the events and suggested that the reasons for failure and the source of betrayal might be found closer to home. He used the pages of his newspaper to defend the maligned survivors of the Río Bravo campaign and to note their honorable attempts to defend Mexico. He also confronted the interim president Mariano Paredes and his allies in print and conducted an impassioned cross-examination of the decision-making that had left Arista so vulnerable. "Why abandon that army of heroes to face the enemy alone and an immense distance from all resources?" he demanded in a column titled "National Honor."

> *Why send an army with no vanguard, center, or rear guard?*
>
> *Why have the reserve forces for the Army of the North happily remained many leagues from the theater of operations?*
>
> *Why did no one believe the words of General Arista when he foretold defeat if the reinforcements in San Luis moved toward the capital instead of the front?*
>
> *Why not carry out the program of the movement of San Luis, have the army establish a government, then return immediately to the border?*
>
> *Why send the least disciplined or least trained units to face a foreign enemy—was it just to get them out of Mexico?*
>
> *Why did the reserve army—composed of units known for their valor and discipline—remain inactive in this capital city?*

> *Why consider maintaining troops in various posts around the nation when there is an invading enemy who compensates for his lack of valor and expertise with the speed of his actions and the measures of his government?*
>
> *Why not try to convince our foreign enemies that there are no divisions among the Mexicans and that there is no clamor other than that of Mexicans crying out in unison of their hate for the deceitful Yankees?*
>
> *Why not frankly publicize all of the causes of our disgrace in order to fuel public spirit and love of country just as we have publicized information about the position of our army and so many other bits of information that should have been kept secret?*

"Why?" he concluded. "So many whys."[13]

García Torres's questions contained their own answers. Like the officers of the Army of the North, Mexico's leaders had been unwilling to set aside political differences and personal ambitions to focus on a common defense. General Paredes appropriated troops that were desperately needed on the northern frontier to place himself on the presidential throne. He then kept the best troops close at hand to preserve his tenuous hold on power. Meanwhile, officials at all levels had chosen to engage in partisan infighting rather than find ways to provide funds, supplies, and matériel to the ragged army on the front line of defense. The Army of the North had suffered the consequences of this inattention, and Arista was being held accountable for the results. That attempt to pin the entirety of the blame on him would ultimately fail. Although Arista would never be able to completely rub away the tarnish on his reputation, allies like García Torres and the loyal officers of the Army of the North would help him recover status and influence. In time, the fallen general would even rise to serve as president of the Mexican Republic.

Arista's personal redemption was one matter. A greater one entirely was Mexico's effort to overcome ambition, partisanship, and political division in order to confront a common enemy. "If Mexicans would unite with the sole objective of making war against a common enemy they would be invincible," Gen. Manuel María Lombardini, military commander of Querétaro, reminded his troops in the aftermath of the disaster on the Río Bravo. "Our forces would destroy the American phalanges—nothing could stop them."[14] But the initial defeats of the war had only sharpened divisions in the country and increased dissention. They had also ushered in a new phase of the conflict in which Mexico no longer fought for lands north of the Rio Bravo but fought instead for its very survival as a nation. As Mexican generals argued over who should command and politicians assigned blame for military failures, US troops continued to move toward the Mexican interior.

During his brief return as general-in-chief of the Army of the North, Francisco Mejía made a final plea to mount an effective challenge to Taylor's planned push toward Monterrey. In an expansive letter to Minister of War Tornel he recounted the abysmal state of his disheveled army, assessed the tactics, strategies, and intentions of the American force, and offered a detailed explanation of what his army needed to counter the inexorable advance. Once again, the letter devolved into a desperate plea for more troops, more food, more weapons and ammunition, and more money. Like Lombardini, Mejía called for the nation to adopt a sense of unity and to send all the forces at its disposal. "The time has arrived," he wrote, "for the rest of the army to come to this frontier to help repel the aggressions of our foreign enemies, or better said to throw them back, if not beyond the Sabine River, at least as far as the left bank of the Río Bravo. Otherwise we are sure to lose other Departments and, in a matter of years, we are likely to see the American flag rise over our capital."[15]

In the aftermath of the crushing defeats in May, it is unclear whether the ailing general truly believed that Mexico could turn the tide of war. Perhaps he was merely exhorting his countrymen to action. But his nation's failure to heed either his words or the lessons of the first campaign insured that his dire prediction would come to pass.

ABBREVIATIONS

AGNL–FM	Archivos Generales del Estado de Nuevo Léon, Fondo Militar
ALPL	Abraham Lincoln Presidential Library
AMHI	US Army Military History Institute
AO	Army of Occupation
ASDN	Archivos Históricos de la Secretaría de la Defensa Nacional, Mexico City
CM	Courts-Martial Proceedings
CP	Captured Papers
FHS	Filson Historical Society
GO	General Orders
LC	Library of Congress
LR	Letters Received
LSU	Louisiana State University Libraries
MHI	US Military History Institute
MHS	Massachusetts Historical Society
NA	US National Archives
OAG	Office of the Adjutant General
OEG	Records of the Office of the Chief of Engineers
OJAG	Records of the Office of the Judge Advocate General
RG	Record Group
UNC	University of North Carolina
USMA	US Military Academy
UT	University of Texas, Dolph Briscoe Center
UTA	University of Texas at Arlington

NOTES

Unless otherwise noted, translations from the Spanish are the author's.

INTRODUCTION

1. Nathaniel Hunter to Sarah R. Hunter, 11 May 1846, Nathaniel Wyche Hunter Papers, Hargrett Rare Book and Manuscript Library, University of Georgia; *Charleston Mercury,* 5 June 1846; in *Monitor republicano,* 2 June 1846; *Monitor republicano,* 27 June 1846.

2. Milton Rickels, *Thomas Bangs Thorp: Humorist of the Old Southwest* (Baton Rouge: Louisiana State University Press, 1962), 119–21; Thomas Bangs Thorp, *Our Army on the Rio Grande* (Philadelphia: Carey and Hart, 1846), 159.

3. John Frost, *The Mexican War and Its Warriors* (New Haven: H. Mansfield, 1848) and *A Pictorial History of Mexico and the Mexican War* (Philadelphia: Charles Desilver, 1848); R. S. Ripley, *The War with Mexico* (New York: Harper, 1849); Brantz Mayer, *History of the War between Mexico and the United States: With a Preliminary View of Its Origins* (New York: Wiley and Putnum, 1848); Nathan Covington Brooks, *A Complete History of the Mexican War: Its Causes, Conduct, and Consequences* (Philadelphia: Grigg, Elliot, 1849).

4. Pedro de Ampudia, *El ciudadano general Pedro de Ampudia ante el tribunal respetable de la opinión pública* (San Luis Potosí: n.p., 1846); *Campaña contra los Americanos del norte* (México: Imprenta de Ignacio Cumplido, 1846). See, for example, José López Uraga, *Sumaria mandada formar a pedimento del Sr. Colonel Don José López Uraga* (México: Imprenta de J. R. Navarro, 1846).

5. *Fallo definitivo del Supremo Tribunal de la Guerra, al examinar la conducta militar del Exmo. Sr. General D. Mariano Arista, en los acciones de guerra que sostuvo al principio de la invasión americana* (Mexico: Imprenta de Vicente García Torres, á cargo de Luis Vidaurri, 1850); Carlos María Bustamante, *El nuevo Bernal Díaz del Castillo, o sea, historia de la invasión de los Anglo-Americanos en México* (México: Imprenta de V. García Torres, 1847); Ramón Alcaraz et al., *Apuntes para la historia de la guerra entre México y los Estados Unidos* (México: Tipografía de Manuel Payno, 1848).

6. See, for example, José María Roa Bárcena, *Recuerdos de la invasión norte-americana, 1846–1848: por un jóven de entónces* (México: J. Buxó, 1883); Eduardo Paz, *La invasión norte-americana en 1846: ensayo de historia patria-militar por el mayor de caballería* (México: C. Paz, 1889); Emilio Castillo Negrete, *La invasión de los norte-americanos en México,* 6 vols. (México: Imprenta del editor, 1890–91); Heriberto Frías, *Episodios militares mexicanos* (México DF: Vda de C. Bouret, 1901); José Fernando Ramírez, *México durante su guerra con los Estados Unidos* (México DF: Vda de C. Bouret, 1905).

7. Roa Bárcena, *Recuerdos de la invasión norteamericana,* x; Negrete, *Invasión de los norteamericanos,* 1:viii.

8. See, for example, José C. Valadés, *Breve historia de la guerra con los Estados Unidos* (México: Editorial Patria, 1947); Alfonso Trueba, *Legítima gloria* (México: Editorial Campeador, 1954); Carlos Alvear Acevedo, *La guerra del 47* (México: Editorial Jus, 1969); Josefina Zoraida Vázquez, *Mexicanos y norteamericanos ante la guerra del 47* (México: Secretaría de Educación Pública, 1972); Gastón García Cantú, *Las invasiones norteamericanas en México* (México: Ediciones Era, 1974); Leopoldo Martínez Caraza, *La intervención norteamericana en México, 1846–1848* (México, DF: Panorama, 1981); Laura Herrera Serna, ed., *México en guerra, 1846–1848: perspectivas regionales* (México, DF: Consejo Na-

cional para la Cultura y las Artes, 1997); Josefina Zoraida Vázquez, *La intervención norteamericana, 1846–1848* (México, DF: Secretaría de Relaciones Exteriores, 1997); José Manuel Villalpando César, *Las balas del invasor: la expansión territorial de los Estados Unidos a costa de México* (México: Miguel Angel Porrúa, 1998); Ángela Moyano Pahissa, *La pérdida de Tejas* (México, DF: Planeta, 1999); Danna A. Levin Rojo and Martha Ortega, coordinadora, *El territorio disputado en la guerra de 1846–1848* (México, DF: Porrúa, 2007); René Zorrilla Vargas, *El encuentro entre México y Estados Unidos, 1803–1848: el nacimiento de una relación difícil* (México, DF: Minos III Milenio, 2008).

9. Ulysses S. Grant, *Personal Memoirs of U. S Grant* (New York: C. L. Webster, 1885). Examples of other memoirs include Samuel Gibbs French, *Two Wars: An Autobiography of General Samuel G. French* (Nashville: Confederate Veteran, 1901); James Longstreet, *From Manassas to Appomattox: Memoirs of the Civil War in America* (Philadelphia: J. P Lippincott, 1895); George G. Meade, *The Life and Letters of George Gordon Meade,* 2 vols. (New York: Charles Scribner's Sons, 1913).

10. Examples of critiques of Smith include Ramón Eduardo Ruiz, "A Commentary on Morality, Lincoln, Justin Smith and the Mexican War," *Journal of the Illinois State Historical Society* 69, no. 1 (1976): 26–34, and Bernard DeVoto, *The Year of Decision, 1846* (Boston: Little, Brown, 1943), 510–11.

11. See, for example, Justin Harvey Smith, "Sources for a History of the Mexican War, 1846–1848," *Military Historian and Economist* 1 (Jan. 1916): 18–32.

12. Justin Harvey Smith, *War with Mexico,* 147, 178, 158–59, 160–78 passim.

13. DeVoto, *Year of Decision,* 510; Frederick Merk, *The Monroe Doctrine and American Expansionism, 1843–1849* (New York: Alfred Knopf, 1966), 147. Merk also notes that Smith presents one argument in the body of this work, but contradicts it in the footnotes.

14. Otis A. Singletary, *The Mexican War* (Chicago: University of Chicago Press, 1960), 5; Robert Selph Henry, *The Story of the Mexican War* (New York: F. Ungar, 1961), 37; John Edward Weems, *To Conquer a Peace: The War between Mexico and the United States* (College Station: Texas A&M University Press, 1974), 3; K. Jack Bauer, *The Mexican War, 1846–1848* (New York: University of Nebraska Press, 1974): John S. D. Eisenhower, *So Far from God: The US War with Mexico,* 1846–1848 (New York: Random House, 1989), xviii; Joseph Wheelen, *Invading Mexico: America's Continental Dream and the Mexican War, 1846–48* (New York: Carroll & Graf, 2007); Felice Flanery Lewis, *Trailing Clouds of Glory: Zachary Taylor's Mexican War Campaign and His Emerging Civil War Leaders* (Tuscaloosa: University of Alabama Press, 2010). In *A Glorious Defeat: Mexico and Its War with the United States* (New York: Hill and Wang, 2007), Timothy Henderson made the case for Mexico's having fought a war of honor.

15. John Shy, "First Battles in Retrospect," in Charles E. Heller and William A. Stofft, *America's First Battles, 1776–1965* (Lawrence: University of Kansas Press, 1986), 327–29, 332, 335, 339.

16. Jacob Brown to W. W. Bliss, 4 May 1846, in "Messages of the President of the United States with the Correspondence Therewith Communicated Between the Secretary of War and Other Officers of the Government on the Subject of the Mexican War," H.R. Doc. No. 30–60 (1st Sess., 1848) (hereafter cited as H.R. Doc. No. 30–60), at 293–4; E. S. Hawkins to W. W. Bliss, 10 May 1846, in "Message of the President of the United States Relative to the Operations and Recent Engagements on the Mexican Frontier," S. Doc. No. 29–388 (1st Sess., 1846)(hereafter cited as S. Doc. No. 29–388), at 31.

CHAPTER 1

1. James Polk, Message to Congress, 2 Dec. 1845, in James D. Richardson, ed., *A Compilation of the Messages and Papers of the Presidents* (Washington, DC: Bureau of National Literature and Art, 1910), 5:2234–43.

2. For detailed examinations of Mexican views on the war, see Josefina Zoraida Vázquez, ed., *México al tiempo de su guerra con Estados Unidos, 1846–1848* (México: Fondo de Cultura Económica, 1998); Paz, *La invasión norte americana en 1846;* David M. Pletcher, *The Diplomacy of Annexation: Texas, Oregon and the Mexican War* (Columbia: University of Missouri Press, 1973; Henderson, *A Glorious Defeat;* Pedro Santoni, *Mexicans at Arms: Puro Federalists and the Politics of War, 1845–1848* (Fort Worth: Texas Christian University Press, 1996).

3. For more detail, see Pletcher, *Diplomacy of Annexation;* Merk, chap. 6 in *The Monroe Doctrine,* and chaps. 3 and 4 in *Manifest Destiny and Mission in American History* (New York: Vintage, 1966); Smith, *The War with Mexico,* 2 vols. (New York: Macmillan, 1919); Glen W. Price, *Origins of the War with Mexico: The Polk-Stockton Intrigue* (Austin: University of Texas Press, 1967).

4. James Polk, Inaugural Address, 4 Mar. 1845, in Richardson, *Compilation of the Messages and Papers of the Presidents,* 5:2230; Bauer, *Mexican War,* 16.

5. One of the clearest discussions of the Texas boundary issue is the chapter titled "A True Boundary" in Merk, *The Monroe Doctrine,* 133–60. See also Bauer, *Mexican War,* 16–19; Gene M. Brack, *Mexico Views Manifest Destiny, 1821–1846: An Essay on the Origins of the Mexican War* (Albuquerque: University of New Mexico Press, 1975).

6. Even if it had been accepted, the secret portion of the Treaty of Velasco merely committed Santa Anna to seek a boundary for Texas, "not to extend beyond the Río Bravo del Norte." This vague wording fell far short of definitively establishing the river as a formal boundary. Brack, *Mexico Views Manifest Destiny;* Alcaraz, *Apuntes para la historia de la guerra,* 20–27; Josefina Zoraida Vázquez et al., *De la rebelión de Texas a la guerra del 47* (México, DF: Nueva Imagen, 1994).

7. In *Niles' National Register* (Baltimore: Franklin Press, 1811), 26 Apr. 1846; Resolution of the Mexican Congress, 7 May 1845, in *Niles' National Register,* 10 May 1845; Herrera speech cited in the *New York Herald Tribune,* 16 July 1845.

8. Bauer, *Mexican War,* 114–15; Marcy to Taylor, 28 May 1845, in "Message of the President of the United States Relative to the Invasion and Commencement of Hostilities By Mexico," H.R. Doc. No. 29–196 (1st Sess., 1846) (hereafter cited as H.R. Doc. No. 29–196), at 68–69; Bancroft to Taylor, 15 June 1845, H.R. Doc. No. 29–196, at 69–70.

9. George Bancroft to Zachary Taylor, 15 June 1845, H.R. Doc. No. 29–196, at 69–70.

10. Bustamente, *Nuevo Bernal Díaz,* 85; Bauer, *Mexican War,* 21.

11. William S. Henry, *Campaign Sketches of the War with Mexico* (New York: Harper and Brothers, 1847), 11–13; Grant to Julia Dent, 6 July 1845, in Mary Drake and William S. McFeely, eds., *Ulysses S. Grant: Memoirs and Selected Letters* (New York: Library of America, 1990), 894–96; Nathan Sturgis Jarvis, "An Army Surgeon's Notes of Frontier Service—Mexican War," *Journal of the Military Service Institution of the United States* 40 (May 1907) and 41 (June 1907). See 40:435.

12. Thomas Wilhelm and Arthur Tracey Lee, *History of the Eighth US Infantry from Its Organization, in 1838,* 2 vols. (New York: Headquarters, Eighth Infantry, 1873), 1:255.

13. Taylor to R. Jones, 20 July 1845, and Marcy to Taylor, 30 July 1845, both in H.R. Doc. No. 29–196, at 70–72; Henry, *Campaign Sketches,* 10–15; Bauer, *Mexican War,* 32–35.

14. Henry, *Campaign Sketches,* 12–17, 27–28; Jarvis, "An Army Surgeon's Notes," 40:435–36.

15. Henry, *Campaign Sketches,* 27–28; Taylor to Adjutant General of the Army, 15 Aug. 1845, H.R. Doc. No. 29–196.

16. Henry, *Campaign Sketches,* 35; Taylor to Adjutant General, 15 Aug. 1845, H.R. Doc. No. 29–196.

17. Taylor to R. Jones, 20 Aug. 1845, and Marcy to Taylor, 23 Aug. 1845, both in H.R. Doc. No. 29–196.

18. William A. DePalo Jr., *The Mexican National Army, 1822–1852* (College Station: Texas A&M University Press, 1997), 94; Arista to Secretary of War, 11 Jan. 1845, Archivo Histórico de la Secretaría de la Defensa Nacional (hereafter cited as ASDN), Clasificación XI/481.3/2063.

19. Arista to Secretary of War: 11 Jan. 1845, 4 Apr. 1845, and 6 Apr. 1845, ASDN, XI/481.3/2064; Arista to Ministro de Guerra y Marina, 15 June 1845, ASDN, XI/481.3/2066 and 15 July 1845, ASDN, XI/481.3/2067; Arista Proclamation, 25 July 1845, ASDN, XI/1481.3/2068.

20. "Opinión del General Arista que manda la 4a. División Militar sobre la guerra que va a abrirse contra los E.U. relativa solamente a la línea del Río Bravo, 2 Aug. 1845, ASDN, XI/481.3/2069; Arista to Ministro de Guerra y Marina: 7 Mar. 1845, ASDN, XI/481.3/2063; 4 June 1845, ASDN XI/481.3/2066; 19 July 1846, ASDN, XI/481.3/2068; and 16 July 1846, ASDN, XI/481.3/2067.

21. Arista to Ministro de Guerra y Marina, 14 July 1845, ASDN, XI/481.3/2067; Manuel Menchaca to Mariano Arista, 26 Dec. 1844, ASDN, XI/481.3/2063; Santiago Rodríguez to Ministro de Guerra y Marina, 10 Jan. 1845, ASDN, XI/481.3/2062; Arista to Ministro de Guerra y Marina, 15 Apr. 1845 ASDN, XI/481.3/2064; *Eco del norte de Tamaulipas,* 3 July 1845; Arista to Governor of Nuevo León, 8 Oct. 1845, Archivos Generales del Estado de Nuevo Léon, Fondo Militar (hereafter cited as AGNL–FM). For a detailed discussion of the conflict between Mexico and Comancheria, see Brian DeLay, *War of A Thousand Deserts: Indian Raids and the US-Mexican War* (New Haven: Yale University Press, 2008).

22. DePalo, *Mexican National Army,* 96; Manuel Balbontín, *Estado Militar de la Republica Mexicana en 1846* (México: Tipo de Ignacio Pombo, 1891).

23. García Conde to Arista, 14 July 1845 and 16 July 1845, ASDN, XI/481.3/2067; Governor of Nuevo León to Arista, 1 July 1845, AGNL–FM; Arista to Governor of Nuevo León, 23 July 1845, AGNL–FM.

24. Arista to Ministro de Guerra y Marina, 25 July 1846, ASDN, XI/481.3/2068.

25. Marcy to Taylor, 30 July 1845, H.R. Doc. No. 29–196, at 70–71; 23 Aug. 1845, at 72–73; and 16 Oct. 1845, at 76–77; Taylor to Adjutant General of the Army, 14 Sept. 1845, H.R. Doc. No. 29–196, at 92–93; 15 Oct. 1845, at 6; and 7 Nov. 1845, at 96–97.

26. Henry, *Campaign Sketches,* 30; Meade, *Life and Letters,* 1:26–27.

27. Taylor to Jones, 30 Aug. 1845, H.R. Doc. No. 30–60, at 104–5; Henry, *Campaign Sketches,* 38–39; Charles Masland to Matthew Masland, 5 Apr. 1846, Charles Masland Papers, US Army Military History Institute (hereafter cited as AMHI), Carlisle Barracks, Pennsylvania; French, *Two Wars,* 34; Henry, *Campaign Sketches,* 44–45; Wilhelm, *History of the Eighth US Infantry,* 259–60. After the war, Forbes Brittan speculated heavily in south Texas properties and became a permanent resident of Corpus Christi.

28. Ephraim Kirby-Smith, *To Mexico with Scott: Letters of Captain E. Kirby Smith to His Wife,* ed. Emma Jerome Blackwood (Cambridge: Harvard University Press, 1917), 19.

29. Darwin Payne, "Camp Life of the Army of Occupation: Corpus Christi, July 1845 to Mar. 1846," *Southwestern Historical Quarterly* 73, no. 3 (Jan. 1970): 328.

30. Payne, "Camp Life of the Army of Occupation," 334; Wilhelm and Lee, *History of the Eighth US Infantry,* 1:258–74 passim. The McLaws incident took place during an extended hunting outing to San Antonio and the vicinity. French, *Two Wars,* 39; John B. Porter, "Medical and Surgical Notes of Campaigns in the War with Mexico," *American Journal of Medical Science* 24 (Jan. 1852): 12–20.

31. James Wood to Mother, 18 Sept. 1845, James Wood Papers, Princeton University.

32. Taylor to Adjutant General, 7 Nov. 1846, H.R. Doc. No. 29–196, at 97; Payne, "Camp Life of the Army of Occupation," 335; Joseph Dorst Patch, *The Concentration of General Zachary Taylor's Army at Corpus Christi, Texas* (Corpus Christi: Mission Printing, 1962), 12–14.

33. Henry, *Campaign Sketches,* 31; Taylor to Adjutant General, 14 Sept. 1845 and 15 Oct. 1845, H.R. Doc. No. 30–60, at 106–7, 110–11.

34. Taylor to Adjutant General, 30 Aug. 1845, 14 Sept. 1845, 11 Oct. 1845, and 15 Oct. 1845, H.R. Doc. No. 30–60, at 104–5, 106–7, 109–10 and 110–11.

35. Taylor to Adjutant General, 4 Oct. 1845, H.R. Doc. No. 30–60, at 107–9.

36. Bustamante, *El nuevo Bernal Díaz,* 93; Bauer, *Mexican War,* 22.

37. Marcy to Taylor, 16 Oct. 1845, H.R. Doc. No. 30–60, at 89–90.

38. Taylor to Adjutant General, 4 Oct. 1845, H. R. Doc. No. 30–60, at 107–9.

39. Patch, *The Concentration of General Zachary Taylor's Army,* 10; Henry, *Campaign Sketches,* 44–47; Porter, "Medical and Surgical Notes," 17–20; Payne, "Camp Life of the Army of Occupation," 332–36; "An Army Surgeon's Notes," 40 (May 1907): 437.

40. Jarvis, "An Army Surgeon's Notes," 40:436–37; Meade, *Life and Letters,* 1:36–37; W. W. Bliss to Edmund Schriver, 12 Dec. 1845, Edmund Schriver Papers, Rare Books and Special Collections Library, Duke University (cited hereafter as Schriver Papers, Duke)

41. Marcy to Taylor, 13 Jan. 1846, H.R. Doc. No. 30–60, at 90–91.

42. Henry, *Campaign Sketches,* 48; Jarvis, "An Army Surgeon's Notes," 40:437; Bauer, *Mexican War,* 36–37.

43. Meade, *Life and Letters,* 1:46; Jarvis, "An Army Surgeon's Notes," 40:437; Henry, *Campaign Sketches;* Bauer, *Mexican War,* 37–38.

44. Jarvis, "An Army Surgeon's Notes," 40:438.

45. Jarvis, "An Army Surgeon's Notes," 40:440; Sibley to Taylor, 21 Feb. 1846, Letters Received, Army of Occupation, Record Group 94 (hereafter cited as LR–AO, RG94): E-133:3, US National Archives (NA).

46. General Order No. 20, 24 Feb. 1846, General Orders, Army of Occupation, National Archives Record Group 94, US National Archives (hereafter cited as GO–AO, RG94, NA); George A. McCall, *Letters from the Frontiers* (Philadelphia: Lippincott, 1868), 437–38; Grant, *Personal Memoirs,* 57; Bauer, *Mexican War,* 37.

47. Henry, *Campaign Sketches,* 51–52, Meade, *Life and Letters,* 1:48; Marcy to Taylor, 2 Mar. 1846, H. R. Doc. No. 30–60; Robert Hazlitt to Mrs. Ingersol, 20 Mar. 1846, Hazlitt Papers, US Military Academy (hereafter cited as USMA), Special Collections, NY.

48. Grant to Julia Dent, 3 Mar. 1846, in Drake, *Ulysses S Grant;* Ethan Allen Hitchcock, *Fifty Years in Camp and Field: Diary of Major General Ethan Allen Hitchcock,* ed. E. A. Croffut (New York: G. P. Putnam's Sons, 1909), 208; Meade, *Life and Letters,* 1:50.

49. Jarvis, "An Army Surgeon's Notes," 40:441; Henry, *Campaign Sketches,* 52; John James Peck, *The Sign of the Eagle: A View of Mexico, 1830 to 1855,* ed. Richard F. Pourade (San Diego: Union-Tribune, 1970), 14.

50. Jarvis, "An Army Surgeon's Notes," 40:441; Henry, *Campaign Sketches,* 52; Peck, *Sign of the Eagle,* 14; Taylor, General Order No. 20, GO–AO, RG94, NA.

51. Joseph King Fenno Mansfield to Wife, 9 Mar. 1846, Mansfield Papers, USMA; Robert Hazlitt to Mrs. Ingersoll, 20 Mar. 1846, Hazlitt Papers, USMA.

52. "Declaraciones dadas por dos comisiones que salieron el 24 de Corpus Cristo," 28 Jan. 1846, ASDN, XI/481.3/2147.

53. Arista to Paredes, 15 Nov. 1845; Paredes to Arista, 19 Nov. 1845; Paredes to Herrera, 19 Nov. 1845; Paredes to Ministro de Guerra y Marina, 19 Nov. 1845; Anaya to Ministro de Guerra

y Marina, 25 Nov. 1845, all in *Contestaciones habidas entre los exmos. señores generales de división, D. Mariano Paredes y Arrillaga, D. Mariano Arista y el supremo gobierno. . . .* (San Luis Potosí: V. Carrillo, 1845); Arista to Ministro de Guerra y Marina, 18 Nov. 1845, and Paredes to Arista, 10 Dec. 1845, both in ASDN XI/481.3/2074.

54. Frank D. Robertson, "The Military and Political Career of Mariano Paredes y Arrillaga, 1797–1849," PhD diss., University of Texas at Austin, 1955, 170–75; Miguel Soto, *La conspiración monárquica en México, 1845–1846* (México, DF: Editorial Offset, 1988), 52.

55. Bustamante, *El Nuevo Bernal Díaz,* 145–50; Justin Smith, *War with Mexico,* 1:54–55; Pletcher, *Diplomacy of Annexation,* 358–61.

56. Arista to Paredes, 15 Nov. 1845, in *Contestaciones habidas entre los exmos. señores generales de división,* 3.

57. Arista to Ministro de Guerra y Marina, 16 Nov. 1845, ASDN, XI/481.3/2074.

58. Arista to Governor of Nuevo León, 12 Aug. 1845, AGNL–FM; *Eco del norte de Tamaulipas,* 21 Aug. 1845.

59. Arista to Ministro de Guerra y Marina, 18 Nov. 1845, ASDN XI/481.3/2074.

60. Ibid., 16 Nov. 1845 and 17 Dec. 1845, ASDN, XI/481.3/2074.

61. Ibid.

62. *Seminario político del gobierno de Nuevo León,* 8 Oct. 1845 and 13 Oct. 1845; Arista to Ministro de Guerra y Marina, 22 Nov. 1845, ASDN, XI/481.3/2074.

63. Arista circular, "To customs agents of Tampico and Matamoros and foreign consuls of these ports," 5 Jan. 1846, ASDN, XI/481.3/2147; Arista to Ministro de Guerra y Marina, 14 Jan. 1846, ASDN. XI/481.3/2147; Almonte declaration, 14 Jan. 1846, ASDN, XI/481.3/2147.

64. Santoni, *Mexicans at Arms,* 105–9; Henderson, *A Glorious Defeat,* 152–55; Robertson, "Military and Political Career of Mariano Paredes y Arrillaga," 180.

65. *Monitor republicano,* 7 Mar. 1846.

66. Ibid., 9 Mar. 1846.

67. Slidell to Buchanan, 14 Jan. 1846, H.R. Doc. No. 29–196, at 42; Buchanan to Slidell, 20 Jan. 1846, H.R. Doc. No. 29–196, at 44–46. Polk was receiving guidance on the issue from Col. Alejandro Atocha, a Spaniard with knowledge of Mexico, who advised the president to pressure Mexico by directing naval troops near Veracruz and Taylor's troops to the Rio Grande. See James K. Polk, *The Diary of James K. Polk during His Presidency, 1845–1849,* ed. Milo Milton Quaife, 2 vols. (Chicago: A. C. McClurg, 1910), 1:225, 233. Also in Robert Merry, *A Country of Vast Design: James K. Polk, the Mexican War and the Conquest of the American Continent* (New York: Simon and Schuster, 2009), 230–31. See also Sam W. Haynes, *James K. Polk and the Expansionist Impulse* (New York: Longman, 1997), 136–8.

68. Díaz de la Vega to Ministro de Guerra y Marina, 8 Feb. 1846, and Almonte to Díaz, 16 Feb. 1846, both in ASDN XI/481.3/2147.

69. Díaz de la Vega to Ministro de Guerra y Marina, 13 Jan. 1846 and 8 Feb. 1846, ASDN, XI/481.3/2147.

70. Anastasio Parrodi to Mariano Paredes, 10 Jan. 1846, ASDN, XI/481.3/2147.

71. Almonte to Mejía, 17 Feb. 1846, ASDN, XI/481.3/2147.

72. Arista to Ministro de Guerra y Marina, 10 Dec. 1845 and 18 Dec. 1845; Ministro de Guerra y Marina to General en Jefe, 4th Division, 29 Dec. 1845; Mejía to Ministro de Guerra y Marina, 21 Jan. 1846; Robinson statement; Mejía to Ministro de Guerra y Marina, 11 Feb. 1846; Robinson statement; George Lake statement; and Erick Hilliard statement, all in ASDN, XI/481.3/2147; *Eco del norte de Tamaulipas,* 31 Dec. 1845, 11, 17.

73. Arista to Ministro de Guerra y Marina, 10 Dec. 1845 and 18 Dec. 1845, ASDN, XI/481.3/2147; Díaz de la Vega to Ministro de Guerra y Marina, 13 Jan. 1846 and 8 Feb. 1846, ASDN, XI/481.3/2147.

74. Mejía to Ministro de Guerra y Marina, 4 Feb. 1846, ASDN, XI/481.3/2147.

75. Ibid.

76. Ibid.

77. *Monitor republicano,* 20 Mar. 1846; Ministro de Guerra y Marina to Pedro de Ampudia, 14 Mar. 1846, ASDN, XI/481.3/2147; Tornel to Ministro de Hacienda, 2 Apr. 1846; Tornel to Parrodi, 24 Apr. 1846; and Tornel to Comandante de Zacatecas, 7 Apr. 1846, ASDN, XI/481.3/2147.

78. Díaz de la Vega to Ministro de Guerra y Marina, 22 Feb. 1846; Tornel to Díaz de la Vega, 6 Mar. 1846; Parrodi to Ministro de Guerra y Marina, 21 Feb. 1846; Mejía to Ministro de Guerra y Marina, 28 Jan. 1846; and Mejía to Díaz de la Vega, 16 Feb. 1846, all in ASDN XI/481.3/2147.

79. Castillo y Lanzas to Slidell, 12 Mar. 1846, H.R. Doc. No. 29–196, at 57–61. The Paredes speech is reproduced in *Monitor republicano,* 25 Mar. 1846.

80. Mejía to Díaz de la Vega, 18 Feb. 1846; Díaz de la Vega to Ministro de Guerra y Marina, 22 Feb. 1846; Ampudia to Ministro de Guerra y Marina, 11 Mar. 1846, 12 Mar. 1846, and 14 Mar. 1846; and Tornel to Ampudia, 15 Mar. 1846, all in ASDN, XI/481.3/ 2147.

CHAPTER 2

1. Grant to Julia Dent, 3 Mar. 1846, in Drake, *Ulysses S. Grant,* 905–7; John Henshaw, "Bombardment of Fort Brown and a Brief Mention of the Battles of Palo Alto and Resaca de la Palma," unpublished manuscript, Henshaw Papers, Massachusetts Historical Society, Boston (hereafter cited as Henshaw Papers, MHS); Peck, *Sign of the Eagle,* 14.

2. Meade, *Life and Letters,* 1:50–51; Jarvis, "An Army Surgeon's Notes," 40:437–39; Henry, *Campaign Sketches,* 52; Hitchcock, *Fifty Years in Camp and Field,* 200, 212.

3 Meade, *Life and Letters,* 1:46; Jarvis, "An Army Surgeon's Notes," 40:437; Kirby-Smith, *To Mexico with Scott,* 22–23; Henry, *Campaign Sketches,* 52–53.

4. Meade, *Life and Letters,* 1:46; Jarvis, "An Army Surgeon's Notes," 40:437; Kirby-Smith, *To Mexico with Scott,* 22–23; Henry, *Campaign Sketches,* 52–53; Charles Masland to Mathew Masland, 5 Apr. 1846, Charles Masland Papers, AMHI; Samuel Gibbs French, *Two Wars,* 41; Richard E. Cochrane to wife, 25 Mar. 1846, Richard E. Cochrane Papers, 1838–1859, Dolph Briscoe Center for American History, University of Texas at Austin (hereafter cited as Cochrane Papers, UT).

5. Wilhelm, *History of the Eighth US Infantry,* 2:402.

6. Henry, *Campaign Sketches,* 51–54; Madison Mills, Diary, 1, Filson Historical Society (hereafter cited as FHS), Louisville, KY; Peck, *Sign of the Eagle,* 14; Charles Masland to Mathew Masland, 5 Apr. 1846, Charles Masland Papers, AMHI; French, *Two Wars,* 41–42; Kirby-Smith, *To Mexico with Scott,* 20–25; Henshaw, "Bombardment of Fort Brown," Henshaw Papers, MHS; Jarvis, "An Army Surgeon's Notes," 40:437.

7. Henshaw, "Bombardment of Fort Brown," 5, Henshaw Papers, MHS: Henry, *Campaign Sketches,* 51–54; Mills, Diary, 1, FHS; Peck, *Sign of the Eagle,* 14; Charles Masland to Mathew Masland, 5 Apr. 1846, Charles Masland Papers, AMHI; French, *Two Wars,* 41–42; Kirby-Smith, *To Mexico with Scott,* 20–25; Henshaw, "Bombardment of Fort Brown," Henshaw Papers, MHS; Jarvis, "An Army Surgeon's Notes," 40:438.

8. William T. H. Brooks to Unknown, 26 Mar. 1846, Brooks Papers, US Military History Institute, Carlisle, PA (hereafter cited as Brooks Papers, MHI).

9. Henry, *Campaign Sketches,* 55–8; French, *Two Wars,* 42; Reeves, C. M., "Five Years an American Soldier," 438; Charles Masland to Mathew Masland, 5 Apr. 1846, Charles Masland Papers, AMHI.

10. Bauer, *Mexican War,* 21; Henry, *Campaign Sketches,* 57–58; Taylor, General Order 32, GO–AO, RG94, NA

11. Jarvis, "An Army Surgeon's Notes," 40:438; Kirby-Smith, *To Mexico with Scott,* 20–25; Henry, *Campaign Sketches,* 53; Richard E. Cochrane to wife, 25 Mar. 1846, Cochrane Papers, UT.

12. Taylor, General Order 33, GO–AO, RG94, NA; Jarvis, "An Army Surgeon's Notes," 40:438.

13. Kirby-Smith, *To Mexico with Scott,* 29; Richard E. Cochrane to wife, 25 Mar. 1846, Cochrane Papers, UT; Taylor to Adjutant General of the Army, 21 Mar. 1846, H.R. Doc. No. 30–60, at 123–25.

14. Mejía Proclamation, 18 Mar. 1846, H.R. Doc. No. 30–60, at 125–27; Taylor to Adjutant General of the Army, 21 Mar. 1846, H.R. Doc. No. 30–60, at 123–25.

15. Taylor to Adjutant General of the Army, 21 Mar. 1846, H.R. Doc. No. 30–60, at 123–25; Wilhelm and Lee, History of the Eighth US Infantry, 1:406; Henry, *Campaign Sketches,* 53; Calvin Benjamin to Isaac B. Tracey, 29 Mar. 1846, Calvin Benjamin Papers, Manuscript Division, Library of Congress (cited hereafter as Benjamin Papers, LC); Richard E. Cochrane to wife, 25 Mar. 1846, Cochrane Papers, UT.

16. Taylor to Adjutant General of the Army, 21 Mar. 1846, H.R. Doc. No. 30–60, at 123–25; William T. H. Brooks letter, 26 Mar. 1846, Brooks Papers, MHI; French, *Two Wars,* 44; John Corey Henshaw, *Recollections of the War with Mexico,* ed. Gary F. Kurutz (Columbia: University of Missouri Press, 2008), 41–42; Reeves, "Five Years an American Soldier," 439; C. F. Smith to Lt. Larkin Smith, 21 Mar. 1846, Charles F. Smith Papers, USMA; Daniel P. Whiting, *A Soldier's Life,* ed. Murphy Givens (Corpus Christi: Nueces Press, 2012), 70.

17. Henshaw, *Recollections of the War,* 41; French, *Two Wars,* 44; Kirby-Smith, *To Mexico with Scott,* 31; Calvin Benjamin to Isaac B. Tracey, 29 Mar. 1846, Benjamin Papers, LC; Richard E. Cochrane to parents, 6 Apr. 1846, Cochrane Papers, UT; Whiting, *A Soldier's Life,* 71.

18. Henshaw, *Recollections of the War,* 42; Kirby-Smith, *To Mexico with Scott;* William T. H. Brooks letter, 26 Mar. 1846, Brooks Papers, MHI; Jarvis, "An Army Surgeon's Notes," 40:442.

19. Peck, *The Sign of the Eagle,* 14–15; William T. H. Brooks letter, 26 Mar. 1846, Brooks Papers, MHI.

20. Henry, *Campaign Sketches,* 60; Kirby-Smith, *To Mexico with Scott,* 31; Grant to Julia Dent, 29 Mar. 1846, in Drake, *Ulysses S. Grant,* 907–8.

21. *Monitor republicano,* 20 Mar. 1846; Díaz de la Vega to Ministro de Guerra y Marina, 11 Mar. 1845, Castillo Lanzas to Ministro de Guerra y Marina, 26 Mar. 1846, and Parrodi to Ministro de Guerra y Marina, 14 Mar. 1846, ASDN XI/481.3/2147

22. Canales to Mejía, 25 Feb. 1846, ASDN XI/481.3/2147.

23. Bauer, *Mexican War,* 36–37; Canales to Díaz de la Vega, 20 Jan. 1846, ASDN XI/481.3/2147; Mejía to General en Jefe, 4th Division, 18 Feb. 1846, ASDN XI/481.3/2147.

24. Tornel to General en Jefe, 4th Division, 6 Mar. 1846, ASDN XI/481.3/2147.

25. Mejía to Ministro de Guerra y Marina, 28 Jan. 1846, 4 Feb. 1846, and 14 Mar. 1846, ASDN XI/481.3/2147.

26. Tornel to Mejía, 24 Mar. 1846, ASDN XI/481.3/2147.

27. Ibid.

28. Ibid.

29. Mejía to Ministro de Guerra y Marina, Mar. 14, 1846, ASDN XI/481.3/2147.

30. Díaz de la Vega to Tornel, 10 Mar. 1846, ASDN, XI/481.3/2147.

31. Mejía to Ministro de Guerra y Marina, 14 Mar. 1846, ASDN, XI/481.3/2147.

32. Probably the spot known today as Laguna Atascosa.

33. Mejía to Ministro de Guerra y Marina, 15 Mar. 1846, cited in Negrete, *Invasión de los norte-americanos,* 1:114; Jean Luis [Jean Louis] Berlandier, "Itinerario: Campaña de Palo Alto y Resaca de Guerrero," Ms. S-310, Jean Louis Berlandier Papers, Yale Collection of Western Americana, Beinecke Rare Book and Manuscript Library, Yale (hereafter cited as Berlandier Papers–Yale), 9–13.

34. Mejía to Ministo de Guerra y Marina, 18 Mar. 1846, cited in *Monitor republicano,* 30 Mar. 1846; Rafael Quintero to Mejía, 20 Mar. 1846, cited in *Monitor republicano,* 13 Apr. 1846.

35. Mejía Proclamation, 18 Mar. 1846, H.R. Doc. No. 30–60, at 125–29.

36. Rafael Quintero to Mejía, 20 Mar. 1846, in *Monitor republicano,* 13 Apr. 1846.

37. Rafael Quintero to Mejía, 20 Mar. 1846, in *Monitor republicano,* 13 Apr. 1846; Berlandier, "Itinerario," 23–25, Berlandier Papers–Yale.

38. Rafael Quintero to Mejía, 20 Mar. 1846, in *Monitor republicano,* 13 Apr. 1846.

39. Mejía to Ministro de Guerra y Marina, 21 Mar. 1846, ASDN, XI/481.3/2147.

40. Henry, *Campaign Sketches,* 60–61; Kirby-Smith, *To Mexico with Scott,* 32; French, *Two Wars,* 44; Mills, Diary, 2–3, FHS; Col. T. Cross to Maj. Gen. Thomas Jesup, 4 Apr. 1846, H.R. Doc. No. 30–60, at 651–52.

41. Taylor, General Order No. 35, 22 Mar. 1846, and General Order No. 34, 22 Mar. 1846, both in GO–AO, RG94, NA.

42. Taylor, General Order No. 35, 22 Mar. 1846, and General Order No. 34, 22 Mar. 1846, both in GO–AO, RG94, NA.

43. Taylor to Adjutant General of the Army, 25 Mar. 1846, H.R. Doc. No. 30–60, at 129–30.

44. Taylor, General Order No. 35, 22 Mar. 1846, GO–AO, RG94, NA.

45. Kirby-Smith, *To Mexico with Scott,* 32; Richard E. Cochrane to wife, 6 Apr. 1846, Cochrane Papers, UT.

46. Henshaw, *Recollections of the War,* 42–43; Henry, Campaign Sketches, 60–62; Kirby-Smith, *To Mexico with Scott,* 32; Whiting, *A Soldier's Life,* 71.

47. Henshaw, *Recollections of the War,* 42–43; Henry, Campaign Sketches, 60–62; Kirby-Smith, *To Mexico with Scott,* 32; Whiting, *A Soldier's Life,* 71.

48. Taylor to Adjutant General of the Army, 25 Mar. 1846, H.R. Doc. No. 30–60, at 129–30; Jarvis, "An Army Surgeon's Notes," 40:443; Kirby-Smith, *To Mexico with Scott,* 33; French, *Two Wars,* 45.

49. Taylor to Adjutant General of the Army, 25 Mar. 1846, H.R. Doc. No. 30–60, at 129–30; Mills, Diary, 4–5, FHS; Jarvis, "An Army Surgeon's Notes," 40:443; Bauer, *Mexican War,* 36–37; Henry, *Campaign Sketches,* 62–63.

50. Juan José Pineda to Zachary Taylor, n.d., H.R. Doc. No. 30–60, at 131–32; Taylor to Adjutant General, 25 Mar. 1846, H.R. Doc. No. 30–60, at 129–30.

51. Taylor to Adjutant General, 25 Mar. 1846, H.R. Doc. No. 30–60, at 129–30; Henry, *Campaign Sketches,* 62.

52. Taylor to Adjutant General, 25 Mar. 1846, H.R. Doc. No. 30–60, at 129–30.

53. Ibid.

54. Wilhelm, *History of the Eighth US Infantry,* 1:408; Richard E. Cochrane to wife, 6 Apr. 1 1846, Cochrane Papers, UT.

55. Taylor to Mejía, 30 Mar. 1846, H.R. Doc. No. 29–56, at 393.

56. Taylor to Mejía, 30 Mar. 1846, H.R. Doc. No. 29–56, at 393; Henry, *Campaign Sketches,* 66–68; Jarvis, "An Army Surgeon's Notes," 40:443; Edmund Schriver to "My Dear Captain," 3 May 1846, Schriver Papers, Duke.

57. Henry, *Campaign Sketches,* 66–68; Fleming, *Life and Letters of Alexander Hays,* 57; Peck, *Sign of the Eagle,* 17; Taylor to Adjutant General, 29 Mar. 1846, H.R. Doc. No. 30–60, at 132; French, *Two Wars,* 45; Dana, *Monterrey Is Ours: The Mexican War Letters of Lieutenant Dana, 1845–1847,* ed. Robert H. Ferrell (Lexington: University of Kentucky Press, 1990), 39; Philip N. Barbour, *Journals of the Late Brevet Major Philip Norbourne Barbour ... and His Wife, Martha Isabella Hopkins Barbour: Written during the War with Mexico–1846,* ed. Rhoda van Bibber Tanner Doubleday (New York: G. P. Putnam's Sons, 1936), 17.

58. Henry, *Campaign Sketches,* 65–66; minutes of an interview between Brig. Gen. W. J. Worth, United States Army, and Gen. Rómulo Díaz de la Vega, of the Mexican Army, held on the right bank of the Rio Grande, 28 Mar. 1846, H.R. Doc. No. 30–60, at 137–38; Barbour, *Journals,* 18–20.

59. Ibid.

60. Ibid.

61. Ibid.

62. Mejía to Minister of War, 26 Mar. 1846, in ASDN XI/481.3/2147.

63. Francisco Mejía to Gen. Zachary Taylor, 31 Mar. 1846, H.R. Doc. No. 30–60, at 394–95.

64. Francisco Mejía to Gen. Zachary Taylor, 31 Mar. 1846, H.R. Doc. No. 30–60, at 394–95.

CHAPTER 3

1. Luther Giddings, *Sketches of the Campaign in Northern Mexico* (New York: George P. Putnam, 1853), 34; John R. Kenly, *Memoirs of a Maryland Volunteer in the War with Mexico* (Philadelphia: J. B. Lippincott, 1873), 34; James Austin to Mr. Owen Gathright, 29 July 1846, Sperry-Gathright Papers 1846, FHS; John Nixon to Mary Nixon, 4 Apr. 1846, John Nixon Papers, Western Americana Collection, Beinecke Rare Books and Manuscript Library, Yale University.

2. Frank Edwards, *A Campaign in New Mexico with Colonel Doniphan* (Philadelphia: Carey and Hart, 1847), 163; George W. Taylor to Lewis H. Taylor, 20 May 1847, Taylor Papers, Manuscripts Division, William Clements Library, University of Michigan, Ann Arbor (hereafter cited as Taylor Papers, University of Michigan); Kenly, *Memoirs of a Maryland Volunteer,* 49; J. A. Hendricks to Friend Hendricks, Oct 4 1846, J. A. Hendricks Papers, Dolph Briscoe Center for American History, University of Texas at Austin; William H. Emory, *Report on the United States and Mexican Boundary Survey,* H.R. Doc. No. 34–135, at 3:59 (1st sess., 1856) (hereafter cited as H.R. Doc. No. 34–135), 3 vols. (Washington, DC: C. Wendell, 1858.

3. H. W. Hawker et al, Soil Survey of Hidalgo County, Texas (Washington, D.C.: Government Printing Office, 1929), 2.

4. Meade, *Life and Letters,* 1:56; Giddings, *Sketches of the Campaign,* 51; George Taylor to Lewis Taylor, 21 July 1847, Taylor Papers, University of Michigan; Thomas Nealy Love, *A Southern Lacrimosa: The Mexican War Journal of Dr. Thomas Neely Love, Surgeon, Second Regiment Mississippi Infantry USA,* ed. H. Grady Howell (Jackson, MS: Chickasaw Bayou, 1995), 74; Henry, *Campaign Sketches,* 121.

5. Emory, *Report on the United States and Mexican Boundary Survey,* H.R. Doc. No. 34–135, at 3:56; Henry, *Campaign Sketches,* 63–64; Daniel Harvey Hill, *A Fighter from Way Back: The Mexican War Diary of Lt. Daniel Harvey Hill, 4th Artillery, USA.,* ed. Timothy D. Johnson (Kent, OH: Kent State University Press, 2002), 2.

6. Giddings, *Sketches of the Campaign,* 40; George W. Taylor to Lewis Taylor, 21 July 1847, Taylor Papers, University of Michigan; Henshaw, *Recollections of the War,* 42.

7. Jonathan Hampton Kuykendall, "Journal through Texas," Kuykendall Family Papers, 1822–1897, 1936, 1963–1994, Dolph Briscoe Center for American History, University of Texas at Austin

(hereafter cited as Kuykendall Papers, UT); Meade, *Life and Letters,* 1:81; William A. Droddy, 2 Aug. 1846, p. 21, "William A. Droddy Diary," 1936, Dolph Briscoe Center for American History, University of Texas at Austin.

8. Milo Kearney and Anthony Knopp, *Boom and Bust: The Historical Cycles of Matamoros and Brownsville (*Austin: Eakin, 1991), 5–15; Frank C. Pierce, *A Brief History of the Rio Grande Valley* (Menasha, WI: George Banta, 1917), 11–12, 15–20; Armando C. Alonzo, *Tejano Legacy: Rancheros and Settlers in South Texas, 1734–1900* (Albuquerque: University of New Mexico Press, 1998), 40–53; Jerry Thompson, *A Wild and Vivid Land: An Illustrated History of the South Texas Border* (Austin: Texas State Historical Association, 2012).

9. Giddings, *Sketches of the Campaign,* 51; George Deas, "Reminiscences of the Campaign," *Historical Magazine and Notes and Queries Concerning the Antiquities, History, and Biography of America* 7 (Jan. 1870): 21; George W. Taylor to Lewis Taylor, 21 July 1847, Taylor Papers, University of Michigan.

10. Manuel de Mier y Terán, *Texas by Terán: The Diary Kept by General Manuel de Mier y Terán on His 1828 Inspection of Texas,* trans. John Wheat, ed. Jack Jackson (Austin: University of Texas Press, 2000), 160; Alonzo, *Legacy,* 85–88; Kearney and Knopp, *Boom and Bust,* 44–47; Kuykendall, "Journal Through Texas," Kuykendall Papers, UT.

11. Alonzo, *Tejano Legacy,* 85–88; Mary Margaret McAllen Amberson et al., *I Would Rather Sleep in Texas: A History of the Lower Rio Grande Valley and the People of the Santa Anita Land Grant* (Austin: Texas State Historical Association, 2003), 10–16; Meade, *Life and Letters,* 1:106.

12. Meade, *Life and Letters,* 1:106; "Plano del pais situado al NE de la ciudad de Matamoros, 1846," in Alcaraz, *Apuntes para la historia de la guerra,* 30; Alonzo, *Tejano Legacy,* 80–81; Mier y Terán, *Texas by Terán,* 165; Alonzo, *Tejano Legacy,* 51–53; 85–88; Daniel, Military Diary, 11, FHS.

13. Jean Luis Berlandier, "Matamoros: Sa descripcion, son immense superficie, sa nature de su edificies," unpublished manuscript, Thomas Phillips Collection, no. 15461, Library of Congress (hereafter cited as Berlandier Papers–LC); Manuel Payno, *El Puerto de Matamoros en 1844,* ed. Vargas Rea (México: Biblioteca de Historiadores Mexicanos, 1951), 17–19; Hill, *A Fighter from Way Back,* 2; Henry, *Campaign Sketches,* 110.

14. Berlandier, "Matamoros: Sa descripción," Berlandier Papers–LC; Kearney and Knopp, *Boom and Bust,* 44–50.

15. Ibid.; Alonzo, *Tejano Legacy,* 70–74.

16. Chauncy Devereaux Stillman, *Charles Stillman, 1810–1875* (New York: C. D. Stillman, 1956), 5; Berlandier, "Matamoros: Sa descripción," Berlandier Papers–LC; Mier y Terán, *Texas by Terán,* 159.

17. Kearney and Knopp, *Boom and Bust,* 32, 50–51, 55; Stillman, *Charles Stillman,* 5–6; Bustamante, *El nuevo Bernal Díaz,* 232–36.

18. Stillman, *Charles Stillman,* 5–6; Kearney and Knopp, *Boom and Bust,* 32, 34; Payno, *El Puerto de Matamoros en 1844,* 20.

19. Jean Louis Berlandier, *Journey to Mexico during the years 1826 to 1834,* trans. Sheila M. Ohlendorf et al. (Austin: Texas State Historical Association, 1980), 429; Mier y Terán, *Texas by Terán,* 166.

20. Mier y Terán, *Texas by Terán,* 166; Berlandier, *Journey to Mexico,* 434–7.

21. Kenley, *Memoirs of a Maryland Volunteer,* 44; William H. Carpenter, *Travels and Adventures in Mexico* (New York: Harper and Brothers, 1851), 16–17; Berlandier, *Journey to Mexico,* 439; Emory, H.R. Doc. No. 34–135, at 3:58; Carpenter, *Travels and Adventures in Mexico,* 18.

22. J. J. Abert, "Map of the Country Adjacent to the Left Bank of the Rio Grande Below Matamoros" (New York: Ackerman's Lith., 1847), in S. Doc. No. 31–65 (1st Sess., 1850); Emory,

Report on the United States and Mexican Boundary Survey, H.R. Doc. No. 34–108, at 3:58; Berlandier, *Journey to Mexico,* 441, 446.

23. Berlandier, *Journey to Mexico,* 446; Payno, *El puerto de Matamoros, en 1844,* 21; Thorpe, *Our Army on the Rio Grande* (Philadelphia: Carey and Hart, 1846), 130.

24. Berlandier, *Journey to Mexico,* 444–45; Emory, *Report on the United States and Mexican Boundary Survey,* H.R. Doc. No. 34–135, at 3:56; Berlandier, *Journey to Mexico,* 444.

25. Giddings, *Sketches of the Campaign,* 29; William H. Daniel, Military Diary, FHS, 5; Carpenter, *Travels and Adventures in Mexico,* 14; Benjamin F. Scribner, *Camp Life of a Volunteer: A Campaign in Mexico, or A Glimpse at Life in Camp* (Philadelphia: Grigg, Elliot, 1847), 18; Berlandier, *Journey to Mexico,* 444; Giddings, *Sketches of the Campaign,* 29–30.

26. Berlandier, *Journey to Mexico,* 444; C. Donnavan, *Adventures in Mexico* (Cincinnati, Robinson & Jones, 1847), 17.

27. Berlandier, *Journey to Mexico,* 444.

28. Emory, *Report on the United States and Mexican Boundary Survey,* H.R. Doc. No. 34–135, at 3:54; Meade, *Life and Letters,* 1:59.

29. "Statement of the Italian," LR–AO, RG94, Microcopy 307, Roll 2, NA.

30. John Sanders to Zachary Taylor, 16 May 1846, LR–AO, RG94, Microcopy 307, Roll 2, NA; Taylor to Ampudia, 22 Apr. 1846, cited in Thorp, *Our Army on the Rio Grande,* 32.

31. Philip N. Barbour, *Journals,* 23.

32. Meade, *Life and Letters,* 1:64; Sanders to Totten, 10 Apr. 1846, Sanders, Smith and Swift Correspondence, Letters Received, Office of the Chief of Engineers, US National Archives, Record Group 77 (hereafter cited as LR–OCE, RG 77, NA): *Recollections of the War,* 44.

33. Manuel Payno, *El Puerto de Matamoros en 1844,* 20–22; Francisco Mejía to Mariano Arista, 16 June 1845, ASDN, XI/481.3/3320.

34. Francisco Mejía to Mariano Arista, 16 June 1845, ASDN, XI/481.3/3320; Scott Cook, *Mexican Brick Culture in the Building of Texas, 1800s–1980s* (College Station: Texas A&M University Press, 1998), 5–12; Berlandier, "Matamoros: La descripción," Berlandier Papers–Yale.

35. Francisco Mejía to Mariano Arista, 16 June 1845, ASDN, XI/481.3/3320.

36. Francisco Mejía to Mariano Arista, 16 June 1845, ASDN, XI/481.3/3320.

CHAPTER 4

1. Mills, Diary, 5, FHS.

2. Cited in *Monitor republicano,* 7 Apr. 1846; Henry, *Campaign Sketches,* 70; Mills, Diary, 6, FHS.

3. *Monitor republicano,* 15 May 1846.

4. Ignacio Mora y Villamil to Ministro de Guerra, 4 May 1846, printed in *Monitor republicano,* 12 May 1846.

5. Ibid.

6. Marcy to Taylor, 13 Jan. 1846, H.R. Doc. No. 30–60, at 90–91.

7. *Congressional Globe,* 29th Cong., 1st Sess., 2 July 1846, 920.

8. I. H. Charles to Jonathan Edward Siddal, 5 May 1846, Isaac H. Charles Letters, Ms. 621, Louisiana and Lower Mississippi Valley Collections, LSU Libraries, Baton Rouge, LA. Detailed discussions of dissent can be found in Samuel Eliot Morison et al., *Dissent in Three American Wars* (Cambridge: Harvard University Press, 1970), John H. Schroeder, *Mr. Polk's War: American Opposition and Dissent, 1846–1848* (Madison: University of Wisconsin Press, 1973), and Amy S. Greenberg, *A Wicked War: Polk, Clay, Lincoln, and the 1846 US Invasion of Mexico* (New York: Knopf, 2012).

9. Grant, *Personal Memoirs,* 25.

10. Taylor to Adjutant General, 6 Apr. 1846 and 29 Mar. 1846, H.R. Doc. No. 30–60, at 132.

11. Henry, *Campaign Sketches,* 68–69; Jarvis, "An Army Surgeon's Notes," 40:445; Mills, Diary, 6, FHS; Richard E. Cochrane to wife, 6 Apr. 1846, Cochrane Papers, UT.

12. Jarvis, "An Army Surgeon's Notes," 40:446; Henry, *Campaign Sketches,* 68–69.

13. Meade, *Life and Letters,* 1:52.

14. Henry, *Campaign Sketches,* 70.

15. *Monitor republicano,* 21 Apr. 1846.

16. Ibid.

17. Ignacio Mora y Villamil to Ministro de Guerra y Marina, 9 May 1846, in *Monitor republicano,* 12 May 1846.

18. Ampudia to Secretary of War, 8 Apr. 1846, ASDN, XI/481.3/2174, 248.

19. Ibid., 250.

20. *Monitor republicano,* 20 Mar. 1846. The Sabine formed the boundary between Texas and Louisiana; therefore raising the Mexican flag on that river represented the recapture of the lost province.

21. Ampudia to Ministro de Guerra y Marina, 28 Mar. 1846 (two letters), 30 Mar. 1846 (two letters), and Ampudia to Mejía, 30 Mar. 1846, all in ASDN XI/481.3/2147, 244.

22. Torrejón to General-in-Chief, three messages dated 7 Apr. 1846, ASDN XI/481.3/2147, 250–52.

23. Joseph Benjamin Ridout, "An Anti-National Disorder: Antonio Canales and Northeastern Mexico, 1846–1852" (Master's thesis, University of Texas at Austin, 1994); Josefina Zoraida Vázquez, "La supuesta Repúblca del Río Grande," *Historia Mexicana*" 36, no. 1 (July–Sept. 1986): 43–44; Ampudia to Ministro de Guerra y Marina, 28 Mar. 1846 (two letters), 30 Mar. 1846, and 7 Apr. 1846, ASDN, XI/481.3/2147, 244.

24. Ampudia to Ministro de Guerra y Marina, 7 Apr. 1846, ASDN, XI/481.3/2147, 244.

25. Ministro de Guerra y Marina to Ampudia, 20 Apr. 1846, ASDN, XI/481.3/2147, 246.

26. Ampudia to Ministro de Guerra y Marina, 8 Apr. 1846, ASDN, XI/481.3/2147, 248.

27. Mejía to Ministro de Guerra y Marina, 2 Apr. 1846, ASDN, XI/481.3/2147.

28. Mejía to Ampudia, 30 Mar. 1846; quote found in Mejía to Ampudia, 29 Mar. 1846; Mejía to Ministro de Guerra y Marina, 2 Apr. 1846, all in ASDN, XI/481.3/2147.

29. Mejía to Ampudia, 29 Mar. 1846, 30 Mar. 1846, 2 Apr. 1846, and 5 Apr. 1846, all in ASDN XI/481.3/2147.

30. Henshaw, *Recollections of the War,* 44; Taylor to Adjutant General, 6 Apr. 1846, H.R. Doc. No. 30–60, at 133.

31. Manfield to Col. Joseph Totten, 2 Apr. 1846, 4 May 1846, and 23 June 1846, LR–OCE, RG77, NA.

32. Taylor to Adjutant General, 6 Apr. 1846, H.R. Doc. No. 30–60, at 133–34.

33. Fleming, *Life and Letters of Alexander Hays,* 58.

34. Taylor to Adjutant General of the Army, 25 Mar. 1846, H.R. Doc. No. 30–60, at 129–30.

35. "Fort Polk: A Letter from Major Sanders," *Southern Literary Messenger* 17, no. 5 (May 1851): 317–18.

36. Meade, *Life and Letters,* 1:60.

37. "Fort Polk: A Letter from Major Sanders," 317–18; Sanders to Totten, 10 Apr. 1846, Sanders, Smith and Swift Correspondence, LR–OCE, RG77, NA.

38. Sanders to Taylor, 2 May 1846, Sanders, Smith and Swift Correspondence, LR–OCE, RG77, NA.

39. Ibid.

40. Sanders to Taylor, 15 Apr. 1846, LR–AO, RG94, Microcopy 307, Roll 2, NA.

41. Sanders to Totten, 10 Apr. 1846, Sanders, Smith and Swift Correspondence, LR–OCE, RG77, NA.

42. Sanders to Taylor, 14 Apr. 1846, LR–AO, RG94, Microcopy 307, Roll 2, NA.

43. Ibid., 15 Apr. 1846, LR–AO, RG94, Microcopy 307, Roll 2, NA.

44. Sanders to Taylor, 15 Apr. 1846, LR–AO, RG94, Microcopy 307, Roll 2, NA; E. S. Hawkins to W. W. Bliss, 10 May 1846, S. Doc. No. 29–388, at 31.

45. Barbour, *Journals,* 31, 35–36, 39–40; Kirby-Smith, *To Mexico with Scott,* 35–36; Taylor to Adjutant General, 15 Apr. 1846, H.R. Doc. No. 30–60, at 138–39.

46. Meade, *Life and Letters,* 1:54.

47. Cochrane to Sally Cochrane, 10 Apr. 1846, Cochrane Papers, UT.

48. Jarvis, "An Army Surgeon's Notes," 40:447; Taylor to Adjutant General, 6 Apr. 1846, H.R. Doc. No. 60; Kirby-Smith, *To Mexico with Scott,* 37; John Hatch to Eliza Hatch, 5 Apr. 1846, Hatch Papers, Library of Congress (hereafter cited as Hatch Papers, LC), Dana, *Monterrey Is Ours Ours,* 41–42.

49. Dana, *Monterrey Is Ours,* 41.

50. Taylor to Adjutant General, 6 Apr. 1846, H.R. Doc. No. 30–60, at 133–34; Smith, *To Mexico with Scott,* 37; Dana, *Monterrey Is Ours,* 45; John Hatch to Eliza Hatch, 5 Apr. 1846, Hatch Papers, LC.

51. Hitchcock, *Fifty Years in Camp and Field,* 214.

52. McIntosh to Bliss, 29 Mar. 1846; Jacob Brown to Z. Taylor, 31 Mar. 1846, both in LR–AO, RG94, Microcopy 307:4, NA.

53. Major Staniford to Taylor, 9 Apr. 1846; McKavett to Taylor, 14 Apr. 1846; Belknap to Taylor, 17 Apr. 1846; Belknap to Bliss, 18 Apr. 1846; charges by J. Staniford against James McIntosh, 3 May 1846, all in LR–AO, RG94, Microcopy 307:4, NA.

54. Worth to Taylor, 2 Apr. 1846, LR–AO, RG94, Microcopy 307:4, NA; Worth to 1st Brigade, 8 Apr. 1846, in James Duncan Papers, USMA.

55. Barbour, *Journals,* 31–32.

56. Cross to Taylor, 3 Apr. 1846, LR–AO, RG94, Microcopy 307:4, NA.

57. Meade, *Life and Letters,* 1:66.

58. Taylor to Ampudia, 15 Apr. 1846, and Ampudia to Taylor, 16 Apr. 1846, both in *Monitor republicano,* 6 May 1846; Robert Gruber, "The Cross, Porter, and Thornton Episodes: America's Inauspicious Entry into the Mexican War," *Military History of Texas and the Southwest* 12, no. 3 (1974): 188; Edmund Schriver to "My Dear Captain," 3 May 1846, Schriver Papers, Duke; Taylor to Adjutant General, 15 Apr. 1846, H.R. Doc. No. 30–60, at 138–39; Barbour, *Journals,* 32–38.

59. Ampudia to Taylor, 12 Apr. 1846, H.R. Doc. No. 30–60, at 140.

60. Taylor to Ampudia, 12 Apr. 1846, H.R. Doc. No. 30–60, at 139–40.

61. Mills, Diary, 9, FHS; Jarvis, "An Army Surgeon's Notes," 40:449; *Cincinnati Gazette,* 7 May 1846.

62. Barbour, *Journals,* 35; Peck, *Sign of the Eagle,* 19.

63. Mills, *Diary,* 9–10, FHS; Jarvis, "An Army Surgeon's Notes," 40:449–50; Taylor to Adjutant General, 15 Apr. 1846, H.R. Doc. No. 60, 138–39.

64. Tornel to Ampudia, 4 Apr. 1846, in *Monitor republicano,* 5 May 1846; Tornel to Ampudia, 11 Apr. 1846, ASDN XI/481.3/2147, 270.

65. Alberto María Carreño, ed., *Jefes del ejército mexicano en 1847: biografías de generals de división y de coronels del ejército méxicano por fines del año de 1847* (México, Imprenta y Fototipia de la

Secretaría de Fomento, 1914), 147–48; DePalo, *Mexican National Army,* 80–81; Negrete, *Invasión de los norte-americanos,* 1:136–37; Thorpe, *Our Army on the Rio Grande,* 106.

66. Tornel to Arista, 4 Apr. 1846, ASDN XI/481.3/2147, 278; Carreño, Jefes del ejército méxicano, 44–49; Joseph Milton Nance, *After San Jacinto: The Texas-Mexican Frontier, 1836–1841* (Austin: University of Texas Press, 1963), 438–39. Arista could be just as cruel as Ampudia. In 1840, after crushing a Federalist revolt by Antonio Zapata, Arista had Zapata tried and executed and preserved his severed head in a cask of mescal. He then had Ampudia carry the head to the town of Guerrero and mounted on a post as a warning to other rebels. See Nance, *After San Jacinto,* 266–67. This was not an uncommon practice in fighting along the frontier, but, for some reason, Arista escaped a reputation for cruelty while Ampudia did not.

67. Ampudia to Tornel, 15 Apr. 1846, in *Monitor republicano,* 5 May 1846.

68. *Monitor republicano,* 5 May 1846.

69 Alcaraz, *Apuntes para la historia de la guerra,* 34–35.

70. Ampudia to Taylor, 22 Apr. 1846, H.R. Doc. No. 30–60, at 144–45; Taylor to Ampudia, 22 Apr. 1846, H.R. Doc. No. 30–60, at 145–47.

71. *Monitor republicano,* 5 May 1846.

72. *Monitor republicano,* 5 May 1846.

73. Meade, *Life and Letters,* 1:67–68; Dana, *Monterrey Is Ours,* 47–48; Jarvis, "An Army Surgeon's Notes," 40:451; Henshaw, *Recollections of the War,* 48–49; Mills, *Diary,* 11, FHS; Gruber, "The Cross, Porter, and Thornton Episodes," 189–90.

74. Mills, *Diary,* 11, FHS; Jarvis, "An Army Surgeon's Notes," 40:451; Meade, *Life and Letters,* 1:67–68; Samuel Gibbs French, *Two Wars,* 46; Dana, *Monterrey Is Ours,* 47–48; C. F. Smith Diary, 21 Apr. 1846, Charles F. Smith Papers, USMA.

75. Dana, *Monterrey Is Ours,* 48.

76. *Richmond Whig,* 8 May 1846; Dana, *Monterrey Is Ours,* 46, 49; Jarvis, "An Army Surgeon's Notes," 40:451; Francisco Mejía to Ministro de Guerra y Marina, 15 Mar. 1846, cited in Negrete, *Invasión de los norte-americanos,* 2:114–15.

77. Taylor to Adjutant General, 15 Apr. 1846, H.R. Doc. No. 30–60, at 138–39.

78. Mills, Diary, 10, FHS; Jarvis, "An Army Surgeon's Notes," 40:451; Meade, *Life and Letters,* 1:67–68; Samuel Gibbs French, *Two Wars,* 46.

79. Thorpe, *Our Army on the Rio Grande,* 38–39; Arista to Taylor, 24 Mar. 1846, in *Monitor republicano,* 8 May 1846.

80. Thorpe, *Our Army on the Rio Grande,* 40; Arista to Taylor, 24 Mar. 1846, in *Monitor republicano,* 9 May 1846.

81. Mills, Diary, 12, FHS; Meade, *Life and Letters,* 1:73–74; Jarvis, "An Army Surgeon's Notes," 40:451–52.

CHAPTER 5

1. James K. Polk, "Hostilities By Mexico: Message From the President of the United States," 11 May 1846, H.R. Doc. No. 30–60, at 4–11.

2. Taylor to Adjutant General, 26 Apr. 1846, H.R. Doc. No. 30–60, at 140–41. In-depth presentations of both the political and social responses to Polk's call for war can be found in Pletcher, *Diplomacy of Annexation,* and Merk, *Manifest Destiny,* 89–106; Robert W. Johannsen, *To the Halls of the Montezumas: The Mexican War in the American Imagination* (New York: Oxford University Press, 1985).

3. Anastasio Parrodi to Ministro de Guerra y Marina, 30 Apr. 1846, in *Monitor republicano,* 6 May 1846.

4. Arista to Gobernador de Nuevo León, 15 Apr. 1846, in *Monitor republicano,* 1 May 1846.

5. *Monitor republicano,* 1 May 1846 and 5 May 1846. See also *War of A Thousand Deserts,* 254–56, 270–73.

6. Arista to Governor of Nuevo León, 15 Apr. 1846, in *Monitor republicano,* 1 May 1846.

7. Cochrane to wife, 3 Apr. 1846, Richard Cochrane Papers, UT.

8. Peck, *Sign of the Eagle,* 18; Rafael Quintero to Mariano Arista, 1 May 1846, Papers Captured with Arista's Baggage (hereafter cited as CP), Ib99, in AO–LR, RG94, NA; sketch of Taylor's camp, CP, Id1, in AO–LR, RG94, NA.

9. J. P. Schatzell to Arista, 20 Apr. 1846, in *Monitor republicano,* 10 May 1846.

10. Arista to Consul of the United States, 29 Apr. 1846, in *Monitor republicano,* 10 May 1846.

11. Arista orderbook, Mexican War muster rolls and orders, 1845–1846, Manuscript Collection, New-York Historical Society, New York; Jauregui declaration, ASDN, XI/481.3/3320; Arista to Secretary of War, 26 Apr. 1846, in *Monitor republicano,* 6 May 1846.

12. Comandante General, Departamento de Tamaulipas to Arista, 29 Apr. 1846, CP, Ib122, in AO–LR, RG94, NA; Arista to Torrejón, 24 Apr. 1846, ASDN, XI/481.3/3320.

13. Arista to Torrejón, 24 Apr. 1846, ASDN, XI/481.3/3320.

14. Ibid.

15. Arista to Ministro de Guerra, 24 Apr. 1846, ASDN, XI/481.3/2174; Arista to Torrejón, 24 Apr. 1846, ASDN, XI/481.3/3320.

16 Arista to Ministro de Guerra, 24 Apr. 1846, ASDN, XI/481.3/2174; Arista to Torrejón, 24 Apr. 1846, ASDN, XI/481.3/3320.

17. Arista to Ministro de Guerra, 24 Apr. 1846, ASDN, XI/481.3/2174.

18. Declaration of Col. José María Carrasco (hereafter cited as Carrasco Declaration), 6 Aug. 1846. ASDN, XI/481.3/3320; Jauregui declaration, ASDN, XI/481.3/3320.

19. Carrasco declaration, Jauregui declaration, ASDN, XI/481.3/3320; Mariano Arista File, ASDN, XI/111/1–120.

20. Canales declaration, ASDN, 481.3/3320; Torrejón to Arista, 26 Apr. 1846, CP, Ib92, in LR–AO, RG94, NA.

21. Meade, *Life and Letters,* 1:73; Mills, Diary, 12, FHS.

22. Thorpe, *Our Army on the Rio Grande,* 41; General Order No. 51, 24 Apr. 1846, GO–AO RG94, NA; Dana, *Monterrey Is Ours,* 52.

23. W. W. S. Bliss to Thornton, 24 Apr. 1846, in Trial of Captain Seth Thornton, July 1846, Records of Judge Advocate General, Courts-Martial Proceedings (hereafter cited as CM–OJAG), RG153, EE255, NA. (The trial is hereafter cited as Thornton CM.) Thornton and Bliss testimonies, Thornton CM.

24. Thornton testimony, Thornton CM; Trial of Captain William Hardee, Hardee testimony, July 1846, CM–OJAG, RG153, EE248, NA. (The trial is hereafter cited as Hardee CM.)

25. US soldiers regularly referred to Sandoval as "Chapita." See, for example, Barbour, *Journals,* 21, 37 and Henry, *Campaign Sketches,* 28, 35, 82. Jean Louis Berlandier states that Mexican troops also identified Sandoval by his nickname, but with the proper spelling of "Chepito." See Berlandier, "Itinerario," Berlandier Papers–Yale, 126. "Chepe" is a common Spanish nickname for José. The diminutive "Chepito" roughly translates as "Little Joe." Details about Sandoval and the departure of the US scout pary are recorded in Thornton and McConnell testimonies, Thornton CM; Hardee testimony, Hardee CM.

26. Thornton, Kane, and Hardee testimonies, Thornton CM; Hardee and Lenz testimonies, Hardee CM.

27. Thornton, Kane, and Hardee testimonies, Thornton CM; Hardee and Lenz testimonies, Hardee CM.

28. Thornton testimony, Thornton CM.

29. Thornton and Lenz testimonies, Thornton CM.

30. Ibid.

31. Hardee to Taylor, 26 Apr. 1846, H.R. Doc. No. 30–60, at 291; Hardee testimony, Hardee CM.

32. Thornton to W. W. S. Bliss, 27 Apr. 1846, H.R. Doc. No. 30–60, at 290.

33. Thornton and Kane testimonies, Thornton CM; Hardee testimony, Hardee CM.

34. Thornton and Kane testimonies, Thornton CM; Hardee testimony, Hardee CM.

35. Thornton and Kane testimonies, Thornton CM; Hardee testimony, Hardee CM.

36. Thornton and Lenz testimonies, Thornton CM; Hardee testimony, Hardee CM; Thornton to Taylor, 27 Apr. 1846, H.R. Doc. No. 30–60, at 290.

37. Thornton testimony, Thornton CM.

38. Ibid.

39. Ibid.

40. Hardee testimony, Hardee CM.

41. Ibid.; *Niles' National Register,* 16 May 1846.

42. Torrejón to Taylor, 25 Apr. 1846, in *Monitor republicano,* 6 May 1846; Hardee to Taylor, 26 Apr. 1846, H.R. Doc. No. 30–60, at 291; Hardee testimony, Hardee CM.

43. Hardee to Taylor, 26 Apr. 1846, H.R. Doc. No. 30–60, at 291; Hardee testimony, Hardee CM.

44. Arista to Secretary of War, 30 Apr. 1846, in *Monitor republicano,* 12 May 1846; Thornton to Taylor, 27 Apr. 1846, H.R. Doc. No. 30–60, at 290.

45. Thornton to Taylor, 27 Apr. 1846, H.R. Doc. No. 30–60, at 290; Thornton statement, Thornton CM. The Carrizos were descendants of the Coahuiltecans people who originally settled the region. They spoke Spanish, had been integrated into northern Mexican society, and had regularly ridden with Antonio Canales in conflicts with the Comanches.

46. José María Clavito to Arista, "Relación de gastos secretos," 23 Aug. 1845, ASDN, XI/481.3/2069; Mariano Arista File, ASDN, XI/111/1–21; Anastasio Parrodi to Ministro de Guerra y Marina, 30 Apr. 1846; Canales to Secretary of War, 26 Apr. 1846; and Arista to Ministro de Guerra y Marina, 30 Apr. 1846, all in *Monitor republicano,* 6 May 1846; Berlandier, "Itinerario," Berlandier Papers–Yale, 126.

47. Torrejón to Arista, 25 Apr. 1846, in *Monitor republicano,* 6 May 1846.

48. Ibid.

49. Ibid.

50. Ibid.

51. Canales to Ministro de Guerra y Marina, 26 Apr. 1846, in *Monitor republicano,* 6 May 1846; Anastasio Parrodi to Ministro de Guerra y Marina, 30 Apr. 1846, both in *Monitor republicano,* 6 May 1846; Ministro de Guerra y Marina to Arista, 9 May 1846, in *Monitor republicano,* 12 May 1846.

52. Canales to Ministro de Guerra y Marina, 26 Apr. 1846, in *Monitor republicano,* 6 May 1846.

53. Arista to Ministro de Guerra y Marina, 30 Apr. 1846, in *Monitor republicano,* 6 May 1846.

54. Berlandier, "Itinerario," 115–16, Berlandier Papers–Yale.

55. Arista to Ministro de Guerra y Marina, 1 May 1846, in *Monitor republicano,* 12 May 1846; Berlandier, "Itinerario," 117, Berlandier Papers–Yale.

56. Arista to Ministro de Guerra y Marina, 26 Apr. 1846, in *Monitor republicano,* 6 May 1846.

57. Mills, Diary, 12–17, FHS; Barbour, *Journals,* 47; C. F. Smith Diary, 26 Apr. 1846, USMA.

58. Meade, *Life and Letters,* 1:74.

59. Hawkins testimony, in Trial of Gen. Edmund P. Gaines, June 1846, CM–OJAG, RG153, EE2591. (The trial is hereafter cited as Gaines CM.) Barbour, *Journals,* 45–46

60. Mills, Diary, 17, FHS; Barbour, *Journals,* 49; McCall to Taylor, 1 May 1846, LR–AO, RG94, NA.

61. Montgomery testimony, in Gaines CM.

62. Mills, Diary, 17, FHS; Barbour, *Journals,* 49.

63. Taylor, General Order No. 47, GO–AO, RG94, M29, NA; Henry, *Campaign Sketches,* 85; Frederick Wilkins, *The Highly Irregular Irregulars: Texas Rangers in the Mexican War* (Austin: Eakin Press, 1990), 25.

64. French, *Two Wars,* 47–48; Meade, *Life and Letters,* 1:76; Dana, *Monterrey Is Ours,* 56–57.

65. Walker to Taylor, 24 Apr. 1846, LR–AO, RG94, NA; Henry, *Campaign Sketches,* 85; Thorpe, *Our Army on the Rio Grande,* 47.

66. Taylor, General Order No. 54, GO–AO, RG94, M29, NA; Taylor to Adjutant General, 3 May 1846, H.R. Doc. No. 30–60, at 288–90.

67. Taylor, General Order No. 55, GO–AO, RG94, M29, NA; Taylor to Adjutant General, 3 May 1846, H.R. Doc. No. 30–60, at 288–90.

68. Jarvis, "An Army Surgeon's Notes," 41:94; Henshaw, *Recollections of the War,* 53.

69. Torrejón to Arista, 28 Apr. 1846, CP, Ib93, in AO–LR, RG94, NA; *Seminario Político,* 7 May 1846.

70. Jauregui declaration, ASDN, XI/481.3/3320.

71. Jauregui declaration, ASDN, XI/481.3/3320; Diario de las operaciones que practican las tropas de la División del norte, sobre la margen izquierda del Río Bravo, 7 May 1846, CP, 1b12, in AO–LR, RG94, NA; Ampudia to Arista, Apr. 30, 1846, CP, Ia6, in AO–LR, RG94, NA.

72. Jauregui declaration, ASDN, XI/481.3/3320; Ampudia to Arista, Apr. 30, 1846, CP, Ia6, in AO–LR, RG94, NA; Mejía to Arista, 1 May 1846, CP, Ib48, in AO–LR, RG94, NA; Rafael Quintero to Arista, 1 May 1846, CP, Ib99, in AO–LR, RG94, NA; declaration of Mariano Ávila and Trial of Mariano Arista, ASDN XI/111/1–21; Diario de las operaciones de la División del Norte, Maya de 1846 (cited hereafter as Diario, Mayo 1846), ASDN, XI/481.3/3320. Sandoval subsequently abandoned the US camp and remained with the Mexican Army for the rest of the campaign.

73. Jauregui declaration, ASDN, XI/481.3/3320; Berlandier, "Itinerario," 37–39, Berlandier Papers–Yale; Cardenas to Arista, 1 May 1846, , in AO–LR, RG94, NA, 1b82; Rafael Quintero to Arista, 1 May 1846, CP, Ib99, in AO–LR, RG94, NA; Diario, Mayo 1846, ASDN, XI/481.3/3320; Ampudia to Arista, 30 Apr. 1846, CP, Ia6, in AO–LR, RG94, NA; declarations of Mariano Ávila and Mariano Arista, ASDN XI/111/1–21; Francisco de Beara, Comandante de la línea, to General en Jefe de la Segunda Brigada de Infantería, 1 May 1846, CP, Ib94, in AO–LR, RG94, NA.

74. Peck, *Sign of the Eagle,* 20; Kirby-Smith, *To Mexico with Scott,* 41–43; Barbour, *Journals,* 50–51; Henshaw, *Recollections of the War,* 53.

75. Canales declaration, ASDN, XI/481.3/3320; Diario, Mayo 1846, ASDN, XI/481.3/3320; Jauregui declaration, ASDN, XI/481.3/3320; Berlandier, "Itinerario," 37–39, Berlandier Papers–Yale.

76. Diario, Mayo 1846, ASDN, XI/481.3/3320; Boletín del Norte, 4 May, 1846, in *Monitor republicano,* 24 May 1846.

CHAPTER 6

1. Henry, *Campaign Sketches,* 86; Mills, Diary, 15, FHS; French, *Two Wars,* 48; Meade, *Life and Letters,* 1:74.

2. Roa Bárcena, *Recuerdos,* 1:61–62; Luis Noriega, "Brigada de Caballerías," 3 May 1846, CP, Ic5, in LR–AO, RG94, NA; Francisco Méjia, "División de Norte—Mayoría General," 3 May 1846, CP, Ic4, in AO–LR, RG94, NA; Bauer, *Mexican War,* 57–58.

3. Deas, "Reminiscences of the Campaign," 101.

4. *Monitor republicano,* 24 May 1846.

5. Pedro García Conde, Mexico's Ministro de Guerra y Marina, in *Niles' National Register,* 1 Nov. 1845; Joseph Hefter et al., *El Soldado mexicano: organización, vestuario, equipo, 1837–1847* (México: Documentos Histórico-Militares, 1958), 50; DePalo, *Mexican National Army.* For detailed anaylsis of the political organization of Mexico, see Henderson, *A Glorious Defeat;* Santoni, *Mexicans at Arms;* and DeLay, *War of A Thousand Deserts.*

6. DeLay, *War of A Thousand Deserts,* 178–79, 184; Sam W. Haynes, *Soldiers of Misfortune: The Somervell and Mier Expeditions* (Austin: University of Texas Press, 1997), 67–68, 74; Fayette Robinson, *Mexico and Her Military Chieftains* (Philadelphia: E. H. Butler, 1847), 252–65; Mariano Arista File, ASDN, XI/111/1–21; Pedro de Ampudia File, ASDN, XI/111/1–221, Antonio Canales File, ASDN, XI/111/2–120; Rómulo Díaz de la Vega File, ASDN, XI/111/1–65; José López de Uraga File, ASDN, XI/111/1–113.

7. DeLay, *War of A Thousand Deserts,* 178–79; Haynes, *Soldiers of Misfortune,* 68; Robinson, *Mexico and Her Military Chieftains,* 260–65; *Monitor republicano,* 24 May 1846; Nance, *After San Jacinto,* 372–74; Joseph E. Chance, *José María de Jesús Carvajal: The Life and Times of a Mexican Revolutionary* (San Antonio: Trinity University Press, 2006); Rómulo Díaz de la Vega File, ASDN, XI/111/1–65; Antonio Canales File, ASDN, XI/111/2–120.

8. Nance, *After San Jacinto,* 263–67; Jauregui declaration, ASDN, XI/481.3/3320; Alcaraz, *Apuntes para la historia de la guerra,* 36–37; Negrete, *Invasión de los norte-americanos,* 168; Mariano Arista File, ASDN, XI/111/1–21.

9. Although Ampudia faulted Arista for a lack of boats, he himself had planned a similar crossing in the weeks before Arista's arrival and had also failed to locate the necessary transports. Ampudia, *El ciudadano general Pedro de Ampudia,* 8; Berlandier, "Itinerario," 39–40; Jauregui declaration, ASDN, XI/481.3/3320.

10. Reeves, "Five Years an American Soldier," 441.

11. Meade, *Life and Letters,* 1:101.

12. For a detailed look at the US military of the period, see Edward M. Coffman, *The Old Army: A Portrait of the American Army in Peacetime, 1784–1898* (New York: Oxford University Press, 1988); Francis Paul Prucha, *The Sword of the Republic: The United States Army on the Frontier, 1783–1846* (New York: McMillan, 1969); and Robert P. Wettemann Jr., *Privilege vs. Equality: Civil-Military Relations in the Jacksonian Era, 1815–1845* (Santa Barbara, CA: Praeger, 2009). Discussions of the frustrations of soldiers who have devoted years to service without promotion can be found in Richard Bruce Winders, *Mr. Polk's Army: The American Military Experience in the Mexican War* (College Station: Texas A&M University Press, 1997), 50–65; William B. Skelton, *An American Profession of Arms: The Army Officer Corps, 1784–1861* (Lawrence: University Press of Kansas, 1992), 181–220; Wettemann, *Privilege vs. Equality,* 122–34, 148–51; Coffman, *The Old Army,* 42–103; Grant, *Personal Memoirs,* 71.

13. Fleming, *Life and Letters of Alexander Hays,* 59; *Richmond Whig,* 15 May 1846; Winders, *Mr. Polk's Army,* 53–57; Coffman, *The Old Army,* 96–103.

14. Winders, *Mr. Polk's Army,* 50–65.

15. For a detailed account of army enlisted men, see Dale Richard Steinhauer, "'Sogers'": Enlisted Men in the US Army, 1815–1860" (PhD diss., University of North Carolina, 1992); Coffman, *The Old Army,* 137–211.

16. *Niles' National Register,* 27 June 1846.

17. *Richmond Whig,* 1 May 1846; Waddy Thompson, *Recollections of Mexico* (New York: Wiley and Putnam, 1846), 172–73.

18. DePalo, *Mexican National Army,* 1:6–7; Manuel Otero, cited in Cecil Robinson, ed., *The View from Chapultepec: Mexican Writers on the Mexican-American War* (Tucson: University of Arizona Press, 1989), 20.

19. Thompson, *Recollections of Mexico,* 173.

20. George Ballentine, *The Mexican War, by an English Soldier: Comprising Incidents and Adventures in the United States and Mexico with the American Army* (New York: W. A. Townsend, 1860), 91.

21. Thorpe, *Our Army on the Rio Grande,* 24–25.

22. *Niles' National Register,* 4 July 1846.

23. Ampudia to Arista, 30 Apr. 1846, CP, Ia6, in LR–AO, RG94 NA.

24. Ibid., CP, Ib15, in LR–AO, RG94, NA.

25. Steinhauer, "'Sogers,'" 124.

26. Winders, *Mr. Polk's Army,* 92–100; Charles M. Haecker and Jeffrey G. Mauck, *On the Prairie of Palo Alto: Historical Archaeology of the US-Mexican War Battlefield* (College Station: Texas A&M University Press, 1997), 59–72 passim; Grant, *Personal Memoirs,* 38.

27. Farnham Bishop, *Our First War with Mexico* (New York: C. Scribner's Sons, 1916), 84; Haecker, *A Thunder of Cannon: Archeology of the Mexican-American War Battlefield of Palo Alto* (Santa Fe: National Park Service, Southwest Regional Office, 1994); Haecker and Mauck, *On the Prairie of Palo Alto,* 59–104 passim; Winders, *Mr. Polk's Army,* 96–100.

28. Ballentine, *Mexican War,* 199.

29. Haecker and Mauck, *On the Prairie of Palo Alto,* 59–104 passim; DePalo, *Mexican National Army,* 50–51, 96–97.

30. Bishop, *Our First War with Mexico,* 86–87; Haecker and Mauck, *On the Prairie of Palo Alto,* 89–90.

31. Ignacio de Mora y Villamil to Ministro de Guerra y Marina, 4 May 1846, ASDN, XI/481.3/2174.

32. Mejía to Ministro de Guerra y Marina, 4 Mar. 1846, ASDN, XI/481.3/2174; Gregory H. Nobles, *American Frontiers: Cultural Encounters and Continental Conquest* (New York: Hill and Wang, 1997), 160; Bishop, *Our First War with Mexico,* 86–87.

33. "History in Tabloid," *FRA Magazine: A Journal of Affirmation,* Jan.–Sept. 1915, 103; Winders, *Mr. Polk's Army,* 89–94.

34. Thorpe, *Our Army on the Rio Grande,* 145.

35. Thorpe, *Our Army on the Rio Grande,* 190–92; J. Thomas Sharf, *History of Western Maryland* (Philadelphia: Louis J. Everts, 1882), 1024–5; James Wynne, *Memoir of Major Samuel Ringgold, United States Army, Read before the Maryland Historical Society, Apr. 1st, 1847* (Baltimore: J. Murphy, 1847).

36. Mejía to Ministro de Guerra y Marina, 4 Mar. 1846, ASDN, XI/481.3/2174.

37. Ignacio Mora y Villamil to Ministro de Guerra y Marina, 4 May 1846, ASDN, XI/481.3/2174.

38. Juan Antonio Ballé Cavazos to General en Jefe, 3 May 1846; Ramón Cabazos Guerra to Mariano Arista, 4 May 1846; Mariano Arista to Ministro de Guerra y Marina, 7 May 1846, all in *Monitor republicano,* 15 May 1846.

39. Zenas Matthews, Diary, Special Collections, Southwestern University, Georgetown, Texas, 12; Mary A Southerland, *The Story of Corpus Christi* (Houston: Rein and Sons, 1916), 10–11.

40. Arista to Ministro de Guerra y Marina, 25 May 1846, ASDN, XI/481.3/2178.

41. John C. Duval, *The Adventures of Big Foot Wallace: Texas Ranger and Hunter* (Macon, Georgia: J. W. Burke, 1870), 173; Smith, *War With Mexico,* 157, 462.

42. Henry, *Campaign Sketches,* 85; Wilkins, *The Highly Irregular Irregulars,* 25; Taylor to Adjutant General, 3 May 1846, H.R. Doc. No. 30–60, at 288.

43. Berlandier, "Itinerario," 116, Berlandier Papers–Yale.

44. Arista to Ministro de Guerra y Marino, 7 May 1846, in *Monitor republicano,* 15 May 1846.

45. Taylor to Adjutant General, 3 May 1846, H.R. Doc. No. 30–60, at 289–90.

46. Ibid., at 289.

47. Arista to Ministro de Guerra y Marino, 7 May 1847, in *Monitor republicano,* 15 May 1846.

48. Ibid.

49. Ampudia to Arista, 30 Apr. 1846, CP, Ia6, in LR–AO, RG94, NA.

50. Arista to Ministro de Guerra y Marino, 7 May 1847, in *Monitor republicano,* 15 May 1846.

CHAPTER 7

1. *Monitor republicano,* 24 May 1846.

2. Whiting, *A Soldier's Life,* 74.

3. Dana, *Monterrey Is Ours,* 59.

4. Brown to Taylor, 4 May 1846, H.R. Doc. No. 30–60, at 293–94; Whiting, *A Soldier's Life,* 74.

5. *Niles' National Register,* 20 June 1846; Dana, *Monterrey Is Ours,* 60; "Bombardment of Fort Brown," *Niles' National Register,* 6 June 1846; Henshaw, *Recollections of the War,* 54–55; Whiting, *A Soldier's Life,* 75.

6. Dana, *Monterrey Is Ours,* 60; "Bombardment of Fort Brown," *Niles' National Register,* 6 June 1846; Henshaw, *Recollections of the War,* 54–55.

7. Josph Mansfield to Totton, 4 May 1846, LR–OCE, RG77, NA; "Bombardment of Fort Brown," *Niles' National Register,* 6 June 1846; Dana, *Monterrey Is Ours,* 60.

8. Whiting, *A Soldier's Life,* 75; "Bombardment of Fort Brown," *Niles' National Register,* 6 June 1846.

9. Mejía to Arista, 5 May 1846; Agustin de Mier y Terán to Arista, 4 May 1846; and Tomás Requena to Arista, 5 May 1846, all in *Monitor republicano,* 15 May 1846; Mejía to Arista, 3 May 1846, CP, Ib51 and Ib55, in LR–AO, RG94, NA; Mier y Terán to Requena, 4 May 1846, CP, Ib122, and Requena to Arista, 5 May 1846, CP, Ib87, in LR–AO, RG94, NA.

10. Mejía to Arista, May 3, 1846, CP, Ib51, in LR–AO, RG94, NA.

11. Mier y Terán to Arista, 5 May 1846, in *Monitor republicano,* 15 May 1846.

12. Henry, *Campaign Sketches,* 21–22.

13. Zachary Taylor to Adjutant General, 4 May 1846, in "Messages of the President of the United States with the Correspondence Therewith Communicated Between the Secretary of War and Other Officers of the Government on the Subject of the Mexican War," H.R. Doc. No. 30–60, at 293–94; Meade, *Life and Letters,* 1:26–27, 75; Henry, *Campaign Sketches,* 88.

14. Peck, *Sign of the Eagle,* 22.

15. Taylor to Adjutant General, 5 May 1846, H.R. Doc. No. 30–60; Meade, *Life and Letters,* 1:75; Henry, *Campaign Sketches,* 88.

16. Arista to Ampudia, 5 May 1846, in *Monitor republicano,* 15 May 1846.

17. Berlandier, "Itinerario," 132–34, Berlandier Papers–Yale.

18. Henshaw, *Recollections of the War,* 55–56.

19. Brown to Taylor, 4 May 1846, H.R. Doc. No. 30–60; Mills, Diary, 14–15, FHS; Henshaw, *Recollections of the War,* 55–56; Jauregui declaration, ASDN, XI/481.3/3320.

20. Brown to Taylor, 4 May 1846, H.R. Doc. No. 30–60; Dana, *Monterrey Is Ours,* 58–59; Henshaw, *Recollections of the War,* 55–56.

21. Henshaw, *Recollections of the War,* 55–56; Dana, *Monterrey Is Ours,* 58–59; Whiting, *A Soldier's Life,* 75.

22. Henshaw, *Recollections of the War,* 55–56; Dana, *Monterrey Is Ours,* 58–59; Barbour, *Journals,* 65; Niles National Register, 23 May 1846.

23. Taylor to Adjutant General, 4 May 1846, H. R. Doc. No. 30–60, 293–94; Meade, *Life and Letters,* 1:75; Henry, *Campaign Sketches,* 88.

24. Berlandier, "Itinerario," Berlandier Papers–Yale, 134–35.

25. Arista to Ampudia, 5 May 1846, ASDN, XI/481.3/2174; Jauregui declaration, ASDN, XI/481.3/3320.

26. Berlandier, "Itinerario," Berlandier Papers–Yale, 136–37; Diario, Mayo 1846, ASDN, XI/481.3/3320; Jauregui declaration, ASDN, XI/481.3/3320; Arista to Antonio Osorio, 4 May 1846, CP, Ib101, in LR–AO, RG94, NA.

27. Arista to Canales, 4 May 1846, CP, Ib17, in LR–AO, RG94, NA; Diario, Mayo 1846, ASDN, XI/481.3/3320; Canales to Arista, 4 May 1846, CP, Ib103, in LR–AO, RG94, NA; Arista to Ampudia, 5 May 1846, ASDN, XI/481.3/2174; Berlandier, "Itinerario," Berlandier Papers–Yale, 140–41.

28. Jauregui declaration, ASDN, XI/481.3/3320.

29. Henshaw, *Recollections of the War,* 55–56; Dana, *Monterrey Is Ours,* 60–63; Whiting, *A Soldier's Life,* 76–77.

30. Henshaw, *Recollections of the War,* 55–56; Dana, *Monterrey Is Ours,* 60–63.

31. Arista to Ampudia, 5 May 1846, in *Monitor republicano,* 15 May 1846.

32. Berlandier, "Itinerario," Berlandier Papers–Yale, 148; Arista to Ampudia, 5 May 1846, in *Monitor republicano,* 15 May 1846; Ampudia to Arista, 6 May 1846, CP, Ib36, LR–AO, RG94, NA; Arista to Ampudia, 6 May 1846, CP, Ib7, in LR–AO, RG94, NA.

33. Ampudia to Arista, 6 May 1846, CP, Ib36, Ib37, Ib38, Ib40, in LR–AO, RG94, NA.

34. Ibid.

35. Arista to Ampudia, 6 May 1846, CP, Ib7, in LR–AO, RG94, NA.

36. Dana, *Monterrey Is Ours,* 60–63; Hawkins to Bliss, 10 May 1846, in "Reports from General Taylor," H.R. Doc. No. 29–209, at 31–35; Ampudia to Arista, 6 May 1846, CP, Ib41, in LR–AO, RG94, NA.

37. Dana, *Monterrey Is Ours,* 61; Hawkins to Bliss, 10 May 1846, H.R. Doc. No. 29–209, at 31–35; Whiting, *A Soldier's Life,* 76–77.

38. Hawkins to Arista, 6 May 1846, H.R. Doc. No. 29–209, at 35–36; Hawkins to Bliss, 10 May 1846, H.R. Doc. No. 29–209, at 31–35.

39. Hawkins to Bliss, 10 May 1846, H.R. Doc. No. 29–209, at 31–35; Henshaw, *Recollections of the War,* 55–56.

40. Arista to Ampudia, 7 May 1846, CP, Ib12, in LR–AO, RG94, NA.

41. Arista to Ampudia, 7 May 1846, CP, Ib11; Ampudia to Arista, 7 May 1846, CP, Ib42–Ib45; and Arista to Mejía, 7 May 1846, CP, Ib9, all in LR–AO, RG94, NA.

42. Taylor to Adjutant General, 7 May 1846, H. R. Doc. No. 30–60, 294–95.

43. John Hatch, Campaign Account, Hatch Papers, Abraham Lincoln Presidential Library (hereafter cited as ALPL), Springfield Illinois; French, *Two Wars,* 53.

44. Mills, Diary, 16, FHS; Hatch, Campaign Account, ALPL; Bauer, *Mexican War,* 52.

45. Longstreet, *From Manassas to Appomattox,* 24.

46. Deas, "Reminiscences of the Campaign," 101.

47. Unlike the Loma Alta (High Hill) and Palo Alto (Tall Trees), in is not clear whether the prairie where battle occurred had an established name. Several Mexican soldiers referred to the site as the Llano El Chiflido or Whistling Prairie, a name that accurately describes the sound of the wind whipping over grasslands. Others indicate that El Chiflido was actually a site several miles south of the prairie. See Berlandier, "Itinerario," Berlandier Papers–Yale, 150–55; Jauregui declaration, ASDN, XI/481.3/3320.

48. Berlandier, "Itinerario," Berlandier Papers–Yale, 150–55; Diario, Mayo 1846, ASDN, XI/481.3/3320; Jauregui declaration, ASDN, XI/481.3/3320.

49. Berlandier, "Itinerario," Berlandier Papers–Yale, 153–57; Diario, Mayo 1846, ASDN, XI/481.3/3320; Jauregui declaration, ASDN, XI/481.3/3320.

50. Berlandier, "Itinerario," Berlandier Papers–Yale, 153–57; Diario, Mayo 1846, ASDN, XI/481.3/3320; Jauregui declaration, ASDN, XI/481.3/3320.

51. Berlandier, "Itinerario," Berlandier Papers–Yale, 153–57; Diario, Mayo 1846, ASDN, XI/481.3/3320; Berlandier, "Batalla del dia 8 de Mayo," Berlandier Papers, Thomas Phillips Collection, Ms.17742, Library of Congress (hereafter cited as Berlandier Papers–LC).

52. Diario, Mayo 1846, ASDN, XI/481.3/3320; Berlandier, "Itinerario," Berlandier Papers–Yale, 153–57.

53. Jauregui declaration, ASDN, XI/481.3/3320; Diario, Mayo 1846, ASDN, XI/481.3/3320; Berlandier, "Itinerario," Berlandier Papers–Yale, 158; Berlandier, "Batalla del dia 8 de Mayo," Berlandier Papers–LC.

54. Berlandier, "Itinerario," Berlandier Papers–Yale, 158; Diario, Mayo 1846, ASDN, XI/481.3/3320; Ampudia, *El ciudadano general Pedro de Ampudia,* 4–7; Jauregui and Torrejón declarations, ASDN, XI/481.3/3320; Arista to Ministro de Guerra y Marina, 8 May 1846, all in ASDN, XI/481.3/2174; Berlandier, "Batalla del dia 8 de Mayo." Berlandier Papers–LC.

55. Barbour, *Journals,* 167–72; Mills, Diary, FHS, 17; George McCall to Capt. Bradford Alden, 5 June 1846, McCall Papers, US Military Academy (cited hereafter as McCall Papers, USMA).

56. Phillip Barbour to Mattie Barbour, 12 May 1846, in Barbour, *Journals,* 167–72; Taylor to Adjutant General, 16 May 1846, H.R. Doc. No. 29–209; Mills Diary, 17, FHS; George McCall to Capt. Bradford Alden, 5 June 1846, Alden Papers, US Military Academy (cited hereafter as Alden Papers, USMA); Deas, "Reminiscences of the Campaign," 101–2.

57. Taylor to Adjutant General, 16 May 1846, H.R. Doc. No. 29 209.

58. Deas, "Reminiscences of the Campaign," 101–3.

59. Grant, *Personal Memoirs,* 38–39.

60. French, *Two Wars,* 48.

61. Ibid., 49.

62. Jauregui declaration, ASDN, XI/481.3/3320.

63. Diario, Mayo 1846, ASDN, XI/481.3/3320; Alcaraz, *Apuntes para la historia de la guerra,* 38–39.

64. Arista to Ministro de Guerra y Marina, 8 May 1846, ASDN, XI/481.3/2174; Berlandier, "Batalla del dia 8 de Mayo," Berlandier Papers–LC; Diario, Mayo 1846, ASDN, XI/481.3/3320; Alcaraz, *Apuntes para la historia de la guerra,* 38–39.

65. Arista to Ministro de Guerra y Marina, 8 May 1846, ASDN, XI/481.3/2174; Diario, Mayo 1846, ASDN, XI/481.3/3320; Berlandier, "Batalla del dia 8 de Mayo," Berlandier Papers–LC; Alcaraz, *Apuntes para la historia de la guerra,* 38–39; Jauregui declaration, ASDN, XI/481.3/3320; Berlandier, "Itinerario," Berlandier Papers–Yale, 157–60; Negrete, *Invasión de los norte-americanos,* 178.

66. Jauregui declaration, ASDN, XI/481.3/3320; Diario, Mayo 1846, ASDN, XI/481.3/3320; Berlandier, "Itinerario," Berlandier Papers–Yale, 157–60. In reports of the battle, Arista was vague

about his troop numbers. He claims a force of about thirty-two hundred men, but this figure does not appear to include the last-minute arrivals who entered the field with Ampudia and Canales. Ampudia's force was listed at well over a thousand, but some of those troops appear to have remained at Longoreña, Paso Real, and Anacuitas to guard crossing points on the river. This suggests a total force at Palo Alto of thirty-nine hundred to four thousand troops. Arista to Ministro de Guerra y Marina, 8 May 1846, ASDN, XI/481.3/2174; Arista to Ampudia, 8 May 1846, CP, Ia9, in LR–AO, RG94, NA.

67. Reeves, "Five Years an American Soldier," 443; Henry, *Campaign Sketches,* 211.

68. Longstreet, *From Manassas to Appomattox,* 25; Styles Hawley to Clarinda B. Carpenter, 20 Aug. 1846, Maebius Collection, San Antonio Texas; D. E. Twiggs to Zachary Taylor, 11 May 1846, H.R. Doc. No. 29–209, at 14–15.

69. Barna Upton to Nehamiah Upton, 14 May 1846, Barna Upton Papers, Beinecke Library, Yale (hereafter cited as Upton Papers, Yale); Grant, *Personal Memoirs,* 38; J. M. Scarritt to Col. J. G. Totten, 12 May 1846, LR–OCE, RG77, NA.

70. Fleming, *Life and Letters of Alexander Hays,* 61; Upton to Nehamiah Upton, 14 May 1846, Upton Papers, Yale; Grant, *Personal Memoirs,* 38, and Scarritt to Totten, 12 May 1846, LR–OCE, RG77, NA.

71. *Campaña contra los Americanos del norte,* 13.

72. Jauregui and Torrejón declarations, ASDN, XI/481.3/3320; Diario, Mayo 1846, ASDN, XI/481.3/3320; *Campaña contra los Americanos del norte,* 10–14.

73. Jauregui declaration, ASDN, XI/481.3/3320; Diario, Mayo 1846, ASDN, XI/481.3/3320.

74. Arista to Ministro de Guerra y Marina, 8 May 1846; and Jauregui, Torrejón, and Canales declarations, all in ASDN, XI/481.3/3320; Diario, Mayo 1846, ASDN, XI/481.3/3320; *Campaña contra los Americanos del norte,* 13–14; Ampudia, *El ciudadano general Pedro de Ampudi,* 9–10; Berlandier, "Batalla del dia 8 de Mayo," Berlandier Papers–LC.

75. Jauregui, Torrejón, and Canales declarations, all in ASDN, XI/481.3/3320; Diario, Mayo 1846, ASDN, XI/481.3/3320; Berlandier, "Batalla del dia 8 de Mayo," Berlandier Papers–LC.

76. Jauregui declaration, ASDN, XI/481.3/3320; Diario, Mayo 1846, ASDN, XI/481.3/3320; Berlandier, "Itinerario," Berlandier Papers–Yale, 157–60; Jean Luis Berlandier, "Batalla del dia 8 de Mayo," Berlandier Papers–LC.

77. Jauregui, Torrejón, and Uraga declarations, all in ASDN, XI/481.3/3320; Berlandier, "Batalla del dia 8 de Mayo," Berlandier Papers–LC; Beaman to Brother, 11 May 1846, Jenks Beaman Papers, Houghton Library, Harvard (hereafter cited as Beaman Papers, Harvard).

78. Mills, Diary, 18, FHS.

79. Ampudia, *El ciudadano general Pedro de Ampudia,* 9–11; *Campaña contra los Americanos del norte,* 11–14; Barbour, *Journals* 40.

80. Jauregui declaration, ASDN, XI/481.3/3320; Diario, Mayo 1846, ASDN, XI/481.3/3320.

81. Berlandier, "Batalla del dia 8 de Mayo," Berlandier Papers–LC; Arista to Ministro de Guerra y Marina, 8 May 1846, ASDN, XI/481.3/2174; Diario, Mayo 1846, ASDN, XI/481.3/3320.

82. Samuel Gibbs French to Brother, 10 May 1846, published in *Philadelphia Public Ledger,* 27 May 1846; John Hatch to Eliza Hatch, 19 May 1846, Hatch Papers, Library of Congress (hereafter cited as Hatch Papers, LC); Barbour, *Journals,* 167–68; McCall to Alden, 5 June 1846, McCall Papers, USMA; McCall, *Letters,* 449–52; Taylor to Adjutant General, 10 May 1846; Twiggs to Taylor, 11 May 1846; Staniford to Twiggs, 10 May 1846; Ridgely to Taylor, 10 May 1846; and Belknap to Bliss, 15 May 1846, all in H. R. Doc. No. 29–209.

83. Beaman to brother, 11 May 1846, Beaman Papers, Harvard; Reeves, "Five Years an American Soldier," 443; McCall, *Letters,* 449–52; Taylor to Adjutant General, 10 May 1846; Twiggs to

Taylor, 11 May 1846; Staniford to Twiggs, 10 May 1846; Ridgely to Taylor, 10 May 1846; and Belknap to Bliss, 15 May 1846, all in H.R. Doc. No. 29–209.

84. Jauregui, Torrejón, and Uraga declarations, ASDN, XI/481.3/3320; Berlandier, "Batalla del dia 8 de Mayo," Berlandier Papers–LC; Alcaraz, *Apuntes para la historia de la guerra,* 41.

85. Ampudia, El ciudadano general Pedro de Ampudia, 9–11; *Campaña contra los Americanos del norte,* 11–14; Berlandier, "Itinerario," Berlandier Papers–Yale; Uraga testimony, ASDN, XI/481.3/3320; Diario, Mayo 1846, ASDN, XI/481.3/3320; Berlandier, "Batalla del dia 8 de Mayo," Berlandier Papers–LC.

86. J. M. Scarritt to Col. J. G. Totten, 12 May 1846, LR–OCE, RG77, NA; Thorpe, *Our Army on the Rio Grande,* 80–81.

87. Alcaraz, *Apuntes para la historia de la guerra,* 40–43, and Arista to Ministro de Guerra y Marina, 8 May 1846, ASDN, XI/481.3/2174; Diario, Mayo 1846, ASDN, XI/481.3/3320; Jauregui declaration, ASDN, XI/481.3/3320; *Campaña contra los Americanos del norte,* 14.

88. Alcaraz, *Apuntes para la historia de la guerra,* 41–43; Diario, Mayo 1846, ASDN, XI/481.3/3320; Arista to Ministro de Guerra y Marina, 8 May 1846, ASDN, XI/481.3/2174; Jauregui declaration, ASDN, XI/481.3/3320.

89. Taylor to Adjutant General, 10 May 1846; Twiggs to Taylor, 11 May 1846; Staniford to Twiggs, 10 May 1846; Ridgely to Taylor, 10 May 1846; Belknap to Bliss, 15 May 1846, all in H.R. Doc. No. 29–209; Mills, Diary, 18–19, FHS; Scarritt to Totten, 12 May 1846, LR–OCE, RG77, NA; French to Brother, 10 May1846, in *Philadelphia Public Ledger,* 27 May 1846.

90. C. F. Smith Diary, 8 May 1846, USMA; Taylor to Adjutant General, 17 May 1846, S. Doc. No. 29–388, at 6–9.

91. Taylor to Adjutant General, 10 May 1846, S. Doc. No. 29–388; John Hatch to Eliza Hatch, 19 May 1846, Hatch Papers–LC.

92. Taylor to Adjutant General, 10 May 1846, S. Doc. No. 29–388; Ampudia, *El ciudadano general Pedro de Ampudia,* 9–11; *Campaña contra los Americanos del norte,* 13–16.

CHAPTER 8

1. Arista to Ministro de Guerra y Marina, 8 May 1846, ASDN, XI/481.2174.

2. Canales to Ministro de Guerra y Marina, [?] May 1846, ASDN, XI/481.3/2174.

3. Canales and Jauregui declarations, both in ASDN, XI/481.3/3320.

4. Taylor to Adjutant General, 9 May 1846, H.R. Doc. No. 30–60, at 95.

5. Mills, Diary, 16–18, FHS.

6. "The Night of Palo Alto," Arthur Tracey Lee, *Army Ballads, and Other Poems* (1871), 98–100.

7. Mills, Diary, 16–18, FHS; Lee, "The Night of Palo Alto," 99–100; Peck, *Sign of the Eagle,* 22–23.

8. Arista to Mejía, 8 May 1846, CP, Ib14, LR–AO, RG94, NA; Ampudia to Morlet, 8 May 1846, CP, Ia18, LR–AO, RG94, NA.

9. Jauregui declaration, ASDN, XI/481/3320; Canales to Ministro de Guerra y Marina, May 1846, ASDN, XI/481.2174.

10. Jauregui declaration, ASDN, XI/481.3/3320; Berlandier, "Itinerario," Berlandier Papers–Yale, 96.

11. Arista to Ministro de Guerra y Marina, 10 May 1846, ASDN, XI/481.3/2174.

12. Barbour, *Journals,* 57; Jarvis, "An Army Surgeon's Notes," 41:98–99; Thorpe, *Our Army on the Rio Grande;* Deas, "Reminiscences of the Campaign," 102–3.

13. J. M. Scarritt to Col. J. G. Totten, 12 May 1846, LR–OCE, RG77, NA; Robert Hazlitt to Sister, 14 May 1846, Hazlitt Papers, Ms. 1531, USMA; John Hatch to Eliza Hatch, 19 May 1846, Hatch Papers, LC; Mills, Diary, 18–19, FHS; Longstreet, *From Manassas to Appomattox,* 24–25.

14. Mills, Diary, 18, FHS; Henry, *Campaign Sketches,* 95; Thorpe, *Our Army on the Rio Grande,* 90; Barbour, *Journals,* 55–56.

15. Mills, Diary, 18, FHS; Meade, *Life and Letters,* 1:80; Barbour, *Journals,* 57–58.

16. McCall to Capt. Bradford R. Alden, 5 June 1846, Alden Papers, USMA; Barbour, *Journals,* 55–56; McCall to Zachary Taylor, 13 May 1846, in Official Reports from General Taylor, H.R. Doc. No. 29–209, at 26–28; Mills, Diary, 18–19, FHS; Henry, *Campaign Sketches,* 94–95.

17. Thorpe, *Our Army on the Rio Grande,* 90; Jarvis, "An Army Surgeon's Notes," 41:98.

18. McCall to Alden, 5 June 1846, Alden Papers, USMA; Lee, "La Muerta de Resaca," *Army Ballads,* 105–6; Thorpe, *Our Army on the Rio Grande,* 91.

19. George McCall to Alden, 5 June 1846, Alden Papers, USMA; George McCall to Zachary Taylor, 13 May 1846, and C. F. Smith to George McCall, 13 May 1846, both in H.R. Doc. No. 29–209.

20. Jauregui declaration, ASDN, XI/481.3/3320; Berlandier, "Itinerario," 177, Berlandier Papers–Yale.

21. *Campaña contra los Americanos del norte,* 12–14; Canales and Jauregui declarations, both in ASDN, XI/481.3/3320.

22. Jauregui declaration, ASDN, XI/481/3320; "Itinerario," 177–79, Berlandier Papers–Yale; *Campaña contra los Americanos del norte,* 16–17; Alcaraz, *Apuntes para la historia de la guerra,* 41–42.

23. *Campaña contra los Americanos del norte,* 12–14.

24. Arista was not aware that Taylor had entrenched most of his supply train at Palo Alto. It is not clear whether knowing this would have led him to modify his strategy.

25. Jauregui declaration, ASDN, XI/481/3320; Berlandier, "Itinerario," 16–17, Berlandier Papers–Yale; Alcaraz, *Apuntes para la historia de la guerra,* 42–43; Jean Luis Berlandier, "Mapa para las posiciones respectivas de las fuerzas beligerantes en la batalla de la Resaca del la Palma el 9 Mayo, 1846," Diario, Mayo 1846, ASDN, XI/481.3/3320; Berlandier Papers–LC, Ms. 17742. Some Mexican and all US troops apparently applied the name of the small pond "Charco de la Palma" to the entire resaca.

26. Arista to Ministro de Guerra y Marina, 9 May 1846 and 13 May 1846, in ASDN, XI/481.3/2174.

27. Arista to Ministro de Guerra y Marina, 10 May 1846, and Canales to Ministro de Guerra y Marina, [?] May 1846, both in ASDN, XI/481.3/2174.

28. Henry, *Campaign Sketches,* 96; Mills, Diary, 18–19, FHS; Barbour, *Journals,* 57–58; McCall to Alden, 5 June 1846, Alden Papers, USMA. Unless otherwise indicated, sources for the American perspective on the battle of the resaca are Taylor to Adjutant General, 17 May 1846; Twiggs to Taylor, 11 May 1846; Garland to Twiggs, 11 May 1846; Allen to Garland, 10 May 1846; Buchanan to Allen, 10 May 1846; Morris to Garland, 10 May 1846; Staniford to Twiggs, 10 May 1846; Ridgely to Taylor, 10 May 1846; May to McDonald, 10 May 1846; Belknap to Taylor, 15 May 1846; McCall to Taylor, 13 May 1846; and Smith to McCall, 13 May 1846, all in H.R. Doc. No. 29–209.

29. French, *Two Wars,* 51.

30. Twiggs to Bliss, 11 May 1846, in S. Doc. No. 29–388, at 13–16; Barbour, *Journals,* 58–59; Henry, *Campaign Sketches,* 97.

31. Taylor to Adjutant General, 17 May 1846, S. Doc. No. 29–388, at 6–9; C. F. Smith Diary, 9 May 1846, USMA; Longstreet, *From Manassas to Appomattox,* 26–27; Deas, "Reminiscences of the Campaign," 102–3; Grant, *Personal Memoirs,* 39–40.

32. Berlandier, "Itinerario," 18, Berlandier Papers–Yale.

33. Requena to Arista, 10 May 1846, cited in Martin Carrera to Ministro de Guerra y Marina, 25 May 1846, ASDN, XI/481.2174; Diario, Mayo 1846, ASDN, XI/481.3/3320.

34. Jauregui declaration, ASDN, XI/481.3/3320; Diario, Mayo 1846, ASDN, XI/481.3/3320; Alcaraz, *Apuntes para la historia de la guerra,* 44–46; Martin Carrera to Ministro de Guerra y Marina, 25 May 1846 and 29 May 1846; Arista to Ministro de Guerra y Marina, 9 May 1846 and 13 May 1846; and Ampudia to Ministro de Guerra y Marina, 14 May 1846, all in ASDN, XI/481.2174.

35. Jauregui declaration, ASDN, XI/481.3/3320; Alcaraz, *Apuntes para la historia de la guerra,* 45–46; Martin Carrera to Ministro de Guerra y Marina, 25 May 1846 and 29 May 1846, ASDN, XI/481.3/2174; Diario, Mayo 1846, ASDN, XI/481.3/3320; José López Uraga, *Sumaria mandada formar a pedimento de . . . José López Uraga* (México: Imprenta de J. R. Navarro, 1846); Arista to Ministro de Guerra y Marina, 9 May 1846 and 13 May 1846, and Ampudia to Ministro de Guerra y Marina, 14 May 1846, all in ASDN, XI/481.3/2174.

36. Berlandier, "Itinerario," Berlandier Papers–Yale, 18; Arista to Mejía, 9 May 1846, ASDN, XI/481.3/2174; Jauregui declaration, ASDN, XI/481.3/3320.

37. Berlandier, "Itinerario," Berlandier Papers–Yale, 19; Diario, Mayo 1846, ASDN, XI/481.3/3320; Canales declaration, ASDN, XI/481.3/3320.

38. Barbour, *Journals,* 58–59; George McCall to Peter McCall, 14 June 1846, in McCall, *Letters* 454–56; French, *Two Wars,* 52; Deas, "Reminiscences of the Campaign," 102.

39. French, *Two Wars,* 53; Longstreet, *From Manassas to Appomattox,* 24–25.

40. French, *Two Wars,* 53; Reeves, "Five Years an American Soldier," 445; Longstreet, *From Manassas to Appomattox,* 27.

41. May to Adjutant General, 10 May 1846, S. Doc. No. 29–388, at 21–22; Reeves, "Five Years an American Soldier," 445–46; anonymous account in New York Herald, 28 May 1846; *New Orleans Daily Picayune,* 5 June 1846.

42. Jauregui and Canales declarations, ASDN, XI/481.3/3320; Diario, Mayo 1846, ASDN, XI/481.3/3320; Arista to Ministro de Guerra y Marina, 9 May 1846, and Ampudia to Ministro de Guerra y Marina, both in ASDN, XI/481.2174; *Campaña contra los Americanos del norte,* 19–20.

43. Twiggs to Taylor, 11 May 1846; Taylor to Adjutant General, 17 May 1846; Garland to Twiggs, 11 May 1846; Allen to Garland, 11 May 1846; Buchanan to Allen, 11 May 1846; Morris to Garland, 10 May 1846; Staniford to Twiggs, 10 May 1846; Ridgely to Twiggs, 10 May 1846; McCall to Taylor, 13 May 1846; Smith to McCall, 13 May 1846; and Belknap to Taylor, 15 May 1846, all in S. Doc. No. 29–388.

44. Grant, *Personal Memoirs,* 39–40; George Wainwright to Aunt, n.d., in *Connecticut Courant,* 27 June 1846; *New Orleans Daily Picayune,* 5 June 1846.

45. McCall to Peter McCall, 14 June 1846, in McCall, *Letters;* Edmund Kirby-Smith to Mother, 13 May 1846, Kirby-Smith Papers, Southern Historical Collection, University of North Carolina (cited hereafter as Kirby-Smith Papers, UNC); Grant, *Personal Memoirs,* 39–40; Mills, Diary, 19, FHS; Alexander Hays to Mrs. R. E. Cochrane, 7 Aug. 1846, Cochrane Papers, UT.

46. May to Adjutant General, 10 May 1846, S. Doc. 29–388, at 21–22; Jauregui declaration, ASDN, XI/481.3/3320; Samuel French to Brother, 10 May 1846, in *Philadelphia Public Ledger,* 27 May 1846. Some of the most enduring images of the battle are the many lithographs and prints depicting May confronting Díaz de la Vega in the fight and taking his sword. The captain was later criticized by others in the US Army who accused him of stealing credit for capturing the Mexican general. It is true that May did not personally capture Díaz de la Vega, who was actually taken by infantry troops. Díaz then asked them for an officer to whom he could formally surrender his sword and soldiers, and his captors led him to May. May never directly stated that he had seized the general, and most of his

peers agreed that he had played a vital and heroic role in the events that led to the general's capture. See Reeves, "Five Years an American Soldier," 445; Deas, "Reminiscences of the Campaign," 102–3; and May to Adjutant General, 10 May 1846, all in S. Doc. No. 29–388.

47. Alcaraz, *Apuntes para la historia de la guerra,* 44–46; *Campaña contra los Americanos del norte,* 19–20; Diario, Mayo 1846, ASDN, XI/481.3/3320; Jauregui and Torrejón declarations, both in ASDN, XI/481.3/3320.

48. French, *Two Wars,* 54; Mills, Diary, 19, FHS; Kirby-Smith to Mother, 13 May 1846, Kirby-Smith Papers, UNC.

49. Smead to John Radcliff, 12 May 1846, Raphael Smead Archive, Lusher Collection, Austin, Texas; Barbour, *Journals,* 58–60.

50. Reeves, "*Five Years an American Soldier,*" 447; McCall to Alden, 5 June 1846, Alden Papers, USMA; Gouverneur Morris, Inventory of Captured Property, S. Doc. No. 29–388, at 11–13; Theodore Clancy to Father, 29 May 1846, Clancy Papers, FHS.

51. Robert Hazlitt to Sister, 14 May 1846, Hazlitt Papers, Ms. 1531, USMA; Meade, *Life and Letters,* 1:81; Styles Hawley to Clarinda B. Carpenter, 20 Aug. 1846, Maebius Collection, San Antonio.

52. Kirby-Smith to Mother, 13 May 1846, Kirby-Smith Papers, UNC; Dana, *Monterrey Is Ours,* 71; Henry, *Campaign Sketches,* 99; McCall to Alden, 5 June 1846, Alden Papers, USMA; *Philadelphia Public Ledger,* 4 June 1846.

53. Mejia to Arista, 10 May 1846, ASDN, XI/481.3/2174; Henshaw, *Recollections of the War,* 63.

54. Henshaw, *Recollections of the War,* 63; French, *Two Wars,* 54.

55. Whiting, *A Soldier's Life,* 78–79; Emily Van Dorn Miller, *A Soldier's Honor: With Reminiscences of Major-General Earl Van Dorn* (New York: Abbey Press, 1902), 23; *New Orleans Daily Picayune,* 21 May 1846.

56. Henshaw, *Recollections of the War,* 63; Robert N. Pruyn, "Campaigning through Mexico with 'Old Rough & Ready,'" *Civil War Illustrated,* Oct. 1963, 12; Whiting, *A Soldier's Life,* 77.

57. Henshaw, *Recollections of the War,* 63; Dana, *Monterrey Is Ours,* 62–63; *New Orleans Daily Picayune,* 21 May 1846.

58. *Niles' National Register,* 6 June 1846.

59. Dana, *Monterrey Is Ours,* 62–63, Henshaw, *Recollections of the War,* 65–66; Whiting, *A Soldier's Life,* 77–78.

60. Dana, *Monterrey Is Ours,* 62–63; Henshaw, *Recollections of the War,* 65–66; Hawkins to Bliss, 10 May 1846, in "Reports From General Taylor," H.R. Doc. No. 29–209, at 31–35.

61. Henshaw, *Recollections of the War,* 67; *New Orleans Daily Picayune,* 21 May 1846, 14; Pruyn, "Campaigning through Mexico,"14; Whiting, *A Soldier's Life,* 77–78.

62. Arista to Ministro de Guerra y Marina, 9 May 1846, ASDN, XI/481.3/2174.

63. Canales declaration, ASDN, XI/481.3/2174.

64. Diario, Mayo 1846, ASDN, XI/481.3/3320; Arista to Gen. Joaquín Morlet, 8 May 1846, CP, Ia19, LR–AO, RG94, NA, Alcaraz et al. Apuntes para la historia de la guerra 45–46.

65. Diario, Mayo 1846, ASDN, XI/481.3/3320; Jauregui declaration, ASDN, XI/481.3/3320; Alcaraz et al. Apuntes para la historia de la guerra, 45–46.

66. Diario, Mayo 1846, ASDN, XI/481.3/3320; Mejía to Arista, 9 May 1846, CP, Ib69, LR–AO, RG94, NA.

67. Jauregui declaration, Torrejón declaration, both in XI/481.3/2174/3320; Arista to Minister of War, 9 May 1846, ASDN, XI/481.3/2174; Alcaraz, *Apuntes para la historia de la guerra,* 46–47.

68. Alcaraz, *Apuntes para la historia de la guerra,* 46–47; Diario, Mayo 1846, ASDN, XI/481.3/3320; Arista to Ministro de Guerra y Marina, 9 May 1846, ASDN, XI/481.3/2174.

69. Requena to Arista, 11 May 1846, cited in Martin Carrera to Minister of War, 25 May 1846, ASDN, XI/481.3/2174.

70. Arista to Ministro de Guerra y Marina, 9 May 1846, ASDN, XI/481.3/2174; Arista to Commander General of Tampico, 9 May 1846, cited in Ysidro Reyes to Ministro de Guerra y Marina, 26 May 1846, ASDN, XI/481.3/2174.

CHAPTER 9

1. Berlandier, "Itinerario," Berlandier Papers–Yale.

2. Panfilo Barasorda, *Pedimentos presentados a la Exma. Primera Sala del Suprema Tribunal de la Guerra y Marina. . . .* (México: Imprenta de Lara, 1849), 24.

3. Arista to Ministro de Guerra y Marina, 13 May 1846, and "Relación de la artillería armas y municiones que existen en la almacenes de esta plaza," 13 May 1846, both in ASDN, XI/481.3/2174; Berlandier, "Itinerario," 114, Berlandier Papers–Yale.

4. Arista to Ministro de Guerra y Marina, 13 May 1846, ASDN, XI/481.3/2174.

5. Ibid.

6. Arista to Ministro de Guerra y Marina, 13 May 1846, XI/481.3/2174; Diario, Mayo 1846, ASDN, XI/481.3/3320; Jauregui declaration, ASDN, XI/481.3/3320.

7. *Campaña contra los Americanos del norte,* 23; Diario, Mayo 1846, ASDN, XI/481.3/3320; Alcaraz, *Apuntes para la historia de la guerra,* 46–47.

8. *Campaña contra los Americanos del norte,* 23–24; Jauregui declaration, ASDN, XI/481.3/3320; Diario, Mayo 1846, ASDN, XI/481.3/3320; Alcaraz, *Apuntes para la historia de la guerra,* 46–47.

9. *Campaña contra los Americanos del norte,* 23–24, Jauregui declaration, ASDN, XI/481.3/3320; Diario, Mayo 1846, ASDN, XI/481.3/3320; Alcaraz, *Apuntes para la historia de la guerra,* 47.

10. *Campaña contra los Americanos del norte,* 23–24; Jauregui declaration, ASDN, XI/481.3/3320; Diario, Mayo 1846, ASDN, XI/481.3/3320; Alcaraz, *Apuntes para la historia de la guerra,* 47; Roa Bárcena, *Recuerdos de la invasión norteamérica,* 85.

11. Samuel Gibbs French, *Two Wars,* 58.

12. Barna Upton to Nehamiah Upton, 14 May 1846, Upton Papers, Yale; Barbour, *Journals,* 61; Porter, "Medical and Surgical Notes," 20–22.

13. Report of the Secretary of War Showing the Names of the Officers and Men Killed, Wounded, or Missing, in the Battles of Palo Alto and Resaca de la Palma, S. Doc. No. 29–4 (2nd Sess., 1846); *Niles' National Register,* 18 July 1846; Jarvis, "An Army Surgeon's Notes," 41:101; Henry, *Campaign Sketches.*

14. *Campaña contra los Americanos del norte,* 24–27; Jauregui declaration, ASDN, XI/481.3/3320; Diario, Mayo 1846, ASDN, XI/481.3/3320; Mills, Diary, 18, FHS; Jarvis, "An Army Surgeon's Notes," 41:101.

15. *Campaña contra los Americanos del norte,* 26–27; Jarvis, "An Army Surgeon's Notes," 41:101. In another version of the event, it was reported that General Díaz de la Vega refused to accept parole because the Mexican government would force him to violate it and compel him to take up arms when he returned to Matamoros. See Thorpe, *Our Army on the Rio Grande,* 114.

16. Henry, *Campaign Sketches,* 103; Kirby-Smith, *To Mexico with Scott,* 53; Mills, Diary, 18–19, FHS.

17. Quote is in Whiting, *A Soldier's Life,* 78; Henry, *Campaign Sketches,* 103.

18. Raphael Smead to Sarah Smead, 11 May 1846, Smead Archive, Lusher Collection, Austin; Meade, *Life and Letters,* 1:82; Taylor to Adjutant General, 12 May 1846, H.R. Doc. No. 30–60, at 297.

19. Barbour, *Journals,* 60 61.

20. Grant, *Personal Memoirs,* 41; Thorpe, *Our Army on the Rio Grande,* 115–16; Taylor to Adjutant General, 12 May 1846 and 18 May 1846, in H.R. Doc. No. 30–60, at 698; Bauer, *The Mexican War,* 81–82; Niles National Register, 16 May 1846, 13 June 1846.

21. General Order No. 60, 12 May 1846, GO–AO, RG94, NA; Maj. Charles Thomas to Gen. Thomas Jesup, 15 May 1846 and 18 May 1846, and Taylor to Jesup, 18 May 1846, all in H.R. Doc. No. 30–60, at 698; Frost, *A Pictorial History of Mexico,* 247–48.

22. Maj. Charles Thomas to Gen. Thomas Jesup, 15 May 1846 and 18 May 1846, and Taylor to Jesup, 18 May 1846, all in H.R. Doc. No. 30–60, at 698; W. W. Bliss, Special Order No. 64, Special Orders, AO, RG94, NA; Frost, *A Pictorial History of Mexico,* 247–48; John M. Ellicott, *The Life of John Ancrum Winslow* (New York: G. P. Putnam's Sons, 1905), 30; Thorpe, *Our Army on the Rio Grande,* 121–22; Van R. Baker, ed., *The Websters: Letters of an American Family in Peace and War, 1836–1853* (Kent, Ohio: Kent State University Press, 2000), 72.

23. Meade, *Life and Letters,* 1:82.

24. Taylor to Adjutant General, 18 May 1846, H.R. Doc. No. 30–60, at 297–98; Maj. Charles Thomas to Lt. Col. T. F. Hunt, 18 May 1846, H.R. Doc. No. 30–60, at 653; Barbour, *Journals,* 61–62.

25. Taylor, General Order No. 62, 17 May 1846, GO–AO, RG94, NA; Taylor to Adjutant General, 18 May 1846, H.R. Doc. No. 30–60, at 297–98; Barbour, *Journals,* 64; Thorpe, *Our Army on the Rio Grande,* 122–23.

26. Arista to Ministro de Guerra y Marina, 10 May 1846, ASDN, XI/481.3/2174; Jauregui declaration, both in ASDN, XI/481.3/3320.

27. Arista to Ministro de Guerra y Marina, 10 May 1846, ASDN, XI/481.3/2174.

28. Antonio Parrodi to Ministro de Guerra y Marina, 19 May 1846, ASDN, XI/481.3/2174.

29. Jauregui declaration, ASDN, XI/481.3/3320; Diario, Mayo 1846, ASDN, XI/481.3/3320; Antonio Parrodi to Ministro de Guerra y Marina, 19 May 1846, ASDN, XI/481.3/2174.

30. Arista to Ministro de Guerra y Marina, 13 May 1846, ASDN, XI/481.3/2174; Jauregui declaration, ASDN, XI/481.3/3320; Diario, Mayo 1846, ASDN, XI/481.3/3320; *Campaña contra los Americanos del norte,* 23–25.

31. Ministro de Guerra y Marina to General en Jefe, Ejército del Norte, 15 May 1846, ASDN, XI/481.3/2174.

32. Juan Álvarez to Ministro de Guerra y Marina, 30 May 1846; Gerónimo Cardona to Ministro de Guerra y Marina, 9 June 1846; Comandante General, Departamento de Durango to Ministro de Guerra y Marina, 29 May 1846; and Antonio Parrodi to Ministro de Guerra y Marina, 19 May 1846, all in ASDN, XI/481.3/2174.

33. *Campaña contra los Americanos del norte,* 26–27; Jauregui declaration, ASDN, XI/481.3/3320; Antonio Parrodi to Ministro de Guerra y Marina, 19 May 1846, ASDN, XI/481.3/2174.

34. *Campaña contra los Americanos del norte,* 26–27; Jauregui declaration, ASDN, XI/481.3/3320; Antonio Parrodi to Ministro de Guerra y Marina, 19 May 1846, ASDN, XI/481.3/2174.

35. *Campaña contra los Americanos del norte,* 26–27; Jauregui declaration, XI/481.3/3320; Diario, Mayo 1846, ASDN, XI/481.3/3320; Antonio Parrodi to Ministro de Guerra y Marina, 19 May 1846, ASDN, XI/481.3/2174.

36. *Campaña contra los Americanos del norte,* 26–27; Jauregui declaration, and Antonio Parrodi to Ministro de Guerra y Marina, 19 May 1846, both in ASDN, XI/481.3/2174.

37. *Campaña contra los Americanos del norte,* 26–27; Jauregui declaration, ASDN, XI/481.3/2174. Several officers later denied supporting the withdrawal and attempted to pin the decision solely on Arista; see Barasorda, *Pedimentos,* 24–26.

38. *Campaña contra los Americanos del norte,* 26–27; Jauregui declaration, ASDN, XI/481.3/3320, and Antonio Parrodi to Ministro de Guerra y Marina, 19 May 1846, both in ASDN, XI/481.3/2174; Berlandier, "Itinerario," 238–40, Berlandier Papers–Yale.

39. Berlandier, "Itinerario," 238–40, Berlandier Papers–Yale; Diario, Mayo 1846, ASDN, XI/481.3/3320; *Campaña contra los Americanos del norte,* 25–26; Jauregui declaration, ASDN, XI/481.3/3320.

40. Berlandier, "Itinerario," 238–40, Berlandier Papers–Yale; *Campaña contra los Americanos del norte,* 25–26; Diario, Mayo 1846, ASDN, XI/481.3/3320; Jauregui declaration, ASDN, XI/481.3/3320.

41. There is some confusion over the number of artillery pieces left behind. Jean Louis Berlandier places the number at two, while *Campaña contra los Americanos del norte* reports three, and Jauregui recalls four. See Berlandier, "Itinerario," 240, Berlandier Papers–Yale; *Campaña contra los Americanos del norte,* 26; Diario, Mayo 1846, ASDN, XI/481.3/3320; Jauregui declaration, ASDN, XI/481.3/3320.

42. Diario, Mayo 1846, ASDN, XI/481.3/3320; Berlandier, "Itinerario," Berlandier Papers–Yale, 239–41.

43. Diario, Mayo 1846, ASDN, XI/481.3/3320.

44. Jarvis, "An Army Surgeon's Notes," 41:102; Barbour, *Journals,* 64; Henry, *Campaign Sketches,* 109; Meade, *Life and Letters,* 1:85–86.

45. Taylor to Dr. R. C. Wood, 19 May 1846, in Zachary Taylor, *Letters of Zachary Taylor from the Battle-fields of the Mexican War,* ed. William K. Bixby (Rochester, NY: Genesee Press, 1908), 3–5; Taylor to Secretary of War, 18 May 1846, H.R. Doc. No. 30–60, at 298.

46. Barbour, *Journals,* 64; Henry, *Campaign Sketches,* 109.

47. Henry, *Campaign Sketches,* 109; Barbour, *Journals,* 64–65; Smith, *To Mexico with Scott,* 54–55.

48. Mills, Diary, 18–19, FHS; French, *Two Wars,* 58–59; Barbour, *Journals,* 65–66; Henry, *Campaign Sketches,* 109–10; Smith, *To Mexico with Scott,* 54.

49. Henry, *Campaign Sketches,* 109; Deas, "Reminiscences of the Campaign," 102; Dana, *Monterrey Is Ours,* 79.

50. Taylor to Adjutant General, 24 May 1846, H.R. Doc. No. 30–60, at 301; Meade to Wife, 24 May 1846, in Meade, *Life and Letters,* 1:88–89; Dana, *Monterrey Is Ours,* 80–81; Henry, *Campaign Sketches,* 113–14.

51. Meade to Wife, 24 May 1846, in Meade, *Life and Letters,* 1:88–89.

52. *Campaña contra los Americanos del norte,* 31–32; Jauregui declaration, ASDN, XI/481.3/3320; Diario, Mayo 1846, ASDN, XI/481.3/3320; Alcaraz, *Apuntes para la historia de la guerra,* 47–48.

53. *Campaña contra los Americanos del norte,* 31–32; Jauregui declaration, ASDN, XI/481.3/3320; Diario, Mayo 1846, ASDN, XI/481.3/3320; Alcaraz, *Apuntes para la historia de la guerra,* 47–48.

54. *Campaña contra los Americanos del norte,* 31–32; Jauregui declaration, ASDN, XI/481.3/3320; Diario, Mayo 1846, ASDN, XI/481.3/3320; Alcaraz, *Apuntes para la historia de la guerra,* 47–48.

55. Campaña contra los Americanos, 32–33; Diario, Mayo 1846, ASDN, XI/481.3/3320; Jauregui declaration, ASDN, XI/481.3/3320; Alcaraz, *Apuntes para la historia de la guerra,* 47–49.

56. *Campaña contra los Americanos del norte,* 32–33; Jauregui declaration, ASDN, XI/481.3/3320; Diario, Mayo 1846, ASDN, XI/481.3/3320; Arista to Ministro de Guerra y Marina, 25 May 1846, both in ASDN, XI/481.3/2174.

57. *Campaña contra los Americanos del norte,* 33; Alcaraz, *Apuntes para la historia de la guerra,* 47–49; Diario, Mayo 1846, ASDN, XI/481.3/3320; Jauregui declaration, ASDN, XI/481.3/3320; Mejía to Ministro de Guerra y Marina, 9 July 1846, ASDN, XI/481.3/2174.

58. *Campaña contra los Americanos del norte,* 33; Alcaraz, *Apuntes para la historia de la guerra,* 47–49; Diario, Mayo 1846, ASDN, XI/481.3/3320; Jauregui declaration, ASDN, XI/481.3/3320; Arista to Ministro de Guerra y Marina, 25 May 1846, both in ASDN, XI/481.3/2174.

59. *Campaña contra los Americanos del norte,* 34–35; Jauregui declaration, ASDN, XI/481.3/3320; Alcaraz, *Apuntes para la historia de la guerra,* 47–49; Raphael Smead to Sarah Smead, 1 June 1846, Smead Archives, Lusher Collection, Austin.

EPILOGUE

1. *New Orleans Daily Picayune,* 18 May 1846; *New Orleans Commercial Bulletin,* 18 May 1846; *New Orleans Bee,* 18 May 1846; *New Orleans Daily Tropic,* 19 May 1846.

2. *New York Courier,* cited in *Charleston Mercury,* 5 June 1846; *Philadelphia Public Ledger,* 4 June 1846.

3. For details of the reaction of popular culture to the battles, see Johannsen, *To the Halls of the Montezumas.*

4. *Cincinnati Catholic Messenger,* 23 May 1846.

5. Henry, *Campaign Sketches,* 112.

6. Henry, *Campaign Sketches,* 112; Dana, *Monterrey Is Ours,* 69; Raphael Smead to John Radcliff, 12 May 1846, Raphael Smead Archives, Lusher Collection, Austin.

7. Dana, *Monterrey Is Ours,* 69–70; *Richmond Enquirer,* 12 May 1846; Charles J. Peterson, *Military Heroes of the War with Mexico* (Philadelpha: W. A. Leary, 1848), 179; Henry, *Campaign Sketches,* 112.

8. Robert Hazlitt to Mary Hazlitt, 14 May 1846, Hazlitt Papers, USMA; Grant, *Personal Memoirs,* 40; Meade, *Life and Letters,* 1:85.

9. Mejia to Ministro de Guerra y Marina, 13 June 1846, 25 May 1846, and 29 May 1846, all in ASDN XI/481.3 /2178.

10. Arista to Governor of Nuevo León, 4 June 1846; "El general Arista a las tropas de la división del Norte," 4 June 1846, in *Monitor republicano,* 27 June 1846.

11. Arista to Minister of War, 12 July 1846, ASDN, XI/481.3 /2174.

12. *Campaña contra los Americanos del norte,* 36–37; Alcaraz, *Apuntes para la historia de la guerra,* 50–51.

13. "Honor Nacional," *Monitor republicano,* 23 May 1845.

14. Manuel Maria Lombardini, "El comandante general de este departmento a las tropas de su mando," Broadside, Jenkins Garrett Collection, Special Collections Library, University of Texas at Arlington.

15. Mejia to Ministro de Guerra y Marina, 13 June 1846, XI/481.3 /2178.

BIBLIOGRAPHY

This bibliography includes only documents and publications that substantially informed or were directly cited in my research. The listed sources provide the foundation for my understanding of the first campaign of the US-Mexican War, but they in no way represent a comprehensive list of primary or secondary materials on the subject.

OFFICIAL ARCHIVAL DOCUMENTS—MEXICO

Archivos Generales del Estado de Nuevo León, Monterrey, N.L.
  Fondo Militar
Archivo Histórico Genaro Estrada de la Secretaría de Relaciones Exteriores, Mexico City
  Archivo de la Embajada de México en los Estados Unidos de America, 1805-1925
Archivos Históricos de la Secretaría de la Defensa Nacional, Mexico City
  Clasificación XI/111: Plana mayor
    Expedientes 1-21, 1-65, 1-113, 1-221, 2-120, 2-478, 2-724
  Clasificación XI/481.3: Operaciones militares
    Expedientes 2061–64, 2066–70, 2074, 2147, 2173–78, 3320

OFFICIAL ARCHIVAL DOCUMENTS—UNITED STATES

US National Archives, Washington, D.C.
  Army of Occupation, Record Group 94
    Letters Received
    General Orders
    Special Orders
  Office of the Adjutant General, Record Group 94
    Letters Received
    Letters Sent
  Records of the Office of the Chief of Engineers, Record Group 77
    Letters Received
  Records of the Office of the Judge Advocate General, Record Group 153
    Courts-Martial Proceedings

ARCHIVED PERSONAL ACCOUNTS

Abraham Lincoln Presidential Library, Springfield, IL
  Christopher Columbus Augur Papers
  John Porter Hatch Papers
Duke University, Rare Books and Special Collections Library
  William A. Gordon Papers
  Edmund Schriver Papers
Filson Historical Society, Louisville, KY
  Richard M. Creagh Letters
  William H. Daniel Military Diary

Madison Mills Diary
Sperry-Gathright Papers 1846
Theodore Clancy letter
Harvard University, Houghton Library
Jenks Beaman Papers
Library of Congress, Washington, DC
Calvin Benjamin Papers
Berlandier Papers
Dyer Collection
Charles Ferguson Smith Papers
John Porter Hatch Papers
Louisiana State University Libraries, Louisiana and Lower Mississippi Valley Collections, Baton Rouge, LA
Isaac H. Charles Collection
Lusher Collection, Austin, TX
Raphael Smead Archives
Maebius Collection, San Antonio, TX
Styles Hawley Letters
Massachusetts Historical Society, Boston
John Henshaw Papers
New-York Historical Society
Mexican War Muster Rolls and Orders, 1845-1846
Princeton University Library
James Wood Papers
Southwestern University, Special Collections, Georgetown, TX
Zenas Matthews Diary
US Military Academy Library, Special Collections, West Point
Bradford Alden Papers
Charles Ferguson Smith Papers
James Duncan Papers
Robert Hazlitt Papers
George McCall Papers
US Army Military History Institute, Carlisle, PA, Mexican War Miscellaneous Collection
Isaac Bowen Papers
William Brooks Papers
Charles Masland Papers
University of Georgia, Hargrett Rare Book and Manuscript Library
Nathaniel Wyche Hunter Papers
University of Michigan, Manuscripts Division, William Clements Library
George William Taylor Papers
University of North Carolina at Chapel Hill, Louis Round Wilson Special Collections Library, Southern Historical Collection
Edmund Kirby-Smith Papers
University of Texas at Arlington, Special Collections Library,
Jenkins Garrett Collection
Broadside Collection

University of Texas at Austin, Dolph Briscoe Center for American History
- Richard Cochrane Papers
- William Droddy Diary
- J. A. Hendricks Papers
- Kuykendall Family Papers

Yale University, Beinecke Library
- Barna Upton Papers
- Berlandier Papers
- Edmund Kirby-Smith Letter
- John Nixon Letter

CONGRESSIONAL SOURCES

Cong. Globe, 29th Cong., 1st Sess., 7 (1846), 920.

Correspondence Between the Secretary of War and Generals Scott and Taylor, and Between General Scott and Mr. Trist. H.R. Doc. No. 29-56, 1st Sess., 1848.

"Map of the Country Adjacent to the Left Bank of the Rio Grande Below Matamoros." S. Doc. No. 31-65, 1st. Sess., 1847.

Message of the President of the United States Relative to the Invasion and Commencement of Hostilities By Mexico. H.R. Doc. No. 29-196, 1st Sess., 1846.

Message of the President of the United States Relative to the Operations and Recent Engagements on the Mexican Frontier. S. Doc. No. 29-388, 1st Sess., 1846.

Messages of the President of the United States with the Correspondence Therewith Communicated Between the Secretary of War and Other Officers of the Government on the Subject of the Mexican War. H.R. Doc. No. 30-60, 1st Sess., 1848.

Report of the Secretary of War Showing the Names of the Officers and Men Killed, Wounded, or Missing, in the Battles of Palo Alto and Resaca de la Palma. S. Doc. No. 29-4, 2nd Sess., 1846.

Report on the United States and Mexican Boundary Survey. H.R. Doc. No. 34-135 1st Sess., 1857.

NEWSPAPERS

El amigo del pueblo (Mexico City)
Charleston (SC) Mercury
Cincinnati Catholic Messenger
Cincinnati Gazette
Eco del norte de Tamaulipas (Matamoros, Tamaulipas)
El diario de gobierno (Mexico City)
El monitor constitucional (Mexico City)
El monitor republicano (Mexico City)
La gaceta del gobierno de Tamaulipas (Victoria)
New Orleans Bee
New Orleans Commercial Bulletin
New Orleans Daily Crescent
New Orleans Picayune
New York Courier
Niles' National Register, Baltimore
Philadelphia Public Ledger
Richmond Enquirer

Richmond Whig
Seminario político del gobierno de Nuevo León (Monterrey)
El tiempo (Mexico City)
Times (London)

PUBLISHED ACCOUNTS AND SECONDARY SOURCES

Alcaraz, Ramón, et al. *Apuntes para la historia de la guerra entre México y los Estados Unidos*. México: Tipografía de Manuel Payno, 1848.

Alonzo, Armando C. *Tejano Legacy: Rancheros and Settlers in South Texas, 1734–1900*. Albuquerque: University of New Mexico Press, 1998.

Alvear Acevedo, Carlos. *La guerra del 47*. México: Editorial Jus, 1969.

Amberson, Mary Margaret McAllen, et al. *I Would Rather Sleep in Texas: A History of the Lower Rio Grande Valley and the People of the Santa Anita Land Grant*. Austin: Texas State Historical Association, 2003.

Ampudia, Pedro de. *El ciudadano general Pedro de Ampudia ante el tribunal respetable de la opinión publica*. San Luis Potosí: n.p., 1846.

Baker, Van R. (ed.) The *Websters: Letters of an American Family in Peace and War, 1836–1853* (Kent, Ohio: Kent State University Press, 2000).

Balbontín, Manuel. *Estado militar de la Republica Mexicana en 1846*. México: Tipo de Ignacio Pombo, 1891.

Ballentine, George. *The Mexican War, by an English Soldier: Comprising Incidents and Adventures in the United States and Mexico with the American Army*. New York: W. A. Townsend, 1860.

Barasorda, Pánfilo. *Pedimentos presentados a la Exma. Primera Sala del Suprema Tribunal de la Guerra y Marina en la causa formada al E. Sr. Gral. Don Mariano Arista*. México: Imprenta de Lara,1849.

Barbour, Philip N. J*ournals of the Late Brevet Major Philip Norbourne Barbour . . . and His Wife, Martha Isabella Hopkins Barbour: Written during the War With Mexico—1846*. Edited by Rhoda van Bibber Tanner Doubleday. New York: G. P. Putnam's Sons, 1936.

Bauer, K. Jack. "The Battles on the Rio Grande: Palo Alto and Resaca de la Palma, 8–9 May 1846." In Heller and Stoffit.

———. *The Mexican War, 1846–1848*. Lincoln: University of Nebraska Press, 1974.

Berlandier, Jean Louis. *Journey to Mexico during the Years 1826 to 1834*. Translated by Sheila M. Ohlendorf et al. Austin: Texas State Historical Association, 1980.

Bishop, Farnham. *Our First War with Mexico*. New York: Charles Scribner's Sons, 1916.

Brack, Gene M. *Mexico Views Manifest Destiny, 1821–1846: An Essay on the Origins of the Mexican War*. Albuquerque: University of New Mexico Press, 1975.

Brooks, Nathan Covington. *A Complete History of the Mexican War: Its Causes, Conduct, and Consequences*. Philadelphia: Grigg, Elliot, 1849.

Bustamante, Carlos María. *El nuevo Bernal Díaz del Castillo, o sea, Historia de la invasión de los Anglo-Americanos en Mexico*. Mexico: Imprenta de V. García Torres, 1847.

Campaña contra los Americanos del norte. México: Imprenta de Ignacio Cumplido, 1846.

Carpenter, William W. *Travels and Adventures in Mexico*. New York: Harper & Brothers, 1851.

Carreño, Alberto María. *Jefes del ejército Mexicano en 1847: Biográfias de generals de división y de coronels del ejército Méxicano por fines del año de 1847*. México: Imprenta y Fototipia de la Secretaría de Fomento, 1914.

Chance, Joseph E. *José María de Jesús Carvajal: The Life and Times of a Mexican Revolutionary*. San Antonio: Trinity University Press, 2006.

Clary, David. *Eagles and Empire*. New York: Bantam, 2009.

Coffman, Edward M. *The Old Army: A Portrait of the American Army in Peacetime, 1784–1898.* New York: Oxford University Press, 1988.

Contestaciones habidas entre los exmos. señores generales de división, D. Mariano Paredes y Arrillaga, D. Mariano Arista y el supremo gobierno. . . . San Luis Potosí: V. Carrillo, 1845.

Cook, Scott. *Mexican Brick Culture in the Building of Texas, 1800s–1980s.* College Station: Texas A&M University Press, 1998.

Cotner, Thomas Ewing. *The Military and Political Career of José Joaquín de Herrera.* Austin: University of Texas Press, 1949.

Crimmins, M. L. "The 2nd United States Dragoons in Texas." *Frontier Times* 15, no. 3 (December 1937): 127–31.

Dana, Napoleon Jackson Tecumseh. *Monterrey Is Ours: The Mexican War Letters of Lieutenant Dana, 1845–1847.* Edited by Robert H. Ferrell. Lexington: University of Kentucky Press, 1990.

De Vega, Mercedes and María Cecilia Zuleta, eds. *Testimonios de una guerra: México 1846–1848.* 2 vols. México, DF: Secretaría de Relaciones Exteriores, 2001.

Deas, George. "Reminiscences of the Campaign on the Rio Grande." *Historical Magazine and Notes and Queries Concerning the Antiquities, History, and Biography of America* 7 (January–May 1870).

DeLay, Brian. *War of a Thousand Deserts: Indian Raids and the US-Mexican War.* New Haven, CT: Yale University Press, 2008.

DePalo, William, Jr. *The Mexican National Army.* College Station: Texas A&M University Press, 1997.

DeVoto, Bernard. *Year of Decision, 1846.* Boston: Houghton Mifflin, 1942.

Donnavan, C. *Adventures in Mexico.* Cincinnati: Robinson and Jones, 1847.

Duval, John C. *The Adventures of Big Foot Wallace: Texas Ranger and Hunter.* Macon, Georgia: J. W. Burke, 1870.

Edwards, Frank. *A Campaign in New Mexico with Colonel Doniphan.* Philadelphia: Care and Hart, 1847.

Eisenhower, John S. D. *So Far from God: The US War with Mexico, 1846–1848.* New York: Doubleday, 1989.

Ellicott, John M. *The Life of John Ancrum Winslow.* New York: G. P. Putnam's Sons, 1905.

Estado militar de la Republica Mexicana en 1846. México: Tipo de Ignacio Pombo, 1891.

Fallo definitivo del Supremo Tribunal de la Guerra, al examinar la conducta militar del Exmo. Sr. General D. Mariano Arista, en los acciones de guerra que sostuvo al principio de la invasión americana. México: Imprenta de Vicente García Torres, á cargo de Luis Vidaurri, 1850.

Fleming, Thornton, ed. *Life and Letters of Alexander Hays.* Pittsburgh: n.p., 1913.

French, Samuel Gibbs. *Two Wars: An Autobiography of General Samuel G. French.* Nashville, TN: Confederate Veteran, 1901.

Frías, Heriberto. *Episodios militares mexicanos.* México, DF: Vda de C. Bouret, 1901.

Frost, John. *The Mexican War and Its Warriors.* New Haven: H. Mansfield, 1848.

———. *A Pictorial History of Mexico and the Mexican War.* Philadelphia: Charles Desilver, 1848.

García Cantú, Gastón. *Las invasiones norteamericanas en México.* México: Ediciones Era, 1974.

Giddings, Luther. *Sketches of the Campaign in Northern Mexico.* New York: George P. Putnam, 1853.

Grant, Ulysses S. *Personal Memoirs of U. S. Grant.* New York: C. L. Webster, 1885.

———. *Ulysses S. Grant: Memoirs and Selected Letters.* Edited by Mary Drake and William S. McFeely. New York: Library of America, 1990.

Greenberg, Amy S. *A Wicked War: Polk, Clay, Lincoln, and the 1846 US Invasion of Mexico.* New York: Knopf, 2012.

Grubar, Robert H. "The Cross, Porter and Thornton Episodes: America›s Inauspicious Entry into the Mexican War." *Military History of Texas and the Southwest* 12, no. 3 (1974): 185–202.

Haecker, Charles M., and Jeffrey G. Mauck. *On the Prairie of Palo Alto: Historical Archaeology of the US-Mexican War Battlefield.* College Station: Texas A&M University Press, 1997.

Haecker, Charles. *A Thunder of Cannon: Archeology of the Mexican-American War Battlefield of Palo Alto.* Santa Fe: National Park Service, Southwest Regional Office, 1994.

Haynes, Sam W. *Soldiers of Misfortune: The Somervell and Mier Expeditions.* Austin: University of Texas Press, 1997.

Hefter, Joseph et al. *El Soldado mexicano: organización, vestuario, equipo, 1837–1847.* México: Documentos Histórico-Militares, 1958.

Heller, Charles E., and William A. Stofft, eds. *America's First Battles, 1776–1965.* Lawrence: University of Kansas Press, 1986.

Henderson, Timothy. *A Glorious Defeat: Mexico and Its War with the United States.* New York: Hill and Wang, 2007.

Henry, Robert Selph. *The Story of the Mexican War.* New York: DaCapo Press, 1950.

Henry, William S. *Campaign Sketches of the War with Mexico.* New York: Harper and Brothers, 1847.

Henshaw, John Corey. *Recollections of the War with Mexico.* Edited by Gary F. Kurutz. Columbia: University of Missouri Press, 2008.

Herrera Serna, Laura, ed. *México en guerra, 1846–1848: Perspectivas regionales.* México, DF: Consejo Nacional para la Cultura y las Artes, 1997.

Hill, Daniel Harvey. *A Fighter from Way Back: The Mexican War Diary of Lt. Daniel Harvey Hill, 4th Artillery, USA.* Edited by Timothy D. Johnson. Kent, Ohio: Kent State University Press, 2002.

"History in Tabloid." *FRA Magazine: A Journal of Affirmation,* January–September 1915.

Hitchcock, Ethan Allen. *Fifty Years in Camp and Field: Diary of Major General Ethan Allen Hitchcock.* Edited by E. A. Croffut. New York: G. P. Putnam's Sons, 1909.

Jarvis, Nathan Sturgis. "*An Army Surgeon's Notes of Frontier Service—Mexican War.*" *Journal of the Military Service Institution of the United States* 40 (May1907): 435–52, 41 (June 1907): 90–105.

Johannsen, Robert W. *To the Halls of the Montezumas: The Mexican War in the American Imagination.* New York: Oxford University Press, 1985.

Kearney, Milo and Anthony Knopp. *Boom and Bust: The Historical Cycles of Matamoros and Brownsville.* Austin: Eakin Press, 1991.

Kenley, John R. *Memoirs of a Maryland Volunteer in the War With Mexico.* Philadelphia: J. B. Lippincott, 1873.

Kessell, John L. *Spain in the Southwest.* Norman: University of Oklahoma Press, 2002.

Kirby-Smith, Ephraim. *To Mexico with Scott: Letters of Captain E. Kirby-Smith to His Wife.* Edited by Emma Jerome Blackwood. Cambridge: Harvard University Press, 1917.

Lee, Arthur Tracey. *Army Ballads, and Other Poems.* N.p.: n.p., 1871.

Levin Rojo, Danna A., and Martha Ortega, coordinadora. *El territorio disputado en la guerra de 1846–1848.* México, DF: Porrúa, 2007.

Lewis, Felice Flanery. *Trailing Clouds of Glory: Zachary Taylor's Mexican War Campaign and His Emerging Civil War Leaders. Tuscaloosa: University of Alabama Press, 2010.*

Longstreet, James. *From Manassas to Appomattox: Memoirs of the Civil War in America.* Philadelphia: J. P Lippincott, 1895.

Love, Thomas Nealy. *A Southern Lacrimosa: The Mexican War Journal of Dr. Thomas Neely Love, Surgeon, Second Regiment Mississippi Infantry, USA.* Edited by H. Grady Howell. Jackson, MS: Chickasaw Bayou, 1995.

Martínez Caraza, Leopoldo. *La intervención norteamericana en México, 1846–1848.* México, DF: Panorama, 1981.

Mayer, Brantz. *History of the War between Mexico and the United States: With a Preliminary View of Its Origins.* New York: Wiley and Putnum, 1848.

McCall, George A. *Letters from the Frontiers.* Philadelphia: Lippincott, 1868.

McCampbell, Coleman. "Zachary Taylor's Encampment at Corpus Christi." *Frontier Times* 11, no. 7 (April 1934), 281–86.

Meade, George G. *The Life and Letters of George Gordon Meade.* 2 vols. New York: Charles Scribner's Sons, 1913.

Merk, Frederick. *Manifest Destiny and Mission in American History.* New York: Vintage, 1966.

———. *The Monroe Doctrine and American Expansionism, 1843–1849.* New York: Alfred Knopf, 1966.

Merry, Robert W. *A Country of Vast Design: James K. Polk, the Mexican War and the Conquest of the American Continent.* New York: Simon and Schuster, 2009.

Mier y Terán, Manuel de. *Texas by Terán: The Diary Kept by General Manuel de Mier y Terán on his 1828 Inspection of Texas.* Translated by John Wheat. Edited by Jack Jackson. Austin: University of Texas Press, 2000.

Miller, Emily Van Dorn. *A Soldier's Honor: With Reminiscences of Major-General Earl Van Dorn.* New York: Abbey, 1902.

Morison, Samuel Eliot et al. *Dissent in Three American Wars.* Cambridge: Harvard University Press, 1970.

Morton, Ohland. *Terán and Texas: A Chapter in Texas-Mexican Relations.* Austin: Texas State Historical Association, 1948.

Nance, Joseph Milton. *After San Jacinto: The Texas-Mexican Frontier, 1836–1841.* Austin: University of Texas Press, 1963.

Negrete, Emilio Castillo. *Invasión de los norte-americanos en México.* México, Imprenta del editor, 1890–91.

Nobles, Gregory H. *American Frontiers: Cultural Encounters and Continental Conquest.* New York: Hill and Wang, 1997.

Pahissa, Ángela Moyano. *La pérdida de Tejas.* México, DF: Planeta, 1999.

Paredes y Arrillaga, Mariano. *Manifiesto del Exmo. Sr. Presidente Interino de la República Mexicana.* México, DF: Imprenta del Águila, 1846.

Patch, Joseph Dorst. *The Concentration of General Zachary Taylor's Army at Corpus Christi, Texas.* Corpus Christi: Mission Printing, 1962.

Payne, Darwin. "Camp Life of the Army of Occupation: Corpus Christi, July 1845 to March 1846." *Southwestern Historical Quarterly* 73, no. 3 (1970), 326–42.

Payno, Manuel. *El puerto de Matamoros en 1844.* Edited by Vargas Rea. México: Biblioteca de Historiadores Mexicanos, 1951.

Paz, Eduardo. *La invasión norte americana en 1846: ensayo de historia patria-militar por el mayor de caballería.* Mexico: C. Paz, 1889.

Peck, John. *The Sign of the Eagle: A View of Mexico, 1830–1855.* Edited by Richard F. Pourade. San Diego: Union-Tribune, 1970

Peterson, Charles J. *Military Heroes of the War with Mexico.* Philadelphia: W. A. Leary, 1848.

Pierce, Frank C. *A Brief History of the Rio Grande Valley.* Menasha, WI: George Banta, 1917.

Pletcher, David. *The Diplomacy of Annexation: Texas, Oregon, and the Mexican War.* Columbia: University of Missouri Press, 1973.

Polk, James K. *The Diary of James K. Polk during His Presidency, 1845–1849. Edited by* Milo Milton Quaife. 2 vols. Chicago: A. C. McClurg, 1910.

Porter, John B. "Medical and Surgical Notes of Campaigns in the War with Mexico during the years 1845, 1846, 1847, and 1848." *American Journal of the Medical Sciences* 23 (January 1852): 13–37; 24 (July 1852): 13–30; 25 (January 1853): 25–42; 26 (October 1853): 297–333; 35 (April 1858): 347–52.

Price, Glen W. *Origins of the War with Mexico: The Polk-Stockton Intrigue.* Austin: University of Texas Press, 1967.

Prucha, Francis Paul. *The Sword of the Republic: The United States Army on the Frontier, 1783–1846.* New York: McMillan, 1969.

Pruyn, Robert N. "Campaigning through Mexico with 'Old Rough & Ready.'" *Civil War Illustrated,* Oct. 1963, 10–15.

Ramírez, José Fernando. *México durante su guerra con los Estados Unidos*, México, DF: Vda de C. Bouret, 1905.

Reeves, C. M. "Five Years an American Soldier," in *Adventures and Achievements of Americans.* Edited by Henry Howe. Cincinnati: Henry Howe, 1859, 429–484.

Reeves, Jesse Siddall. *American Diplomacy Under Tyler and Polk.* Baltimore: Johns Hopkins Press, 1907.

Richardson, James D., ed. *A Compilation of the Messages and Papers of the Presidents.* Washington, DC: Bureau of National Literature and Art, 1910.

Rickels, Milton. *Thomas Bangs Thorpe: Humorist of the Old Southwest.* Baton Rouge: Louisiana State University Press, 1962.

Ridout, Joseph Benjamin. "An Anti-National Disorder: Antonio Canales and Northeastern Mexico, 1846–1852." Master's thesis, University of Texas at Austin, 1994.

Ripley, R. S. *The War with Mexico.* New York: Harper, 1849.

Roa Bárcena, José María. *Recuerdos de la invasión Norteamérica.* México: Edición de la Librería Madrileña de Juan Buxó, 1883.

Robertson, Frank D. "The Military and Political Career of Mariano Paredes y Arrillaga, 1797–1849." PhD. diss., University of Texas at Austin, 1955.

Robinson, Cecil, ed. *The View from Chapultepec: Mexican Writers on the Mexican-American War.* Tucson: University of Arizona Press, 1989.

Robinson, Fayette. *Mexico and Her Military Chieftains*, Philadelphia: E. H. Butler, 1847.

Rodríguez, Mario. *La revolución americana de 1776 y el mundo hispánico: Ensayos y documentos* (Madrid: Editorial Tecnos, n.d.).

Ruiz, Ramón Eduardo. "A Commentary on Morality, Lincoln, Justin Smith and the Mexican War," *Journal of the Illinois State Historical Society* 69, no. 1 (1976): 26–34.

Sanchez, Javier E. "Valor Wrought Asunder: The Mexican General Officer Corps in the US-Mexican War, 1846–1847." Master's thesis: University of New Mexico, 2011.

Sanders, John. "Fort Polk: A Letter from Major Sanders," *Southern Literary Messenger* 17, no. 5 (May 1851): 317–18.

Santoni, Pedro. *Mexicans at Arms: Puro Federalists and the Politics of War, 1845–1848.* Fort Worth: Texas Christian University Press, 1996.

Schroeder, John H. *Mr. Polk's War: American Opposition and Dissent, 1846–1848.* Madison: University of Wisconsin Press, 1973.

Scribner, Benjamin F. *Camp Life of a Volunteer: A Campaign in Mexico, or A Glimpse at Life in Camp.* Philadelphia: Grigg, Elliot, 1847.

Sharf, J. Thomas. *History of Western Maryland.* Philadelphia: Louis J. Everts, 1882.

Shy, John. "First Battles in Retrospect." In Heller and Stoffit.

Singletary, Otis. *The Mexican War.* Chicago: University of Chicago Press, 1960.

Skelton, William B. *An American Profession of Arms: The Army Officer Corps*, 1784–1861. Lawrence: University Press of Kansas, 1992.

Smith, Justin Harvey. "Sources for a History of the Mexican War, 1846–1848." *The Military Historian and Economist* 1 (January 1916): 18–32.

———. *The War with Mexico.* 2 vols. New York: Macmillan, 1919.

Soil Survey of Hidalgo County, Texas. Washington, D.C.: Government Printing Office, 1929.

Soto, Miguel. *La conspiración monárquica en México*, 1845–1846. México, DF: Editorial Offset, 1988.

Southerland, Mary A. *The Story of Corpus Christi.* Houston: Rein and Sons, 1916.

Steinhauer, Dale Richard. "'Sogers': Enlisted Men in the US Army, 1815–1860." PhD diss., University of North Carolina, 1992.

Stillman, Chauncy Devereaux. *Charles Stillman, 1810–1875.* New York: C. D. Stillman, 1956.

Thompson, Jerry. *A Wild and Vivid Land: An Illustrated History of the South Texas Border.* Austin: Texas State Historical Association, 1997.

Thompson, John R. "The Military Establishment of the United States." *Southern Literary Messenger* 17, no. 2 (February 1851): 65–78.

Thompson, Waddy. *Recollections of Mexico.* New York: Wiley and Putnam, 1846.

Thonhoff, Robert H. "Taylor's Trail in Texas," *Southwestern Historical Quarterly* 70, no. 1 (1966): 7–22.

Thorpe, Thomas Bangs. *Our Army on the Rio Grande.* Philadelphia: Carey and Hart, 1846.

Traas, Adrian. *From the Golden Gate to Mexico City: The US Army Topographical Engineers in the Mexican War, 1846–1848.* Washington, DC: United States Army, 1993.

Trueba, Alfonso. *Legítima gloria.* Mexico: Editorial Campeador, 1954.

Uraga, José López. *Sumaria mandada formar a pedimento del Sr. Coronel Don José López Uraga. . . .* México: Imprenta de J. R. Navarro, 1846.

Valadés, José C. *Breve historia de la guerra con los Estados Unidos.* México: Editorial Patria, 1947.

Vargas, René Zorrilla. *El encuentro entre México y Estados Unidos, 1803–1848: el nacimiento de una relación difícil.* México, DF: Minos III Milenio, 2008.

Vázquez, Josefina Zoraida. *De la rebelión de Texas a la guerra del 47.* México, DF: Nueva Imagen, 1994.

———. *La intervención norteamericana, 1846–1848.* México, DF: Secretaría de Relaciones Exteriores, 1997.

———. *Mexicanos y norteamericanos ante la guerra del 47.* México: Secretaría de Educación Pública, 1972.

———, ed. *México al tiempo de su guerra con Estados Unidos, 1846–1848.* México: Fondo de Cultura Económica, 1998.

———. "La supuesta República del Río Grande. *Historia Mexicana* 36, no. 1 (July–September 1986), 49–80.

Villalpando César, José Manuel. *Las balas del invasor: la expansión territorial de los Estados Unidos a costa de México.* México: Miguel Ángel Porrúa, 1998.

Ward, Henry George. *Mexico in 1827.* London: H. Colburn, 1828.

Weems, John Edward. *To Conquer a Peace.* College Station: Texas A&M Press, 1974. Wettemann, Robert P., Jr. *Privilege versus Equality: Civil-Military Relations in the Jacksonian Era, 1815–1845.* Santa Barbara, CA: Praeger, 2009.

Wheelen, Joseph. *Invading Mexico: America's Continental Dream and the Mexican War, 1846–48.* New York: Carroll & Graf, 2007.

Whiting, Daniel P. *A Soldier's Life.* Edited by Murphy Givens. Corpus Christi: Nueces Press, 2012.

Wilhelm, Thomas, and Arthur Tracey Lee. *History of the Eighth US Infantry from Its Organization, in 1838.* 2 vols. New York: Headquarters, Eighth Infantry, 1873.

Wilkins, Frederick. *The Highly Irregular Irregulars: Texas Rangers in the Mexican War.* Austin: Eakin Press, 1990.

Winders, Richard Bruce. *Mr. Polk's Army: The American Military Experience in the Mexican War.* College Station: Texas A&M University Press, 1997.

Wynne, James. *Memoir of Major Samuel Ringgold, United States Army, Read Before the Maryland Historical Society, April 1st, 1847.* Baltimore: J. Murphy, 1847.

INDEX

Note: Page numbers in the endnotes are designated by the addition of an "n" followed by the note number.